W9-ALM-437

FEMINIST ORGANIZING FOR CHANGE

THE CONTEMPORARY WOMEN'S MOVEMENT IN CANADA

NANCY ADAMSON
LINDA BRISKIN
MARGARET McPHAIL

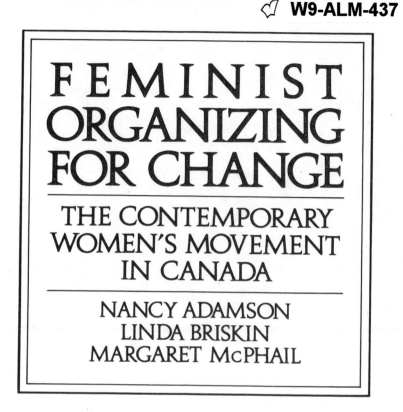

To Percy —
a friend & fellow
feminist in the struggle
for change.
Nancy

TORONTO
OXFORD UNIVERSITY PRESS

Oxford University Press, 70 Wynford Drive, Don Mills, Ontario, M3C 1J9

Toronto   Oxford   New York   Delhi   Bombay   Calcutta   Madras   Karachi
Petaling Jaya   Singapore   Hong Kong   Tokyo   Nairobi   Dar es Salaam
Cape Town   Melbourne   Auckland

and associated companies in
Berlin   Ibadan

CANADIAN CATALOGUING IN PUBLICATION DATA

Adamson, Nancy
Feminist organizing for change

Bibliography: p.
Includes index.
ISBN 0-19-540658-3

1. Feminism – Canada.   I. Briskin, Linda, 1949–.
II. McPhail, Margaret.   III. Title.

HQ1453.A28 1988   305.4′2′0971   C88-093823-4

Cover design based on a poster by Barbara Klunder.
© Nancy Adamson, Linda Briskin, Margaret McPhail 1988
OXFORD is a trademark of Oxford University Press
2 3 4 - 1 0 9
Printed in Canada

Contents

Acknowledgements

It is impossible to thank each of the many feminists with whom we worked over the years, but without the shared experiences of constructing a movement, building organizations, and struggling for change, this book would not have been possible.

Many women generously shared their time to provide information and to critique our work. Our thanks to Sandy Steinecher, who participated in the discussions leading up to this book; Alice de Wolff, Debbie Field, Maureen FitzGerald, Tori Smith, and Lynda Yanz, who read an early draft and offered very important comments and suggestions; Meg Luxton, Anne Molgat, and Lorna Weir, who made detailed and insightful comments on portions of the first manuscript; Patricia Bush, our research assistant, who did excellent work compiling the bibliography; and Sally Livingston of Oxford University Press, for her careful editing of the manuscript. This is a better book because of them; however, any errors or omissions are entirely our own.

This project was supported by grants from the Ontario Arts Council's Writers' Stimulation Grants, administered by the Women's Press, and from the small grants program of the Social Sciences and Humanities Research Council of Canada, administered by York University. We would also like to thank Secretarial Services, York University, for help with the data entry.

Without the Canadian Women's Movement Archives we could not have written the history chapter, nor could we have illustrated the other chapters with Canadian examples; our thanks to the collective for bending some of the rules to make our research easier.

The three of us were supported through the long process of writing this book by friends and family and owe many individual debts, too numerous to mention.

Finally, we would like to thank each other. This project has been a long one, at times difficult and discouraging, at times challenging and exhilarating. We have struggled to be supportive and constructively critical of each other's work throughout this process; the existence of this book is a testament to our success.

I

SETTING THE STAGE

1

Entering the World of the Women's Movement

THE IMPACT OF THE WOMEN'S MOVEMENT

The women's movement has been and is still one of the most significant and successful social movements in Canada. In its recent re-emergence in the last twenty years—what we call the second wave, in contrast to the first wave when women organized for suffrage, property rights, and so on in the nineteenth and early twentieth centuries[1]—it has challenged images of women and of femininity; the sexual division of labour in the home and the workplace; outdated laws and inadequate social services; the organization and delivery of health care to women; and the reproduction of stereotypic choices for girls and women within the education system. It has uncovered and named violence against women—sexual harassment, incest, rape, and wife abuse; it has identified the discrimination women face in the workplace, such as lack of access to the male-dominated trades, to training, or to executive promotion ladders; it has exposed the heterosexism and racism that pervade the entire social system and contribute to the double and triple oppression of lesbians, immigrants, and women of colour.[2] This list is far from complete.

These challenges and revelations have led to some changes. We might begin by noting the legislative changes that have occurred as a result of organized pressure by women. In 1988 the Supreme Court ruled that the federal abortion law, which had seriously restricted women's access to abortion services, was unconstitutional.[3] In 1986 the federal government passed Bill C-62, dealing with affirmative action for women, visible minorities such as native Canadians, and the disabled; in 1985 the Manitoba government passed equal-value legislation. In 1981 the Ontario Human Rights Code was amended to include protection against sexual harassment; also in 1981 women's right to equality was inscribed in section 28 of the new Canadian constitution.[4]

Despite financial restraints, governments have been increasing the funding to services required by women. In 1987 the federal government announced major funding initiatives to deal with the problem of wife abuse in response to a new report, *Battered But Not Beaten*, which estimated that one million women in Canada were abused each year;[5] over the last fifteen years the numbers of licensed child-care spaces have risen significantly (from 28,373 in 1973[6] to 192,374 in 1986[7]) and both federal and provincial governments are promising large-scale initiatives in this area.

Perhaps the most important victories lie in the change in public consciousness. These may be the hardest to document, but there is no doubt that the public consciousness about and acceptance of women's issues have altered dramatically in the last twenty years. Even a cursory glance at a recent report on public-opinion polls, released by the Women's Bureau of Labour Canada, shows such evidence:[8]

> Most Canadians thought that women could run most businesses as well as men, and this increased over time, from 58 per cent of the respondents in 1971 to . . . 83 per cent in 1983. . . . Although Canadians increasingly believed that women can run most businesses as well as men, they were equivocal about whether men and women have equal chances. In fact in response to the question on whether or not women in Canada get as good a break as men, the percentage indicating 'yes' declined over time. Nearly two thirds said yes in 1971. . . . By the early 1980s, over half of the Canadians polled believed that women did not get as good a break.[9]

> . . . Canadians increasingly believe that married women [without children] should take a job outside the home. . . . In 1960, nearly two thirds of the respondents thought that married women should take a job outside the home . . . in 1982 87 per cent polled indicated agreement.[10]

> . . . in 1960, only one out of twenty Canadians indicated that married women with young children should take a job outside the home, by 1982 38 per cent held similar views.[11]

A recent update of this poll, released by Gallup in 1987, showed that Canadians are now almost evenly divided on whether married women with young children should work: 47 per cent favour married women with young children taking jobs, a dramatic increase of 9 per cent in only five years.[12]

These few examples show increased acceptance of women's rights as well as increased awareness of women's inequality. The statistics are strongly reinforced by our subjective experience of the last twenty years. For example, the legitimacy accorded to women's demands in newspapers like *The Globe and Mail* and *The Toronto Star*, inside the trade-union movement, and by the government contrasts sharply with the recent past, when women's issues were completely ignored and the women's movement ridiculed.

Another dramatic change has been in the self-organization of women themselves. In 1965 in Canada there were few women's organizations, no women's bookstores (because there were almost no books about women), and no women's studies courses in schools and universities. In contrast, today almost all large urban centres, as well as many small towns and rural communities, have rape crisis centres, shelters for battered wives, self-defence courses, women's bookstores/music events/art galleries; all universities have women's studies courses (and many have extensive degree-granting programs in women's studies) as well as women's centres and/or centres to deal with campus sexual harassment; and the numbers of women's groups continue to grow. For example, the National Action Committee on the Status of Women, the umbrella organization to which most women's groups in Canada belong, had 530 member groups in 1987; in 1984 it had 280, and in 1977 only 130.[13]

These changes in legislation, services, self-organization, and public consciousness have occurred in the context of shifting social and economic realities for women: perhaps most important, the increase of women in the work-force, especially married women with young children. In 1900 women made up about 13 per cent of all workers; by 1983 this figure had risen to 42 per cent. This massive increase in women's participation is one of the most significant economic changes in Canada in this century. The number of women entering the work-force has risen steadily since the beginning of the century, except for a small drop immediately after World War II, reaching 38 per cent by 1970 and 53 per cent by 1983, an increase of 2.3 million.[14]

Although the women's movement cannot take all the credit, the coincidence of its growth and these changes is significant. Too often the movement's role in initiating discussion of these issues, in pressuring the government to pass legislation and increase funding, in changing social consciousness, has been relatively invisible.

Yet important as it is to make the role of the women's movement visible and to highlight the improvements outlined above, it is also necessary not to overestimate the extent of the changes. Despite the increase in opportunities and the changes in legislation, attitudes, and social consciousness, women still face escalating violence, inadequate wages, discrimination in the workplace, continuing responsibility for child-care and housework, and restrictions on control of our bodies. We have not eradicated the problems of sexual harassment, racism, heterosexism, sexual objectification, or the double day of labour. The litany of oppression is substantially the same today as it was in the late 1960s; in fact, as we uncover more about women's experience the scope of our concerns has expanded—for example, in our identification of the feminization of poverty.

The majority of women are mocked by the media image of the superwoman of the 1980s who combines a successful career with a fulfilling family life. The attempt to combine the two is very stressful for professional women, who now face all the pressures in the workforce in addition to the responsibility for the family. And well-educated women continue to earn considerably less than their male counterparts. For example:

> In 1981, men between 35 and 44 years of age with a university or first professional degree earned an average of $33,500 compared to $17,475 earned by women within the same age group and with the same level of education.[15]

Furthermore, the superwoman image is a completely fallacious portrayal of the reality faced by the majority of women. Far from pursuing 'exciting' careers and being on a financial par with men, most women are segregated in female job ghettoes doing monotonous work (in 1984, 60 per cent of all employed women were in clerical, sales, or service jobs)[16] and earning about two-thirds of what men earn.[17] Whatever fulfilment is available to them in the family is limited by their continuing responsibility for housework and child-care. In truth, the ideology of the modern 'superwoman' represents a not-very-sophisticated justification for the double day of labour. It does not reflect the kind of structural change necessary to the liberation of women.

The women's movement has not made the breakthroughs we sought. It has not transformed the society in fundamental structural ways, although it may have changed the rhetoric, the ideology, and perhaps even the expectations of society—changes not to be underestimated but also not to be confused with a more far-reaching vision of women's liberation. Elizabeth Wilson and Angela Weir, in their assessment of women's position in Britain, come to a similar conclusion: 'While women's right to equality is increasingly (if grudgingly) recognised, the material basis for equality and independence is denied.'[18] Perhaps in Canada we might say that the two central barriers that women face today are their economic dependence and their lack of reproductive rights.

Increasing numbers of excellent Canadian books are identifying and researching these issues that affect women. Few, however, look at the women's movement itself. *Feminist Organizing for Change* sets out to examine not the issues addressed by the women's movement, but rather the movement itself: its history, its forms of organizing, its ideology, its success or lack thereof in achieving change.

Our examination of the women's movement and its effectiveness in making change is influenced by our own experience as activists and our sense of the movement's unfulfilled potential: that is, the gap between the changes that have occurred and the radical visions that informed the early years of its second wave in Canada. Once this fundamental transformation in women's lives seemed within our grasp, certainly within our lifetime. But although much has changed, the radical vision has not been fulfilled. Writing this book was motivated in part by our desire to understand more fully the contradictions and limitations that face the movement in living up to its goals for social change.

Achieving such change, by definition the goal of the women's movement, is our central unifying theme. To make change is to challenge women's powerlessness and social inertia; to make change is to create a new set of possibilities. Furthermore, legitimizing the role of social movements such as the women's movement in making change challenges the conventional narrow emphasis on electoral politics, thereby redefining what constitutes the 'political'. We will return to this discussion in Chapter 4.

DEFINING THE WOMEN'S MOVEMENT

One of the complexities of this project has been to clarify what constitutes 'the women's movement'. This is not a straightforward task. The women's movement has a shifting, amoeba-like character; it is, and has always been, politically, ideologically, and strategically diverse. It is not, and has never been, represented by a single organizational entity; it has no head office, no single leaders, no membership cards to sign. Indeed, much of the widespread support for women's liberation has had no organizational identification at all.

One of the confusions about the movement relates to the fact that men are often excluded from women's groups. This is incorrectly taken to be a sign of 'man-hating'. Although we would not want to underestimate or trivialize the degree of anger and alienation that some women feel towards men, it is important that the autonomous nature of the movement not be understood only in terms of women's relationship to men, which would reproduce the tendency in our society to define women in relation to men. Women choose to organize separately from men because of their bonds with women and because of the commonality of their experience as women, as second-class citizens, as second-class workers, as sex objects, as bearers (and rearers) of children, and so on. In Chapter 6 we will discuss in more detail the ideology of the 'autonomous' women's movement.

To the extent that we define the women's movement organizationally, it is made up of hundreds of groups: some small, some large, some focused on single issues, some with a complex and wide-ranging political perspective. Some organize around legislative issues, some provide services, others focus on organizing women into unions. The constituency of some organizations is homogeneous: immigrant women, lesbians, women of colour, business and professional women, women in trades. Others have a heterogeneous constituency and focus on specific issues such as day-care, or on supporting a political perspective, as does the women's committee of the New Democratic Party (NDP). Some are based in large institutions like universities and government ministries; some are located in small communities. Some use traditional methods of organizing themselves; others have developed unconventional organizational structures, a topic we will explore in Chapter 7. The diversity and political heterogeneity is enormous and is further complicated by the fact that the practice of the women's movement—the way it organizes for change—is also constantly being transformed through self-criticism, through experience, and by changing historical circumstances.

Generalizing about the women's movement in a country like Canada is made more difficult by our geography, regional diversity, and size. The women's movement in Calgary is quite unlike its counterpart in Vancouver, Halifax, or Thunder Bay. We are aware of the important differences in feminist organizing in Quebec and the rest of Canada, especially as a result of the Quebec movement for national liberation.[19] Unfortunately, limitations of both space and our own experience have forced us to treat these differences less thoroughly than we would have liked. For all our caution about overgeneralizing, however, we also wish to stress the internationalism of feminism and the women's movement, despite regional diversities. In almost every country in the world there is a women's movement. Although the priorities, politics, organizations, and ide-

ology of each one reflect cultural, economic, and political specific-
ities, the degree of commonality is surprising. We have struggled in
the text to hold onto a level of commonality and generality without
sacrificing specificity and difference. But we would remind readers
to frame our discussions with regional specificity and uniqueness on
the one hand, and internationalism on the other.

It is also true that what is considered to be a 'woman's issue' is
constantly shifting and expanding. As the complexity of women's
position in society is unravelled, feminists have come to understand
that all economic and social-policy decisions have an impact on
women. This explains, for example, the 1987 emphasis of the
National Action Committee on the Status of Women on organizing
against free trade, which will detrimentally affect many of the sectors
within which women work,[20] or the intervention of other women
into the public hearings on the Meech Lake Accord, which by changing the constitutional arrangements in Canada may undermine social
programs of importance to women.[21]

Finally, we might point out that this constant expansion, both in
the definition of what constitutes a woman's issue and in the number
and kind of women's groups in Canada, is solid evidence that the
movement is not dead, despite the media's oft-repeated suggestions
to the contrary.[22]

DEFINING FEMINISM

Not only is the women's movement a diverse, complex, and shifting
reality, but feminism itself is not a unified political ideology. At the
core of all feminisms are certain commonalities in political perspective: all believe in equal rights and opportunities for women;
all recognize that women are oppressed and exploited by virtue of
being women; and all feminists organize to make change. But within
these broad parameters of commonality are extensive differences:
in political strategy, in vision about what constitutes women's liberation, in attitudes to men, in understanding the roots of women's
oppression, in setting priorities, in identifying constituencies and
allies.

These differences are often categorized by reference to what are
called the currents of feminism: liberal feminism, radical feminism,
and socialist feminism.[23] Each of these has its roots in a long history
that pre-dates the second wave of the movement, and each needs to
be understood in relation to mainstream political traditions such as
liberalism and marxism. However, our clarity is after the fact. For

the currents of feminism, as we now understand them, did not exist in a fully articulated way at the beginning of the second wave; they emerged during and were shaped by that developing women's movement. In fact, most feminists in the late sixties knew little, if anything, about the long history of women organizing.

To summarize briefly and differentiate between the feminist currents is no easy task. Inevitably, what follows will not do justice to the richness and complexity of the political character, traditions, vision, and strategy of each.[24] Indeed, it will no doubt suggest a greater degree of coherence than actually exists. Nonetheless it will help to contextualize our expanded exploration of socialist feminism in Chapter 3 and our comparative discussion of feminist practice, organizations, and ideology in Part III.

The central theme of liberal feminism is equality of opportunity: each individual in society should have an equal chance to compete for the resources of that society in order to rise within it as far as talents permit, unhindered by law and custom; wealth, position, and power should not be distributed on the basis of inherited qualities such as sex and race. Liberal feminists do not argue against the existence of inequalities of wealth, position, and power, however, once the barriers to equality are removed.

Rather than a restructuring of the economic and social order, the liberal-feminist vision includes a redistribution of opportunity in order to give women access to the power and opportunities of men. In order to even up the chances for women, what are seen as the barriers to competition must be removed. Liberal-feminist strategy therefore concentrates on improving educational opportunities for women in order to give them the tools to compete, on changing socialization patterns that shape a feminine personality uncomfortable with competing, and on removing legislation that actively discriminates against women.

Radical feminism provides some sharp contrasts to liberal feminism. Radical feminists identify women's unique capacity to give birth to children as central both to women's experience and to the material basis of their oppression. Women's role in biological reproduction (and often child-rearing) is seen to be the basis upon which male privilege is established and the root of male control of women's bodies, which is expressed in exploitative patterns of female/male sexuality and in violence against women.

Moreover, radical feminists identify fundamental emotional, social, and political differences between men and women. Unlike liberal feminism, which identifies the power of men as a goal for women, radical feminism validates the differences between women and men and in fact argues that we need a anti-militaristic, non-hierarchical co-operative society organized on the female values of life-giving and nurturance.

The importance of a radical feminist perspective to the growth of the women's movement cannot be overestimated. It might even be appropriate to say that in the early years of the second wave of the women's movement, most self-identified feminists were radical feminists. Radical feminism named the differences between women and men and thus made women's oppression visible.

Strategically, radical feminism has been largely responsible for the development of a woman-centred culture that takes the form of alternative businesses, art, music, living arrangements, and so on, and that provides a contrast to 'male-stream' institutions and culture.[25] Radical feminists have also organized all across Canada against male control of women's bodies, through rape crisis centres, Take Back the Night demonstrations, shelters for battered wives, and anti-pornography actions, among others.

Since we will examine in detail the politic of socialist feminism in Chapter 3, we will limit our comments here to a few comparisons. Socialist feminists analyze women's oppression through four intertwining categories: gender, class, race, and sexual orientation. Unlike liberal feminists, who see the social and economic system as fundamentally acceptable and argue for equal opportunity, socialist feminists challenge the power relations of that system and argue that equality of opportunity can never be attained in Canadian society as long as there are fundamental differences in wealth, privilege, and power based on class, gender, sexual orientation, and race. We might call this a systemic approach to women's oppression.

Unlike radical feminists, who focus on the conflicts between men and women, socialist feminists believe that although in some areas men and women have a conflict of interest, in others they have a commonality. So, for example, in the workplace women and men often have common interests concerning health and safety, working conditions, and pay levels; but when it comes to the sharing of housework men have certain privileges that create conflicts between them and women.

Useful as it is to differentiate among feminisms by reference to these three currents, several provisos should be pointed out. In the first place, the labels are somewhat misleading. Socialist feminism is as much about a critique of socialism as it is about socialism; liberal feminism is not uniquely related to tolerance but to the political tradition of liberalism; and, given their challenge to established beliefs, all feminisms rightly qualify to be labelled radical.

Second, these currents do not always accurately reflect the actual practice of feminists (a subject we will return to in Chapter 5), and in many smaller Canadian centres the feminist community may not identify itself by these labels. In fact, and partly for this reason, we have found it useful throughout this text to speak not only of the political currents of feminism, but also of grass-roots and institutionalized feminism. Institutionalized feminism operates within traditional institutions—inside political parties and government ministries, for example—while grass-roots feminism is more community-based, emphasizing collective organizing, consciousness-raising, and reaching out to women 'on the street'. And though liberal feminism is more often institutionalized, while both radical and socialist feminism are community-based, the locations of particular forms of feminist organizing also vary depending on economic, political, and ideological conditions.

Although all feminists agree more than they disagree, to understand the women's movement we must understand not only the commonalities but also these differences. The heterogeneity of both the women's movement and feminism is not very visible to the majority of Canadians. In part this invisibility is a result of specific strategies of isolation pursued by some women's groups, which have been compounded by distorted media portrayals of feminism and the women's movement. In part, too, it is a function of the hegemony of liberal democracy. Hegemony is a complex political and ideological process by which a society comes to appear a coherent whole built on consensus and unity. It means not only the domination of a particular political point of view, but also the tendency for other political views, and especially the recognition of conflicting interests (based, for example, on race, class, or gender), to be made invisible or, if visible, marginalized. As a result of this process of hegemony, the public face of feminism is that of a unified ideology closely related to mainstream Canadian political traditions.

Before we leave this discussion of feminism, it seems important to investigate the reluctance of many women to identify themselves as feminists. Two factors help to explain this phenomenon. In the first place, there has been, and in fact continues to be, active media distortion of the images and issues of feminists. These distortions reflect the resistance to feminism that is embedded in the dominant ideology and mainstream institutions, both of which are challenged by feminism.

Examples of such distortion are widely available. Even a paper like the *Toronto Star*, which tends to cover women's issues in a supportive way, could still print, in 1982, the following commentary on feminism by Frank Jones:

> The movement to put men in dresses is growing fast. The latest breakthrough came last week when the East York Women's Centre began what is called a 'confidence building' course for men. Like everything else these days, of course, the name really means the opposite of what it says. The real aim of such male consciousness raising efforts is to make men soft, sensitive, pliant, in a word, manageable. . . .
>
> The men I see emerging from the universities after years of conditioning the feminists favour are of little use to anyone. They are so sensitive it's sickening. They are inept, unimposing with their birds-nest beards, and spineless. They are mere fodder for their strong willed mates to chew up and spit out.[26]

Such attacks are an easy way of avoiding the substantive issues involved. It is not surprising that thirty-one-year-old Mary Smith, when interviewed by the *Star* a week later, also focused on feminists as individual women, rather than on the issues of feminism: ' "When I hear the word feminism I see a bunch of ugly dogs. I see women who aren't attractive, and who scream and yell a lot. I see women who hate men." '[27] Ironically, Smith, an accountant,

> admits she has . . . freedoms her mother probably never knew. She knows men still have the edge in the world, She also knows the only way to keep moving forward is to keep on fighting. She believes in equal pay for work of equal value.[28]

Herein lies a central contradiction: most women are in favour of equal rights for women, support the issues of feminists, and are glad of the changes that have resulted from the work of feminists and the women's movement, but are uncomfortable with the label 'feminist'.

But the media distortions of feminism are not the only problem. As we have already pointed out, the concept of feminism includes the idea of organizing to make change. This implies a belief in the power to make change and, to some extent, in the efficacy of collective action: '. . .the fact is that feminism isn't simply another word. It implies an understanding of the world and has the potential to empower those who claim it.'[29]

Yet women often feel powerless to change their lives. This powerlessness is rooted in the material conditions of their work and home lives and is reinforced by the ideology of change in our society (a subject we will return to in Chapter 4). Marie O'Shea, in an article on why some women remain outside the women's movement, reports the following:

> Most of the secretaries and clerical workers with whom I spoke described themselves and their co-workers as having an apathetic attitude, with little sense of control over their situation. They felt there was a general unwillingness to challenge the system or engage in unconventional behaviour. 'I would feel uncomfortable actively pushing for some of the things feminists stand for.'[30]

A very powerful letter written to the feminist magazine *Spare Rib*, in England, spoke eloquently of this feeling of powerlessness. Sue, a woman physically abused by her husband, wrote to express gratitude to the Women's Aid Centre in Cardiff for its help. She also expressed some of her contradictory feelings about the women's movement:

> In *Spare Rib* I always feel we see, apart from the interviews with women working under bad conditions . . . women who are already strong; who may have suffered, but know how to stand up for themselves in their personal and political lives. That is a good thing. . . . Sometimes it has made me feel inferior, and has made me feel your magazine is for other women who are more together than I am, who are prepared to fight where I am not; but please make room for us who don't know where we are going, or what we are doing, who only feel that we are failing because of the pressure we are under.[31]

This sense of failure, powerlessness, and pressure, combined with the lack of economic independence that most women face, can make the women's movement attractive; on the other hand, it can turn women towards an anti-feminist ideology. Karen Dubinsky, in her exploration of anti-feminism in Canada, points out that 'the material basis of anti-feminism, therefore, is exactly the condition of women's lives which spawned feminism to begin with';[32] that is, despite what the media and the new right would have us believe, feminism is one response to, not the cause of, the difficulties women face. Deirdre English, in 'The War Against Choice', details the reasons why women are attracted to anti-feminist movements like the anti-choice movement.[33] She points out that it is very difficult for women to survive in nontraditional ways in a society that pays women so little, burdens them with child-care responsibilities, does not protect them from extensive violence, and so on. Women who are opposed to easy divorce, equal pay, and day-care are recognizing how limited their options are:

. . . men have reaped more than their share of benefits from women's liberation. Woman's meager economic independence, a result of her new-found presence in the job market, and her sexual liberation have allowed men to garner great new freedoms.

Because there is no 'trick of nature' to make the link between sex and fatherhood, and little social stigma on he who loves and leaves, women face the abdication of any male responsibility for pregnancy—let alone for any ensuing children. If a woman gets pregnant, the man who 20 years ago might have married her may feel today that he is gallant if he splits the cost of an abortion. . . . Divorce leaves women putting a higher percentage of their incomes and their time into child care. Nationwide, more than 50 percent of men default, in whole or in part, on their child-support payments—not alimony, child support—within one year after divorce. *Under these circumstances, the fear has awakened that feminism will free men first—and might never get around to freeing women.*[34]

But there is no doubt that a large part of women's discomfort with the label 'feminist' is related to what they assume men's response will be: 'Women are unwilling to be too visible in their support of feminist ideology for fear that this would threaten their relationships with fathers, brothers, friends and lovers.'[35] Given the comments of Frank Jones, above, it would be unrealistic and naive to suggest that men are not threatened by feminism, especially given the privileges that accrue to them as a result of women's inequality. However, growing numbers are sympathetic to the concerns of women;[36] perhaps as important, men are increasingly recognizing that their own lives may change for the better with the implementation of feminist demands. In a society where few families can live on a single income, and where men are no longer the only breadwinners, inevitably there is pressure on male roles, pressure that is often blamed on feminism but arises out of changing economic and social conditions in the home and the workplace.

Perhaps the greatest irony is that the changes feminists are struggling for, rather than increasing the hostility between men and women, may provide the material basis for improving their relationships. Economic independence for women may alleviate financial pressures on men; availability of child-care decreases the tensions in families where both parents need to do waged work; eliminating violence against women improves the level of trust between women and men;[37] reproductive rights and freedoms allow women greater access to their own sexuality, creating the conditions for them to relate to men in new ways and to rely on them less. In fact, Joseph Pleck, a well-known writer on male roles, suggests that the women's movement may not go far enough, in that it does not mount a challenge to the patriarchal relations that exist between men:

> While the patriarchal oppression of women may be lessened as a result of the women's movement, the patriarchal oppression of men may be untouched. The real danger for men posed by the attack that the women's movement is making on patriarchy is not that this attack will go too far, but that it will not go far enough. Ultimately, men cannot go any further in relating to women as equals than they have been able to go in relating to other men as equals.[38]

Writer Mary Kay Blakely[39] concludes that the real manhaters are not feminists who are hopeful of relationships between equals, but rather women who believe that men are stupid and vain enough to be manipulated by tactics such as those suggested by Marabel Morgan in her very popular book *The Total Woman*:

> Women need to be loved; men need to be admired. . . . Have you ever wondered why your husband doesn't just melt when you tell him how much you love him? But try saying, 'I admire you,' and see what happens. . . . Remember that compliments will encourage him to talk. Admire him as he talks to you. Concentrate on what he's saying. . . . Even if you don't care who won yesterday's football game, your attention is important to him and he needs you. Let him know he's your hero.[40]

This section has attempted to demonstrate, briefly, the complexity of feminism as a political ideology and as a strategy and indeed, the complexity of the public response to it, from women and from men.

POINT OF VIEW

We hope this book will make the heterogeneity of the women's movement more evident by focusing on grass-roots feminism, our study of which is informed by a socialist-feminist perspective. Neither grass-roots nor socialist feminism has had much exposure in the mass media, and both are therefore largely invisible to public consciousness.

The complexity of feminism and the women's movement means that many histories of the movement need to be told and many analyses put forward. This book does not attempt to do justice to them all, but rather accepts the necessity to write about feminism from a particular political and personal point of view. We feel much like the German socialist feminist Frigga Haug, who was initially delighted when she was commissioned to write a history of the German women's movement: 'At last there would be an account in which the role of socialist feminists, who from the beginning constituted a major part of the movement, would not be passed over in silence or at best mentioned briefly, and negatively, like a kind of historical error.'[41] Confronting the complexity of the task, however, finally she

> came to the conclusion that the history of a movement in which one was and still is active always requires a construal of the meaning of one's own actions. One arrives at a history by grasping oneself historically, at least in retrospect. Therefore my aim could no longer be just to reproduce the multifarious record of the movement as objectively as possible. On the contrary, I would have to work my own partisanship into the story in such a way that the socialist and feminist perspective would be identifiable as its procedural material.[42]

We would go further than Haug. Not only would we argue that as feminist activists our writing must, and will inevitably, reflect our own experiences but, further, that all writing about politics must make explicit the vision, politics, and point of view of the authors. All writing in the social sciences, including that on feminism and the women's movement, has a particular point of view, for all such writing, explicitly or inexplicitly, makes underlying assumptions about how the world ought to be. These judgements are the essence of politics.

The best social science openly acknowledges its point of view, allowing readers to see the implications of what is being argued and providing the context within which it can be evaluated. Readers must become active participants; they must develop a critical perspective and seek their own truth and reality.

In contrast, the cloak of objectivity disguises the necessity, and indeed the inevitability, of a point of view and suggests the existence of one absolute truth. It makes readers passive, mere recipients of that 'truth' rather than active judges. Not surprisingly, women have suffered a lot throughout history because of assumptions about objective truths.

For example, it is often assumed that women could take care of children better than men, that women were weaker than men and needed protection, or that women's place was in the home. Feminist scholars now cite numerous examples of historical times and societies when this ideology of women and men, and the forms of social organization they reflect, were not the norm. Rather than being objective truths, these points of view arise out of specific historical circumstances, reflect a particular vision of how the world ought to be, and support the interests of certain sectors of society over others. Challenging our often inexplicit assumptions about objectivity and universalism has been one of the most important contributions of feminist methodology.

Each one of us has a point of view in the world. It is constructed out of our experience in families, in schools, with friends, in the culture within which we live, from the particularities of our class, race and sex experience. Some points of view are more familiar than others; some are more acceptable. Familiarity is often confused with objectivity and correctness, and we often mistakenly assume that because a point of view matches that of others it must be right and true.

Yet certain points of view dominate. Rather than assuming that they are more true than others, we need to ask political questions. Who benefits from that perspective? What politics and vision about the future emerge from that perspective? Whose interests does it reflect?

Perhaps more than any other subject, the study of women must ask these kinds of questions. For women have been subjected to the constraints of 'objective truth' for centuries: the 'truths' that restricted their activities and choices, that subjected them to husbands and unfair laws, that defined them in terms of their ability to have children, that denied their sexuality and desire.

Having argued forcefully for the writing of social science from an explicitly articulated point of view, let us lay ours out. We write as socialist-feminist activists, as theorists, each of us involved in diverse organizations of the women's movement for about fifteen years, at various times in the United States and England, in Quebec and Ontario. We are heterosexual and lesbian. We have children, have chosen not to have children, and have been unable to have children. We rent and own our homes. We live collectively, in a nuclear family, and alone. In some ways, however, our experience is limited: we are all white, English-speaking, and university-educated, and we all live in a large urban centre.

Throughout this text we have tried to maintain the presence of our own voices and experiences as a reminder of the context from which we speak, and of both the scope and the limits of that experience. We do this most explicitly in Chapter 2, on the history of the women's movement, where we self-consciously intertwine our own experiences with a more general chronicle of events.

As important, we do not want to objectify our experiences or set ourselves up as outside, impartial observers studying the women's movement, a stance that is virtually impossible anyway. We have been and still are active participants in the English Canadian women's movement, and this exerts a powerful influence on what we say. Although we are not writing only about socialist feminism, our analysis is informed by that perspective, which necessarily influences our interpretation of events and our criticism.

In attempting to highlight our own experiences and point of view, we faced a serious problem with the use of 'we'. There are three 'we's' of which we are a part: the three of us who have written this book; the 'we' that includes socialist feminists; and the 'we' that involves the larger women's movement. In general we have tried to confine our use of 'we' to the three of us, but we felt uncomfortable referring to socialist feminists or the women's movement as 'they'. We did not want to use an all inclusive 'we', which suggested that our point of view was overly representative; at the same time, we did not want the language to mask our activist involvement.

There is another problem with the use of 'we'. Hazel Carby concludes her article 'White Women Listen! Black Feminism and the Boundaries of Sisterhood' with: 'of white feminists we must ask, what exactly do you mean when you say "WE"??'[43] We want to emphasize that we speak as white women who have participated in a largely white women's movement, and that this is necessarily reflected in our text. However, the issue of racism in the women's movement is an important and recurring theme throughout what follows. For example, in discussing the ideology of sisterhood we consider the particular problems faced in building alliances between white women and women of colour; when we outline the politic of socialist feminism we focus on the intertwining of class, race, gender, and sexual orientation as central analytic categories.

We have struggled not only to clarify our own standpoint in the text, but also to identify our audience. In the early stages of the project we were writing to other socialist-feminist activists. Gradually our audience widened as we set ourselves the goal of making the book accessible and meaningful to the many women interested in feminism and the women's movement. In fact, we saw this as an opportunity to demonstrate the viability of socialist feminism as a world view and to profile its contribution to the women's movement.

Aiming for a wide audience can sometimes mean that the final product is not entirely successful for anyone. For those who are already feminist activists and scholars, some of what we say may seem obvious and elementary; for women new to the movement, we might assume too much. Whatever the weaknesses, we are committed both to theorizing our experiences and to making the history and debates of the women's liberation movement accessible to a wide spectrum of readers.

SELF-CRITICISM AND AGENCY

We want to understand how to make change. The lack of fundamental structural improvement in the conditions of women makes us turn a critical eye on the women's movement. We are struck by the contrast between the relatively unchallenging movement of today and the heady mobilizations of earlier stages. We are concerned that the women's movement has become overly institutionalized and that this may undermine our ability to achieve change in the future, especially in the face of attacks by neo-conservatives who want to turn back the clock on the few gains we have made.

Why has the women's movement not accomplished what we once thought it would? Why has our earlier, more radical vision remained unfulfilled? And where are the thousands of women whose ideas have been changed and who have welcomed changes in women's rights? Are they active today? If not, why not?

This is not to suggest that there have been no successes, but only that our vision has been far greater than its realization. In fact, not only has the women's movement an impressive record, but the Canadian one may be unique in the western world. In particular we can point to the successes of the women's movement vis-à-vis the trade-union movement,[44] and to the viability of socialist feminism as both an activist and a theoretical current in the Canadian movement. It is precisely the strength of Canadian socialist-feminist theorizing and organizing that has created the conditions for us to ask the questions that we do in this book. Cultural imperialism often leads us to ignore these particular realities.

Our questions have forced us to deal with what it means to be publicly critical of the women's movement. Since the women's movement has faced so much ridicule, feminists have often felt a need to protect its internal processes from public scrutiny. It is a sign of the strength and increasing legitimacy of the Canadian women's movement that feminists are beginning to openly debate their strategic and political differences.

In trying to assess the women's movement we have recognized a tension between criticism of our own actions and a realistic appraisal of the material conditions that limit the movement's potential. There are tremendous constraints on our ability to make change. The choices of feminist practice are necessarily shaped by political, economic, and social conditions: the nature of public consciousness, the level of development of the women's and other progressive movements, the degree of state repressiveness, the state of the economy, and so on. Indeed, we are more realistic now than we were twenty years ago. We know that women's oppression is more deep-rooted, the structures and power relations more intransigent, and mobilization so much more difficult to sustain than we realized.

However, while it is important to acknowledge the limitations of the given social and political situation, it is not enough to attribute the unfulfilled character of the socialist-feminist vision entirely to that material situation. Too often, in emphasizing the degree to which historical conditions shape our choices we lose sight of the fact that the very premise of a socialist-feminist politic is a belief in agency—in the ability to affect the course of events through collective action. Thus in this book we try to analyze and evaluate the organizations, ideology, and strategies of the women's movement.

The purpose of this self-criticism is not to 'blame' the women's movement for the difficulties faced in transforming women's lives; we do not mean to imply that if such and thus had been done differently our victories would have been greater. We do not know that. But we do know that we must address the question of where the women's movement and, in particular, socialist-feminist activists go from here. And to do that, we need to come to terms with where we have already been.

The underlying premise of this book is that change is possible, despite the difficulties that confront us. This implies a belief in our own agency and the ability of organized movements to make a difference. We suggest that self-criticism is part of the recognition of agency. If what we did made no difference, then we would have no agency and would be but passive victims of the world around us. To exercise our agency, however, involves some degree of self-criticism, of public scrutiny, of strategic debate. In the long run, increasing the level of self-consciousness about feminist practice will make strategic and tactical choices more effective.

THE STRUCTURE OF THIS BOOK

This book is divided into three parts. The first introduces the reader to the women's movement, in the general discussions in this chapter and in the historical overview of Chapter 2. In the second part we elaborate our theoretical perspective: on socialist feminism and on the politics of making change. This perspective informs the rest of the book, in which we investigate in detail the feminist practice, organizations, and ideologies of the contemporary Canadian women's movement. Let us expand on this brief overview.

Chapter 2, 'Our History/Histories', begins to record the complex, and mostly untold, history of feminist organizing in Canada. We argue that the contemporary women's movement has important links with the first wave, in which we can see the origins of institutionalized and grass-roots feminism. While this chapter is necessarily only a brief account of some key events, it is important, not only because there are almost no other writings on this subject, particularly on grass-roots feminism, but also because it provides a context for our discussion of the contemporary women's movement.

The next two chapters set the stage for a detailed examination of the women's movement in Canada. Chapter 3 outlines what we consider to be the distinctive features of a socialist-feminist politic. It begins by elaborating the socialist-feminist vision of women's liberation and the centrality of difference expressed in the intertwining of the categories of gender, race, class, and sexual orientation. After dealing briefly with the sexual division of labour, the public and the private, the role of the state, and socialist-feminist method, we conclude by situating socialist feminism in its historic, international, and Canadian contexts.

Chapter 4 addresses the problem of making change in Canadian society. We analyze the prevailing social consciousness about change through an examination of our society's endemic fear of change, its emphasis on individualism, and its identification of representative democracy as the only legitimate route to social change. This 'ideology of change' we contrast to a socialist-feminist perspective, which emphasizes the possibilities for change and focuses on changing material structures through popular political movements.

In Chapter 5 we develop a model of feminist practice, differentiating among feminist practices on the basis of their understanding of the process of change. Two key politics of change emerge, both of which are necessary to the feminist vision: disengagement (desire to create alternative structures and ideologies based on a critique of the system and a standpoint outside of it) and mainstreaming (desire to reach out to the majority of the population with popular and practical feminist solutions to particular issues). Each of these options, however, has a strategic risk. Disengagement can easily lead to the marginalization and invisibility of feminists and their demands; mainstreaming, to the co-optation and institutionalization of those demands. The chapter concludes with the argument that socialist feminism, with its unique vision of change and strategic orientation, has the potential, albeit unfulfilled, to reconcile the tension between disengagement and mainstreaming.

In Chapter 6 we examine the ideology of the women's movement: 'the personal is political' and 'sisterhood is powerful'. This ideology has been and is a source of strength to the women's movement, and offers important insights into the nature of disengagement and mainstreaming. At the same time, however, it has proved insufficient as a basis for reconciling these politics. As a result, the ability of feminism—and in particular, socialist feminism—to develop an effective public strategy for change has been limited.

Chapter 7 turns to the issues of feminist organizations and process. As feminists challenged traditional organizational notions, two different feminist models emerged: one a modified form of the traditional norms and the other a new grass-roots approach to structure and organizational process. This chapter focuses on that grass-roots model and details the successes and the difficulties the women's movement has had in structuring organizations and in effectively reaching out to, educating, and recruiting women. In order to examine the daily practice and process of feminism, we explore the development of the feminist critique of traditional organizational models, examine issues of feminist organizing, and finally focus on the particular organizational dilemmas that emerge from a socialist-feminist politic.

In our conclusion we return to our central theme—making change—and our political perspective: socialist feminism. We examine the attitude to change inside the women's movement itself and the challenges facing both socialist feminists and the women's movement at large in the years ahead.

Writing the first book on the second wave of the women's movement in Canada was no easy task. In addition to presenting history and analysis, we have attempted to articulate some conceptual tools and frameworks that will be useful to the continued exploration of the movement: the distinction between grass-roots and institutionalized feminism, the model of feminist practice, and the concept of the ideology of the women's movement, for example.

We have also developed two important resources that will facilitate further research in this area: first, an extensive bibliography on the women's movement in Canada and a selective one on feminist organizing in other Western countries; and second, what we hope is a representative selection of unpublished documents of the Canadian women's movement dealing with some of the issues raised in this book. These resources provide a further entry into the complex and controversial life of the Canadian women's movement.

NOTES

[1]Some also distinguish between the 'woman's movement' of the nineteenth century and the 'women's liberation movement' of the late twentieth century. In popular vernacular, however, we now talk of the 'women's movement'. Some attribute the dropping of the word 'liberation' to practicality, that is, shortening a mouthful of words. Others see it as a reflection of the dominance of a more limited feminist vision, one that does not include real liberation.
[2]The term 'women of colour' continues to be a controversial one because it does not reflect the variety of experiences of 'non-white' women: black women, native women, Asian women, etc. For some women, it is also too reminiscent of the term 'coloured people', which resonates with racism. Although it is not entirely effective as an inclusive term, other terms such as 'non-white women', or 'visible minority women' are no more successful, since in our estimation they overly privilege the dominant category of white experience.

For a trenchant analysis of the problem with the category of 'visible minorities' see Himani Bannerji, 'Popular Images of South Asian Women', *Tiger Lily* Nov./Dec. 1986. Bannerji says: 'The category of "visible minorities" is a perplexing one. On the surface it seems to be a simple euphemism. It seems to work as a way of classifying or categorizing, without appearing to be in any way racist. . . . But its first impact is one of absurdity to anyone who bothers to reflect on it. . . . All people, black and white, South Asian or Scandinavian, are visible. So in what way are we more visible than others? . . . There must be something "peculiar" about some people which draws attention to them. . . . "Visibility" in such a case means that people are "selected-out" as not only being different, but also as inferior or inadequate. . . . To be labelled "visible" is to be told to become invisible. . . .' pp. 25–6.
[3]Chief Justice Brian Dickson stated: 'Section 251 (of the Criminal Code) clearly interferes with a woman's physical and bodily integrity. Forcing a woman by the threat of criminal sanction, to carry a fetus to term unless she meets certain criteria . . . is a profound interference with a woman's body and thus an infringement of security of the person.' Quoted in the *Toronto Star* 29 Jan. 1988, p. 1.
[4]In 1981, thousands of women rallied in support of Clause 28. The story of this process is recounted in Penny Kome, *The Taking of Twenty Eight: Women Challenge the Constitution* (Toronto: Women's Press, 1983).
[5]Linda MacLeod, *Battered But Not Beaten . . . Preventing Wife Abuse in Canada* (Ottawa: Canadian Advisory Council on the Status of Women, 1987) p. 7.

[6]*Women in Canada: A Statistical Report* (Statistics Canada, March 1985), Table 22, p. 21.

[7]'Fact Sheet: Daycare in Canada' (Ottawa: Canadian Daycare Advocacy Association, n.d.).

[8]Monica Boyd, *Canadian Attitudes toward Women: Thirty Years of Change* (Women's Bureau, Labour Canada, 1984).

[9]Ibid., pp. 18–19.

[10]Ibid., p. 11.

[11]Ibid., p. 12.

[12]Results reported in the *Toronto Star* 23 March 1987.

[13]The National Action Committee began in 1972 with a few member groups; by 1977 it had 130; by 1980, 150; by 1984, 280; and by 1987, 530. Judy Campbell, Executive Co-ordinator of the National Action Committee on the Status of Women, supplied these figures.

[14]*Women in Canada: A Statistical Report*: 'During the same period, the number of men in the labour force increased by only 1.5 million and male participation rate declined slightly'(p. 41).

[15]'Women and Work' Fact Sheet (Canadian Advisory Council on the Status of Women, Feb. 1985).

[16]Ibid.

[17]In fact, Labour Canada's most recent figures show that the gap is widening: 'In 1985, women employed for the full-year (49 to 52 weeks either full-time or part-time) earned, on average, 59.6 per cent of men's average earnings, a slight decrease from 60.1 per cent in 1984. . . . In 1985, women employed full-time earned only 64.9 per cent of the average earnings of men, down from 65.5 per cent in 1984.' *Women in the Labour Force, 1986-7 Edition* (Ottawa: Labour Canada, 1987), p. 35.

[18] Angela Weir and Elizabeth Wilson, 'The British Women's Movement', *New Left Review* 148 (Nov./Dec. 1984), p. 102.

[19]See, for example, Diane Lamoureux, 'Nationalism and Feminism in Quebec: An Impossible Attraction', in Heather Jon Maroney and Meg Luxton, eds, *Feminism and Political Economy*, (Toronto: Methuen, 1987); also, Violette Broduer et al., *Le mouvement des femmes au Québec* (Montreal: Centre de formation populaire, 1982).

[20]See, for example, Marjorie Cohen, *The Macdonald Report and Its Implications for Women* (Toronto: National Action Committee on the Status of Women, Nov. 1985) and Isa Bakker, 'Free Trade: What's At Risk?' *Feminist Action/féministe* vol. 2, 7 (1987), pp. 1–2.

[21]See, for example, *Brief on the 1987 Constitutional Accord*, presented to the Special Joint Committee of the Senate and the House of Commons on the 1987 Constitutional Accord by the National Action Committee on the Status of Women, 26 Aug. 1987.

[22]This book focuses explicitly on the range of feminist organizing. It is the case, however, that not all women who organize for change, and not all organizations that focus on significant issues for women see themselves as feminists or as part of the women's movement. For example, a tenant housing group may be very concerned with housing issues for single parents, most of whom are women, yet not see themselves as a part of the women's movement. Further, women organize in explicitly anti-feminist women's groups, such as the Canadian group REAL Women.

[23]These labels are not necessarily agreed upon. Sometimes liberal feminism is called reform feminism or bourgeois feminism; sometimes socialist feminism is called marxist feminism; and sometimes radical feminism, which is a less coherent perspective, is referred to by one of its more specific expressions, such as cultural feminism, separatist feminism, eco-feminism, etc.

[24]The following discussion draws heavily on Alison Jaggar, *Feminist Politics and Human Nature* (Totowa, N.J.: Rowman and Allanheld, 1983).

[25]Mary O'Brien in *The Politics of Reproduction* (Boston: Routledge and Kegan Paul, 1981) introduces the term 'male-stream culture' to replace 'mainstream culture', in order to make visible the domination of men.

[26]Frank Jones, 'Next thing you know feminists will have all men wearing dresses,' *Toronto Star* 19 Oct. 1982.

[27]Leslie Fruman, 'How feminism became a dirty word', *Toronto Star* 29 Oct. 1982.

[28]Ibid.

[29]Lois Sweet, 'Feminism has become a dirty word', *Toronto Star*, 18 Feb. 1985.

[30]Marie O'Shea, 'Clerical and Secretarial Workers: Why some women remain outside the women's movement', *Breaking the Silence* Spring/Summer 1986, p. 24.

In the same issue of *Breaking the Silence*, Dorothy O'Connell, in 'Income Makes all the Difference', explores the image of feminism held by low-income women, many of whom do not believe that feminism has any benefits to offer them.

It is interesting to contrast these two articles with 'Speaking Up: A Labour Women's Roundtable', by Ruth Scher, also in the same issue. She interviews women in the union movement about their attitudes to the women's movement. No sense of apathy and power-lessness is reflected in that discussion. This suggests that when women participate in collective organizing for change, in unions or in the women's movement, their sense of empowerment grows.

[31]Quoted in Elizabeth Stanko, *Intimate Intrusions: Women's Experience of Male Violence* (London: Routledge and Kegan Paul, 1985), p. 54.

[32]Karen Dubinsky, *Lament for a 'Patriarchy Lost'? Antifeminism, Anti-abortion, and R.E.A.L. Women in Canada* (Ottawa: CRIAW/ICREF, 1985).

Linda Gordon, in her review of Claudia Koonz's *Mothers in the Fatherland: Women, the Family and Nazi Politics* (New York: St. Martin's Press, 1987), points out that 'one of Koonz's central arguments is that women joined these organizations for many of the same reasons they have joined progressive and feminist movements: they were rebelling against the low status and confinement of women's conventional role and were seeking recognition, an arena for political activism and power'. See Linda Gordon, 'Review Essay: Nazi Feminists', *Feminist Review* no. 27 (Autumn 1987), p. 97.

[33]Deirdre English, 'The War Against Choice', *Mother Jones* Feb./March 1981.

[34]Ibid. (emphasis added).

[35]O'Shea, 'Clerical and Secretarial Workers'.

[36]A recent collection of articles edited by Michael Kaufman, *Beyond Patriarchy: Essays by Men on Pleasure, Power and Change* (Toronto: Oxford Univ. Press, 1987) is a pro-feminist book that explores these concerns.

[37]A 1987 poll done for the *Toronto Star* ('What a difference a year makes. . .' [29 Dec. 1987]) showed that 57 per cent of males felt 'very safe' walking alone in their neighbourhood after dark in contrast to 22 per cent of females; 1 per cent of males felt 'very unsafe' compared to 18 per cent of females. What women fear is the violence of men.

[38]Joseph Pleck, 'Men's Power with Women, Other Men and Society: A Men's Movement Analysis', in Robert Lewis, ed., *Men in Difficult Times* (Englewood Cliffs: Prentice Hall, 1981), p. 242.

[39]In 'Who are the real man-haters?' *Vogue* April 1983, quoted in Carol Tavris and Carole Wade, *The Longest War* (San Diego: Harcourt Brace Jovanovich, 1984), p. 5.

[40]Marabel Morgan, *The Total Woman* (Markham: Simon and Schuster, 1973), pp. 63–7.

[41]Frigga Haug, 'The Women's Movement in West Germany', *New Left Review* 155 (Jan./Feb. 1986), p. 51.

[42]Ibid.

[43]In Centre for Contemporary Cultural Studies, *Empire Strikes Back* (London: Hutchinson, 1982), p. 233.

[44]See Linda Briskin and Lynda Yanz, eds, *Union Sisters: Women in the Labour Movement* (Toronto: Women's Press, 1983).

2

Our History/Histories

When it emerged in the 1960s, the second wave of the women's movement appeared to be a new and potentially revolutionary force; at the time we had no sense of a history of women organizing for change. Gradually, however, we uncovered and reclaimed a long history of active organizing by women to change society. As feminists we did not lose our sense of being pioneers, but we came to understand that we are also part of a long tradition. What follows is a brief history of active organizing by women to change society, with an emphasis on the grass-roots women's movement, interwoven with our individual experiences.

This chapter is necessary because the little that has been written about the contemporary Canadian women's movement has focused on the issues it has addressed, rather than the movement itself. For those readers who are not familiar with the movement, the chapter will provide a context for the analysis to follow. For those who are, we hope our narrative can be related to similar experiences across Canada.

Even within the women's movement we have very little sense of our history; we often seem reluctant to recognize its importance. But our personal experiences have convinced us that it is important:

VOICE 1: When I got involved in the women's movement in Toronto, I had already five or six years of experience in the Montreal women's movement. What was discouraging was not so much that we faced the same issues (what kind of leadership structure and membership requirements, what size group did we want, what was our basis of unity, how would we make decisions, etc.) but rather that we faced them as if the women's movement, our women's movement, had no history of trying to address them. We tried out solutions as if none had been tried before. For me and others who had been involved for years, there was a sense that our histories and past experiences were not valued, that somehow trying to share that experience and learn from it was pulling rank. We were often effectively silenced by the power of the present and the disdain for the past, even our own past. I always found it very ironic that at the same time we were discovering 'herstory' we were often ignoring the history that we ourselves had made.

Although little has been written about the contemporary women's movement, women's historians in the universities have now done considerable research into the history of women across time. In the late 1960s we felt that we were initiating a new movement, and in a way we were, because the history of the previous women's movement was largely unwritten; we were almost totally ignorant of the women who had preceded us, their politics, their strategies, their organizations. In telling our personal histories and the general story of the women's movement since the late 1960s, we need to be always aware of these two contradictory realities: a long history of active organizing by women to change society and the sense of creating a new movement. While many historians treat the first and second waves as two separate movements, we believe there are important ideological links between them. Thus in this chapter we will briefly examine the first wave, in order to understand more fully the origins of the contemporary movement.

Deciding how to present this history has been difficult. We could have simply told our own three stories, but that seemed too limited and individualistic. After all, our experiences were shaped by being part of a larger movement, and to take them out of that context would make them meaningless and minimize the importance of the movement itself. On the other hand, it is impossible to write the history of the Canadian women's movement in one chapter. We have no agreed-upon history, no consensus on 'what happened'. In fact, it may never be possible to have one, for such an approach suggests that there is some kind of 'objective' truth the historian can uncover and record. As noted in Chapter 1, we do not believe such a 'truth' exists; instead we argue that it is important to reveal one's point of view, or bias. Hence, rather than try to accurately reflect all points of view,[1] we have chosen to weave together our own personal experiences with a very general history of the development of the women's movement in English Canada. We do not attempt to tell the story of the Canadian francophone women's movement, either in Quebec or outside it. Although in different places and at various times English- and French-speaking women have worked together, on the whole the two have remained distinct. Our experiences are within the anglophone women's movement, and that is what this book is about.

To explain the currents, politics, or strategies of the women's movement in a book such as this, we have to reduce them to clear and concrete statements; but the reality is rarely so neat and tidy. In Chapter 1 we described the politics and strategies of the currents within the women's movement today. But when we look back to the late 1960s and early 1970s we cannot talk about these currents, because they did not exist as such then; we can only identify elements of what later became liberal, radical, and socialist feminisms. To supply the labels in retrospect would be misleading, and so instead we are using the terms 'institutionalized feminism' and 'grass-roots feminism', introduced in Chapter 1.

The contemporary women's movement in Canada had two distinct origins. On the one hand were women from such established orga- nizations as the Canadian Federation of University Women and the YWCA, who lobbied for the Royal Commission on the Status of Women (RCSW). Many of these were professional women who oper- ated within traditional institutions and wanted more opportunities for women within them. As the different currents of feminism dis- tinguished themselves, this current came to be called 'liberal fem- inism', but for the early period we will refer to it as 'institutionalized feminism'.

The other origin of the contemporary women's movement is more community-based. These women were drawn into the movement from the left, from the universities, from their homes and work- places, and knew little or nothing about the institutional expressions of feminism. Although they had no clearly defined strategy to differ with institutionalized feminism, we can see differences, notably in their emphasis on collective organizing, consciousness-raising, and reaching out to the 'woman on the street'. We will refer to this current as 'grass-roots feminism'. Again, however, a caution: these terms are somewhat misleading because they suggest a self-con- sciousness on the part of each about the existence of the other, and clear distinctions between the two.

In this chapter we will begin by examining the contemporary movement's roots in the first wave of feminism. Then we will briefly chart the development of the second wave in Canada, beginning with the material and ideological context of the 1960s and moving through the establishment of the women's movement in the late 1960s and early 1970s; its consolidation in the mid-1970s; its expansion through alliances and coalitions in the later 1970s and early 1980s; and, finally, the period of the early to mid-1980s, when the move- ment was defending its gains against the right and enlarging its definition of feminism.

LINKS WITH THE FIRST WAVE OF FEMINISM

The contemporary Canadian women's movement is in fact part of a long history of women organizing to change their position in society. The earlier women's movement is referred to as the 'first wave'. Canadian women's rights advocates began organizing around women's issues such as suffrage, pregnancy rights, education, and economic independence in the late nineteenth century. The first Canadian suffrage organization was founded in Toronto in 1876 by Dr Emily Howard Stowe. A wide variety of social reformers mobilized under the suffrage banner, until by 1922 women had obtained the provincial franchise throughout English Canada (Manitoba, Alberta, Saskatchewan, and British Columbia, in that order, in 1916; Ontario in 1917; Nova Scotia in 1918; New Brunswick in 1919; Prince Edward Island in 1922). Quebec women, who had been organizing around suffrage since the late nineteenth century, did not get the provincial vote until 1940,[2] although the federal franchise had been granted to all women in 1918. When the battle for the vote was won, most suffragists turned their attention once again to the questions that had previously preoccupied them.

The granting of suffrage has generally been considered to mark the end of the first wave of the women's movement. But Nancy Cott, in *The Grounding of Modern Feminism*, offers a new interpretation, arguing that the decades between 1910 and 1930 were a period of transition in which the nineteenth-century 'woman movement' was transformed and modern feminism emerged. In contrast to the nineteenth-century 'cause of woman' or claim for 'woman's rights'—in which the singular noun symbolized the unity of women—the feminism of the early twentieth century recognized the increasing heterogeneity and diverse loyalties among women, and championed individual variability.[3] Indeed, individual Canadian women remained active in a variety of causes and issues throughout the years 1920–60, but it was not until the sixties that they came together again in what is referred to as the second wave of the women's movement.[4]

While first- and second-wave feminists shared a vision of women as equal to men, they differed in their analysis of the reasons for the existing inequality and the means for redressing it. These differing analyses are what have shaped the distinct currents of feminism: it is out of analysis that specific strategies flow for making change.

The basic political strategies of the second wave—liberal feminism (reform), radical feminism (the creation of alternatives), and socialist feminism (structural change)—have their origins in the political struggles of first-wave feminists, although the names of those strategies have changed. In the nineteenth-century maternal-feminist claim of female superiority and the link between biology and morality we can see the seeds of contemporary radical feminism. Equal-rights feminism, with its focus on suffrage and property and custody laws, foreshadowed the political strategies of today's liberal feminism. And the focus of socialist and trade-union women on the plight of female wage-earners has been influential in shaping today's socialist-feminist politics. Understanding the links between these past and present forms of feminism, and the experiences and strategies of the first wave, reminds us that today's feminists did not invent the movement. We organize around many old issues as well as new ones, frequently using strategies similar to those of the first wave.

As women in the late nineteenth century tried to understand their role as women and the possibilities for change, an analysis emerged that we now refer to as 'maternal feminism'. In 1984 Lady Aberdeen of the National Council of Women of Canada put it this way:

> But in the meantime, how can we best describe this woman's mission in a word? Can we not best describe it as 'mothering' in one sense or another? We are not all called upon to be mothers of little children, but every woman is called upon to 'mother' in some way or another; and it is impossible to be in this country, even for a little while, and not be impressed with a sense of what a great work of 'mothering' is in a special sense committed to the women of Canada.[5]

In the words of Nellie McClung, maternal feminism's foremost Canadian advocate:

> The woman movement . . . is a spiritual revival of the best instincts of womanhood— the instinct to serve and save the race. . . . Women are naturally the guardians of the race, and every normal woman desires children. . . . It is woman's place to lift high the standard of morality.[6]

The main assumption of maternal feminism was 'the conviction that woman's special role as mother gives her the duty and the right to participate in the public sphere'.[7] As the National Council of Women maintained, it was woman's 'mothering'—the nurturing qualities common to all women—that made her the ideal reformer. Women had an obligation to use their moral superiority and ability to bear children to make the world a better place for everyone. According to McClung, the woman movement's focus was wide—

from how best to raise children to be good citizens to the issues of temperance, peace, and social services. Many maternal feminists were active in other social-reform movements; their larger purpose was to broaden women's role, from guardians of family morality to guardians of public morality.[8]

Radical feminism did not inherit maternal feminism's political agenda or philosophy; instead it inherited the latter's belief in women's moral superiority. Much radical-feminist writing, especially on issues of peace and violence against women, has in it the unarticulated assumption that men are inherently aggressive, violent, and self-serving. The other side of this assumption, also rarely stated explicitly, is that women are inherently different from men: women are *not* naturally aggressive, violent, individualistic, or self-serving. If women ran the governments we would have peace, equality, cooperation between nations; there would be no poverty and no exploitation. To a large extent this view is based on the belief that women's special status comes from their ability to procreate. For example, Yolande Cohen discusses 'women's capacity for procreation and the *values this implies*'.[9] She goes on to comment that women are 'particularly vulnerable to this threat [nuclear destruction]—their foetuses as well as *their life-creating values* are all especially liable to destruction', and states that feminists 'achieve an essential link in positing our [feminine] values as the foundation of a new society'.[10] Patricia Hughes writes that

> reproduction is the epitome of creativity, the ultimate creative act, and belongs particularly to women. . . . For feminists, birth, not death, and creation, not destruction, are at the centre of human existence. Feminists intend to change women's condition in a substantial way by transforming that which has been the root of women's oppression, the ability to reproduce, into the foundation of revolutionary activity which will result in life and creation *becoming the organizing force of society*.[11]

This assumption of female moral superiority, though often unspoken, is operative in much radical-feminist thought. The radical feminists' analysis of the roots of our oppression as women would not be familiar to maternal feminists, but the tone of much of their writing would.

Although maternal feminism had become the predominant public feminist analysis in North America by 1910, it was not the only feminist analysis of women's situation. Another argument for women's rights, especially suffrage, was based on natural rights: the idea that certain rights are human rights, regardless of gender. The focus of much of the equal-rights feminist movement was on changing laws so that women might have the same rights as men, among them suffrage, ownership of property, and access to higher education and the guardianship of their children. The first organizational expression of equal-rights feminism in Canada was Dr Emily Howard Stowe's Toronto Women's Literary Club, founded in 1876; in 1883 it took a name more revealing of its politics: the Toronto Women's Suffrage Association. While it fought for the franchise at every political level, it did not focus solely on woman suffrage; it also fought for improved educational opportunities for women, in 1883 supporting the opening of the Ontario Medical College for Women and in 1886 putting pressure on the University of Toronto to admit female students. Stowe argued that notwithstanding her maternal function, woman should be 'as free to choose her vocation as her brother, man, tethered by no conventionalities, enslaved by no chains either of her own or man's forging'.[12] For equal-rights feminism, suffrage was just one aspect in the struggle for equal human rights.

Flora MacDonald Denison was another equal-rights feminist.[13] Born in Ontario in 1867 and active in the Toronto suffrage movement, she differed from many other suffragists because 'she did not succumb to the dominant view that the women's vote represented a vote for purity, nor did she envision woman's contribution as merely social housekeeping'.[14] Denison called equal-rights feminists like herself 'the real suffragists' and argued that 'men and women should be born equally free and independent members of the human race'.[15] She had little sympathy for the temperance movement or for organized Christianity; she supported birth control and divorce and was a critic of the nuclear family. Despite such radical views, she worked within suffrage organizations with many social reformers and was head of the Canadian Suffrage Association from 1911 to 1914,[16] when she resigned because of controversy over her support of the militant English suffragettes.

Equal-rights and liberal feminisms shared a political philosophy that assumed the equality of women and men, and neither challenged the fundamental organization of the state. Both sought change within existing institutions. Like the former's strategy, the latter's has focused on the entrenchment of that equality in public institutions (among others, the law, the church, the family, the medical profession, and the educational system).

A third analysis of the situation of women emerged from the activities and discourse of women who were socialists and trade unionists. Though this feminism had in common with equal-rights feminism a belief in equality, and with maternal feminism the occasional suggestion that women might clean up public life, unlike them it addressed the economic inequalities of capitalism. Socialists believed that full equality was impossible under capitalism. Suffrage was useful only if it was part of a broader package of social and economic reforms. In 1910 the Woman's Labor League of Winnipeg endorsed woman suffrage 'as a practical political necessity to secure the other objects of the league', among them equal pay for equal work, the abolition of 'the evils that promote woman's degradation', the active participation of women in the trade-union movement, and improved education in domestic and health matters.[17]

In the first wave most women who were socialists made a clear separation between themselves and the women's movement. While they did not call themselves feminists or see themselves as part of the movement, they did address the problem of women's inequality. The early socialist movement regarded class alliances as more important than alliances among women against men. The Socialist Party of Canada (SPC) denounced 'all individual reforms as deceptive manoeuvres of "respectable wage-skinners" (capitalists)' and argued that the 'only demand relevant . . . was the abolition of capitalism'.[18] Socialist women challenged that one-issue focus and pushed the SPC to adopt a pro-suffrage position at their 1909 convention. Arguing with male SPC leaders over the importance of women's issues, Toronto socialist activist Edith Wrigley wrote in a letter to the editor of the SPC's *Western Clarion*: 'I have come in contact with women full of the spirit of revolt and very often it is not because "some man is a socialist" but because of some man she is working for. . . . She is "sex-conscious" as well as "class conscious" and recognizes the SPC as the only existing force in society that will help her attain her freedom.'[19]

The focus on working women and the assumption of the need for some fundamental changes can be seen in the activities of a number of Canadian women in this period. One example was Helena Rose Gutteridge, who immigrated to British Columbia from London, England, accompanied by a number of British suffragettes, in 1911.[20] There she helped to organize the B.C. Women's Suffrage League 'to deal with all matters connected with the interests of women, particularly those things that affect women out in the labour market'.[21] Gutteridge was a strong supporter of suffrage because the ballot would allow working-class women to make 'significant changes in industrial legislation governing working conditions and pay rates, thereby eliminating sweated labour, the undervaluing of women's work and poverty-induced prostitution'.[22] Her interest in working-class women lead her to participate in a variety of trade-union activities, and eventually she became a prominent member of the Vancouver Trades and Labour Council. While active in that organization she became a socialist, joining first the Federated Labour Party, in 1918, then the Socialist Party of Canada, and finally the Co-operative Commonwealth Federation (CCF) in 1933.[23] In March 1937 she was elected as a CCF representative to the Vancouver City Council, the first woman to be elected to the Council. Gutter-idge's political activities brought together her interests in suffrage, labour, politics, women, and community affairs.[24] She was just one of a number of working-class women who were politically active in the early twentieth century.[25]

Both the unease with which socialist women and trade-union activists regarded the first wave of the women's movement and the struggle to raise women's issues within socialist organizations, workplaces, and trade unions are, as we will see, all too familiar to today's socialist feminists. Just as early feminist socialists and trade-union activists pushed their organizations to take up women's issues, socialist feminists today have played a similar role with many left and far-left parties and within trade unions. Socialist feminists have challenged radical organizations to adopt more progressive positions on women's issues.

The Canadian suffrage movement was led by middle-class women. As Veronica Strong-Boag has pointed out, 'their perspective and views on proper behavior and standards infused the feminist movement, making it at times intolerant of ethnic and class diversity and often unwilling to confront profound inequities in capitalist society'.[26] In spite of these attitudes, working-class women were active in the first wave of the women's movement. While involved to some extent in suffrage activities, they were primarily interested in working conditions, in encouraging the use of union labels on products, and in arranging strike support for both organized and unorganized women workers. Recent research in Manitoba documents the role of working-class men and women and their organizations in the struggle for suffrage. *The Voice*, a Winnipeg labour newspaper, was the first paper in the west to endorse suffrage for women, in 1895; in the same year the Winnipeg Trades and Labor Council supported the franchise for women. In 1910 the Woman's Labour League also endorsed equal suffrage. Individual trade-union activists, both men and women, were active in so-called middle-class suffrage organizations such as the Equal Suffrage Club and the Political Equality League. Anne Molgat concludes her study of these activities by noting that 'it is true, as *The Voice* itself acknowledged, that the leadership [of the suffrage movement] came from the middle class. It is not true that, as Carol Bacchi and others have suggested, credit for the victory belongs solely to . . . middle-class professionals'.[27]

Black women were also active in the first wave, although the full extent of their involvement has not yet been researched. Like middle-class white women, they participated in reform societies. D'Oyley and Braithwaite note that 'the Canadian black woman, until recently, made her greatest contributions through humanitarian pursuits'.[28] Adrienne Shadd has briefly documented some of these organizations: 'The Victoria Reform Benevolent Society offered aid to indigent women in mid-nineteenth century Chatham [Ontario]. In 1882, the Women's Home Missionary Society of Amherstburg, Ontario was formed . . . in Halifax, Nova Scotia in 1914, female members of the church organized . . . a group called Women at the Well, to help raise funds for the establishment of a normal and industrial school in that city.'[29] The Colored Women's Club of Montreal began in 1900 as a social club and organization to assist black people in whatever way they needed.[30] The extent to which black women and other women of colour were involved in the suffrage movement is not yet known.

The activities and experiences of Canada's many immigrant and ethnic women in the late nineteenth and early twentieth centuries are just beginning to be documented.[31] Some groups of ethnic women were very active in the suffrage struggle—for example, Icelandic women in Manitoba. Anne Molgat goes further and argues that the latter kept the issue of suffrage in the public eye when there were no high-profile middle-class Anglo-Saxon suffrage societies to do so.[32]

The work done by the feminists of the first wave was tremendously important in making the current women's movement possible. Although we are too often unaware of who they were and what they did, every day we reap the benefits of that work. Our right to vote and to own property, to participate in the world of politics and government, and our access to higher education, divorce, and guardianship of our children, all owe much to those women.

As we look at the first wave we can see that women were organizing in a number of different ways, with different philosophies and strategies. The early women's movement was as varied and complex as ours is today. At the same time we can see that much has changed.

Although each of the major contemporary currents of feminism has a forerunner in the earlier women's movement, they are all, in a certain sense, new approaches. The world has changed enormously, and our analyses have become much more complex. The second wave has been able to take for granted certain basic rights and build on those. Changes in women's work, an increasingly urbanized society, the growth of technology, and changes in family life have raised different problems and issues for contemporary women. We are both a new movement and a part of a long history of women organizing for change.

THE BEGINNINGS OF THE SECOND WAVE: THE 1960s

The ideological and material beginnings of the contemporary women's movement in Canada can be traced to the early 1960s. While the terms and concepts of 'women's liberation', 'feminism', 'sexism', and 'discrimination against women' were not used in this period, the material conditions for the development of the contemporary women's movement had appeared. The widespread political, economic, and social changes that were occurring in those years provided the context in which the women's liberation movement would grow. This section will focus on two key factors in the re-emergence of a politically active women's liberation movement: new education and work patterns for women, and the emergence of several popular movements.

In 1900 women made up about 13 per cent of all workers; by the early 1980s that figure had risen to 39 per cent. This massive increase is one of the most significant economic changes in Canada in this century. Except for a small drop immediately after World War II, the number of women entering the work-force has risen steadily since the beginning of the century. Since the early 1950s the percentage of working-age women who have jobs or are looking for work has increased steadily across Canada, reaching 48.9 per cent in 1979; this increase is true for all age groups and for both single and married women.[33]

As married women became a permanent part of the work-force, their families came to depend increasingly on two incomes. Unfortunately, women's participation in the work-force has not made any substantial difference in their responsibilities in the home. Women continue to work a double day. As the tension between family and work, and between domestic and wage labour, increased, women came to feel that their situation was unjust.

In addition, important changes took place in women's educational patterns. The educational system in Canada expanded in the 1960s, partly because of the baby boom of the post-war period and partly because of changing career goals, but most importantly as a result of changing expectations about careers and lifestyles.

Universities were made more accessible to large numbers of students in several ways: low tuition fees, easily obtainable student loans and grants, and the expansion of universities themselves. A number of universities were founded in this period, among them York, Simon Fraser, Trent, and Sir Wilfred Laurier. Universities were also in a state of tremendous upheaval as a result of the student movement, which was itself influenced by the civil- and native-rights movements, the draft resistance to the Vietnam war, and the struggle for Quebec's right to self-determination. They were accessible, politically active places, where every aspect of the organization of society was being questioned.

Most women were unable to reap the alleged benefits of education. Women were going to colleges and universities in increasing numbers, but they still could not find the kinds of jobs they had been led to believe were available to them. Increasingly, women were forced to recognize the contradictions between the promises of education and the reality of the labour market. Appealing to the system for freedom, equality, and justice produced no real changes. Despite women's best efforts, the system showed itself unable and unwilling to accommodate them. Women's increasing consciousness of their oppression as women politicized them.

> VOICE 2: It is a measure of the contradictory messages of the times that throughout high school in the 1960s, I never doubted that I would go to university or be a career woman. Nor did I have any doubts about my measure as a person compared to males.
>
> At the same time, in 1968, I was able to write an essay concerning the 'essential' character of mothering, and how this was woman's most important job. My essay was a diatribe against those 'women's libbers' and what I perceived their goals to be.

The 1960s are remembered as a decade of upheaval, change, revolutionary ideas, and resistance to any authority. The changes in women's work and educational patterns examined above took place in the context of a series of popular movements in which everything was questioned. This questioning was expressed in new lifestyles, language, music, dress, ideas, and values.

> VOICE 2: I had a tremendous sense of being young and powerful.

The 'swinging sixties', long hair, communal living, jeans, dope, loud
rock music—all the things our parents hated—showed us how powerful we were.

Myrna Kostash, who has examined these years in Canada, sees the
beginning of this turbulent period in the protests of the 'peaceniks'
of the early 1960s.[34]

Women were active in the peace movement in Canada from its
beginnings. *Toronto Star* columnist Lotta Dempsey wrote a column,
on 21 May 1960, about the seemingly inevitable drift toward nuclear
war and concluded by asking: 'What can women do?'[35] As Kay
Macpherson and Meg Sears remember, that column triggered an
enormous response, which led to the calling of a mass meeting in
Toronto's Massey Hall. Out of that meeting the Voice of Women
(VOW) was founded on 28 July 1960, 'to unite women in concern for
the future of the world' and 'to provide a means for women to
exercise responsibility for the family of humankind'.[36] By the fall of
1961 this non-partisan women's organization had a membership of
5,000 and a newsletter with a circulation of over 10,000. Although
largely a peace organization, VOW began to take up other issues of
concern to its members. Its second president was Thérèse Casgrain,
and under her leadership VOW took up the issue of biculturalism and
established itself as a bilingual organization. In addition, it began to
address women's health and safety issues: it first raised the issue of
radioactivity in breast milk, and at its 1964 conference adopted a
position in favour of the legalization of the distribution of birth-
control information.[37]

In addition to the peace movement, there was growing support
and activity in Canada for the civil-rights movement and against the
U.S. war in Vietnam. In Canada some women who became active
in the women's liberation movement had previously been in the
native-rights movement. Many lived and worked on reserves, doing
organizing in Indian, Métis, and Inuit communities. Like many
women in the mid-nineteenth-century abolition movement, and like
their U.S. counterparts active in civil rights, they were led through
this work to the women's movement.[38]

The emerging New Left in Europe and North America challenged
the limited orthodox economistic view of communism by insisting
that the definition of what was political be expanded beyond economics. New Left activist groups such as the Student Union for
Peace Action (SUPA) were established on many Canadian university
campuses. These groups gave new life to the left in Canada and

challenged many of its accepted positions. Many of the women who joined either traditional left or New Left organizations played an important role in the contemporary women's movement.

VOICE 2: Although I was aware of the women's movement before I joined the Young Socialists, my activist involvement in it was certainly precipitated and shaped by joining this trotskyist political organization.

In 1963 the first Front de libération du Québec (FLQ) was organized. Its manifesto declared that 'the Quebec Liberation Front is a revolutionary movement of volunteers ready to die for the political and economic independence of Quebec'.[39] Many radicals outside Quebec supported the province's right to self-determination. At the same time native people began to question their treatment by the Canadian government and to resist white authority.

VOICE 2: The War Measures Act of 1970 was a really significant event for me. Somehow this event—in *my* country, with arrests of people I *knew*—brought all the pieces of the past few years together. The political messages—René Lévesque, the anti-Vietnam protests, the civil-rights movement in the States and the student unrest in France—combined with the personal aspect—hootenannies and social protest music, hippieism, and lifestyle challenges. The political transformation jelled and I made a self-conscious leap from social democracy and the NDP to revolutionary socialism and the Young Socialists.

The sixties generation also challenged how people organized and lived their personal lives; it challenged traditional notions of sex, family life, and marriage, and advocated new types of relationships and new ways of thinking about personal lives. When the birth-control pill became available in Canada, in 1966, it became possible for women to be sexually active without fear of pregnancy, though in retrospect we can see that this 'sexual revolution' did little to challenge traditional male/female sex roles, nor did it concern itself with female sexual pleasure. The structure of family life was challenged by an alternative, the co-op or collective house, and the necessity of both marriage and children was questioned. These challenges to how people organized and lived their personal lives were later taken up in the context of the women's movement.

VOICE 1: For complex personal reasons, I was a rebel concerned with justice and fairness during my adolescence. It was largely an unhappy and confusing period in which I felt very isolated, not having yet discovered others who were as angry about and critical of the world as I was.

When I entered university in 1966 I rapidly discovered a whole world of rebels and radicals. I early became interested in marxism; in particular the 1844 manuscripts, the most humanist writings of Marx, had a profound effect on me.

From 1968–70 I was involved in the McGill student movement. Looking back, however, I can see that I was on the periphery. Women were not really 'let in'; almost all of the women who were involved, myself included, were connected to political men. It was clearly our ticket in. I can remember meetings where nothing that a woman said was taken seriously.

VOICE 3: Although I didn't think of myself as politically aware or active in the 1960s, looking back I can see that they were a very formative time for me. I was living in a small town in the southern U.S.A. On the one hand in school I learned that 'all men were created free and equal' and that the U.S. was the most democratic and free society in the world and that I should 'love my neighbor as myself'. And then I looked around and saw 'For Whites Only' signs and blacks having to use separate schools, churches, bathrooms, water fountains, etc. I shocked my parents and teachers by refusing to accept such a dual system. My initial objections came from the illogic of such a society rather than a political critique.

My first year in university (1969) was an exciting one—the black students occupied part of the college and at the end of the year we all went on strike to protest the killing of students by the National Guard at Kent State University in Ohio. For me that was a very significant year. I began to develop a political view of the world—it was a simplistic and uneven analysis, but it was also a base on which to build later. I was idealistic and I believed that our society could be changed and the civil rights and anti-war movements of the 1960s provided some basis of analysis and a sense that together people could make change.

During the 1960s several other important milestones for women contributed to the emergence of the second wave of the women's movement. One was the 1963 publication of Betty Friedan's *Feminine Mystique*.[40] Although written from an American perspective, the 'problem without a name' spoke to the experience of many Canadian women, and was the first widely read liberal-feminist analysis of women's oppression. Following Doris Anderson's appointment as editor of *Chatelaine* magazine in 1959, in the early 1960s *Chatelaine* increased its circulation and published articles on Friedan's book, needed changes in divorce laws, poverty among women, and birth control. Gradually women began to insist that their issues were public ones, a process that led to the development of the ideology of 'the personal is political' (to be discussed in Chapter 6).

It is in the 1960s that we see the ideological and material setting for the re-emergence of the women's liberation movement. The traditional women's organizations were still active in their areas, usually quietly. These groups, established in the first wave of the women's movement, included the YWCA, the WCTU, the Canadian Federation of University Women, the National Council of Women, the Business and Professional Women's Clubs, and Women's Institutes. Though their memberships were still small and their influence in the political sphere almost non-existent, they provided an important training ground. The political and organizational skills developed in these organizations played an important role in the development of the women's movement.

THE EMERGENCE OF THE WOMEN'S LIBERATION MOVEMENT: 1967–71

The women's liberation movement emerged as a separate activist movement in Canada in the late 1960s and the early 1970s, as feminists put forward analyses of women's oppression, proposed strategies for change, and formed organizations. In describing this period it is difficult to capture the intensity and the strength of the almost spontaneous eruption of feminist ideas and questions. The dominant mood was one of anger as the enormity of our oppression dawned on us, mixed with relief that we could now make sense of our personal histories. The following section focuses largely, though not exclusively, on the growth and development of the grass-roots women's movement. It was this segment of the movement that was completely new, emerging from the 1960s social movements and women's critique of their position in society. Institutionalized feminism continued to operate in much the same way it had for years, but in the late sixties it focused its attention on the formation of a royal commission on the status of women, discussed at greater length later in this chapter.

The grass-roots women's liberation movement was activist, optimistic, and externally focused. Feminists talked about, wrote about, made speeches about, demonstrated about, had meetings about everything. We had boundless energy and sought eagerly to collectivize our experience, to move away from our isolation and powerlessness. Those years had an almost evangelical tone to them; feminists wanted to spread the good news, and we were ready to take on the world and male chauvinism in all its manifestations. As grass-roots activists we saw ourselves leaving no stone unturned in the quest to identify all the ways in which we experienced our oppression. The progress made during this brief period was nothing short of phenomenal. In a very few years the movement had put the issue of women's liberation on the social and political map, and it was characterized by an exciting and seemingly endless growth.

VOICE 2: The turmoil and excitement created by feminist ideas really pushed the Young Socialists and League for Socialist Action. Certainly the size and intensity of the movement forced the organization to relate to it both inside and out. Many feminists thought that socialists were just 'using' the women's movement for our own ulterior purposes, but the reality was that many women in the revolutionary left were personally affected and personally committed. Inside the organizations, there was lots of protest and anger, discussion and change as women challenged organizations of the left to be actively involved in the struggle. This meant not only changing their political ideas and orientation, but also trying to clean up the chauvinism inside the organization. It was a pretty strife-ridden period.

VOICE 1: One woman was reading women's-liberation material coming out of the U.S. We started talking about it, almost in a secretive way. Marlene Dixon, an American feminist, came to Montreal to teach at McGill University and a group formed around her in 1969. I have little memory of what we actually talked about, but I think it was certainly one of the first self-consciously feminist women's groups in Montreal.

VOICE 3: I wasn't involved in the women's liberation movement in these early years, but I certainly remember hearing about it in the media—a bunch of bra-burning, man-hating crazies. I wanted nothing to do with such women. I responded to claims that women were discriminated against with what I have come to recognize as a fairly typical liberal individualist defensive response: 'I can do whatever I want and if I'm good at it no one will stand in my way'. I thought there were much more important issues to deal with, such as discrimination against blacks or the war in Vietnam.

In the early years we formed study groups, avidly read the few books available on women (Friedan, de Beauvoir, Mitchell, and Morgan for example),[41] organized large public meetings on women's liberation, listened to speakers from England and the States, distributed pamphlets published by small presses or gestetnered by hand, arranged for illegal abortions . . . In Montreal women's liberation meetings were held weekly at University Settlement, and each week many new women came. Much of the discussion focused on the abortion issue. These meetings were frequently dominated by American women who had come to Canada with draft dodgers; although their American-centric point of view was a problem, many of them were politicized and experienced organizers, from whose skills and analyses we learned a great deal. Similar meetings were held in cities across Canada.

At Simon Fraser University in B.C. a women's caucus of the Students for a Democratic Union (SDU) group was formed in June 1968 and quickly became the off-campus Working Women's Association and Vancouver Women's Caucus. Women's caucuses of the SDU were also formed at the University of Alberta and the University of Regina. In Toronto in late 1967 a group of women involved in SUPA began to meet to discuss their oppression as women. They prepared a brief on abortion and in December 1967 personally presented it to the House of Commons. This group, largely made up of women associated with the University of Toronto, continued to meet through the academic year 1968–69.[42] The University of Toronto Women's Caucus of SUPA formed the Toronto Women's Liberation Movement (TWLM) in the fall of 1968, which then formed a working women's committee, modelled on Vancouver's Working Women's Association, and did strike-support work. By February 1970 Regina Women's Liberation was active and had organized a co-op day-care centre on the University of Regina campus. And later in the year Fredericton Women's Liberation Movement held its first public forum, on abortion, which drew 150 people. Many of the women's groups initially formed within universities made conscious decisions to move outside in order to reach larger numbers of women.[43] Although often seen as negative, this process of forming larger numbers of organizations with clear political analyses reflected the growing maturity and deepening political commitment of the grass-roots women's movement.

In this early period, feminists devised a form of organizing unique to our movement: consciousness-raising (CR). Consciousness-raising groups were usually made up of eight to ten women who met regularly over a period of time. They operated without a leader, and discussion could include any topic of interest to the members. It often focused on aspects of women's lives such as personal relationships with men, sex and sexuality, body image, or friendships and attraction between women. In an article in *Canadian Woman Studies*, Patricia Carey argues that 'the survival and consistent progress [of feminism] can be attributed, I think, to one of its most frequently trivalized symbols and political vehicles: the consciousness raising session'.[44]

The CR group emerged very quickly as a powerful tool for grass-roots organizing. By focusing on the reality of each woman's life, it was able to reach and, ultimately, activate women in a way that more abstract calls to organize around an issue would not have done. These CR groups encouraged women to think about acting politically. More formal political meetings were essential to organize those women who had been reached, but it was the CR group that got so many out to those meetings in the first place.

Women came together in these groups because they needed the support of other women and because they wanted to figure out how to make changes in their lives. In this period it was difficult to work as a feminist in the community or workplace—we were too few, our ideas were too new and often regarded as 'crazy'.

VOICE 2: Although I was not involved in consciousness-raising groups as such, there were women's caucuses inside the Young Socialists, and later, the Revolutionary Marxist Group. And although they weren't set up for this purpose, these caucuses often acted much like consciousness-raising groups and we discussed personal issues as well as organizational ones.

VOICE 1: Probably one of the most successful Montreal ventures that I was involved in was the organization of CR groups through the women's centre on Ste-Famille during the early seventies. We publicized widely that we were facilitating these groups; we would use the free announcements on radio and women could call and indicate what night they would like to meet. When we had a list of ten names for a particular night we would convene the first meeting. One of us would attend one or perhaps two sessions to get the group under way and then the women were left on their own. The Ste-Famille women's centre organized dozens of these groups. At the same time women were initiating such groups on their own, and there existed an extensive network of consciousness-raising groups across the city of Montreal (though I suspect confined to the English middle-class community, although not entirely based in or around the university.)

Abortion was one of the issues around which the women's liberation movement organized in the early 1970s. Many women's experiences of illegal abortions and the difficulty of obtaining birth control made it a powerful personal as well as political issue. In 1968 the McGill Student Society published *The Birth Control Handbook*, although the distribution of information on birth control was still illegal in Canada.[45]

The book rapidly became an underground best-seller across North America. In August 1969 the federal government legalized the sale of birth-control devices, the dissemination of information about birth control, and abortion when approved by a Therapeutic Abortion Committee (TAC). Although the legalization of abortion through such committees went some way towards meeting women's demands, it did not give them full control over their bodies, and many feminists were outraged. The first demonstration calling for the repeal of the new Canadian abortion law was held on 14 February 1970 in Vancouver, B.C.[46] In April 1970 the Vancouver Women's Caucus asked women across Canada to join a caravan that would travel from Vancouver to Ottawa, stating: 'We consider the government of Canada is in a state of war with the women of Canada. If steps are not taken to implement our demands by Monday, May 11, 1970, at 3:00 P.M. we will be forced to respond by declaring war on the Canadian government.'[47] From Vancouver to Kamloops to Edmonton to Regina to Winnipeg to the Lakehead to Toronto and finally to Ottawa, women marched with a coffin to symbolize all the women who had died from illegal abortions.[48]

VOICE 1: While I was at McGill I arranged an illegal abortion for a friend of mine (before the Morgentaler clinic was open). It was a horrible experience; the man wore a greasy housecoat, had Playboy pinups on the wall, and in fact did not perform a proper abortion. My friend developed tetanus and almost died. It was this experience, in part, that made the Abortion Caravan so exciting for me. It was a public, political and defiant challenge to the Canadian state on the part of women; it posed such a sharp contrast to the seedy, underground and ugly experience with that backstreet abortionist. I still have the sign from the demonstration that read, 'THIS UTERUS DOES NOT BELONG TO THE STATE'.

Along the way, from Vancouver to Ottawa, thousands of supporters signed a petition calling for repeal of the abortion laws. Women demonstrated outside the Parliament buildings, marched to 24 Sussex, chained themselves to seats in the visitors' gallery, and disrupted the proceedings of Parliament. We felt strong, powerful and united; anything was possible. In assessing the Abortion Caravan in November 1970, the Saskatoon Women's Liberation (SWL) group stated that 'in Canada the abortion caravan was a catalyst for the movement, generating new groups and increasing women's awareness of their collective strength'.[49]

Day-care was another important issue around which feminists

organized. At Simon Fraser University feminists were active in setting up a parent-run day-care co-op in 1968. The sFu Co-op Family grew out of a sit-in at the Board of Governors meeting room in the spring of 1968: 'Some students and faculty who agreed with the sit-in brought their children there for a number of days. When the sit-in ended the nursery also ended, but the idea of an on-campus nursery was born.'[50] In 1969 the TWLM occupied a building on the University of Toronto campus as a day-care centre. As one sit-in participant remembers:

> Our intelligence agents filtered out . . . lists of university-owned houses and we put several under surveillance. When we found one occupied only by crashers we simply moved in, letting negotiations, which had been fruitless before our action, continue. It was direct action. . . . There we were painting, collecting cribs, high-chairs, toys, hauling in an old fridge and getting excited.[51]

In June 1971 a national day-care conference was held. As John Foster commented in 1971: 'Day care is newly present in the public mind. It's been on a lot of mothers' and fathers' minds for a long time.'[52] The National Action Committee made day-care a priority from its beginning. At one of its earliest meetings a motion was carried, that 'the expansion of daycare centres in its broadest and widest concept be a matter of priority'.[53] A submission to the government of Canada a year later revealed the mixed feelings of the women's liberation movement about day-care: was it a part of the women's movement, or was it a separate movement of parents? The submission quoted child-care specialist Barbara Chisholm:

> I believe that further consideration of day-care should not be undertaken within the context of the [RCSW] Report. . . .This is because the focus of the Report is, rightly, on women. Day-care, while inseparable from that focus as one of its aspects, has many more. Perhaps its most important focus is not the mother and her needs, but the child and his needs. And perhaps all of those can only be planned effectively in terms of the Canadian family and its needs.[54]

In later years some day-care activists remarked that the women's movement had more or less ignored day-care in favour of other issues. Perhaps Chisholm's statement explains some of the ambiguity on the part of the women's liberation movement. However, NAC, other feminist organizations, and many individuals remained supportive of and active in the day-care movement.

The debates over whether to focus on one or several issues occupied much time in the early years. For many women, entry into the movement was through a specific issue, and as they organized in that area their specific concerns gradually became linked to a range of other women's issues. In the late sixties and early seventies much of this debate focused on whether or not to concentrate on repeal of the abortion laws. In 1972 the collective of the Canadian Women's Educational Press wrote:

> Those concerned with a single-issue orientation began coalitions for a national movement for repeal of the abortion laws. This group has become synonymous with women's liberation for many sectors of the Canadian population. This is unfortunate as it demonstrates the failure of the Canadian movement to develop a comprehensive strategy. While the control of our bodies is fundamental to the liberation of women, taken in isolation and within the context of the existing political structure, the demand for repeal of abortion laws will do little to change the general situation of women.[55]

Organizing around single issues instead of the more general theme of women's liberation has always been the subject of debate within the women's movement. With hindsight we can see that single-issue organizing can make it appear that women's oppression is an isolated problem: for example, if women had full access to abortion, then they would no longer be oppressed. While most single-issue organizations did not themselves hold such a simplistic view, their rhetoric was often guilty of suggesting the answer was that simple. Multi-issue organizations and politics, on the other hand, stress the interconnectedness of issues and therefore point out the systemic character of women's oppression. In both the first wave and the contemporary movement, feminists have organized around both general and specific issues.

The first national conference on the women's movement was held in Saskatoon in November 1970. Over two hundred women attended, half of them from outside Saskatoon. The purpose of the conference was to determine where and how the women's movement should proceed. *The Pedestal*, a Vancouver feminist newspaper, summed up the debate:

> Most participants held one of two completely different ideas of what the conference was all about. One group, led by, but not exclusively composed of YS/LSA [Young Socialist/League for Socialist Action] women, came to argue for a national strategy focused on a national day of protest against the abortion laws. The other group, much less conscious of itself as a group, hoped to discuss and analyze immediate problems of various groups: how to become more than campus-based

groups, how to avoid becoming a social service bureau around abortion counselling, how to develop a political analysis and strategy that will lead to revolutionary change.[56]

At that same conference Marlene Dixon, then a sociology professor at McGill and the featured speaker, attacked the notion of a movement uniting all women. She argued that race and class divide women too much to build a common movement and urged women to unite with other revolutionary forces rather than to form an autonomous movement. The Toronto feminist newspaper *The Velvet Fist* reported that while

> many women at the conference were sympathetic to the idea that all of the demands of the movement could ultimately be met only within a socialist society, they were unsure about converting the movement into a movement of only socialist women. Several women voiced this feeling; as one said, 'Since I've been in the movement I've become more of a socialist, but if it had been a socialist movement I was joining, I know I would never have joined at all.'[57]

> VOICE 2: The debate over whether or not the struggle for women's liberation should be organized around a single issue or as a composite struggle was also waged inside all the revolutionary left organizations I was a part of—the League for Socialist Action, the International Marxist Group in England, and the Revolutionary Marxist Group. And it was over the same questions too: which was the best way to develop consciousness, and collective struggle among women. Some argued that single issues meant that we could draw in women who weren't yet prepared to go for the 'whole package', and offered a way to focus our united strength so that we could win victories. The League for Socialist Action argued this over the abortion issue.

> Others argued that there was certainly a place for organizing on a single-issue basis—in order to fight the Birch proposals on day-care, we didn't have to argue for a full program of women's liberation. But the women's movement should not restrict itself to any one issue on a continuous and restrictive basis. This not only cut off our access to women who were concerned about other issues, it also cut up and narrowed the scope of women's struggle for social change. This was a problem if we were to be able to develop a revolutionary consciousness.

> But perhaps most importantly, restricting the women's movement to one issue at a time was not satisfactory to those who were committed feminists already. In any struggle for change, it was important to be able to sustain those who were already conscious and active.

The organizational expression of this debate between single and multi-issue focuses is seen in the splits and factions within organizations. For example, in the fall of 1968 the TWLM was formed out of the University of Toronto women's caucus of SUPA. By 1969 the radical feminists and lesbians had left the TWLM to form the New Feminists. In 1970 another group withdrew from the TWLM to form the Leila Khaled Collective to focus on Third World solidarity; they called themselves 'revolutionaries' and distinguished themselves from the 'feminists' of the TWLM. Also in 1970, a group of women withdrew from the New Feminists to form the Toronto Women's Caucus, a group that was heavily influenced by the trotskyist League for Socialist Action, to focus on abortion as the key issue in women's liberation. In September 1970 the Vancouver Women's Caucus expelled members of the League for Socialist Action and Young Socialists, who then founded a new organization, the Vancouver Women's Alliance, 'on the basis of mass actions to mobilize women from all sectors of society, non-exclusion and a responsible democratically-elected leadership'.[58] Different politics and different strategies began to emerge, and it became clear that 'feminism' had no one meaning.

The debates within grass-roots feminism coincided with the emergence of a consciously socialist-feminist analysis. In 1966 Juliet Mitchell published her article 'Women: The Longest Revolution' in *The New Left Review*; this was the first widely available statement of marxist feminism.[59] By 1967 women who considered themselves feminists as well as part of the Canadian left were beginning to write about their experiences. In the fall of 1967 Judy Bernstein, Peggy Morton, Linda Seese and Myrna Wood, activists in SUPA, wrote an article, 'Sisters, Brothers, Lovers . . . Listen', tracing the role of women in the New Left in Canada.[60]

For socialist feminists the split between socialism and feminism was to be the major challenge, both theoretically and practically, in the years to follow. In these early years women were socialists and feminists but had little, if any, sense of socialist feminism. In their introduction to *Women Unite!*, the first publication, in 1972, of the Canadian Women's Educational Press, the Press collective argued that

> an important distinction from their American sisters was that Canadian women more uniformly developed an analysis of their oppression based on a class notion of society. This was an important development not only because it is the first major divergence from the American movement but because the Marxist perspective has since been central to the development of the Canadian women's liberation movement.[61]

Looking back, it is clear that many of the elements we now see as important aspects of socialist feminism were beginning to be voiced: an emphasis on moving the women's movement out of the universities and into the community, a focus on the concerns of working women, an effort to develop broad-based and broadly focused organizations, and an insistence on the need for fundamental social and political change. In the early 1970s there seems to have been widespread agreement on the need for revolutionary change if the demands of the women's movement were to be achieved. The challenge for those women who were socialists and feminists was to learn to integrate the issues of class and gender.

While grass-roots feminists were taking the movement to the streets and declaring war on the government, institutionalized feminism made the government the target of its campaign to end women's inequality. In 1966 Laura Sabia, then president of the Canadian Federation of University Women, called a meeting of all established women's organizations to discuss what could be done to change the status of women in Canada. That meeting, held on 3 May, was attended by fifty women representing thirty-two organizations.[62] Some of those women formed the Committee for Equality of Women in Canada (CEW), which called on the federal government to establish a royal commission on the status of women. The need for a commission was presented as arising out of concern for human rights, a position reminiscent of equal-rights feminists' justification for suffrage.[63] That same year women in Quebec organized the Fédération des femmes du Québec (FFQ). On 3 February 1967 the Royal Commission on the Status of Women (RCSW) was appointed; it submitted its report in September 1970. It is no accident that the first calls for a royal commission came from women involved in established women's organizations. They had previously lobbied governments, often successfully, and believed in the state as an agent of change. They were able to put into action an 'old-girls' network' that gave them not only a sympathetic media voice (*Chatelaine*), but sympathetic MPs and government officials (for example, Grace McInnis and Judy LaMarsh).[64]

While in many parts of the country the RCSW and provincial Action Committees became the focus of women's activity, many women in large urban areas looked elsewhere. The size of the movement in cities such as Montreal, Toronto, and Vancouver gave feminists many outlets for their political activities: single-issue and general-action groups, community and social-service work, a variety of political ideologies, and student and socialist organizations. Feminists elsewhere focused on the RCSW as an important route for change and a way of organizing women.

Many women active in left organizations were critical of the RCSW, dismissing it as just one more government pretence of reform. Opinion was not unanimous, however. Other socialist feminists saw great potential in the RCSW report. Pat Schultz, for example, a member of the Toronto Women's Caucus, wrote: 'Critics of the Report. . .see only its limitations, but fail to recognize its potential for mobilizing women initially around its demands but eventually going far beyond. We have in this report a weapon that we can use in our coming struggles.'[65]

Early in January 1971 Laura Sabia called a meeting of the CEW, which had been dormant while awaiting the report of the Royal Commission. Sabia cautioned CEW member groups that 'only in *joint action* can we be sure that the Report will not gather dust on some Parliamentary shelf'.[66] The CEW decided to dissolve itself into The National Ad Hoc Action Committee on the Status of Women (NAC), whose purpose was to pursue the implementation of the RCSW recommendations. The list of member groups on NAC's first steering committee in April 1971 suggests that these women had a particular, somewhat limited, view of the women's movement:

Canadian Federation of Business and Professional Women
Canadian Federation of University Women
Canadian Home Economics Association
Canadian Union of Public Employees
Catholic Women's League of Canada
Federated Women's Institute of Canada
Federation of Labour (Ontario)
Federation of Women Teachers Association of Ontario
National Chapter of Canada, IODE
National Council of Jewish Women of Canada
National Council of Women
New Feminists
Women's Coalition (for the Inclusion of the Word 'Sex' in the Ontario Human Rights Code)
Women's Liberation Movement [Toronto]
YWCA[67]

By December 1971 NAC had forty-two member groups.[68] In January 1972 a motion was made at a general meeting to enlarge the steering committee to include the National Voice of Women (VOW), the Single Parents' Association, the Association for the Repeal of the Abortion Law, and the Ontario Committee on the Status of

Women. In early 1972 the group dropped the 'ad hoc' from its name and became The National Action Committee on the Status of Women.

The list of steering-committee members reveals that while NAC had made some attempt to include the grass-roots women's movement from its inception, it was largely a coalition of institutionalized feminist organizations, many of which had existed since the early twentieth century. The challenge for NAC in the years to follow was to become a coalition that would truly represent the variety and range of the women's movement in Canada.

By the end of 1971 the women's movement was established as a force in Canadian society. The abortion law had been modified; feminists had mounted a national campaign to protest the limited nature of that change; the RCSW had been formed, had done its research, and had reported to the government on the need for wide-spread changes to improve the status of women; women's organizations had been formed in major urban areas and universities across Canada; the first issue of a women's newspaper, *The Pedestal*, had been published in Vancouver; the first gay liberation group in Canada, the University of Toronto Homophile Association, had been formed; and the first women's studies course had been given at the University of Toronto.

By this time grass-roots feminism was already articulating a sense of itself as different from institutionalized feminism. The Discussion Collective that produced *Women Unite!* wrote in its introduction:

> The [women's liberation] movement differs greatly from the middle-class women's rights groups which consist mostly of professional and church women. Although the broad base of both is the improvement of the quality of life for women in Canada, the philosophy of the women's rights groups is that civil liberty and equality can be achieved *within* the present system, while the underlying belief of women's liberation is that oppression can be overcome only through a radical and fundamental change in the structure of society.[69]

CONSOLIDATING THE WOMEN'S LIBERATION MOVEMENT: THE 1970s

After the initial period of founding organizations and establishing the issues, the women's movement passed into a period of consolidation. The tremendous number of existing feminist organizations addressed a wide range of issues and provided a variety of services to the movement and to women in general. As the movement grew, the two currents within it—grass-roots and institutional feminisms—began to move in clearly different directions. As we shall see, grass-roots feminism became marginalized because of its focus on internal questions of strategy and direction. At the same time liberal feminists became well established in the eyes of the public as the spokeswomen of the women's liberation movement.

1. Organizational growth

Through the 1970s the women's movement expanded enormously, both in the numbers of women's organizations it included and in the range of issues it addressed. Feminists were developing theories about the nature and basis of women's oppression; women's studies programs were created, books and journals published, lecture tours organized, and much collective discussion held. It is difficult today to appreciate how little research or writing on women existed in the early 1970s. Feminists were hungry for reading material, and each new publication was eagerly seized and passed on from friend to friend. Pamphlets printed privately or by small presses, many of them from Britain and the United States, had wide circulation. Such early publications as *Sisterhood is Powerful, Century of Struggle, Notes from the First (and Second) Year*, and later *Women Unite!* and *Women, Resistance and Revolution*, were widely read and discussed.[70]

All contributed to the development of a wide-ranging and deeply probing body of material and analysis. In fact, the increasing emphasis on theory resulted in the growth of many different ideas and groups. At the time many feminists felt the unity of the women's movement was being splintered as factions pitted themselves against one another: radical feminists against socialist feminists, supporters of a 'Wages for Housework' analysis against those of traditional marxism, unaligned feminists against revolutionary vanguard parties, and heterosexual feminists against lesbians.

The number of women's organizations and services started up in the seventies is staggering. The women's movement was able to build on a broad base of support established in its early years, and to focus in more detail on the provision of social services, the development of political strategies and theory, the growth of a women's culture, and the further expansion of the movement through new organizations. In British Columbia in 1969 there were two established women's groups; in 1970, five; in 1971, twelve; in 1972, twenty-four; and by 1974, approximately one hundred women's groups.[71] One B.C. activist recalls that 'there were women's groups popping up like popcorn all over the provinces'.[72] By November 1979 there were thirty-nine women's centres across Canada, at least one in every province and territory.[73]

National women's organizations such as Indian Rights for Indian Women, NAC, the Canadian Women's Educational Press, the Canadian Alliance for the Repeal of the Abortion Law (CARAL),[74] Women for Political Action, the federal government's Advisory Council on the Status of Women, the National Association of Women and the Law, and the Feminist News Service were formed. Provincial organizations such as the B.C. Federation of Women (BCFW), the Ontario Daycare Organizing Committee, and the Ontario Committee for the Repeal of the Abortion Law began. National conferences were held by lesbians in June 1973 in Toronto, and by rape crisis centres in June 1975. A broad variety of women's journals and newspapers began publishing.

One of the most popular types of grass-roots organization in the early and mid-1970s was the women's centre. Some of these centres were established in colleges and universities, but most were organized by women to serve the population of a region or city. The philosophy behind them was explained in a 1975 funding proposal by a B.C. centre:

> Most women's centres are founded on the premise that while changes in the law are crucial to achieving equality for women, these must be supplemented by the work of women in the community. As long as women are treated unequally in society, they will require compensatory services such as those offered by women's centres.[75]

One of the results of the RCSW was that government funding for women's groups was made available through several sources: the Secretary of State, Opportunities for Youth (OFY) grants, and Local Initiative Programme (LIP) grants were important in providing the initial funding for many women's centres. The Prince George Women's Centre, founded out of a women's discussion group in Prince George, B.C., in the fall of 1972, was typical of the many women's centres established across Canada.[76]

Its aims were to 'provide a wide range of information for women; . . . a referral service to women who are new to the community or who are frightened to approach more specific community services alone; and . . . a space where women could meet to share their concerns'.[77] A meeting was held to determine the major concerns of

Prince George women, including 'the need for more diversified day care centres, a greater variety of job opportunities for women, expanded family planning facilities and the mental health of young housewives'.[78] The activities of the Prince George Women's Centre from 1972 to 1976 mirror those of other centres across Canada: co-ordinators came and went, the group established women's services (in this case a transition house), started a newsletter, held workshops, and organized conferences. Regular membership fluctuated back and forth from a medium-sized group to a tiny core of women.[79]

Once we had named our oppression and begun to understand its extent, we felt the need to provide a variety of feminist alternatives. Many women turned to setting up services such as rape crisis centres, battered-women hostels, bookstores, and information and counselling services. In Toronto, for example, the Rape Crisis Centre was established, as well as women's shelters such as Interval House and Nellie's, and the Women's Credit Union. In Vancouver the first women's bookstore in Canada was opened on 16 July 1973.[80]

Some women focused on staging feminist cultural events and promoting feminist artists; others concentrated on developing feminist lifestyles. Once a range of women's services had been established, a strategy emerged: if the system would not provide what women needed, feminists would establish alternatives and through them exert pressure for change. While the creation of feminist alternatives to some extent marginalized the women's movement, it also provided a bridge to certain working-class women. By making these services accessible to them, the movement set up an important challenge to the prevailing media image of feminists as white middle-class women interested in getting ahead in the corporate world. The growth in size of the women's movement made it possible to begin to address the variety of needs and issues women were voicing.

2. Issues

Just as the number of organizations grew, so did the range of issues the women's movement addressed. That the three legal challenges discussed below were raised by women and men not formally aligned with the women's movement attests to the movement's growing, though sometimes invisible, influence. Feminists throughout the country followed, and sometimes actively supported, the Murdoch, Corbière-Lavell, and Morgentaler cases. The other two issues to emerge in this period, sexual orientation and race, were challenges to the women's movement itself. Grass-roots feminists had begun to expand the base of the movement, and now lesbians, immigrant women and women of colour demanded that the movement include them and address their issues.

In 1971 Irene Murdoch, an Alberta farmer's wife, launched a court challenge to the notion of male ownership of family property and the devaluation of women's work in the family. She argued that her domestic labour and help with the farm during her twenty-five year marriage should be considered a financial contribution and entitle her to part ownership of 'her husband's' farm upon the break-up of the marriage. An Alberta court refused her title to any of the property, and instead awarded her $200 per month. When, in 1974, the Supreme Court of Canada upheld that decision, farm wives organized in protest and lobbied for recognition of their labour. The Murdoch case opened the doors to a redefinition of family property and a revaluation of women's unpaid work in the family.[81]

In the same period, between 1970 and 1973, Jeannette Corbière-Lavell, a status Indian, challenged Section 12(1)(b) of the Indian Act by which she lost her Indian status when she married a non-Indian; not only did males who married non-Indians not lose their status, but their wives were made status Indians. In October 1971 the Federal Court of Appeal ruled that the Indian Act was discrim-inatory and illegal. But when the case was taken to the Supreme Court the lower court's decision was overturned by a five to four decision.[82] (The issue was finally resolved in 1985, when Indian women were allowed to marry non-Indians without losing their Indian status.)

Abortion, as we have seen, has been an important focus of the second wave, and not surprisingly, it too moved into the court system in the early 1970s. The abortion-related charges laid against Dr Henry Morgentaler in 1970 initiated almost two decades of court battles. Those battles are summed up in the following table:

June 1970:	First charges laid in Quebec
November 1973:	Morgentaler acquitted by jury in Montreal
April 1974:	Quebec Court of Appeal overturns jury acquittal and orders Morgentaler to appear for sentencing
March 1975:	Supreme Court of Canada upholds Court of Appeal action
June 1975:	Morgentaler acquitted by another Montreal jury
September 1976:	Morgentaler acquitted again at retrial of original charges after serving only ten months of an eighteen-month sentence

December 1976:	Quebec government orders a halt to prosecutions of Morgentaler
June 1983:	Manitoba government charges Morgentaler and seven others
July 1983:	Morgentaler and two others charged in Toronto
July 1984:	Ontario Supreme Court rules against Morgentaler's challenge that Canada's abortion laws violate the Charter of Rights and Freedoms
November 1984:	Toronto jury acquits Morgentaler and others
October 1985:	Ontario Court of Appeals overturns acquittal and orders new trial
October 1986:	Morgentaler appeals to Supreme Court of Canada
January 1988:	Supreme Court of Canada overturns Ontario Court of Appeals decision and declares that TACs violate women's right to choose[83]

Although the Supreme Court's 1988 decision declaring TACs unconstitutional is a tremendous victory for the women's movement, it is not the end of this long and difficult fight.[84]

Two other major issues were raised within the context of the women's movement itself. At the founding convention of the British Columbia Federation of Women, in September 1974, Vancouver feminist activist Pat Smith posed a question that many women across Canada were beginning to ask with increasing regularity: 'Why no lesbian policy?'[85] The issues of lesbians and heterosexism emerged during the 1970s as controversial, yet crucially important to the women's movement. The acrimonious debates in the U.S. organization NOW over lesbianism and its place in the feminist agenda, and the subsequent division between lesbian and heterosexual feminists, are now part of feminist legend.[86] The history of these issues in Canada is different. Lesbians and gay men began developing organizations, separately and together, in this period. The gay movement developed alongside and sometimes in conjunction with the women's movement. Inevitably the women's movement had to deal with the issues of sexual orientation and gay rights, and the gay movement with the issue of feminism.[87]

Lesbians had been working within all currents of feminism, but were largely invisible except within radical feminism. Lesbian feminists' critique of society in this period resulted in a strategy we have come to call lesbian separatism. Skeptical of the ability of men or society to change, these women argued that lesbians should separate from male-dominated society and focus on creating woman-positive places for women. The comment 'feminism is the theory, lesbianism is the practice'[88] found a receptive audience.

Such a position was clearly more compatible with radical feminism because of the latter's analysis of the origins of women's oppression, although not all radical feminists were lesbians, nor were all lesbians radical feminists.

VOICE 1: In 1973 I was involved in yet another women's centre, also on St-Laurent; in Montreal we seemed to have an endless optimism about the viability, possibility and necessity for a women's centre. What I remember most clearly about this centre was the tremendous conflict that developed around lesbian separatism (and, I suppose, homophobia, though we did not have the word for it in those days). The activists in the centre were divided between a group of 'socialist feminists' and a group of 'lesbian separatists'. We kept a notebook in the hallway near the telephone where women could write comments/suggestions/criticisms about the centre. It became the venue for a vituperative attack on a straight woman. Although I remember few of the details, the woman, a friend of mine, was devastated by the intensity and anger of the attack. As a straight woman it was a difficult time: to come to grips with both personal homophobia and curiosity as well as confusion about what kind of redefinition of feminism was necessary to make sense of lesbian separatism and lesbian experience. For the first time I recall experiencing a sharp divide about what it meant to be a feminist.

VOICE 3: I came out as a lesbian and discovered feminism at the same time. I wasn't very politically sophisticated, didn't know about different currents of feminism, etc., but I did have a clear sense that the women's movement was where I wanted to be. However, after a few visits to women's liberation groups, I realized that while a number of the women were lesbians, that was not an acceptable topic of discussion or political activity. And so I turned to lesbian organizations. There I found the support and community that I needed as I struggled with what my love for women meant. Although I didn't think it was practical to completely separate from men, the notion of separatism appealed to me and seemed like a plausible political strategy. I thought that if we all just lived our lives differently and created separate places for women, that we would soon develop a parallel society of lesbians, feminists, and perhaps a few men.

Lesbian feminism has had a tremendous impact on the women's movement, forcing the discussion of issues of sexuality and insisting that feminists grapple with heterosexism. The struggle to legitimize those issues was a long, difficult, and sometimes bitter one. Heterosexual feminists felt judged as women who had 'sold out' to men;

lesbians felt heterosexual women did not appreciate the privileges our society accorded them for living with and loving men. But while there were many tensions, in Canada we continued to work together within the women's movement.

Initially many lesbians felt the need to organize autonomously as lesbians, regardless of larger individual political analyses, for many of the same reasons women first came together in CR groups: the need for support and a safe place for self-definition, to explore the existence of a lesbian feminist politic and to understand feelings of discomfort within the women's movement. However, after this early period women discovered that being a lesbian in itself was not necessarily a sufficient basis for organizing. Lesbians have a variety of different political analyses and strategies, which make it difficult to organize on the basis of sexual orientation. The struggle was, and remains, to insist that the women's movement take up the issues of lesbianism and heterosexism. The ease with which heterosexual feminists and lesbians have discussed these issues has varied across the country. Julia Creet's study of the British Columbia Federation of Women suggests that the raising of lesbian issues was difficult, but on the whole positive. When Toronto feminists organized a day-long event, called 'A Fine Kettle of Fish', to explore the differences and common ground between lesbians and heterosexual feminists, the result was mixed—an imaginative exploration of the topic by the event's organizers and savage personal attacks in the discussion groups.[89] As lesbian issues and the concept of heterosexism became more accepted aspects of the grass-roots women's movement, many lesbians moved into other feminist organizations and activities, while some continued to organize as lesbians. (As we are fond of saying, lesbians are everywhere.)

Another important set of issues was raised by immigrant women as, throughout the 1970s, they began to organize services, associations, and resources to meet their needs and those of their communities.[90] While the following examples are from Toronto, similar organizations were being set up in major cities across Canada. In 1973 a group of Spanish-speaking women in Toronto established the Centre for Spanish Speaking Peoples (CSSP).[91] At the time these women and the CSSP were not seen as a part of the women's movement either by themselves or by feminists. While women of colour, immigrant women, and native women were all involved in the movement, women's issues were still narrowly defined in a way that reflected the racial (white) and class (middle) assumptions of its founders. Individual feminists were supportive of such organizing efforts, but the women's movement as a whole did not regard such organizations as an integral part of its struggle. In 1974 two important immigrant women's organizations were formed in Toronto. The first, Women Working with Immigrant Women (WWIW), began when women who worked with immigrant women in service agencies met to learn more about their needs.[92] By 1976 WWIW had asked government employees to leave the organization and the immigrant women had taken over its direction. The other organization formed in 1974 was the Women's Community Employment Centre (WCEC). Formed by a group of immigrant and refugee women in Toronto, WCEC focused on the needs of immigrant women concerning labour issues and the job market.[93]

Women's organizations in the 1970s almost always included on their agendas some mention of the concerns of black and native as well as immigrant women. Although more research needs to be done, it seems that the women of colour actively involved in feminist organizations were few. The reasons are complex: the origins of the women's movement, the definition of 'women's issues', and racism. It was not until the early 1980s that the women's movement began, at the insistence of organizations of women of colour, to incorporate an analysis of racism in Canada into their politics.

THE EMERGENCE OF DIFFERENT FEMINISMS

While feminists have always had different analyses and strategies, in the early years of the women's liberation movement the emphasis was on the similarities—a shared sisterhood—rather than the differences in politics. It was in that period that one found organizations called simply 'Women's Liberation Movement'. In the seventies, especially in the early years, the women's movement began, as we have noted, to recognize and articulate the differences, although still within the rhetoric of sisterhood.

Although at the time feminists felt that the movement was being splintered into numerous small groups with different politics, with hindsight it is clear that this shift represented a healthy and much-needed diversification. The underlying differences in political analyses and strategies had always existed, but in the excitement of naming our oppression and organizing for change, we lost sight of them. Looking back, we can see that the integration of feminism into the gamut of political strategies and analyses was a sign of the strength and importance of the women's movement. At the time, however, we struggled with the fear that our movement was breaking into small factions. Now we can see that such debates forced us to articulate our different politics in ways that were positive. The political analyses of the institutionalized and grass-roots feminist movements became more clearly differentiated, and within the grass-roots movement radical and socialist feminists began to distinguish themselves.

1. Institutionalized feminism

In the period after 1970 many institutionalized feminist organizations were being set up in response to the generation of ideas and activism of the earlier stages. In 1973 the federal government established the Canadian Advisory Council on the Status of Women and most provincial governments followed suit, establishing provincial status of women councils.[95] Other groups like NAC, CCLOW, and the National Association of Women and the Law began to assume public leadership.

In 1979 Lynn McDonald, then NAC president, described the basic orientation of these groups:

> The distinctive characteristics of the Canadian Women's Movement . . . included, first, a political position slightly left of centre, progressive/reformist, revolutionary in certain respects, but with little questioning of capitalist institutions. . . . Second . . . solidarity across class lines, and, to a lesser extent, across ethnic and religious barriers. . . .
>
> Finally, there is a commitment to the ordinary political process, public education and persuasion of politicians and parties within the system; conversely, avoidance of partisan politics and radical political theory. . . .
>
> The reformist position has largely meant advocating greater state intervention (short of state ownership of the means of production) by way of protective legislation, equal pay, and the creation of a broad range of social services. . . .[96]

McDonald referred to the 'Canadian Women's Movement' when she meant the institutionalized feminist Canadian women's movement. The non-partisan equality-for-all stance of these organizations made them acceptable to the media and the government, and they have come to be regarded as *the* women's movement. Assuming the position of spokeswomen for the movement was made easier by the hostility with which grass-roots feminists regarded the media.

VOICE 1: I remember in the early years of the women's movement in Montreal that I was approached by *The Montreal Star* (now defunct) to be interviewed, along with other feminists, for their Saturday magazine. We had a discussion about this in whatever group I was in at the time, and we drew up a list of conditions under which we would be prepared to participate in the interview: conditions such as seeing the finished piece, not having our names used, etc. Not surprisingly, the *Star* declined to interview me under these circumstances and in the end interviewed women with much more conservative politics. When I read the interviews I regretted not having spoken to them, but I also felt that they would have 'distorted' what I and other more political feminists might have said. In retrospect, I do feel that we abandoned the struggle with the mainstream media and in so doing forced them to find women prepared to speak for the women's movement. Although there is no doubt that our voices would have been distorted, the struggle to be heard in the media was an important one; to some extent we silenced ourselves.

The National Action Committee's report on the 1972 'Strategy for Change' convention is an excellent example of the political analysis of the institutionalized women's movement:

A prime value of the conference was a two-fold realization: on the one hand, by 'conservative' elements, that confrontation techniques are sometimes effective strategies in situations where change is not part of normal expectations; on the other, by 'radical' elements, that reasoned argument based on substantial fact goes further in the pursuit of real justice than does partisan emotion.

It is . . . essential to know that *behind* some apparent flagrant discriminations there exists historical oversight—even a cultural barrier which should not be interpreted as intentionally hostile. It is essential, too, for women seeking change to understand thoroughly the practical procedures and legislative 'machinery' so that they can harness, rather than destroy, the potential energy of established political, economic and social power.[97]

The year 1975, proclaimed International Women's Year (IWY) by the United Nations, was very important to institutionalized feminism as a rallying point. The Canadian government launched a 'Why Not?' campaign around women's issues, and many of its activities were co-ordinated by the provincial Advisory Councils and the Federal IWY Programme. The National Action Committee identified four principal areas of concern: equal pay, child-care, abortion, and family property.[98]

Grass-roots feminists, on the whole, were suspicious of IWY but participated in some of the activities. For example, the Saskatoon

Women's Liberation Organization (SWL) informed its members in April 1975 that it was 'organizing a multi-issue demonstration and rally on May 10 in conjunction with other major centres in Canada', but then pointed out that 'we want to bring to the attention of the public and the government that the IWY government program has so far been a farce in dealing with the issues that the women's movement has raised time and time again'.[99] In May 1975 a consultation meeting was held in Ottawa regarding the IWY World Conference to be held in Mexico. The SWL representative reported that 'This meeting was a gesture as [were] all the other activities of the IWY program. . . . The Government of Canada has well demonstrated that it has no intentions of making the fundamental changes that are required to partly alleviate the oppression of women in Canada. . . . [The way this meeting was handled is] again an indication of the lack of seriousness of government in regards to grass-roots participation.'[100] The Toronto newspaper *The Other Woman* dismissed IWY as 'male-decreed', 'elitist', and 'capitalistic'.[101] And Yukon women drew up a list of resolutions protesting government allocation of money for regional and national conferences and calling for that money to be used instead 'to support relevant impoverished women's organizations in the Yukon'.[102]

Within institutionalized feminism there were various types of women's groups. Most feminists regarded the governmental status-of-women councils with suspicion, as reflecting the politics of the party in power and hence having no independent critical voice. Grass-roots feminists were also suspicious of institutionalized feminist organizations like CCLOW and NAC. Yet throughout this period women became increasingly active in other institutions such as churches, trade unions, the medical profession, and the educational system. Like grass-roots feminism, institutionalized feminism had a variety of faces.

2. Grass-roots feminism

The task of grass-roots feminists was more complex than that of institutionalized feminists because we had to start from scratch and develop our politics, theories, organizational models, and processes—which it was possible to do only by focusing intently on our internal development and politics. Grass-roots feminists never lost sight of the fact that the ultimate goal was to involve large numbers of women in the struggle for change. However, the reality of that task—the tremendous time, energy, and commitment it took to form organizations and to understand women's oppression and communicate it to others—meant that in the early to mid-1970s grass-roots feminists virtually ceased to do the kind of massive outreach that had characterized the period of the Abortion Caravan and national women's liberation movement conferences. In the struggle to define our different politics and strategies, we were sometimes narrow-minded and harsh. The acrimony of the theoretical debates made it difficult to work together the way we had in 1969.

The initial political split was between institutionalized and grass-roots feminists. At the NAC-organized 'Strategy for Change' convention, in 1972, about sixty women attended an emergency meeting to criticize NAC and form a 'radical caucus of women'.[103] At that time the term 'radical' referred to all women who rejected NAC's belief in the liberal-democratic system. Gradually this unity of radical women was broken. Those who would later form the radical-feminist current turned towards the creation of social and political alternatives to the existing society and concentrated particularly on the issue of violence against women. Those who would form the socialist-feminist current turned to theoretical discussion and tended to concentrate on workplace issues.

In the early 1970s it was difficult to articulate the need to develop feminist theory because of the anti-theoretical stance of the grass-roots movement. Grass-roots feminists regarded theories as 'male', and initially concentrated on documenting our experiences as women. These writings later formed the basis for feminist theories, but they were originally written from an anti-theoretical position. Gradually both radical and socialist feminists moved away from this anti-theoretical stance and have since created a large body of feminist theory.

Radical feminism. Radical feminism as an articulated theory and organizational form is difficult to locate in the records of the women's movement in the 1970s. This came as a surprise to the three of us, as in the seventies we had the impression that radical feminism was the dominant grass-roots politic. The reasons for this dearth of records probably lie in radical feminism's attitude to structure and theory. In its attempt to overthrow all vestiges of male domination, radical feminism tended to look on both formal organizations and theory with more suspicion than other currents did. Institutionalized feminism accepted a fairly traditional organizational structure, which had a built-in emphasis on record-keeping. And the socialist-feminist politic emphasized the importance of both organization and a clearly articulated political position. The example of the New Feminists, a radical-feminist group founded in Toronto in 1969, is suggestive of those attitudes. When the group was founded, they explained that they left the 'marxist-dominated' Toronto Women's Liberation Movement because 'New Feminists were feminists essentially, rather then being primarily concerned with politics'.[104] The distinction between feminism and politics is an interesting one, and perhaps suggests one of the reasons why a number of radical feminists turned to cultural organizing, women's services, and women's businesses.

One of the earliest Canadian descriptions of the radical-feminist politic was published in 1972 in *Women Unite!* Bonnie Kreps, the author of the article, rejects the notion that men and women are different 'in their nature[s]'. She argues that radical feminism

> chooses to concentrate exclusively on the oppression of women as *women* and not as workers, students, etc. [Radical feminism] therefore concentrates its analysis on institutions like love, marriage, sex, masculinity, and femininity. It would be opposed specifically and centrally to sexism rather than capitalism . . . and would not be particularly concerned with 'equal rights' [or] 'equal pay for equal work.[105]

U.S. author Ellen Willis argues that this early 1970s radical feminist politic had completely disappeared in the U.S. by 1975 and has been replaced by 'cultural feminism'. Although cultural feminism grew out of radical feminism, Willis argues that the two are completely different:

> . . . radical feminism in its original sense barely exists today. The great majority of women who presently call themselves 'radical feminists' in fact subscribe to a politics more accurately labelled 'cultural feminist'. That is, they see the primary goal of feminism as freeing women from the imposition of so-called 'male values', and creating an alternative culture based on 'female values'. Cultural feminism is essentially a moral, countercultural movement aimed at redeeming its participants, while radical feminism began as a political movement to end male supremacy in all areas of social and economic life, and rejected the whole idea of opposing male and female natures and values as a sexist idea, a basic part of what we were fighting.[106]

Willis argues that in the U.S. radical-feminist ideas were very popular and reached large numbers of women who had no general radical political critique:

> These women experienced sexual inequality in their own lives, and radical feminism raised their consciousness. But their awareness of

their oppression as women did not make them radicals in the sense of being committed to overall social transformation, as the early radical feminists had naively assumed it would. Instead they seized on the idea of women's oppression as the primary oppression and took it to mean not that feminism was or should be inclusive of other struggles, but that left politics were 'male' and could be safely ignored.[107]

Gradually cultural feminism developed the argument that women possessed 'female values' and that these were the same as the traditional feminine virtues. Certainly this current of feminism exists in Canada, as we saw earlier in this chapter in the quotes from Cohen and Hughes. Whether or not 'true' radical feminism has disappeared in Canada remains to be seen. However it has developed, radical feminism was an important current in this country in the 1970s, and its history is still to be written.

Socialist feminism. For women who were socialists and feminists the challenge in the 1970s was to understand how to integrate the issues of class and gender. In some parts of the women's movement, when socialist feminists raised the issue of class they were seen as being 'too sympathetic to men' and thus selling women out. And when they tried to raise women's issues among marxists they were accused of being 'bourgeois feminists'.[108] In an attempt to resolve this apparent contradiction, and to distinguish themselves from radical feminists, socialist feminists began developing their own theory.

Gradually a small body of writings by Canadian women on socialist feminism was published: by Charnie Guettel in 1974, Dorothy Smith in 1977, Roberta Hamilton in 1978, the Vancouver Women's Study Group in 1979.[109] In struggling with these issues socialist feminists made a number of important theoretical advances: the rediscovery of the notion of a historical-materialist basis for women's oppression; the beginning of the discussion of how to unite the concepts of patriarchy and capitalism; and the discovery of women's resistance. We are able to write Chapter 3 of this book only because of this long process of articulating socialist feminism as a distinct entity.

Canadian socialist feminists struggled to develop theory and practice in a number of different ways. Some turned to the academic world and pursued studies there. Others were actively involved in revolutionary organizations, within which they were struggling to understand the relationship between revolutionary socialism and feminism. Still others focused on the women's movement itself and argued that theory should emerge directly from practice.

VOICE 1: At this time there were certain appealing things about joining a revolutionary socialist organization, especially for someone coming from the women's movement. Perhaps the most important was the certainty with which these organizations presented their program and strategy. They appeared to have a clear class perspective, and to integrate socialism and feminism. They confidently developed a view of how revolution would come about; this made it so much easier to see the day-to-day work, politics, meetings and hassles in some larger perspective. I rapidly was disillusioned about the possibilities of such a plan and program, but for a period of time it spelled some relief from the fragmented experience of the women's movement.

It is also true that revolutionary organizations were an excellent training ground for organizational and political skills: because there was an acknowledgement of different skill levels, it was easier to turn our attention more directly to training new members. In retrospect and even at that time I was aware of how much of a dilemma the organizational question was. The left was unable to incorporate the best lessons of the women's movement in terms of organization, but the left also understood some things about how to organize. Two polarities, both problematic and certainly not yet resolved. Later, when I moved from the women's movement into the trade-union movement, I was confronted again with the question of organization. The unions resolve the question of organization in yet another way: not more successful than the women's movement or the left. If only we could learn the lessons of each.

In addition to developing skills and political theory, women in the left were also developing a practice uniting their socialism and their feminism.

VOICE 2: In 1974–75, I was still a member of a revolutionary left organization. There were several of us in the organization in Toronto who were excited by the developments in the women's movement, and in the left. We felt that all this political movement meant that we should be able to develop strong collective actions and consolidate a socialist-feminist slant within the women's movement.

But we were frustrated by our own organization's growing workerism and unwillingness to see women's liberation as highly important in the struggle for social change—there was definitely a hierarchy of struggles. We were also frustrated by factionalism within the women's movement—one current against another, and almost everyone against the revolutionary left organizations. There didn't seem to be a way to pull the struggle for socialism together with the struggle for women's liberation, despite the fact that socialists saw women's liberation as part of its program for change, and many currents of the women's movement identified themselves as anti-capitalist, and even socialist.

In 1973 Selma James from England's Wages for Housework campaign toured Canada.[110] The debate on wages for housework was an important theoretical and strategic turning point for many socialist women. The traditional marxist focus had been on women's waged labour, but James argued that housework was like any other work. This insight led to a new political economy of women: housework came to represent what was different in women's experience. This was especially important to women coming from a marxist analysis of work. James's argument created the framework in which to develop an analysis based on a marxist approach, but that acknowledged women's different experiences.

To radical feminists the notion of housework as women's work confirmed their notion of women as a class. The Wages for Housework analysis galvanized both currents of grass-roots feminism, but in two different directions: socialist feminists towards a political economy of women, and radical feminists towards women as a class.

VOICE 1: The Selma James tour in 1973 was an important theoretical and strategic turning point for me. And it had a galvanizing impact in Montreal. Theoretically I thought the questions she raised were very important; strategically I did not agree with the Wages for Housework strategy. In those days we talked about the fact that it reinforced women's place in the home; in many ways the wages-for-housework demand has been translated into mainstream demands . . . eg., for a guaranteed annual income or pension for homemakers.

Socialist-feminist practice during the 1970s included events and issues outside the women's movement and 'women's issues'. In 1971, at the Ste-Famille women's centre in Montreal, the issue of Quebec's right to self-determination was heatedly debated and eventually supported. The debate was complicated by Quebec nationalism, American imperialism (because of the presence of so many draft-dodgers and American feminists) and English Quebecers.

VOICE 1: I can remember hitching a ride in 1972 with a man (in the days when hitching was not so dangerous!). He was a Québécois and we had a conversation in French about the public-sector general strike. He couldn't believe that as an English Quebecer I would speak French, or support Quebec's right to self-determination. It was an eye-opener for me about the tremendous gap.

Women's solidarity pickets were organized for the Artistic Wood-workers strike in Toronto in 1973, and women supported local actions such as the hospital workers' strike—partly for equal pay—at Toronto Western Hospital in 1972. Some women's groups had emphasized the importance of focusing on working women and their issues from the beginning of the movement, and this tradition was confirmed by many of us who later called ourselves socialist fem-inists. In the early and mid-1970s we were struggling within the two different movements of socialism and feminism to create a united socialist/feminism. Briskin reflected the attempt to redefine social-ism when she wrote in 1974 that 'there is no longer a place for the separation of the women's question from the mainstream socialist movement. . . . Socialism must be redefined'.[111]

The first self-conscious socialist-feminist organization in Canada was Saskatoon Women's Liberation (SWL), founded in the late 1960s.[112] According to the group's history, the early founders were 'a group of women on the left working towards equality for all women'. By 1977 SWL had a position paper on its political analysis that called for the group to 'affirm that it is a Feminist-Socialist women's group, with the perspective that women's true liberation will occur only under socialism, and that socialism will only be established with the liberation of women'.[113] The group continued to exist until 1981, making it one of the longest-lived socialist-feminist organizations in Canada.

By the late 1970s, then, the character of the women's movement had changed substantially. The movement in its earliest stages had opened up the political terrain with its assault on public conscious-ness, its externalized orientation, and its mass outreach. But the concentration on theory and on the creation of feminist alternatives combined to take the grass-roots movement out of the social and political mainstream. In the absence of any other strong feminist perspective, the liberal-feminist current managed to gain public prominence and assumed hegemony over the territory. More and more, we heard women say, 'I'm no women's libber, but I am for women's rights'. The media had clearly succeeded in characterizing the grass-roots women's movement as a bunch of crazy women, and those who lobbied for equal rights (the liberal-feminist current) were deemed to represent women's legitimate concerns. The grass-roots movement became clearly differentiated into two distinct currents: radical feminism and socialist feminism. Both currents began to articulate their own strategies and analyses and increasingly focused on different issues within the women's movement.

FORMING ALLIANCES AND COALITIONS: THE LATE 1970s TO MID-1980s

The period of the late 1970s and early 1980s was characterized by a gradual move towards re-establishing a broader and more public character for the grass-roots women's movement. In particular, rec-ognition was growing of the need to organize collectively and pub-licly in a way that encouraged the participation of a variety of people. For instance, there was a return to the large public demonstrations typical of the early 1970s for International Women's Day and spe-cific issues such as abortion or day-care. Another aspect of this strategy was the forming of alliances and coalitions with other orga-nizations and social movements, a process made easier by the fact that women were working largely at the local, and sometimes prov-incial, level. At the national level NAC continued to operate as *the* Canadian women's coalition.

Within the women's movement the three currents were often dis-tinct and active in different areas. Radical feminists focused on violence against women as their main issue, while socialist feminists concentrated on various aspects of women's work, and liberal fem-inists continued to lobby the government for legal changes.

1. Activities of the three currents

Liberal feminists. During this period liberal feminists were con-solidating their political power. Their success was evident in 1981, when the wide range of contacts liberal feminists had in government and the media were put to the test in the debates regarding the new Canadian constitution. The inclusion of Section 28(b) in the consti-tution represented a major victory for the women's movement. Although its leaders were almost all liberal feminists, feminists of all political persuasions were involved in the Ad Hoc Committee of Canadian Women on the Constitution, and lobbied for the inclusion of a guarantee of equality for women in the constitution.[114]

In the late 1970s through the mid-1980s liberal feminists consol-idated their political power through NAC, which presented itself as a national voice and represented women's interests to the government as a non-partisan political lobby group. It began in 1972 with 30 member groups; by 1981 it had approximately 170; by 1984, over 290; and, by 1987, approximately 450.[115] Although Toronto control remained strong, NAC slowly began to change to make itself more truly a national organization; in 1980 ten regional representatives were added to the executive.[116] Then-president Jean Wood's statement in the fall of 1981 that 'NAC really is 'the grass-roots women's groups of Canada'[117] reveals NAC's perception of itself as widely representative of Canadian women. From a grass-roots perspective, while 170 member groups were impressive, they did not begin to represent the range and diversity of the Canadian women's movement.

Radical feminists. By the late 1970s violence against women was becoming a key issue, particularly for radical, or cultural, feminists. Indeed, many radical-feminist political organizations emerged specifically because of it. For example, in September 1977 Women against Rape in British Columbia proposed a 'national Day of Protest against Violence against Women', to be held on 5 November. In Toronto the rally became a march down Yonge Street, ending with a demonstration in front of a pornography cinema; the demonstration became violent and some women were arrested. The following Sunday two hundred women and men protested the arrests. Out of this series of demonstrations the radical-feminist political organization Women against Violence against Women (Toronto) (WAVAW) was formed.[118]

Initially the political orientation of that organization was not clear, and many socialist feminists attended the early meetings. But that lack of clarity did not last long: 'WAVAW maintains that sex oppression is universal and functions as the model for all other systems of oppression. . . .Men have created the structure of society and, as a whole, are the oppressors of women. Class, race and national divisions are all products of masculinist ideology.'[119] Other WAVAW groups were formed across Canada and led many important campaigns.

In planning for the 1978 International Women's Day celebration in Toronto, WAVAW argued that men should be excluded from the events: 'After an unfortunately acrimonious debate (in the coalition) and a vote (2 to 1), WAVAW and its supporters walked out.'[120] The issue remained controversial, and when in the 1979 IWD preparations it re-emerged, WAVAW's position was again defeated. The group attended the rally to distribute leaflets criticizing the 'male left military style' of the planning coalition. This criticism was supported in an editorial in a new radical-feminist newspaper from Toronto, *Broadside*, published by a number of WAVAW members. The editorial argued that the coalition was controlled by the male left, 'lacked any feminist content, soft-pedalled women's liberation and was unconsciously coy on the subject of lesbians'.[122]

In the west radical feminism also expressed itself in feminist therapy. Alice de Wolff, active in Vancouver in the early years of the women's movement, remembers that a number of the women in her CR group became interested in developing feminist therapy as a political extension of a radical-feminist analysis.[123]

In early 1979 a number of women began meeting in Toronto to discuss the formation of a women's political party. The Feminist Party of Canada was launched at a public meeting, on 19 June, attended by over 600 women and a few men. While the founding members did not give the party's politics a specific label, their motivation and writing is reminiscent of the maternal feminism of the first wave and the radical feminism of the second. One report of the Feminist Party's founding noted that

> it was the failure of the traditional parties to fulfill a moral responsibility to represent the female electorate that formed the Feminist Party's most compelling reason to participate in elections. . . . [Their] vision is based, they stress, on values and an analysis opposed to the present male, profit-motivated political system. Values such as non-violence, environment and health protection, the control of excessive profit, and the opportunity for ongoing education have not been given a chance. The Feminist Party believes it is possible to build a radical organization which cuts across class lines and which incorporates these values.[124]

The Feminist Party was fairly shortlived, from 1979 to 1982, but it caught the imagination of a number of Canadian women, and chapters were formed across the country. In the end, however, the category of woman was not enough to build a political party around.

Lesbian organizing and organizations remained strong in this period. National lesbian conferences were held, newsletters were published, and many confrontations took place between lesbian and heterosexual women over the issues of homophobia and heterosexual privilege. In Canada the deep lesbian/straight splits that characterized the American movement in this period continued to be avoided, perhaps because so many lesbians were prepared to go unacknowledged as such both within the women's movement and without. The role lesbians have played in all aspects of the women's movement is far larger than has ever been acknowledged.

Lesbian feminism was seen by many as a current of the women's movement, though in retrospect it appears to have been an element of radical feminism rather than a distinct entity. Lesbians represented a variety of political analyses. Some were feminists, some were not; among those who were feminists all three political currents were represented. For lesbians who were socialist feminists this was a difficult period. We found ourselves torn between what seemed to be two different camps. Many of us dealt with that problem by remaining active in both socialist-feminist and lesbian organizations and raising the issues of each to the other.

> VOICE 3: It was no problem for me to call myself a lesbian feminist and a socialist feminist—trying to put the two different labels together was the problem! Socialist-lesbian feminist? Socialist-feminist lesbian? Lesbian-feminist socialist? I was all of those labels and for me they weren't really separable. I finally stopped working actively in the autonomous lesbian organizations because it became clear to me that there was no common political basis among lesbians any more than there was a common political basis among women. But it has remained very important for me to identify myself as a lesbian, and to push the women's organizations I've been involved in to take up 'lesbian' issues—because those issues are, or should be, every woman's issues.

For lesbians who were radical feminists this split did not really exist. Although not all radical feminists were lesbians, in the late 1970s and early 1980s those two politics seemed to coexist relatively easily.

Socialist feminists. The re-emergence of an externalized and publicly activist direction within the women's movement attracted the attention of many socialists. Some of these women came out of revolutionary left organizations they had joined in the early 1970s. Some had left the women's movement in the early 1970s to focus on their personal lives or education or to work in other areas, and a number of these were now drawn back into the women's movement.

> VOICE 2: As the active women's movement began to re-emerge after 1975, the left organization to which I belonged became more inter-

ested and involved in it. One sign that there was a shift taking place and a regroupment of forces was the fact that the women in my left group were able to set up a series of discussions with women not in our organization who had until recently been very hostile towards us (and vice versa). It seemed as if we were all willing to work towards some common ground in order to get an active and larger movement going again.

The different currents were also beginning to work together. The International Women's Day Conference and the May 10th demonstration in 1975, the Equal Pay campaign, the day-care campaigns, the emergence of Organized Working Women, the WAVAW actions, the abortion demonstration in 1978 were not without their hassles and factionalism, but they were a beginning of working together.

As I remember, it was socialist feminists—both in left groups and outside of them—who began to make a major move towards activism and who started to become involved in a whole range of new areas. Looking back, it seems that socialist feminists were the ones who tried to bridge the gaps between the currents. Certainly we were part of each one of the key campaigns and events mentioned above.

For socialist feminists this was a largely successful period. The emerging socialist-feminist analysis recognized the importance of making allies within the women's movement and with other important social movements. One of the earliest articulated recognitions of this was the Toronto International Women's Day Committee's basis of unity, adopted in 1979:

It is clear that we have little to gain by lobbying the government. Rather, we must put our energies into building mass actions and a mass, united movement of women which can begin to challenge the system in a more direct and serious way. We will need allies for this battle. Our primary allies are to be found in the various groups which presently form the women's movement. We also want to work with all those who challenge the economic, social and governmental forces which promote our oppression. In particular, the trade union movement can become an important and powerful force for the liberation of women.[125]

Our vision as socialist feminists carried us through the difficult realities of making allies and working in coalitions. It was at this point, when socialist feminists came to see the need for allies, that we were able to realize how unrepresentative we were. As a result we tried to integrate the concerns of lesbians, immigrant women, women of colour, and trade-union women. While we were not always (some would say, not often) successful in truly integrating these concerns, we consistently sought out those groups as allies and attempted to understand how to support their struggles.

Socialist feminists have struggled with issues of organization and structure and established socialist feminism as a major current in the women's movement. We have in many specific instances pushed liberal feminists to take up issues we felt were important and have influenced their position on others. We have addressed many theoretical issues so that it is now possible to talk about a socialist-feminist politic, as we will in the next chapter. Nevertheless, many of us feel demoralized as we now confront the limits of what we have understood to be a mass-action strategy.

In the early and mid-eighties two factors particularly pointed out the limits of our strategy. The first was the nature of alliances. Although we made some important ones, we came to understand how fragile they were. The laying of charges against Dr Morgentaler by the NDP government in Manitoba is one example. Another is the disregard shown by the leadership of the B.C. trade-union movement for groups such as Women against the Budget in the struggle against provincial budget cutbacks. The second obstacle to our mass-action strategy has come from the right wing, which we will examine later in this chapter.

The three of us came together in the early 1980s in the International Women's Day Committee of Toronto (IWDC). We arrived with three different backgrounds in the women's movement: the trotskyist left, the Montreal left and women's movement, and the Toronto lesbian community. All of us were involved in helping to create the IWDC as a self-consciously socialist-feminist organization that would function in a more open way than left organizations.

The Toronto IWDC was formed in 1978 by a group of women who had helped to plan the 1978 IWD celebrations. At the evaluation meetings of IWD-1978 'many women expressed a need for an ongoing group which could put into practice some of the ideas we had discussed in the building of the celebrations'.[126] In the spring and summer of 1979 the committee went through a series of discussions in an attempt to define its politics and strategies. A basis of unity was adopted and the IWDC named itself an anti-capitalist, anti-patriarchal organization in an attempt to contain the politics of a variety of women.[127] Its strategies included continuing to initiate a coalition of Toronto women's groups to plan IWD; making outreach to women in unions a priority; and integrating the concerns of lesbians into its politics and actions.[128]

While the Toronto IWDC was successful in many areas, it was unable to come to terms with the issues of organization and structure, political line or strategy, and, especially, recruitment, education, and expansion. The three of us left the IWDC one by one over the years 1980 to 1984, always over the issues of organization and structure. The IWDC has continued to exist, though we feel its effectiveness as a strong socialist-feminist voice in the Toronto women's movement and the Ontario trade-union movement has greatly declined. [129]

Other socialist-feminist organizations have not fared even that well. Saskatoon Women's Liberation ceased to exist in early 1981 after over ten years of activity; Bread and Roses, a Vancouver socialist-feminist group formed in late 1980, survived only until early 1982. [130] Its demise was largely a result of its inability to balance theory and practice. In this period we all experienced the frustration of socialist feminists everywhere, constantly re-inventing the wheel—structurally we never seemed to move ahead to a point from which we could begin to build a mass movement and/or organization. In later chapters we will examine some of these problems of structure and organization, the areas the three of us initially focused on as the 'causes' of our problems.

In the same period some trade-union activists were trying to raise women's issues within their movement, building on a wide basis of working-class consciousness and feminism. In the early 1970s women had become increasingly active in their trade unions and in organizing. [131] The question of how to go about taking feminism into the union movement generated a debate among feminists and union activists: should that struggle involve non-unionized women as well as women already in trade unions? At the founding meeting of Organized Working Women (OWW), in March 1976, the members narrowly defeated 'a motion which would have made it into a working women's association open to all non-union as well as union women and with a priority on organizing the unorganized. OWW instead restricted its membership to women already in unions'. [132] This, together with a policy of working only on a provincal level, resulted in a small membership, especially after 1979 when a number of active feminists left OWW.

VOICE 2: During the years when I was an active member of OWW, there was an ongoing struggle between those who wanted OWW to be a widely-based, activist organization of working women, and those who saw it primarily as a pressure group within the structured trade-union movement. This was the question behind the debate over membership at the Founding Convention in 1976—and it remained the key dividing line around every major issue over the next few years. There were a few golden years when the activists dominated and OWW made some significant gains through its active support for the Fleck strikers and for the Toronto Public Health nurses' equal pay complaint, or through its involvement in the Wives' Supporting INCO campaign or Ontario Federation of Labour conventions and committees. However, when the balance of power on the Executive shifted back towards the other side, executive members who were committed to an activist OWW got fed up and left the organization. We thought that OWW would probably die or that it could be outflanked, and that it was easier to start afresh around organizing working women than it was to continue these never-ending, often subterranean battles. But we were wrong—OWW did not die and there is no alternative organization. I think now that we should have stayed and fought.

A somewhat similar organization, Saskatchewan Working Women (sww), took the other route. The idea for sww came out of a Saskatchewan Federation of Labour Women's Conference in February 1978, and the organization was officially founded in September 1979. Membership was open to all women, 'unionized or non-unionized, paid or unpaid, who agree with the objectives of the organization'.[133] The group had four chapters (Saskatoon, Regina, Swift Current, and Prince Albert) and by 1980 had 150 members.[134] Over the years of its existence sww did strike-support work; focused on the issues of child-care, parental benefits, and affirmative action; lobbied the Saskatchewan Human Rights Committee to support freedom of sexual orientation and to end discrimination against people with children; conducted educationals on women's issues; and published a provincial newsletter. Denise Kouri, sww president in 1980–81, summed up the organization's politics:

> We are an activist organization . . . concerned with being public, outward, and militant while we believe it is important to pressure governments to make changes . . . we know that governments are not about to solve the problem for us. We do not see ourselves working through an elected party or individually lobbying government members. . . . We do not see the problems of working women as being strictly job-related, but . . . we place them in the context of women's position in the family and society as a whole.[135]

Socialist feminism developed enormously in these years, growing from socialism and feminism into a distinct and integrated theory. While still largely a phenomenon of large urban centres and universities, socialist feminism has had a significant impact on the women's movement. Because there have been only a few socialist-feminist organizations in which to work, socialist feminists have been active in every aspect of the women's movement—political, service, and cultural organizations.

2. Coalition-building

In the late 1970s through the mid-1980s the women's movement was engaged in the important process of moving beyond a white middle-class viewpoint and attempting to open itself up to represent the concerns of all women. This is an on-going process, but important steps have been taken in forming alliances and coalitions with a range of organizations, both inside and outside the autonomous women's movement. One of the primary areas that grass-roots feminism focused on was the trade-union movement.

One of the IWDC's most important contributions to the Toronto women's movement was the alliance it achieved with the women's committees in various unions, the Ontario Federation of Labour, and the Ontario New Democratic Party, as well as Organized Working Women. It was the common efforts of these groups that brought the feminist community out in support of strikes such as those against Fleck in 1978, Radio Shack in 1979, Fotomat in 1980, and Irwin Toy in 1982.[136] That alliance was also one link in the chain that has increased active trade-union support for issues such as day-care, abortion, and equal pay. Today we have come to take this alliance with the union movement for granted. However, the steps taken by the women's movement towards actively seeking and building alliances within its own community and with others represent a significant advance in the development of an activist strategy.

In Toronto IWDC attempted to impart its vision of the women's movement to other grass-roots women's organizations through the March 8th Coalition, a group of Toronto women's organizations that planned the celebrations for International Women's Day; from 1979 through 1984 IWDC played the major leadership role in that coalition. The success of IWDC and the March 8th Coalition in broadening the base of the women's movement is difficult to measure, but we think it was significant in Southern Ontario. The IWDC's height coincided with a period in which the trade unions and the Ontario New Democratic Party took up women's issues in a more serious and concrete way than they had before. In 1976 the Canadian Labour Congress (CLC) held the first conference for women trade-union activists, and in 1977 the Ontario Public Sector Employees Union (OPSEU) voted to have a full-time equal-opportunity co-ordinator. Starting in 1978, large numbers of women organized support pickets and actions for a series of 'women's strikes', such as those at Fleck and Puretex. That same year the CLC held its second women-trade-unionists conference, and in Quebec the Common Front won twenty weeks' paid maternity leave and five days' paternity leave. In 1980 the Ontario Federation of Labour (OFL) launched a major day-care campaign, and in 1981 its women's committee decided on a strategy of promoting mandatory affirmative action. The IWDC, together with independent socialist feminists, was active in all of these events. Recognized by many Ontario progressives as an important voice of the grass-roots women's movement, it tried to carry the concerns of trade-union women into the larger women's movement.

The SWW group operated in a similar way. The annual report from 1979–80 noted that its Labour Solidarity Committee had made contact with a number of unions: the Saskatchewan Government Employees Association, the Canadian Union of Postal Workers, the Canadian Union of Public Employees hospital workers, and the Public Service Alliance of Canada. Like IWDC, SWW did not confine itself to union struggles: an SWW representative attended a Childcare Association Conference, SWW co-sponsored both an all-candidates meeting during the federal election and a social event for IWD, held meetings for Zimbabwean day-care workers touring Canada with CUSO, and presented briefs to the Warman Uranium and Childcare Review hearings. Members were active regarding women's issues in the Prince Albert area and the organization protested unemployment insurance cutbacks.[137] At the 1981 convention a motion was passed 'to build links with other working women's organizations in Canada to exchange information and determine areas of possible coordination of activities in the future'.[138]

The IWDC and SWW were representative of the trend towards coalition-building. The grass-roots women's movement had a sense of itself as broad-based, addressing a wide range of issues. Slowly the definition of women's issues expanded beyond the parameters originally established by its largely white, middle-class founders.

After 1975 the grass-roots women's movement shifted its orientation. Rather than further diversification in the activist wing, there was a gradual coalescing of forces into three distinct and acknowledged currents of feminism. Rather than focusing inwards on creating social and personal alternatives, or on internal theoretical debates, we once again tried to make the women's movement outwardly directed, by turning our attention towards politicizing large numbers of women. Certainly there continued to be important differences on both theoretical issues and strategic approaches: the debates and developments of this consolidation period did not just dissolve into thin air. In real terms, however, the movement was increasingly dominated and directed not by our differences, but by the reappearance of an activist orientation seeking to re-establish a more public, participatory, and confrontational presence for the women's movement. This was accompanied by an ever greater awareness on the part of feminists from a variety of theoretical persuasions that women must work together to challenge the existing social structures successfully.

3. Our story

Our own personal histories in this period are illustrative of what was happening to many feminists who had been active since the early 1970s. We were working at eight-hour-a-day jobs, having children, buying houses, struggling to make our alternative personal and housing situations work; we were tired of arguing the same old points. We no longer had the time or the energy that socialist-feminist organizations and organizing seem to require. We did not cease to be political, but by 1984 none of us were active in women's political organizations any longer. Instead we chose to work politically in a variety of other settings, for a variety of reasons.

> VOICE 2: In 1979, after my first child, I was still able to remain active. By 1982, when my second daughter was born, I was no longer living in a collective household and was continuing to work at a full-time job. I no longer had the energy to put into working with IWDC. If it had been a question of simply contributing to an organization whose overall direction and structure I felt comfortable with, that would have been okay.
>
> But by 1982, IWDC needed more energy than I had to spare in order to develop serious political roots and offer effective political leadership. I had nothing to offer IWDC at this point, nor was IWDC able to offer me the sense of political growth and involvement that I wanted.
>
> Both OWW and IWDC had been so promising and fulfilling, and I had really felt that we were accomplishing things. Now I could not be so involved, and neither organization offered the same sense of accomplishment. I wanted to build something solid, something concrete, something I had some control over—so I joined the parent committee for my daughters' day-care.

VOICE 1: By 1984 I was coming to the end of five years of intense activity in the Ontario Public Service Employees Union (OPSEU). I had been committed to organizing women and to organizing from a rank-and-file perspective. We had some degree of success on both fronts, but I was also aware of the tremendous bureaucracy we were forced to confront. I remember at an early OPSEU convention we spent hours organizing to get a motion on the floor. When we were successful in ensuring that the motion would come up I remember feeling a sense of elation. And yet we had won nothing: we might lose the motion when it did come up. The longer I worked in the trade-union movement, the better I got at measuring the victories in very small steps; eventually the steps were too small, the victories seemed meaningless, and I knew I needed a break.

At the same time I was teaching women's studies in a community college; this gave me an opportunity to confront the tremendous conservatism and fear of the women's movement on the part of many 'ordinary' women. As a result of my frustration with union meetings, my desire for some concrete results, and my firm belief that we could reach out to women despite the conservatism, I got involved in a variety of projects. Out of this period came *The Day the Fairies Went on Strike*, a pro-union, non-sexist children's story, (co-written with Maureen FitzGerald), *Rising up Strong*, an hour-long video documentary on the women's movement in Ontario (co-produced with Lorna Weir), and *Union Sisters*, an anthology of thirty articles on women in the labour movement by union women (co-edited with Lynda Yanz).

VOICE 3: I left IWDC in the fall of 1983. I decided not to join another political organization—not that there was much choice! I was in the midst of a major career change, dealing with health problems and I didn't have the energy for another organization. I was also putting a lot of time and energy into my collective household, and on setting up an alternative 'family' system for myself. I felt I needed time to reflect on my experience in IWDC. I knew that many of the problems and issues that had come up there were familiar from other organizations, and I was tired of struggling with the same old questions and never making any progress. I could remain active and informed through my involvement with the Canadian Women's Movement Archives and through teaching in Women's Studies, and that seemed enough.

In the spring of 1984 the March 8th Coalition of Toronto suggested that the possibility of an ongoing coalition of women's groups be explored. The three of us joined the Women s Liberation Working Group (WLWG). Members of the March 8th Coalition and the WLWG felt frustrated by the disparate and often disunified character of the

Toronto women's movement. The coalition format seemed to represent a mechanism by which the different parts of the women's movement could remain organizationally and politically autonomous, but work together on an ongoing basis. Despite several public meetings, the WLWG's proposal never got off the ground.[139] Several of us decided to meet to try to understand this 'failure' and to detail our criticisms of the way the proposal was handled.

As we discussed our experiences in IWDC and with the WCWG proposal, we came to see that the problems we had encountered were not specific to those organizations, but were endemic to the women's movement as a whole. We sought means of melding theory and practice into a coherent and effective whole within the context of our socialist-feminist politic. The result is this book.

NEW CHALLENGES

This most recent period of the women's movement has been characterized by the demise or consolidation of many local women's political groups and the struggle to preserve our gains and services in the face of widespread economic conservatism and cutbacks, conservative governments, and growth of the right wing. It has also seen minority women, especially women of colour, black, and disabled women, challenge the extent to which the women's movement represents their issues.

1. Women of colour organize

A significant and positive development for the Canadian women's movement in the 1980s is the presence of black women and women of colour, immigrant and native women. While these women have been represented in the movement since its beginning, they have usually acted as individuals and been treated as tokens, and so lacked the power to push the movement to take up their concerns or the issue of racism in an effective way. Specific organizations of black, immigrant, and native women have also existed since the early years of the contemporary women's movement; however, because they frequently addressed issues that were not seen by the feminist movement as 'women's issues', they were not considered part of the movement. Not surprisingly, they were uninterested in joining a movement that did not understand their different oppressions.

Currently both white women and women of colour are struggling to understand how best to confront racism and to integrate the concerns of women of colour into all women's organizations. Some women of colour want to organize separately in their own organizations; others feel the best way to fight racism is to become members of existing organizations (which have had few, if any, women of colour as members). Some want to push white women to publicly acknowledge their own racism and that of the women's movement. Many white women are very frightened by the anger women of colour feel towards them.

The experience of lesbians in the women's movement, while different from that of women of colour, is in some ways similar, which suggest that the results of this struggle to encompass an anti-racist politic will benefit all women. Initially lesbians found it imperative to organize autonomously within the women's movement in order to understand how lesbian oppression operates. With the support of other lesbians, it was possible to challenge the women's movement to include lesbian issues as an integral part of feminism. Out of that experience came an understanding of how heterosexism functions to limit *all* women's choices, heterosexual or lesbian. Through the process of separation and challenge, lesbian issues were integrated into the women's movement, and we now view them as necessary for the liberation of all women. The struggle to get to that point was a long and often difficult one, but ultimately all feminists have benefited from it.

In Toronto the challenge to the representativeness of the women's movement has come most strongly from women of colour and black women, though the last few years have witnessed rapid growth in the organizations representing immigrant and native women as well. In 1983 the Visible Minority Women's Coalition was formed, the first consciously political (as opposed to service or cultural) group bringing together women of colour from a variety of backgrounds. By 1986, nineteen out of the fifty-eight groups listed as endorsers of the International Women's Day events were organizations representing women of colour, black, immigrant, and native women. Women of colour played a very important role in the coalition that planned the events for IWD 1986, challenging the entire planning process and raising questions about organization, decision-making, and leadership. This process made concrete to the other participants some of the ways in which white women unconsciously reproduce racism in the women's movement. The challenge of these groups of women to our definition of feminism is a profound one. The potential for growth is great; in fact, the success of the women's movement depends on our dealing successfully with this challenge, and understanding and incorporating an anti-racist position into our feminist politics.

2. *The rise of the new right*

The 1980s ushered in a period in which right-wing forces appear to be gaining power in many parts of the Western world. First there was Margaret Thatcher in Britain, then Ronald Reagan in the U.S., and now the growth of the new right and religious fundamentalism in Canada. Although here the new right is not yet closely identified with the conservative political party, as it is in the U.S. and Britain, we can begin to see those links being made. Lorna Weir has described this phenomenon:

> The reasons for the rise of the New Right authoritarian conservatism are many. We can point to rising inflation, slow economic growth and increasing unemployment; countries which do not have our high rates of inflation and unemployment haven't witnessed the rise of the New Right. Then too, there's an ongoing crisis of legitimacy: basic social and political institutions, like patriarchy, the family, and maybe even compulsory heterosexuality don't seem to have the unquestioned backing they once had. The New Right is in a sense a patriarchal backlash to the women's movement, the gay movement and stagnation.[140]

Calling for a return to an imaginary past when women and men were happy in clearly defined sex roles, the new right treats the women's movement as a crazy radical fringe, which the government does not need to take seriously. They have an ideal image of woman as mother and helpmate to man, an ideal that has little room for lesbians, single mothers, or independent women.

For women's organizations and services this rise of the new right has meant a constant battle for survival. The election of conservative provincial and federal governments has been followed by cutbacks in funding, many of which seriously endanger women's advances in social services. In 1983, when Premier William Bennett of B.C. decided to balance his budget, women's organizations such as the Rape Crisis Centre, the Vancouver Women's Health Centre, women's hostels, and transition houses, and the Vancouver Status of Women Committee suffered sharp funding cuts, which meant reducing some services and eliminating others.[141] Although B.C. women formed Women Against the Budget, one of the most successful and imaginative groups to take on the Bennett government, they were ultimately unable to stop the cutbacks.[142]

The new right has particularly targeted reproductive rights, specifically abortion. Although a 1983 Gallup poll shows that 72 per cent of the Canadian public is in favour of abortion services, their availability is decreasing across Canada. Ontario decided to follow the earlier example of the Quebec government and appeal the jury acquittal of Drs Henry Morgentaler, Leslie Smolling, and Robert Scott for providing abortions in a free-standing abortion clinic and, while that case was on appeal to the Supreme Court, laid new charges against Morgentaler and Scott, along with Dr Nicki Colodny. The NDP government in Manitoba also laid charges against Morgentaler for operating a free-standing abortion clinic in Winnipeg.

In local areas the right has become increasingly well organized and joined hospital boards, school boards, and local government. It has used these positions to cut off or decrease funding to women's centres, services, and organizations because they provide abortion counselling and/or support for lesbians. Women's groups in small towns and rural areas are particularly vulnerable to such tactics. As feminists we have organized many times to combat the right in similar actions, but it is discouraging to be fighting yet again for our right to an abortion, or the right to choose our sexual orientation. The right wing has managed not only to put us on the defensive, but to create the illusion that it represents the concerns of most women. Feminists know that this is not true. While the new right seeks to control and limit women's choices, the goal of the women's movement is for all women to have choices in all areas of our lives. A 1985 *Chatelaine* survey showed that most Canadian women have understood this: 47 per cent called themselves feminists, and a further 40 per cent supported the aims of the women's movement such as equal pay for work of equal value, the right to participate equally in the work-force and armed forces, and the need for men to take equal responsibility for household chores and children.[143] A 1987 poll showed that 73 per cent of those surveyed believed that overall the feminist movement has had a positive effect on Canadian society.[144]

Right-wing women's groups first emerged as a serious opposition to the women's movement in 1982 with the formation of Realistic, Equal, Active and for Life (REAL) Women. As their name suggests, they are skillful manipulators of the language of the women's movement. Feminists should not dismiss these women too lightly; as the P.E.I. Advisory Council on the Status of Women noted:

Right-wing women's groups have mounted a very slick campaign against most of the goals of feminism. In doing so, they have become a serious threat to the very concept of equality for women.[145]

Members of REAL Women call themselves 'pro-family': 'The family is the basic unit of society; strong families make strong nations, and for women to have equality we must also recognize that women are equal *and* different.'[146] Their strategy for women's equality includes opposition to abortion (under any circumstances), sex education, and contraception (a B.C. member said that the 'birth control pill knocks the libido out of many women and leaves them hostile to men');[147] no-fault divorce; subsidized day-care; the concept of equal pay for work of equal value;[148] affirmative action; Section 28 of the Charter of Rights (they call it 'enforced genderlessness'); and homosexuality ('one of the gravest threats to society').

Right-wing women's groups such as REAL Women pose a serious challenge to the improvements in women's lives made by feminists. While REAL Women claimed in 1985 to have a membership of 200,000, unlike national feminist organizations they refuse to publish their membership list, and their estimates vary dramatically.[149] Unfortunately the media are giving groups like REAL Women a serious hearing and suggesting that the number of women they represent is comparable to that represented by NAC. This false impression makes it important for us to stand up and be counted as feminists and to lay claim to our successes in supporting the issues and legislation that ensure that women can make choices: sexual-orientation legislation *and* pensions for housewives; the availability of birth control, abortion, *and* improved day-care facilities, and so on.

CONCLUSION

This brief overview of the many activities and points of view of the women's movement reveals a strong and vigorous movement, both past and present. A survey of women's organizations done by the CWMA/ACMF in 1988 lists approximately 1500 organizations representing nearly four million women. That list demonstrates the enormous range and diversity of the movement—single-issue to multi-issue groups, local to national, small to large, homogeneous to heterogeneous; some are self-identified as feminist, some see themselves as a part of the women's movement, and others define themselves only as women's organizations.[150] And new organizations continue to form. As we write, lesbians have formed the

National Lesbian Forum; women in Toronto, a Women against Free Trade Committee; and women in B.C., the B.C. Coalition for Abortion Clinics.

On 28 January 1988, exactly seventy-two years after women in Canada were first given provincial suffrage (in Manitoba), the Supreme Court of Canada handed down a major decision on abortion for which the women's movement can rightly take much credit. The Court declared therapeutic abortion committees unconstitutional and confirmed that such restricted access to abortion interfered with a woman's right to control her body. 'Control of Our Bodies' has long been a slogan for the women's movement. Although the struggle for that control is not yet over, the court's decision is a victory for women.

This chapter is only a beginning. In it we have provided an interpretation that links the first and second waves of the women's movement together, and also argued for the fundamental difference between the institutionalized and the grass-roots women's movements; in addition, this chapter provides the context in which to read the rest of this book. Much more research and writing needs to be done on the history of the contemporary Canadian women's movement; for example, the history of each current needs to be more fully explored. To do so, feminists need to recognize that we are making history, and to be more self-conscious about preserving the documents—the minutes and correspondence of women's groups; the oral histories, group and individual; the photos; even the posters and buttons—that will allow us to write our story as it unfolds.

NOTES

[1]An example of such an attempt is an article by Sandra Burt, 'Women's Issues and The Women's Movement in Canada since 1970' in *Politics of Gender, Ethnicity and Language in Canada*, vol. 34: Studies as part of the Research Program of the Royal Commission on the Economic Union and Development Prospects for Canada, coordinated by Alan Cairns and Cynthia Williams, Toronto, University of Toronto Press, pp. 111–69. Burt makes one mention of radical feminism and socialist feminism (pp. 114–115) in a short paragraph based on Allison Jaggar's work. She then proceeds to talk almost exclusively about national women's organizations. Since Burt never reveals her point of view (that of institutionalized, or liberal, feminism), she leads the reader to believe that hers is, as her title claims, a discussion of *the* women's movement in Canada. In fact, Burt is discussing only institutionalized feminism and seems unaware of the large and active grass-roots women's movement in Canada.

[2]Catherine Cleverdon, *Woman Suffrage in Canada* (Toronto: Univ. of Toronto Press, 1950); Veronica Strong-Boag, 'Ever a Crusader: Nellie McClung: First Wave Feminist' in Veronica

Strong-Boag and A. C. Fellman, eds, *Rethinking Canada: The Promise of Women's History* (Toronto: Copp Clarke, 1986), pp. 178–89.

3Nancy Cott, *The Grounding of Modern Feminism* (New Haven, Conn.: Yale Univ. Press, 1987).

4Following are some examples of the women's organizations started in the period between the women's movements. In 1930 the Canadian Federation of Business and Professional Women's Clubs, the 'B and P's', was formed; they supported 'programs supporting social legislation and reform of legal inequalities, and were concerned with the largely overlooked claims of unemployed women workers of all classes' (Lynne Teather, 'The Feminist Mosiac' in Gwen Matheson, ed., *Women in the Canadian Mosiac* [Toronto: Peter Martin, 1976], p. 309). In the period after World War II, the Congress of Canadian Women emerged as a branch of the Women's International Democratic Federation and was supported by women in ethnic and immigrant groups. They organized on issues that concerned them such as high prices, peace, and the education of women in world issues (Teather, p. 311). In 1951 the Canadian Negro Women's Club was formed in Toronto 'to be aware of, appreciate and further the merits of the Negroes in Canada'. In April 1973 this club initiated the formation of the National Congress of Black Women (Rella Braithwaite, ed., *The Black Woman in Canada* [n.p., n.d.], p. 58). In 1958 the Caribbean Club was sponsored by the YWCA of Toronto. This Club was made up of 'single West Indian women who came to Canada under household workers' permits. On the average twenty women met on Thursday evenings, which were "maid's days out" in Toronto. A YWCA worker/volunteer provided counselling for the women and facilitated group activities. This Club lasted for 22 years' (Tania das Gupta, *Learning from Our History: Community Development by Immigrant Women in Ontario, 1958–1986* [Toronto: Cross Cultural Communication Centre, 1986], p. 17). For an example of an individual socialist feminist in this period, see Joan Sangster, 'The Making of a Socialist Feminist: The Early Career of Beatrice Brigden, 1888–1941', *Atlantis* vol. 13, no. 1 (Fall 1987), pp. 13–28.

5From R. Cook and W. Mitchinson, eds, *The Proper Sphere* (Toronto: Oxford Univ. Press, 1976), pp. 200–2.

6Nellie McClung, *In Times Like These* (Toronto: Univ. of Toronto Press, 1972), pp. 22, 34, 66.

7Linda Kealey, 'Introduction', *A Not Unreasonable Claim* (Toronto: Women's Press), p. 7.

8Deborah Gorham, 'Flora MacDonald Denison: Canadian Feminist' in Kealey, *A Not Unreasonable Claim*, p. 48.

9Yolande Cohen, 'Thoughts on Women and Power' in Angela Miles and Geraldine Finn, *Feminism in Canada: From Pressure to Politics* (Montreal: Black Rose Books, 1982), p. 230 (emphasis added).

10Ibid., p. 246 (emphasis added).

11Patricia Hughes, 'Fighting the Good Fight: Separatism or Integration?' in Miles and Finn, *Feminism in Canada*, p. 287 (emphasis added).

12Roberts, pp. 20–1.

13Kealey, *A Not Unreasonable Claim*, p. 11.

14Gorham, 'Flora MacDonald Denison', p. 47.

15Quoted in Carol Lee Bacchi, *Liberation Deferred? The Ideas of English Canadian Suffragists, 1877–1918* (Toronto: Univ. of Toronto Press, 1983), p. 40.

16Based on Gorham, 'Flora MacDonald Denison'.

17*The Voice*, Winnipeg, Manitoba, 15 July 1910, p. 3.

18Wayne Roberts, 'Rocking the Cradle for the World: The New Woman and Maternal Feminism, Toronto, 1877–1914', in Kealey, *A Not Unreasonable Claim*, pp. 42–3.

19Ibid., p. 43.

20Susan Wade, 'Helena Gutteridge, Votes for Women and Trade Unions', in Barbara Latham and Cathy Kess, eds., *In Her Own Right: Essays on Women's History in British Columbia* (Victoria, B.C.: Camosun College, 1980), p. 188.

21Ibid., p. 188.

[22]Ibid., p. 191.

[23]Ibid., p. 198.

[24]Ibid., p. 199.

[25]For another example, see the political interests of Ada Muir in Anne Molgat, 'The Voice and the Women of Winnipeg, 1894–1918' (M.A. thesis, Univ. of Ottawa, 1988).

[26]Strong-Boag, 'Ever a Crusader' in Rethinking Canada, p. 180.

[27]Molgat, 'The Voice'.

[28]Enid D'Oyley and Rella Braithwaite eds, Women of Our Times (Toronto: Sheppard and Sears, 1973); quoted in Adrienne Shadd, '300 Years of Black Women in Canadian History: Circa 1700–1980', Tiger Lily vol. 1, issue 2, p. 10. Tiger Lily and all other newsletters and periodicals cited in this book are available at the Canadian Women's Movement Archives/ Archives canadiennes du mouvement des femmes (hereinafter cited as CWMA/ACMF).

[29]Shadd, '300 Years'.

[30]Braithwaite, Black Woman in Canada, p. 59.

[31]For example, see Jean Burnet, ed., Looking Into My Sister's Eyes: An Exploration of Women's History (Toronto: Multicultural Society of Ontario, 1986).

[32]Molgat, 'The Voice'.

[33]Carole Swan, 'Women in the Canadian Labour Force: The Present Reality' in Naomi Herson and Dorothy Smith, eds, Women and the Canadian Labour Force, proceedings from a workshop to evaluate strategic research needs in women and the Canadian Labour Force, Univ. of British Columbia, Jan. 1981 (Ottawa: Social Sciences and Humanities Research Council, 1982).

[34]Myrna Kostash, Long Way From Home: The Story of the Sixties Generation in Canada (Toronto: James Lorimer & Co. 1980), pp. 3–68.

[35]Kay Macpherson and Meg Sears, 'The Voice of Women: A History', in Gwen Matheson, ed., Women in the Canadian Mosiac (Toronto: Peter Martin, 1976), p. 71.

[36]CWMA/ACMF, Voice of Women Papers, Constitution, 1961.

[37]Macpherson and Sears, 'Voice of Women', pp. 73, 74; Kay Macpherson, 'Persistent Voices: 25 Years with Voice of Women', Atlantis vol. 12, no. 2 (Spring 1987), pp. 60–72.

[38]Meg Luxton pointed out this progression to us. For more information on the native-rights movement see Kostash, Long Way from Home, pp. 147–65.

[39]Ibid., p. 215.

[40]Betty Friedan, The Feminine Mystique (New York: Dell Publishing Co., 1963).

[41]Simone de Beauvoir, The Second Sex (New York: Alfred Knopf Inc. 1952); Juliet Mitchell, 'Women: The Longest Revolution' New Left Review, Nov./Dec. 1966; Robin Morgan, Sisterhood is Powerful (New York: Random House, 1970).

[42]Women Unite, p. 9.

[43]Kostash, Long Way from Home, pp. 166–87.

[44]Patricia Carey, 'Personal is Political', Canadian Woman Studies/les cahiers de la femme vol. 2, no. 2, p. 5.

[45]Donna Cherniak and Allan Feingold, 'Birth Control Handbook', in Women Unite! (Toronto: Women's Press, 1972), pp. 109–13.

[46]CWMA/ACMF, Sound Recording 20/1, Abortion Meeting, Vancouver, 1970.

[47]Kostash, Long Way from Home, p. 176.

[48]For contemporary feminist coverage of the campaign see The Pedestal, a monthly newspaper published by the Vancouver Women's Caucus, especially vol. 2 (1970). The Other Woman reprinted information on the Abortion Caravan in its vol. 4, no. 1.

[49]CWMA/ACMF, Saskatoon Women's Liberation Papers, 'A Proposal for Action—By the Birth Control and Abortion Caucus of Saskatoon Women's Liberation', Nov. 1970.

[50]Melody Killan, 'Children are only Littler People or The Louis Riel University Family Co-op' in Women Unite! (Toronto: Women's Press, 1972), p. 94.

[51]Ibid., p. 100.

[52]John Foster, 'Sussex Day Care' in Women Unite!, p. 108.

[53]CWMA/ACMF, NAC Papers, Minutes, 29 March 1971.

[54]CWMA/AFMF, NAC Papers, Submission, Dec. 1971, p. 3.

[55]*Women Unite!*, p. 12.

[56]*Pedestal* vol. 2., no. 10 (Dec. 1970), p. 2.

[57]*Velvet Fist* vol. 1, no. 2 (Dec. 1970), pp. 4–5.

[58]Ibid., p. 7.

[59]Mitchell, 'Women'.

[60]*Women Unite!*

[61]Ibid., p. 10.

[62]Cerise Morris, 'Determination and Thoroughness: The Movement for a Royal Commission on the Status of Women in Canada', *Atlantis* vol. 5, no. 2 (Spring 1980), p. 10.

[63]Ibid., p. 11.

[64]Ibid., pp. 1–21.

[65]*Velvet Fist* vol. 1, no. 4 (March 1971), p. 6.

[66]CWMA/ACMF, CEW Papers, Correspondance, 6 Jan. 1971.

[67]CWMA/ACMF, NAC Papers, 15 April 1971.

[68]CWMA/ACMF, NAC Papers,'Submission to: The Government of Canada, from National Ad Hoc Action Committee' (Dec. 1971), p. 2.

[69]*Women Unite!*, p. 9.

[70]Eleanor Flexner, *Century of Struggle* (Boston: Harvard Univ. Press, 1959); Morgan, *Sisterhood*; Anne Koedt, ed., *Notes from the First (Second) (Third) Year* (New York, 1969, 1970, 1971); Sheila Rowbotham, *Women, Resistance, and Revolution* (London: Allen Lane, 1972); *Women Unite!*.

[71]Julia Creet, 'A Test of Unity: Lesbian Visibility in the British Columbia Federation of Women, 1974 & 1975' (unpublished essay, April 1986). A copy is available at the CWMA/ACMF.

[72]Ibid.

[73]*Status of Women News* vol. 2, no. 3 (Nov. 1975), pp. 30–1.

[74]Now called the Canadian Abortion Rights Action League.

[75]Bev Le François and Helga Martens Enns, *Story of a Women's Centre* (Pt. Coquitlam Area Women's Centre, B.C. [Vancouver: Press Gang, 1979]), p. 5. A copy is available at the CWMF/ACMF.

[76]H.E. Norman and A.Micco, 'A History of the Women's Movement in Prince George, 1972–1985', p. 3 (CWMA/ACMF). For another history of a women's centre see Liz Willick and Sue Berlove, *Building the Women's Movement: From One Women's Centre to Another* (Kitchener, Ont.: Kitchener-Waterloo Woman's Place, 1975). A copy is available at the CWMF/ACMF.

[77]Norman and Micco, 'History', p. 4.

[78]Ibid.

[79]Ibid., pp. 3–14.

[80]CWMA/ACMF, Sound Recording 'Bookstore—Vancouver: Interview by Pat Leslie with the Bookstore Collective' (Aug. 1976).

[81]Based on 'The Economics of Marriage: The Case of Irene Murdoch', in Paula Bourne, ed., *Women in Canadian Society*, rev. ed. (Toronto: Ontario Institute for Studies in Education, 1978), pp. 1–5, and Nancy Hall and Gene Hayden, 'Equal Partner or "Just a Wife" ', First National Farm Women's Conference, 2–4 Dec. 1980, CWMA/ACMF.

[82]Marlene Pierre-Aggamaway, 'Native Women and the State', in Joan Turner and Lois Emery, eds, *Perspectives on Women in the 1980's* (Winnipeg: Univ. of Manitoba Press, 1983), pp. 66–73; Sherill Cheda, 'Indian Women: An Historical Example and a Contemporary View' in Marylee Stephenson, ed., *Women in Canada*, rev. ed. (Don Mills: General Publishing Co., 1977), pp. 195–208; Kathleen Jamieson, *Indian Women and the Law in Canada: Citizens Minus* (Ottawa: Advisory Council on the Status of Women and Indian Rights for Indian Women, 1978).

[83]Adapted from Kirk Makin, 'And the verdict is. . . .', *Globe and Mail* 23 Jan. 1988, p. D8.

[84]Eleanor Wright Pelrine, *Abortion in Canada* (Toronto: New Press, 1971) and *Morgentaler:*

The Doctor Who Couldn't Turn Away (Toronto: Gage Publishing, 1975); Henry Morgentaler, *Abortion and Contraception* (Toronto: General Publishing Co., 1982).

[85]Creet, 'Test of Unity', p. 10.

[86]Sidney Abbott and Barbara Love, *Sappho was a Right On Woman* (Toronto: Stern & Day, 1972). See ch. 5 below for a full account of this debate within NOW.

[87]For an example see Ed Jackson and Stan Persky, eds, *Flaunting It: A Decade of Gay Journalism from the Body Politic* (Vancouver: New Star Books, 1982), pp. 177–96; Lorna Weir and Eve Zaremba, 'Boys and Girls Together: Feminism and Gay Liberation', *Broadside* vol. 4, no. 1 (Oct. 1982), pp. 6–7.

[88]This phrase has been wrongly attributed to Ti-Grace Atkinson. For an account of its history, see Cheris Kramarae and Paula Treichler, *A Feminist Dictionary* (London: Pandora Press, 1985), p. 10.

[89]Creet, 'Test of Unity', and CWMA/ACMF, Sound Recordings, Fine Kettle of Fish.

[90]Das Gupta, *Learning from Our History*.

[91]Ibid., p. 19.

[92]Ibid, pp. 20–1.

[93]Ibid., p. 21.

[94]See Carolyn Egan, 'Toronto's International Women's Day Committee: Socialist Feminist Politics', in Heather Jon Maroney and Meg Luxton, eds, *Feminism and Political Economy* (Toronto: Methuen, 1987); Das Gupta, *Learning*, p. 32.

[95]Micheline Dumont, 'The Women's Movement: Then and Now', *feminist perspectives féministes*, CRIAW, Ottawa: 1986, n.p.

[96]Lynn McDonald, 'The Evolution of the Women's Movement in Canada', *Branching Out* vol. 6, no. 1, pp. 39–43.

[97]CWMA/ACMF, NAC Papers, 'Report of Strategy for Change Convention of Women in Canada', Toronto, Ont., 7–9 April 1972, (CWMA).

[98]John Cleveland, 'The Mainstreaming of Feminist Issues: The Toronto Women's Movement, 1966–1984', unpublished ms., p. 17 (CWMA/ACMF).

[99]CWMA/ACMF, SWL Papers, Correspondence, 18 April 1975.

[100]CWMA/ACMF, SWL Papers, Correspondence, 8 May 1975.

[101]*The Other Woman* vol. 3, no. 3 (Winter 1975), p. 1.

[102]Ibid., p. 1.

[103]CWMA/ACMF, NAC Papers, Report, p. 23. The total attendance at the conference was approximately 500.

[104]CWMA/ACMF, New Feminists Papers.

[105]*Women Unite!*, pp. 74–5.

[106]Ellen Willis, 'Radical Feminism and Feminist Radicalism', in Sohnya Sayres, ed., *The Sixties Without Apology*, (Minneapolis: Univ. of Minnesota Press, 1984), p. 91.

[107]Ibid., p. 107.

[108]One account of this experience can be found in Vancouver Women's Study Group, 'Women & Socialism: Accounting for our Experience' (Vancouver: 1979). A copy is available at CWMA/ACMF.

[109]Ibid.; Dorothy Smith, *Feminism and Marxism, A Place to Begin, A Way to Go* (Vancouver: New Star Books, 1977); Charnie Guettel, *Marxism and Feminism* (Toronto: Canadian Women's Educational Press, 1974); Roberta Hamilton, *The Liberation of Women: A Study of Patriarchy and Capitalism* (London: Allen & Unwin, 1978).

[110]For a statement of the Wages for Housework viewpoint that was widely circulated in pamphlet form, see Mariarssa Dalla Costa, *The Power of Women and the Subversion of the Community: Women and the Subversion of the Community*; Selma James, *A Woman's Place* (Bristol: Falling Wall Press, 1972). This pamphlet was distributed in Canada by the Canadian Women's Educational Press.

[111]Linda Briskin, 'Toward Socialist Feminism?', *Our Generation* vol. 10, no. 3 (Fall 1974), p. 26.

[112]CWMA/ACMF, SWL, History File, n.d. (before Oct. 1977).

[113]CWMA/ACMF, SWL, 'Position Paper for S.W.L.', 14 Oct. 1977.

[114]Audrey Doerr and Micheline Carrier, eds, *Women and the Constitution in Canada* (Ottawa: Canadian Advisory Council on the Status of Women, 1981); Penny Kome, *The Taking of Twenty-Eight: Women Challenge the Constitution* (Toronto: Women's Press, 1983).

[115]See Joan Riggs, 'N.A.C.: Responsive or Redundant', *Breaking the Silence* vol. 5, no. 3 (Sept. 1987), Table A, p. 7.

[116]John Cleveland, 'Mainstreaming of Feminist Issues', pp. 61, c37, c46–47. In 1983 'the NAC Conference reject[ed] a motion to move the headquarters to bilingual Ottawa by just one vote due largely to the determined opposition of the Toronto old guard' (p. c61).

[117]Jean Wood, 'Who Represents Canadian Women?' *Status of Women News/La Revue Statut de la femme* vol. 7, no. 1 (Fall 1981), p. 4.

[118]Cleveland,'Mainstreaming of Feminist Issues', p. c23.

[119]CWMA/ACMF, WAVAW Papers, International Women's Day Statement, 1983.

[120]Egan, 'Socialist Feminism', p. 110.

[121]CWMA/ACMF, WAVAW Papers, 'For Women Who Woke Up This Morning Thinking "Here We Go Again" ', Toronto, 1979.

[122]*Broadside*, Introductory Issue (May 1979), p. 19.

[123]Conversation with Alice de Wolff, Oct. 1987; for examples, see Alison Griffith, 'Feminist Counselling: A Perspective' in Dorothy Smith and Sara David, *I'm Not Mad I'm Angry: Women Look at Psychiatry* (Vancouver: Press Gang, 1975), pp. 149–54.

[124]Maureen Hynes, 'Feminist Party of Canada: Entering the Electoral Mainstream', *Branching Out* vol. 7, no. 1 (1980), p. 8.

[125]CWMA/ACMF, IWCD Papers, 'Basis of Unity', 1979.

[126]Nancy Adamson and Kathy Arnup, 'A Committee for All Seasons', *Broadside* vol. 3, no. 5 (March 1982), p. 4.

[127]See CWMA/ACMF, IWDC Papers, Minutes, 1979.

[128]John Cleveland, 'Mainstreaming', pp. 44–7; Egan, 'Socialist Feminism', pp. 109–18; Adamson and Arnup, 'Committee'.

[129]For a different assessment see Egan, 'Socialist feminism', pp. 109–18.

[130]CWMA/ACMF, Bread & Roses Papers, Minutes 1980–1982.

[131]See Heather Jon Maroney, 'Feminism at Work', in Maroney and Luxton, *Feminism and Political Economy*, pp. 85–107, for an account of what she sees as the growth of working-class feminism in the 1970s. For feminist coverage of some of these activities see, for example, *The Other Woman* vol. 2, no. 6 (July 1974), p. 8, or *The Pedestal* vol. 2, no. 1, p. 5.

[132]Cleveland, 'Mainstreaming', p. 35.

[133]CWMA/ACMF, SWW Papers, Leaflet, n.d.

[134]CWMA/ACMF, SWW Papers, Board of Directors meeting minutes, 1981–82; Press Release, 2 Dec. 1980.

[135]CWMA/ACMF, SWW Papers, Draft of Opening Remarks by Denise Kouri for SWW Convention, 1981.

[136]For an account of the Fleck strike see Maroney, 'Feminism at Work', pp. 93–4. The International Women's Day Committee of Toronto was active in organizing women's movement support for these strikes; see their organizational files at CWMA/ACMF.

[137]CWMA/ACMF, SWW Papers, Annual Report, 20 June 1980.

[138]CWMA/ACMF, SWW Papers, 1981 Convention.

[139]CWMA/ACMF, Women's Liberation Working Group Papers, Minutes, Correspondence, Proposals, 1984.

[140]CWMA/ACMF, Lesbians Against the Right Papers, Lorna Weir, *Lesbians are Everywhere: Fighting the Right*, n.p., n.d.

[141]For feminist analysis and coverage see *Kinesis*, 1983–1984

[142]CWMA/ACMF, Women against the Budget Papers, 1983–1985.

[143]Chatelaine Consumer Council, Womanpoll IV, 1985.

[144]*Globe and Mail*, 21 Jan. 1987, p. 1; 12 per cent neither agreed nor disagreed, 11 per cent disagreed; and 4 per cent did not know.

[145]P.E.I. Advisory Council on the Status of Women, 'Position Paper on Right Wing Groups', printed in *Common Ground: A Journal for Island Women* vol. 6, no. 1 (Jan. 1987) pp. 14–17.

[146]Val Sears, 'Will the real women please stand up?', *Toronto Star* 3 Jan. 1987, p. B4.

[147]CWMA/ACMF REAL Women Papers, Leaflets, 'Laws Protecting Homosexuals'.

[148]P.E.I. Advisory Council 'Position Paper', pp. 15–16.

[149]Ibid., p. 15; Karen Dubinsky, 'Lament for a Patriarchy Lost? Anti-feminism, anti-abortion, and REAL Women in Canada', *feminist perspectives féministes* no.1 (Ottawa: CRIAW/ICREF), p. 30.

[150]CWMA/ACMF, FemDirect: A Listing of Women's Groups in Canada, 1988.

II

CONSTRUCTING A FRAMEWORK

3

Socialist Feminism: An Analysis of Power

SOCIALIST FEMINISM: A UNIQUE SYNTHESIS

In the introduction to this book we stressed our commitment, and by definition that of the women's movement, to making change. Such a project depends upon a deep understanding of the process of, and the resistance to, making change. It is to enhance this understanding that we now turn to an analysis of the relations of power in Canadian society, and to the politics of making change. For us, socialist feminism provides the only adequate explanation of those relations of power and the basis for developing an analysis of the resistance to change. It is for this reason that this part of the book elaborates the politic of socialist feminism. In this chapter we will focus on the socialist-feminist analysis of power relations; in the next we will use this analysis to elaborate a systematic perspective on social change. These chapters will provide the context for our analysis, in Part III, of the contemporary women's movement in Canada, and in particular of the current dilemmas facing socialist feminism.

We will begin by articulating the underlying assumptions of the socialist-feminist vision. In the section following, three central aspects of socialist-feminist analysis will be explored: first, the unequal distribution of power organized through the social relations of class, gender, race, and sexual orientation; second, the contradictions faced by the majority of women, expressed through the tension between domestic labour and wage labour, the role of the state, and the relation between the public and the private; and third, socialist-feminist method. In the final section socialist feminism will be situated in its historical and international context, within which the unique character of Canadian socialist feminism will be identified.

Socialist feminism emerges out of the complex, and not uncontradictory, interaction of the politics/practice/history of feminism and of socialism. It arises out of the political practice of feminism and of left-wing parties in the West, out of the study of socialist revolutions and so-called socialist societies, out of the history of women's experience not only in advanced capitalism but in other modes of production. What has emerged from this interaction is a unique synthesis that challenges the confines of traditional socialism and expands the scope of feminism as conventionally understood in relation to women's rights. Socialist feminism is not an additive politic: it is not feminism with a bit of socialism thrown in; nor, conversely, socialism with a few concessions to the women's issue. Socialist feminism does not represent an uncomplicated unity of socialism and feminism, however much it is rooted in the struggle to create a relation between the two.

Nonetheless, certain common and erroneous assumptions are often made about it, no doubt in part because of the words themselves: socialism and feminism. Most of these assumptions relate to a view that socialism is the primary politic to which feminism is added; or that class liberation is more important than, or must precede, women's liberation. These assumptions imply a distinction between socialism and feminism contrary to our vision of socialist feminism, a vision that challenges and reconstructs not only feminism but what has traditionally been understood as socialism. Socialist feminism is not only about women's liberation; it is also a reclaiming and reconstitution of socialism. Socialist feminism is not only a current of feminism but also a current of socialism. Socialist feminism does not privilege either class or gender but understands class, gender, race, and sexual orientation in a complex and contradictory relation to one another.

THE SOCIALIST-FEMINIST VISION

We do not have a blueprint for a socialist-feminist society, in large part because we believe the forms of a new society will be discovered in struggle and in practice. Nonetheless, self-identification as socialist feminist rests on certain beliefs. First, socialist feminism is simultaneously about a transformation in the relations of domination between men and women and about a redistribution of political and economic power between classes and races. Central to the world view of socialist feminism as a new synthesis is the understanding that the one is not possible without the other. Neither class, gender, nor race is privileged as *the* primary source of oppression. Rather, the fundamental interconnectedness between the structures of political and economic power—in our society, capitalism—and the organization of male power—what we might refer to as 'patriarchal relations'—is emphasized. Thus we use the concept of 'patriarchal capitalism' rather than just 'patriarchy' or 'capitalism'.[1]

Within this conceptual framework women's liberation is not understood to be the sum of reforms on various issues of concern to women (more day-care, better sexual-assault laws, more shelters for battered wives, affirmative-action programs, etc.). Rather, the strategic and analytic interconnectedness of these issues points to the necessity for dramatic social reorganization. Situating these demands in the political-economic context of patriarchal capitalism highlights the class nature of women's oppression, the impact of racism and heterosexism, and the role of the state in reinforcing women's oppression.

This is not to suggest that socialist feminists do not struggle for and support reforms, for the winning of reforms not only alleviates the burdens of women's daily lives, but also plays a critical role in developing the consciousness for, and the structures of, the mass movement necessary to social change.

The exploitation and oppression of women are rooted in the structures of patriarchal capitalism. Sexism is so deeply ingrained in the social relations of patriarchal capitalism that a fundamental transformation of these structures is necessary. At the same time, the liberation of women rests not only on a liberation from sexism but also on a transformation of the relations of power that characterize all social relations in a patriarchal-capitalist society. In fact, socialist feminism is a vision of a society entirely transformed. It is not only about women's liberation.

The second assumption of socialist feminism rests on the belief that non-exploitative relations between women and men are possible; that is, that the domination of men over women is not biologically based. This approach presents a sharp contrast to conservative political traditions that use 'nature' to justify current relations between men and women, as well as to 'scientific' arguments by sociobiologists who attempt to explain complex social and historical realities, such as the sexual double standard, with reference to biology alone.[2] Socialist feminists see the exploitative relations between the sexes as rooted in social and economic factors; hence these relations can be transformed through human intervention. Change is possible; biology is not over-determining.

Third, certain values predominate in the socialist-feminist vision: co-operation over competition; need over profit; peacefulness over militarism. Perhaps implicit in each of these is the most significant challenge—to common assumptions about the relations between the group/collective/community and the individual, assumptions that are part of the dominant ideology in Canada.[3]

An underlying assumption of that ideology is that individual rights and freedoms are always more important than the rights of the community. The pursuit of individual self-interest—what might be called a philosophy of individualism—is emphasized over collective interest. Despite this emphasis on the individual, however, there is also an often grudging recognition that we have to give up some individual rights to a central co-ordinating body (state/government) to define the common good, such as law and order or a national road system, and to regulate and legislate accordingly. Currently, conservative governments in many countries are attempting to restrict the areas that will be dealt with by that central authority; for example, by allowing—indeed, encouraging—private business to run hospitals, schools, prisons, and day-care centres for profit.

Underlying the commitment to individualism are two other assumptions. First, the belief that human beings are naturally greedy and self-seeking suggests that individualism and the pursuit of individual self-interest are expressions of human nature, part of the natural (and unchangeable) order of things.

The second assumption is that the needs of the individual are fundamentally and necessarily in opposition to the needs of the community or society. Each individual is always competing against the rest for her/his part of the power and privilege; what s/he wins will necessarily be at the expense of someone else, at least in part because resources (of power, for example) are scarce or limited. This belief often emerges in reference to public discussions of women's liberation. Then questions are asked: Do men have to give up power for women to have it? Do women want power over men?[4] The model of power underlying such questions is based on competition and scarcity of resources.

The belief in a group-individual conflict also assumes that community rights will, by definition, infringe on the rights of the individual. This assumption rests partly on the assumption of scarce resources, but also on the notion that community or collective rights will necessarily be exercised in an autocratic, manipulative, and undemocratic way. The collective is seen as requiring the submission of self and negation of the individual; in contrast, individuality is seen as expressing itself through separation from the group, a standing apart from the crowd.

Socialist feminism's view of the relationship between the individual and the collective/community is in a sharp contrast to that of individualism. It rests on entirely different assumptions. To begin with, socialist feminists draw a distinction between individualism (which prizes the rights of individuals over the rights of the collective) and individuality (which focuses on the development of individual potential). Socialist feminists envision a society that would develop individuality but shift the balance from individual rights towards the rights of the majority and the collective, and that would validate the pursuit of the common good rather than individual self-interest.

Socialist feminists believe that individuality can be most fully developed and expressed within a collective context; in other words, the collective creates the material and emotional support necessary for the individual to fully meet her/his needs and develop her/his potential. This belief challenges both the view of human nature as greedy and self-seeking, and the view of the collective as totalitarian and authoritarian.

The fact that human beings act in selfish, greedy, and violent ways can be explained by the social and economic conditions in which they find themselves. When resources are owned and controlled by a few, the majority are forced to compete for what is left in order to survive. Given these conditions, it is not surprising that we see our interests as being in conflict with those of others. But it is unnecessary to attribute such behaviour to inherent and unchangeable human nature: 'the contemporary prevalence of egoistic behaviour must be understood as the inevitable response to a capitalist society which rewards only the relentless pursuit of individual self interest.'[5]

The socialist-feminist understanding of the collective is not of some autocratic or authoritarian body, but of one in which a shared vision and collectively determined structures allow for the resolution of conflict. Rather than requiring the submission and negation of self, it means the liberation of self from isolation and competition. Rather than enforcing sameness and conformity and sacrificing individuality and difference, the collective can be the context in which difference is supported and encouraged. Juliet Mitchell makes this point:

> 'equality' in capitalist society is based on class inequality; in a classless society there will still be differences or inequalities, inequalities between individuals, strengths or handicaps of various kinds. There will be differences between men and women, differences among women and among men; a truly just society based on collective ownership and equal distribution would take these inequalities into account

and give more to he who needed more and ask for more from he who could give more. This would be a true recognition of the individual in the qualities that are essential to his humanity.[6]

Individualism is fiercely propagated by the dominant ideology, and the group is feared as autocratic and undemocratic. Yet at the same time there is enormous pressure to conform, and indeed few social resources are allocated to allow for the development of what we have called individuality: unique personalities, lifestyles, and so on. In fact, those who don't conform are labelled as deviant, and are frequently feared and punished; this despite the fact that mythology and ideology tell us to act as individuals, and apparently value individuality and individualism. In the next chapter we will return to the concept of the 'collective' and expand it to include the 'collective action' that is central to the socialist-feminist approach to social change.

SOCIALIST-FEMINIST ANALYSIS

1. The challenge of difference: gender, class, race, and sexual orientation

Socialist-feminist analysis arises, in part, out of the attempt to elaborate the complex links between sex and class. The recognition of these links challenges the primacy of class in socialist theory and its tendency to seek a clear homogeneity of interests; by contrast, it sets in place an analytic approach which places difference rather commonality at its centre. This in turn provides the basis on which to deconstruct the unified category of 'woman' sometimes found in feminist analysis. Socialist-feminist theory, then, can provide a framework within which an increasingly sophisticated appreciation of what difference entails can be developed. Canadian socialist feminists, both in theory and in practice, are struggling to work with the implications of difference based on class, race, sex/gender, sexual orientation and ethnicity.[7]

Categories of difference are not neutral, but reflect complex relations of power. Central to socialist-feminist analysis is a recognition of, and a desire to change, the unequal distribution of power inherent in gender, class, and race relations. Although each set of relations operates in a historically and ideologically specific way, they also combine to form a racist heterosexist patriarchal-capitalist society.

Socialist-feminist analysis seeks to understand, and socialist-feminist practice to organize around, the operation and intersection of these power relations. In what follows we will examine briefly the specific operation of the relations of power based on sex/gender, class, race, and sexual preference.

A key contribution of feminist theory and research over the last twenty years has been the recognition and exploration of the centrality of sex/gender to organizing women's lives. The vast majority of women in Canada share the experience of a double day of labour, almost total responsibility for housework and child care, fear of violence at the hands of men, lack of reproductive freedoms, and difficulty in attaining even minimal economic independence. The difference between the life experiences of women and men is increasingly self-evident. There is also no doubt that the distribution of power between men and women is unequal, and therefore that women's oppression cannot be understood without a concept of male privilege and male domination. Yet at the same time socialist feminists challenge the use of an undifferentiated category of woman, for despite the commonalities of women's experience, their life circumstances differ considerably on the basis of race, class, and sexual orientation.

Class is a difficult concept, and debate continues over how to understand/use and, in particular, apply it to women.[8] Fundamentally, however, 'class' refers to differential amounts of social and economic power. This power can take a variety of forms. In a classic marxist sense it is power over the means of production. This translates into power over what is produced (the kinds of products: housing versus military weapons, for example); how it is produced (the work process: a speeded-up assembly line or a situation in which those doing the work have some control over the work process); and control over the product (including the process of distribution, the profits that accrue, and the disposable income available to spend). This economic power often intersects with control over political, ideological, and military decisions.

'Class' also refers to differing degrees of access to choice, be it over type of employment, extent of education, location of residence, kind of vacation and leisure activity, or type of medical treatment available. For example, in Canada a woman's access to abortion has depended upon her class position, which has translated into access to gynecologists, skills to manage the bureaucracy of the therapeutic-abortion-committee process, and/or money to take a trip to the

United States, where abortions are more readily available. It is too soon to tell whether the 1988 Supreme Court decision to overturn the abortion law will erase the class bias in abortion access.

Despite what many Canadians would like to believe—that we are all middle class—there are enormous disparities in wealth, power, and privilege in this country. The brief examples given above barely touch the surface. Diane Francis, in *Controlling Interest: Who Owns Canada*, tells us:

> Canada's 32 wealthiest families, along with five conglomerates, already control about one-third of the country's non-financial assets, nearly double what they controlled just four years before. Combined their revenues in 1985 were nearly $123 billion, far greater than the federal government's income of around $80 billion.[9]

Furthermore, a Statistics Canada study of the rich revealed the following figures. In 1986 each of Canada's 63,350 richest families earned $212,000; the remaining 6.3 million Canadian families earned an average of $39,626—clear evidence of a huge divide between the rich and the majority.[10] Such studies do not make evident the growing numbers of Canadians living below the poverty line. In fact, nearly 1.5 million Canadian women—more than one out of every five—live in poverty; and this trend, referred to as the 'feminization of poverty', continues.[11]

Unlike the category of sex/gender, class allows us to see what divides women: differences in power, resources, and choice. But unlike individualism, which explains these differences with reference to individual particularities and peculiarities, class—a social category—allows us to understand the differences between *groups* of women.

Class also highlights the shared interests and experiences of groups of women. The vast majority of women have limited power, restricted choices, and a wide variety of shared experiences, as outlined above. As a result, the possibility exists to bring women together to challenge these conditions. But class also reveals the experiences and interests shared by women and men of the same class. In contrast to both women and men with professional employment, most working-class women and men alike face economic insecurity, monotonous and stressful work, and serious occupational health and safety hazards—conditions that help to explain their attraction to trade unions. Class can bring women together, and women and men together; it can also divide them. It is as a result of this complexity that we do not argue, as some feminists have, that women themselves form a class. Such a position hides the differences in power and choice between women, on the one hand, and, on the other, the possibilities of alliances between women and men of the same class.

Despite the importance of class and sex/gender as organizing concepts to understand women's experience, in themselves they are insufficient to reflect the complexity of women's experience. One of the important elaborations provided by feminist theory is the understanding of how sexual orientation also divides and brings women together. Despite common mythology, heterosexuality is not just a sexual preference; it is also an institution often referred to as 'compulsory heterosexuality'.[12] For a woman it means the assumption that her life will be organized by and defined in relation to a man, and it means structures and social practices that actually force her in this direction:

> What do the following have in common? Tax benefits; pensions; health insurance; common-law relationships; family unit; dependent; next-of-kin; sex education; femininity; tomboy. . . . They are all defined in heterosexist terms. It is assumed that every woman has a sexual, social and economic relationship with a man. Alternative sexual expression, living arrangements, interpersonal relationships and contractual agreements are ignored or penalized. This heterosexism is borne out in law, government, social policy, social services, school curricula, even in casual conversation. It's the language of income tax forms and employment contracts, family court and hospital visiting policy. It's the language of Monday mornings in the staffroom and Friday afternoons in the elevator.[13]

A secondary wage inadequate to economic independence is a part of compulsory heterosexuality in that it reproduces women's dependence on men:

> Heterosexism is also at work in the social perception of women's poverty. Poor women who are single or widowed are treated as special cases, whose poverty is attributed to the lack of a male provider. . . . Compulsory heterosexuality perpetuates the wage gap and job ghettoization by telling women that they are at some point going to be taken care of by men.[14]

Compulsory heterosexuality, although it affects lesbians disproportionately, oppresses all women. In a strongly-worded and oft-repeated quote, Charlotte Bunch says that 'no females will ever be free to choose to be anything until we are also free to choose to be lesbians, because the domination of heterosexuality is a mainstay of male supremacy.'[15] Compulsory heterosexuality is not simply about a sexual preference, but rather about the way that sexual preference is mobilized to reproduce and to justify women's lack of choices in a whole range of areas, in particular at work and in marriage.

We might conclude, then, that heterosexism, or compulsory heterosexuality, serves to unite all women, and to some degree this is the case; but it is also true that heterosexual women, as a result of their sexual preference, have certain privileges. Such privileges range from the legitimacy accorded their love relations, to their access to male financial support, to their ability to have children inside socially accepted relations and to keep those children should the family break down and divorce ensue. This discussion demonstrates the complexity of understanding what unites and what divides women. In the case of heterosexism and heterosexual privilege, there is a complex relation and an uneven balance between privilege and oppression. Since heterosexism affects all women, it provides the basis for an alliance between heterosexual and lesbian women, albeit at times uneasy because of heterosexual privilege. It is also the case that heterosexism affects gay men, and in so doing, creates some common interests between lesbians and gay men.[16]

Likewise, race can bring women together and divide them. In Canadian society racism limits women's power, choice, and access to resources—in the workplace, in education, in politics. For example, women of colour are concentrated in low-paying, low-status jobs doing cleaning, laundry, and maintenance work in hospitals, hotels, and textile factories.[17] Furthermore,

> surveys of income levels of Canadians have concluded that even when education, experience, skills and the job itself are considered, minority workers earn less than dominant group workers. For example, women who are West Indian born Canadians earn $6000 less a year than their British Canadian counterpart with the same qualifications and work experience.[18]

Like heterosexism, racism is not just a set of attitudes but a set of social practices embedded in the structure and organization of social institutions. Carol Allen and Judy Persad stress this point:

> We do not believe that racism is merely a misunderstanding among people, a question of interpersonal relations, or an unchanging part of human nature. Racism, like sexism, is an integral part of the political and economic system under which we live. This system uses racism and sexism to divide us and to exploit our labour for super-profits and it gives some women privilege.[19]

In multi-ethnic and multi-racial Canada one of the most insidious forms of racism is the assumption that all people of colour are necessarily immigrants. From this perspective it is possible to incorrectly suggest that the problems of race are really temporary problems of assimilation. This makes invisible the serious problem of racism in Canada.[20]

The tension between power/privilege and oppression that we identified in looking at the relations between compulsory heterosexuality and heterosexual privilege can help us to look at the question of racism, and in particular at the potential for building alliances between women of colour and white women.

Racism operates to affect all women. For example, the low wages of black women pull down the wages of all women, and there is no doubt that racism divides women in their struggle against women's oppression. This is emphasized by Barbara Smith:

> White women don't work on racism to do a favour for someone else, solely to benefit Third World women. You have to comprehend how racism distorts and lessens your own lives as white women—that racism affects your chances for survival, too, and that it is very definitely your issue. Until you understand this, no fundamental change will come about.[21]

Angela Davis makes the same point in her discussion of the link between racism and rape:

> Racism has always drawn strength from its ability to encourage sexual coercion. While Black women and their sisters of color have been the main targets of these racist-inspired attacks, white women have suffered as well. For once white men were persuaded that they could commit sexual assaults against Black women with impunity, their conduct toward women of their own race could not have remained unmarred. . . . This is one of the many ways in which racism nourishes sexism, causing white women to be indirectly victimized by the special oppression aimed at their sisters of color.[22]

Nevertheless, the balance between privilege and oppression that creates the basis for the unique pattern of alliances between lesbian and heterosexual women is constituted differently on the issue of race. This is because the privilege that accrues to white women far outweighs any disadvantage. Hazel Carby stresses that 'white feminist theory and practice have to recognize that white women stand in a power relation as oppressors of black women'.[23] An example is the situation of West Indian domestics in Toronto who work for white women.[24]

Perhaps most important for our discussion is the racism inside the women's movement itself:

> The distrust women of colour, black women and native women feel towards the women's movement is justified. We have felt continuously excluded from the women's movement. History has shown us this. Although we share a common oppression as women, we must work together to overcome the issues that divide us. This will not be easy because the society we live in continuously tries to highlight the differences between us and make it difficult for us, as women, to come together, acknowledge our differences and find ways to move forward.[25]

As we develop our analysis throughout this book, we will explore some of the dynamics of this racism.

The complexities of this relation of power help us to understand the difficulties faced in building alliances between women of colour and white women, and also to understand the unique alliance possible between women and men of colour. The Black Feminist Statement by the Combahee River Collective emphasizes this latter relation: 'Our situation as black people necessitates that we have solidarity around the fact of race, which white women of course do not need to have with white men.'[26]

Notwithstanding, it is important to stress that women of different races may share experiences of class, sex/gender, and sexual orientation that do provide the basis for strategic alliances, and, further, that differences do not by definition mitigate against the possibility of alliance.

To summarize, although women never have power by virtue of their sex, some women have power by virtue of their class, race, or sexual orientation. Strategically this means that not all women are 'sisters' by virtue of their biology; class, race, and sexual orientation do divide women, but the pattern of common experience can also bring them together in complex patterns of alliances: 'Women do not need to eradicate difference to feel solidarity. We do not need to share common oppression to fight equally to end oppression.'[27]

An analysis in which difference is a central theme provides the basis for an international perspective on women's oppression and liberation. It allows for a vision of international solidarity among women that not only accepts difference but recognizes the unequal power relations between women of the first and the third worlds.[28]

This emphasis on difference provides the basis for socialist feminism to move beyond what Lorna Weir has characterized as a tendency to class reductionism reflected in an 'internal hierarchy of issues'[29] and beyond the gender reductionism of other currents of feminism. We have put forward a view of socialist feminism in which the relations of power inherent in class, race, gender, and sexual orientation are not prioritized or ranked in any abstract way; rather, the focus is on the ways they intertwine, reinforce, and contradict each other. The relative strength and import of these relations to groups, individuals, and political practice is determined within the context of particular historical conjunctures. This means that the prioritizing of issues, a necessity to successful political struggle, must not occur on the basis of abstract principle (what Weir is criticizing), but rather in relation to material, economic, political, and ideological conditions.[30]

Our theorizing of difference also illuminates the basis upon which we argued earlier that socialist feminism transcends the limits of both socialism and feminism. Weir does not agree:

> I disagree with a tendency to construe socialist feminism as the total politic—the new, reconstituted socialism. I can see no a priori reason why the oppression of women should be politically privileged over racial oppression, a claim which underlies suggestions that socialist feminism would form the basis of a transformed socialism.[31]

Our perspective, however, does not suggest the disappearance or liquidation, in practice, of all popular movements into socialist feminism. Hence our vision of the changed relations of power does not call for the *elimination* of difference (such a perspective might arise out of liberal feminism) but rather the neutralizing of difference in terms of the distribution of power and resources. We agree with Housman's challenge to the 'tendency within the Left to regard difference merely as an occasion for oppression and power relations, rather than offering a source of potential celebration and appreciation'.[32] A political standpoint that deconstructs the category of woman and recognizes the centrality of difference, in both its oppressive and potentially liberatory forms, provides the real basis for alliances with other popular movements.[33] To the extent that socialist feminism can theorize about difference and organize from this perspective, it may become an informing politic for other popular movements.[34]

In fact, the ability to build sisterhood on the basis of difference may be central to the survival of the women's movement as a movement to make change. Lynne Segal identifies a growing pessimism among British feminists about the possibilities of making change, a pessimism fueled by the limited gains of the last twenty years, attacks of the new right on those gains, and what is seen as a fragmentation of the women's movement. This pessimism has resulted in a tendency to seek a recreated sisterhood based not on difference, but on the 'timeless truths of women's lives', which produces a strategic orientation away from change, rather than towards it.[35]

Socialist feminism presents a complex and systemic analysis of the roots of women's oppression and of the structures that reproduce that oppression, some of which we have elaborated above. It has also investigated women's daily life experience in order to understand the actual operation of the structures of patriarchal capitalism and the ideologies of oppression. Since extensive discussion of this experience is beyond the scope of this chapter, we will focus briefly on three key contradictions that face the majority of women: first, the sexual division of labour expressed in particular in the tension between wage work and domestic work; second, the role of the state in reproducing women's oppression; and third, the relation between the public and the private.

2. The sexual division of labour

Socialist feminism stresses the importance of the sexual division of labour—inside the workplace, inside the household, and between the two. Inside the workplace women are segregated (from men) in a few occupational classifications (in particular, clerical, sales and service work)[36] where the wages, degree of unionization, extent of benefits, and chances for promotion are low. The current sexual division of labour between the household and the workplace in Canada means, for example, that the care of young infants is generally located inside the household and is a form of unpaid labour performed mostly by women.[37] Finally, the sexual division of labour inside the household assigns women disproportionate responsibility for housework,[38] despite the fact that increasing numbers of women are working for wages.[39]

Women face disadvantages as a result of these forms of the sexual division of labour; in particular they experience a unique tension between the demands of domestic and wage labour. All women who work for wages do a double day of labour: at the end of their paid jobs, they face hours of domestic work. Their responsibility for domestic labour has an impact on their success in the work-force, not only because it limits the extent of their participation in it (for example, women tend to be responsible for sick children and are often forced to take time off work for this reason), but also because the ideology that domestic labour is a woman's responsibility is used to justify job ghettoization ('Women are naturally suited to cleaning, cooking, and serving') and limited opportunities in the wage work force ('Can't promote her; she'll get pregnant and leave').

Perhaps the most insidious assumption is that all women are home-makers, economically dependent on male breadwinners. In fact, in 1985 women made up 42.6 per cent of the labour force.[40] The ideology that women's place is in the home is used to justify low wages (approximately 60 per cent of men's), despite that fact that those wages are increasingly necessary to family/household survival (either in conjunction with the wage of a spouse or because she is the single head of the household). In fact, by 1982 the husband was the sole income earner in only 16 per cent of Canadian families.[41]

This double labour shapes women's experience in the family / household and in the workplace and creates the conditions for exploi-tation and oppression. Although we have spoken of the double day as if it affected all women equally, the point needs to be made that class, race, and sexual orientation influence the particular experience of the double day. For example, class privileges some women by allowing them to purchase services that other women perform them-selves; racial exploitation means that a higher percentage of black women are forced to work for wages, often as domestics, and are therefore proportionally more often faced with the double day.[42]

Despite these differences, the sexual division of labour as it is organized within patriarchal capitalism works against the interests of all women. As a result socialist feminism seeks to understand and strategically neutralize, if not abolish completely, the sexual division of labour as an organizing principle, both inside the family/house-hold and in the workplace. This does not imply eliminating the differences between men and women but, rather, eliminating sex/gender as the basis for assigning work and for valuing different kinds of work.

3. The role of the state

Socialist feminism identifies the state/government (along with the workplace and the family) as a site of patriarchal capitalist relations of power and therefore a participant in the reproduction of women's oppression.[43] To speak of the reproduction of women's oppression in this way is to recognize that, within institutions, structures and social relationships exist that by their very organization and functioning effect the continuation of women's oppression. So rather than identifying a 'villain', so to speak, who is to blame for women's oppression, our analysis of the state focuses on practices and processes that are outside the self-conscious acts of particular individuals.

To speak of the state/government as a site of the patriarchal capitalist relations of power has two implications. First, it suggests that the inequalities of patriarchal capitalism (based on class, race, gender, and sexual orientation) affect the way that individuals and groups enter into relations with the state/government. Second, the state/government, both in its functioning and in its policy/legislative decisions, privileges men over women, the capitalist/corporate class over others, white people over people of colour, and heterosexuals over lesbians and gay men. Individuals and groups do not enter into relations with the state/government on an equal footing, and this inequality is exacerbated by the fact that they are not treated equally by the state/government. It is for these reasons that we would argue that the state/government is not politically neutral.

As capitalist and patriarchal, the state/government represents the interests of the large corporations and the capitalist ruling class: it offers tax breaks for the rich, bail-outs for failing corporations,[44] patronage appointments for relatives or party supporters; it refuses to limit contracting-out, to provide adequate first-contract legislation, or to ensure effective health and safety provisions,[45] all of which would cost employers money. In so doing, it often marshals and reinforces certain patriarchal norms: from the literal control of government and state by men (in the form of judges, appointees to government bodies, and elected politicians)[46] to the myriad mechanisms for controlling women and children through prostitution laws, conditions placed on the provision of family benefits, and wholly inadequate protection of women from violence. And through its immigration laws and hiring practices it reproduces racism.

At this point it is useful to distinguish between the state and the government. Although both are sites of patriarchal-capitalist relations of power, the mechanisms by which these relations are reproduced in each differ considerably. The government is the site of the legislative and electoral process. Representatives chosen through the electoral process reshape old and introduce new laws. The government has a high public visibility and it is (generally) seen to be both responsive to citizens and responsible for the shape and success of Canadian society. Although we may not have a lot of direct contact with our representatives in government, formal mechanisms exist for interacting with them: through voting and to some extent through lobbying. Moreover, these representatives are publicly visible and often have high profiles as individuals; in fact, discussions about government often focus on the personalities, private lives, and personal values of MPs and MPPs. Neither the electoral nor the legislative process, however, operates in a politically neutral fashion, in part because of the inadequacies of representative democracy. (In the next chapter, when we analyze routes to social change, we will examine these inadequacies in detail.)

The nature of the state, and of women's relation to it, is different. The state is a powerful and complex force that intervenes daily in all citizens' lives; yet, unlike the government, it is largely invisible and unnamed. Its power extends beyond elections and elected representatives. It includes agencies such as child welfare, immigration, and housing and coercive forces such as the police. The state is more amorphous—less a question of people and personalities than a process of regulation, administration, and bureaucracy. It is more difficult to identify the state processes that intervene in our lives, and fewer established mechanisms exist by which to challenge them.[47]

To understand the reproduction of women's oppression we need to examine both the state and the government, since many important issues for women cannot be dealt with directly through the electoral process. For example, consider the schools. Feminists have long been concerned about the streaming of girls away from maths and sciences, the stereotypic presentation of girls/women in readers, and the inadequate funding of girls' sports, to name a few issues. Decisions about what actually gets taught in the classroom and how the schools are run are shaped, however, not by the electoral process but by bureaucratic processes, physical space, the professional training of teachers, and the resources available. Thus governments, and even their policies on education and their desire to respond to women's concerns, may change, but what happens in the schools may remain basically the same. As a result of the complex relationship between elected representation and the actual process by which decisions are made and enforced, women must interact with the state as well as the government in order to effect the change they desire.

The state is very powerful. Its activities reach into the lives of every Canadian woman. The state often appears invisible, because it is not named for what it is and is often confused with the government. But a woman confronts the state whenever she enters a school, an immigration office, a police station, or a welfare office; whenever she applies for unemployment insurance, registers a newborn baby, gets married or divorced. Women experience the state as employer,

as educator, as funder, as legislator, as service-provider, as a source
of financial support, and as a cost in the form of taxation. In each
of these circumstances and relationships women experience the
power of the state to intervene in and regulate their lives.

Women are also in a constant process of negotiation with the state
about the provision of caring services. In this regard women relate
to the state in three intertwining roles. First, the state relies on
women to provide a whole range of caring services to children, and
to the sick and old, through families, partly as a result of an ideology
that sees nurturing as part of women's natural role, and partly as a
result of the complex division of labour outlined above, which structures women as secondary workers.

Second, women rely on the state to provide a range of caring
services to the sick, the elderly, and the young. However, these
services are usually inadequate, not only in terms of their availability
but also because of the way they are provided. They make women
overly responsible, often control their behaviour, and limit their
choices and options. For example, only in November 1987 did the
Ontario government revise its 'spouse in the house' guidelines. Until
then a woman on family benefits could lose them if she had a relationship with a man who slept in her apartment. The assumption was
that if he had an intimate relationship with her, he must be head of
the household and responsible for the financial support of her and
her children. In this way the regulations shaped women's behaviour
and privileged a certain form of the family over others (a point we
will return to), as was evident in the response of the Peel Region
Council to the changes: it warned that they would 'lead to the dis-
integration of the family'.[48]

Finally, women are employees of the state as child-care workers,
welfare officers, social workers, and teachers. Women negotiate
with the state about the social division of the labour of caring in all
three roles, which are not discrete but related in a complex way. For
example, when governments cut back on social services the employees that are fired are often women. Not only do these women lose
their jobs, but often they find their own access to services further
restricted. This in turn increases their responsibility for caring within
the family unit and can exacerbate the difficulty of finding another
job. Socialist feminists argue that women need not only a reorganization and redistribution of responsibility around caring, but also
an increased role in shaping and controlling the kinds of services
that are provided and the role that women will play within them. In
fact, writing about the welfare state in the United States, Frances

Piven makes the point that women's centrality in the provision of caring inside and outside of the state provides the basis for them to have a strong political voice and upon which to build a movement.[49]

However, women's demands vis-à-vis caring services are complicated by the fact that in addition to playing a powerful role in regulation and control, the state is not politically neutral, and does not judge each claim by an abstract set of governing principles. The state represents and responds to racist, patriarchal, heterosexist, and capitalist interests by its very functioning and structures; it systematically privileges and acts in the interests of men, corporations, and white heterosexual society.

As a result, women enter into the power relations of the state on different terms and with differing amounts of power, not only because of their gender, but also because of their class, race, and sexual orientation. For example, a black woman's experience of Canada Employment and Immigration differs from that of a white woman immigrant, and it would certainly differ from that of the immigration worker, who also may be a woman. The credentials of a teacher who also happens to be a lesbian are, by definition, suspect.

What we think of as our private relations are also touched differentially by the state. For example, certain forms of the family are privileged and sanctioned by the state over others. Unlike a common-law heterosexual couple, a lesbian couple living together does not qualify for family benefits on the Ontario Health Insurance Plan (OHIP)[50] and will have difficulty with the custody of children and even with municipal building codes, some of which limit the number of 'unrelated' people permitted to live together.

Despite these criticisms of its functioning, socialist feminism does not argue for less state. Our concern is to get the state to work for women rather than against them. We resist the arguments for less state because women depend upon and have a right to the services it provides. And, in fact, women's work is central to the functioning of state agencies.

This position contrasts with periodically recurring arguments from the right wing, especially under the leadership of conservatives such as Ronald Reagan, Margaret Thatcher, and Brian Mulroney, for less government and less intervention, cutbacks in social services, privatization of Crown corporations, a decrease in the support for day-care, and so on. When the state generates or responds to such arguments it acts against the interests of women. For example, decreasing support for child-care services increases women's responsibility and thereby the difficulty women have combining wage work and housework; the current (1987) free-trade initiatives that call for removal of government tariffs will not only lead to extensive job loss in economic sectors where women work (such as the garment industry)[51] but may also challenge universal social programs such as medicare (which the United States might see as unfair wage subsidy). Privatization has often meant the loss of hard-won gains in union contracts, as well as contracting-out and an increase in part-time work, both of which have the most serious impact on women workers.

The state is a web that surrounds us, intrudes into and shapes our experience, limiting the control we have over our lives. We need to reveal and challenge the ways the state intervenes in our lives. Such a challenge is not only necessary but possible, for the state is not a monolith: it does respond to pressure. In the next chapter we will elaborate this point as we examine the process of organizing for social change.

4. The public and the private

Finally, socialist feminists explore and challenge the way the dominant ideology mobilizes the distinction between the public (the realm of government, politics, and the workplace) and the private (family, sexuality, intimacy). The separation of public and private is used to relegate women to the private sphere while devaluing and depoliticizing it.

The realm of the private is often seen as 'natural', unchanging throughout human history. On the one hand, this naturalization of the private provides a justification for avoiding necessary social intervention—for example, in a family where a husband is physically abusing his wife. On the other hand, it masks the already existing and extensive social intervention in this realm. For example, the state shapes and regulates the private experience of sexuality, in part through its definition of deviance ('homosexual/lesbian' as deviant), in part through its control of birth-control/sex education, in part through its abortion legislation. As we explained in the previous section, it also shapes the way we live through the structure of welfare and social-security benefits.

A feminist analysis of women's experience must focus on both the private and the public. However, not all feminists agree about the relative importance of the two. Some focus on the public sphere, in particular on laws that discriminate against women; others emphasize the private sphere, the responsibility women have for domestic work and the extensive violence that prevails there. Socialist-feminist analysis is especially concerned to understand the way the two spheres reinforce, recreate, and contradict each other.[52] Such an analysis explores the complex interconnections between the public and the private, between the family, the workplace, and the state.

This approach to the public and the private highlights the socialist-feminist emphasis on the interconnectedness of issues and the systemic character of women's oppression. Socialist feminists not only identify particular problems that women face, but attempt to develop an analysis that understands the relationship between these problems. Carolyn Egan, in her discussion of the strategy of the Ontario Coalition for Abortion Clinics (OCAC), demonstrates the complexity of the issue of reproductive rights:

> When we use the word 'choice' we are addressing something beyond formal, legal freedom: real possibilities for all women. For working-class, native and black women and other women of colour, full access to free abortion means not just the legal right to choose, but good, free clinics under their control, located in their communities, and staffed by people who speak their language and understand their culture. . . . Reproductive rights [must] also include the right to have children. OCAC also takes the position that we require economic independence, paid parental leave, free universal childcare, and custody rights for lesbian mothers, if the choice to have a child is to be a real one. . . .
>
> We are asking for greater access to abortion not only because the economic crisis makes it more difficult to raise children, but as part of a challenge to conventional views on motherhood and gender roles. . . . OCAC attempts to link economic, ideological and sexual aspects of women's oppression. It stresses the class exploitation of women in the workplace who are denied paid parental leave and childcare, whose inadequate wages leaves us the largest percentage of the poor. It also speaks of racism, rape, violence, the forced or coerced sterilization of native and other women, the denial of the right to determine our own sexuality, and the role of the state, as well as the fact that we still bear the major responsibility for domestic work and childraising. By raising the demand for abortion rights within this broader context, OCAC exemplifies a socialist feminist perspective.[53]

SOCIALIST-FEMINIST METHOD

Intrinsic to any analysis is a method. Method, a way of studying the problem at hand, is always based on certain assumptions about what kind of change is perceived to be possible, how change occurs, and what constitutes a good society. Method is implicitly *political*.

In this section we will briefly consider the historical-materialist method of socialist feminism. This method provides the basis for a challenge to the concept of patriarchy and to a political strategy based on changing attitudes, ideas, and values. The latter point we will take up in the next chapter.

Our 'historical-materialist' method, derived from marxism, is both historically specific and focused on the material conditions of women's lives: how we organize for survival; how the basic necessities of life are produced, reproduced, shared, organized; the level of technological development available to that process of production (for example, the level of mechanization in agriculture) and of reproduction (for example, the level of development of birth control).

Not surprisingly, these conditions change over time and between places. Thus the socialist-feminist analysis put forward in the previous sections is historically specific; it arises out of and is developed in reference to the society in which we live. Socialist-feminist method and the categories of analysis explored above could be used to study another society, such as South Africa, but the specific analysis generated would reflect the unique conditions of that society.

Each society, however, is not just the sum of its particular conditions; it is characterized by a dominant mode of social organization that provides the context within which these conditions can best be understood. In twentieth-century Canada we make sense of the material conditions of women's lives in the context of patriarchal capitalism.

A historical-materialist approach to understanding women's oppression, which is rooted in particular historical modes of production such as patriarchal capitalism, contrasts sharply with studying women's oppression through a concept such as patriarchy. The latter is a transhistorical concept: one that is seen to explain, and be relevant to, all societies at all times. Because of the wide scope with which they are used, transhistorical concepts are generally fairly abstract. They are forced, necessarily, to seek out the lowest common denominator that will make them relevant to all societies. In the case of patriarchy, this means saying that in all societies men have, in some ways, dominated women.

No doubt forms of male domination of women can be documented throughout almost all recorded history. However, the focus on this kind of evidence leads almost inevitably to a distortion of its meaning in each historically specific society, and to pessimism about the possibilities for change. The high level of abstraction and generality involved in a concept like 'patriarchy' masks the co-operation and negotiation that does take place between women and men and makes invisible the instances in which women have resisted particular forms of male domination. If we see the signs of patriarchy unremittingly throughout human history, it is hard to conclude that there is indeed a solution. The concept of patriarchy thereby reinforces the (radical-feminist) view that women and men are fundamentally different and necessarily have opposing interests.[54]

In contrast, the historical-materialist method allows socialist feminists to focus on the ways that domination is organized and reproduced, and to discover the ways to challenge it. More important than apparent continuity are the historically specific forms that domination has taken. Studying societies in this way allows us to see that the relations between women and men are negotiated through a process of struggle, not laid down with an iron inflexibility. Furthermore, it allows us to discover, document, and celebrate women's resistance to domination.

Socialist feminism rests on the historically specific study of women's oppression. It does not focus on an abstract or transhistorical analysis of the relations of domination between men and women, but on the forms of this domination under patriarchal capitalism, the dominant form of social and economic organization in twentieth-century Canada. It is within this historically specific experience that we can make sense of women's experience and find the route to change. This discussion of the method of historical materialism and its contrast to transhistorical concepts should demonstrate the way in which method is implicitly political, for it is out of method that political vision and strategy emerge.

SOCIALIST FEMINISM: THE HISTORICAL, INTERNATIONAL, AND CANADIAN CONTEXTS

To fully understand contemporary socialist feminism, we must situate it within the context of the historical struggle to build a relationship between socialism and feminism—theoretically, organizationally, and strategically— and at the same time within an international perspective, but one that takes account of the unique political, economic, and ideological terrain on which socialist feminism develops in any particular country. Although it is beyond the scope of this chapter to do this in any detail, this brief section gives contemporary socialist feminism an important degree of historical legitimacy as well as serving as a reminder of the historically specific nature of socialist feminism, consistent with the historical-materialist method outlined above.

It might be accurate to argue that a coherent politic and practice of socialist feminism have emerged only in the second half of the twentieth century. Nonetheless, it is also true that there exists a long history of attempts to construct a relationship between socialism and feminism, some of which mirror contemporary issues to a startling degree. Feminist historians have been painstakingly rediscovering these traditions.

One of the traditions that prefigure contemporary socialist feminism can be found in the histories of the socialist and communist parties and in the challenge posed by their 'feminist' membership to take up issues of concern to women.[55] In that tradition the writings of Alexandra Kollontai, during the early years of the Russian revolution, have an important place. She took up issues of morality, sexuality, new family relations, and the double day in a surprisingly contemporary way and articulated an early form of the 'personal is political'.[56] Or we might turn to the texts of Clara Zetkin, not only those in the women's newspaper *Gleichheit*, which she edited (in 1914 it had a circulation of 125,000),[57] but also in her speeches to workers' organizations and in particular to the Congresses of the Social Democratic Party in Germany, at the end of the last century, in which she argues, for example, in favour of socialist women's right to organize autonomously.[58]

Another historical thread currently being unearthed by feminist historians is that of a socialist feminism outside of socialist and communist parties. Perhaps one of the most fascinating studies is Barbara Taylor's account of the Owenite socialists in the early part of the nineteenth century in England.[59] Their '"stupendously grand" vision of a communist feminist society'[60] included a critique not only of socially defined femininity but also of socially defined masculinity[61] : a clear recognition of the need for a substantial transformation in the relations between the sexes. Taylor tells us that 'at the heart of their analysis was a systematic critique of . . . the marriage system, that is, patriarchal marriage and the nuclear family'.[62] At the heart of their vision was 'the collectivization of all reproductive labour'.[63] The Owenites recognized that 'only a complete transformation of family life and sexual attitudes would free women and only the new Social System would revolutionize personal relationships in this way'.[64] We see in Owenite ideology the early

Socialist Feminism: An Analysis of Power | 121

expression of what has come to be one of the fundamental principles of socialist feminism: the necessary relation between a transformation in the public sphere (the organization of work and politics) and in the private sphere (family and sexual relations). The Owenites were unable to sustain their vision in the face of the expansion and entrenchment of capitalist relations of production, but the struggle of the Owenite women is an important part of the history of socialist feminism.

Equally important were the struggles by women to build cross class alliances in late-nineteenth- and early-twentieth-century America. Meredith Tax in *The Rising of the Women* details attempts to organize what she calls a 'united front of women'; that is, 'the alliance, recurring through time in various forms, of women in the socialist movement, the labour movement, the national liberation movements and the feminist movement.'[65] In any discussion of contemporary socialist feminism, this theme of alliance emerges as central.

These brief historical comments indicate the long tradition of which socialist feminism is a part. However, it is equally important to remember, as we pointed out in Chapter 2, that the recovery of this tradition is very recent. In the late 1960s, as the second wave of the women's movement was beginning, feminism and women's liberation appeared to be a new discovery, at least for a short period. It was, in part, the discovery of its history that challenged the assumption that feminism had a unitary character.

The international nature of socialist feminism must also be recognized. This does not mean that socialist feminism takes the same form in every country; such an approach would be contrary to the historical-materialist method, which assumes that socialist feminism in any given country grows on a unique political, economic, and ideological terrain made up of many intertwining threads. In the third world, for example, where imperialism rather than advanced capitalism dominates, the forms of feminism and socialist feminism are quite different.[66] In particular, the structure of nationalist politics provide an important, perhaps the most important, framework within which socialist feminism develops.

In the West socialist feminism grows on a terrain influenced by numerous factors, including the traditions of feminism; the existence and strength of left-wing parliamentary parties and of extra-parliamentary left organizations; the legitimacy of revolutionary points of view and the depth of revolutionary moments; the history of labour organizing and the strength of the trade-union movement; the embeddedness of traditions of liberal democracy, welfare statism, or, conversely, of fascism; the level of development of the economy, and so on. In any given country the particular constellation of factors differs. These establish the context within which socialist feminism emerges and in each case create a historically and culturally specific pattern of socialist feminism.

For example, in countries with strong extra-parliamentary left organizations, socialist feminism will necessarily be linked to them and will be forced to define itself in relation to them. This may take the form of a separation from these organizations, an attempt to transform them to take up a socialist-feminist perspective, or a liquidation into them. Equally important to the shape of socialist feminism is the extent of the development of organizations of the working class. For example, in Britain

> because . . . of the particular history and role of the British labour movement and the existence of a nonmarxist Labour Party as the parliamentary arm of the working class, the relationship of feminism to the organizations of the working class took a specific form. . . .
> British feminists did not have to relate to, or react against, large Communist parties as was the case in France and Italy.[67]

Frigga Haug, discussing the women's movement in West Germany, speaks of the ostracism of socialist feminists, which she attributes in part to the 'virulent all-purpose anti-communism in our country'.[68] And in Spain, a country with limited democratic traditions and a long history of fascism, the women's movement has been slow to cohere, and the issues of 'class-struggle' feminism are different.[69]

France presents a sharp contrast, with a revolutionary tradition that begins in 1789 and is expressed in revolutionary upheavals in 1848, again in 1861, and most recently in May 1968.[70] This is the context from which a French socialist-feminist politic emerges; yet, despite these traditions, demands for an autonomous 'current' inside the French Socialist Party were quashed.[71]

The situation in the United States offers an interesting comparison. Socialist feminism there develops in the context of weak traditions of social democracy and the absence of a viable socialist or communist party. It is not entirely surprising that in such a context a socialist-feminist perspective might be difficult to sustain, although it would be an over-simplification to attribute this difficulty to these factors alone.[72] Lisa DiCaprio, a member of the Chicago Women's Liberation Union, which served as a centre of socialist-feminist activity from 1969 to 1977, identified the current location of socialist feminism in the United States. She speaks of a 'defensive posture of the women's movement':

> With the collapse of socialist feminist organizations, two develop-ments emerged: (1) a tremendous growth of women's scholarship and practical organizing experience, and (2) a loss of the multi-issue approach once characterizing women's liberation.[73]

Barbara Epstein, in a more pessimistic assessment of American socialist feminism, concludes that 'socialist feminist theory has been narrowed and hobbled by academic environs; it's been shaped to the demands of academia, and it's been cut off from any kind of move-ment'.[74] This obviously very schematic treatment of these issues is put forward to remind the reader of the historical and international character of a socialist-feminist politic and to provide a context in which to outline some of the factors that face Canadian socialist feminism.

CANADIAN SOCIALIST FEMINISM

The practice of Canadian socialist feminism must be understood in a historically specific way in relation to the constellation of socialist, feminist, and mainstream political practices that exist, both parlia-mentary and extra-parliamentary.[75] Currently in Canada there is no large, popular, or legitimate parliamentary communist or socialist party, and in fact Canadian traditions in this regard are weak. Con-sequently Canadian socialist feminism does not have to contend with clarifying its organizational, ideological, and strategic relationship to a parliamentary left. As a result socialist feminism here is not as polarized out of the women's movement as it is or has been in countries where socialist-feminist discourse has been dominated by discussions about its relationship to the left.[76]

Despite the absence of left parliamentary parties, there is a long tradition of social democracy expressed in the third party in Can-ada—the New Democratic Party—which garners about 20 per cent of the popular vote federally and has formed governments at the provincial level in Manitoba, Saskatchewan, and British Columbia in the last decade. The existence of the NDP and its commitment to a progressive platform on women's issues, at least in principle,[77] has had an impact on the development of the socialist-feminist stra-tegic orientation to the government and state apparatus.[78] For exam-ple, it might be possible to argue that the NDP's commitment to women's issues, combined with the fact that political parties shape their platforms in terms of public policy on economic and social issues, has meant that feminism in Canada (in particular socialist feminism, because of its closer political affinity to the NDP) has focused more on public-policy issues—child-care, pensions, labour legislation, etc.—than feminism in the U.S., which has attempted to use the Constitution to make change.[79] It is also the case that many socialist feminists have chosen to work with the NDP, especially inside its women's committees. The impact of such a strategy on developing Canadian socialist feminism, and the degree to which such a strategy is seen as a viable route to change for women, has generated on-going debate.[80]

Traditionally Canada has been dominated by a unique form of liberalism committed to the welfare state as well as to state intervention in the economy. Although in the late 1980s the federal government under Conservative Party leadership is decreasing the amount of state intervention in the economy (for example, through the privatization of Crown corporations), nonetheless it is forced to remain committed to improvements in pension schemes, expansion of day-care services, and centrally organized strategies to deal with 'woman abuse'. This commitment, although contradictory, presents a sharp and interesting contrast to the United States and British conservative governments under Reagan and Thatcher, and obviously constructs a different political task for socialist feminists (especially in relation to the potential responsiveness of the state).

Canada has a reasonably strong trade-union movement (about 38 per cent of workers are organized) with a formal alliance to the NDP. It has suffered under the recessions of the seventies and eighties and has faced attacks by the state and employer in the form of wage controls, barriers to organizing, and challenges to union rights, especially the right to strike.[81] Nevertheless, the last decade has also witnessed the emergence of a strong, organized, and relatively successful movement of union women, heavily influenced by a socialist-feminist politic.[82]

In fact, Heather Jon Maroney suggests that by the end of the seventies, what she calls 'working class feminism' based in the trade unions is a distinct current in the women's movement:

> [The] radicalization of working women . . . has profoundly altered the organizational and ideological balance of forces within the movement as a whole. This radicalization is significant not just in itself or in the opportunity it provides for broadening the struggle, but because

the widening of the class basis of feminism deepens our understanding of the way class and gender oppression condenses a global system of domination.[83]

Other historically specific factors important to understanding Canadian socialist feminism include the fact that for a short time in the 1970s far-left maoist and trotskyist groups provided a 'breeding ground' for socialist feminism, not so much as a place for a coherent socialist-feminist practice to emerge, but rather as a context in which a politic that challenged that of the orthodox far left could develop.

Socialist feminism has been part of the autonomous women's movement as a named politic, though not a completely coherent one, almost since the beginning of the second wave of the women's movement in Canada. In fact, in the introduction to *Women Unite!*, one of the very earliest Canadian anthologies (1972) of writings about women,[84] the editors state:

> Canadian women more uniformly developed an analysis of their oppression based on a class notion of society. . . . The marxist perspective has since been central to the development of the Canadian women's liberation movement.[85]

In 1987 Mariana Valverde confirmed that assessment:

> In the unions, in the New Democratic Party (the social democrats), in the reproductive rights movement, in the area of culture and sexual politics, even in the mainstream of women's coalition (the National Action Committee), left feminism is a formidable force.[86]

Socialist feminism has always had a practice; it is not overly identified with the academy;[87] it is not seen to be on the decline; and in fact a socialist-feminist politic has been influential in shaping the politic and practice of other currents of Canadian feminism.

Canadian socialist feminism has had an extensive and fertile ground on which to take root. Perhaps this explains the importance and strength of socialist-feminist theory and practice in Canada. In other countries socialist feminism has been connected to a far greater degree to organized left or labour-party formations, or to the academy; as a result it has occupied less space inside the autonomous women's movement. It is also true, however, that Canadian socialist feminism does not have a high profile, if any, in the public consciousness, in part because feminism is pictured as a unitary politic—that is, hegemonized by liberal feminism—and in part because of the strategic dilemma of building socialist-feminist organizations (to be discussed in Chapter 7).

Given these complexities, it is not surprising to find little public consensus inside the contemporary women's movement, or among socialist feminists, about socialist feminism. Indeed there is often a reluctance to articulate (especially in print) a clear set of guiding principles, a reluctance that stems in part from the fact that such principles present a clarity that is only possible at a fairly abstract level of analysis, removed from the complexities and confusions of daily political activity. We are more than aware that these kinds of principles and theory do not always provide solutions to the dilemmas of activists, and that in daily struggle their apparent clarity can become opaque. For this reason, in Chapter 5 we will try to articulate our understanding of socialist feminism in the more concrete terms of actual feminist practice.

But the fact that the principles and theory of socialist feminism do not provide a step-by-step blueprint to practical struggle or to the future, and in fact often blur in the context of real political struggle, does not mean that they are useless, of concern only to those who like to debate esoteric issues. On the contrary, these principles establish a framework that helps to sort through the muddiness of reality. Just as concrete practice acts as a kind of reality-test of our guiding principles, those principles in turn offer a framework within which to situate the myriad of issues and details that often threaten to overwhelm feminist activists.

The synthesis developed in this chapter represents our attempt as activists and theorists to present a coherent account of socialist feminism. It may not reflect the views of all those who would call themselves socialist feminists. Notwithstanding, the articulation of these principles provides the reader with the framework that informs our exploration, in the final part of this book, of the current practice, ideology, and organizational strategies of the Canadian women's movement.

CONCLUSION: THE LESSON OF HISTORY

History reminds us that contemporary socialist feminism is not the first radical vision of change, of socialism, or of women's liberation; it also reminds us that to a large extent most of them have failed. Although later chapters in this book will look at some of the dilemmas facing contemporary Canadian socialist feminism, we continue to believe that this vision is a timely and accessible one. In fact, it is the strength of socialist feminism that provides the basis for us to understand and see beyond the current dilemmas.

Historians of the first wave of the women's movement, in Canada and elsewhere, have endeavoured to understand why radical visions in the women's movement were unfulfilled. For example, Wayne Roberts seeks to document and explain, for Canada, the 'rise of a conservative brand of women's social activism and . . . its triumph, particularly within the suffrage movement, over earlier reform conceptions of women's place in politics and society'.[88]

He suggests that the 'key . . . can be found in the distorted and contradictory growth patterns which governed women's entry into the new professions'.[89] These patterns emphasized the role of women as mothers, as self-sacrificing nurturers, rather than as economically independent professionals. Given the important leadership role that professional women played in the suffrage movement, and the lack of sustained alternative leadership from the labour or socialist movements, maternal feminism came to dominate over equal-rights feminism.

Ellen Dubois asks a similar question for the nineteenth-century American suffrage movement. Emphasizing the radicalism of its politics in the early years, she asks why this radicalism gradually disappeared. She suggests that as 'suffragism began to take on the character of a social movement'[90] and acquire a constituency, the politics of the movement were constrained by the material conditions of the majority of women:

> The acquisition of a constituency acted to restrain the sexual and economic radicalism to which suffragists were otherwise inclining. The objective social conditions of women's lives in the mid-nineteenth century, their dependence on marriage and the sexually segregated nature of the labour force, constituted the basic framework within which suffragism had to develop.[91]

In light of these arguments, we might suggest that the material basis for widespread acceptance of socialist feminism exists in Canada today. The increase in the permanent character of married women's wage work (and the continued participation by single women) suggests that an analysis and a strategy that place the double day at their centre most accurately reflect the concerns of women and the material conditions they face. And unlike the nineteenth-century Canadian movement in which, as Roberts argues, no sustained radical leadership existed, today such leaders can be drawn from among these women workers, and in particular from the women's movement and the movement of union women.

This is not to suggest that gaining acceptance will be easy. The resistance to change is powerful, from those who currently hold a lot of power and even from women themselves. (We will explore this resistance to change in the next chapter.)

This chapter has presented socialist feminism as a coherent politic able to deepen our understanding of the relations of power—sex, class, race, and sexual orientation—under patriarchal capitalism, and of women's experience of the sexual division of labour, the state, and the public and the private. This socialist-feminist theory and the method of historical materialism lay the basis for a socialist-feminist analysis of the politics of making change.

NOTES

[1]There is a long-standing debate among feminists about the appropriate use of the term 'patriarchy', or 'patriarchal'. See, for example, Gayle Rubin, 'The Traffic in Women: Notes on the "Political Economy" of Sex', in Rayna Reiter, ed., *Toward an Anthropology of Women* (New York: Monthly Review Press, 1975); Veronica Beechey, 'On Patriarchy', *Feminist Review* 3 (1979); Sheila Rowbotham, 'The Trouble with Patriarchy', in Raphael Samuel, ed., *People's History and Socialist Theory* (London: Routledge and Kegan Paul, 1981) and Val Burris, 'The Dialectic of Women's Oppression: Notes on the relation between Capitalism and Patriarchy', *Berkeley Journal of Sociology* 27, 1982.

[2]One of many critiques of socio-biology can be found in Carol Tavris and Carole Wade, *The Longest War: Sex Differences in Perspective*, 2nd ed. (San Diego: Harcourt Brace and Jovanovitch, 1984), pp.126–35. For a discussion of the problems of using biological determinism to explain the patterns of women's work force participation, see Pat and Hugh Armstrong, *The Double Ghetto*, rev. ed. (Toronto: McClelland and Stewart, 1984), ch. 4.

[3]The dominant ideology is a set of ideas and practices about how the world works and how it ought to work. These are widely if subtly propagated, and are often deeply internalized in our social practices and personal psyches. This ideology, albeit dominant, is not unchallenged. For example, the challenge posed by socialist feminism to the dominant 'ideology of change' is examined in the next chapter.

[4]This question seems to have been significant ever since women began to articulate demands for equality. In 1792, in the first systematic treatise on women's rights, *Vindication of the Rights of Woman* (Harmondsworth: Penguin, 1985), Mary Wollstonecraft wrote, 'I do not wish [women] to have power over men; but over themselves' (p. 154).

[5]Alison Jaggar, *Feminist Politics and Human Nature* (Totowa, N.J.: Rowman and Allanheld, 1983), p. 60.

[6]Juliet Mitchell, 'Women and Equality', in Juliet Mitchell and Ann Oakley, eds, *The Rights and Wrongs of Women* (Harmondsworth: Penguin, 1976), p. 397.

[7]The challenge of difference has confronted all feminists and has been reflected, in differing degrees, in the practice of all feminisms. However, we suggest that the socialist-feminist paradigm provides a framework within which difference, as we have defined it, can be theorized; this analysis, and its implications for socialist-feminist practice, are certainly incomplete, but the potential for this elaboration exists.

A seminal article on the relation between sex and class is Heidi Hartmann, 'The Unhappy Marriage of Marxism and Feminism: Towards a More Progressive Union', in Lydia Sargent, ed., *Women and Revolution* (Boston: South End, 1981).

[8]A recent collection of articles dealing with this subject is, Rosemary Crompton and Michael

Mann, eds, *Gender and Stratification* (Cambridge: Polity Press, 1986). See also Anne Phillips, *Divided Loyalties: Dilemmas of Sex and Class* (London: Virago, 1987).

[9]Quoted in 'All Canadians pay the price of corporate concentration', *Toronto Star* 9 Sept. 1986.

[10]Quoted in 'Canada's 63,250 richest families earn $212,000 a year', *Toronto Star* 8 July 1986.

[11]Figure from 'Women and Poverty' Fact Sheet, Canadian Advisory Council on the Status of Women, Feb. 1985.

[12]See Adrienne Rich, 'Compulsory Heterosexuality and Lesbian Existence', *Signs: A Journal of Women in Society* vol. 5, no. 4 (Summer 1980).

[13]Helen Lenskyj, 'From Prejudice to Policy', *Broadside* vol. 8, no. 6 (April 1987), p. 4.

[14]Mariana Valverde, *Sex, Power and Pleasure* (Toronto: Women's Press, 1985), pp. 83–4.

[15]Charlotte Bunch, 'Lesbian Feminist Theory', in Michael Zak and Patricia Moots, eds, *Women and the Politics of Culture* (New York: Longman, 1983), p. 416.

[16] For a discussion of the complexity of the historical and political relations between lesbians and gay men, see Lorna Weir and Eve Zaremba, 'Boys and Girls Together: Feminism and Gay Liberation', *Broadside* vol. 4, no. 1 (Oct. 1982), pp. 6–7.

[17]'How Racism Works', Fact Sheet #3, Ontario Federation of Labour, n.d.

[18]Ibid.

[19]Carol Allen and Judy Persad, 'Fighting Racism and Sexism Together', in Keynote Speech to International Women's Day, Toronto, 1987. Reprinted by International Women's Day Committee (also reprinted in Appendix A, p. 293 below).

[20]Marlene Philip talks of the racism inherent in the substitution of the category of immigrant for women of colour and the way it allows white feminists to avoid confronting the problems of racism inside the women's movement: 'I don't believe this substitution of words was inadvertent; I believe it represents a certain world view that many white Canadian feminists have of women of colour and Black women. . . . One's colôur, if not white, identifies one as immigrant with all the problems consequential upon that. . . . Essentially what it does is allow for the continued avoidance of confrontation with the problems of racism in the women's movement.' See 'Solitary Dialogue', *Broadside* vol. 7, no. 5 (March 1986), p. 5.

This connection between race and immigration is evident in many of the workplace, legislative, and cultural practices in Canadian society. For a recent overview of the issues facing immigrant women, see *Resources for Feminist Research*, Special Issue on Immigrant Women, vol. 16, no.1 (March 1987).

[21]Barbara Smith, 'Racism and Women's Studies', quoted in Kum Kum Bhavnani and Margaret Coulson, 'Transforming Socialist Feminism: the Challenge of Racism', *Feminist Review* 23 (June 1986), p. 91.

[22]Angela Davis, *Women Race and Class* (New York: Vintage, 1981), p. 177.

[23]Hazel Carby, 'White Women Listen! Black feminism and the boundaries of sisterhood', in Centre for Contemporary Cultural Studies, *The Empire Strikes Back* (London: Hutchinson, 1982), p. 214.

[24]See Makeda Silvera, *Silenced* (Toronto: Williams-Wallace Publishers, 1983).

[25]Allen and Persad, 'Fighting Racism and Sexism Together'.

[26]The Combahee River Collective, 'A Black Feminist Statement', in Zillah Eisenstein, ed., *Capitalist Patriarchy and the Case for Socialist Feminism* (New York: Monthly Review Press, 1979), p. 365.

[27]Bell Hooks, 'Sisterhood: Political Solidarity Between Women', *Feminist Review* no. 23 (Summer 1986), p. 124.

[28]Maria Mies, in *Patriarchy and Accumulation on a World Scale: Women in the International Division of Labour* (London: ZED Books, 1986), looks at some of the contradictions in the relations between Third World and Western women, and also seeks to understand the way the international division of labour has structured their experiences in common.

Canadian feminist politics have been infused with a new awareness of the issues of Third World women as a result of the conferences held in Nairobi in 1985 to mark the end of the decade for women, which had been initiated by the United Nations in 1975. The official conference of governmental delegates ratified the Forward-Looking Strategies for the Advancement of Women to the Year 2000. Perhaps more important, 'Forum '85 brought together 13,000 women from non-governmental organizations from around the globe to assess the progress women had made in the decade.' (Janet Laidlaw, 'Forum '85: The "Unofficial" Conference', *Canadian Woman Studies* vol. 7, no. 1/2 [Spring/Summer 1986]. This entire issue is devoted to the Nairobi experience.)

[29]Weir sees this class reductionism reflected in the 'internal hierarchy of issues, with those issues having the most apparent class content at the top and those with the least at the bottom. One gets many points for helping to organize a support picket for striking women workers, but few for putting together a lesbian conference. This ranking scheme is partly inherited by socialist feminists from socialism.' See 'Socialist Feminism and the Politics of Sexuality', in Heather Jon Maroney and Meg Luxton, eds, *Feminism and Political Economy* (Toronto: Methuen, 1987), pp.75–6.

Although Weir is correct in her assessment of this hierarchy in socialist-feminist practice, identifying the centrality of difference to socialist-feminist theory and practice allows for a challenge to that hierarchical framework.

[30]Lynne Segal makes a somewhat similar point: 'We should not be looking for the primacy of sex, class or race, nor to isolate them as separate structures when they have fused together historically. Socialist feminists in Britain need to start from the contemporary reality of a racially and sexually **divided** capitalist class society' (emphasis in original). In *Is the Future Female?: Troubled Thoughts on Contemporary Feminism* (London: Virago, 1987), p. 67.

[31]Weir, 'Socialist Feminism', pp. 81–2.

[32]Judy Housman, 'Mothering, the Unconscious and Feminism', *Radical America* vol. 16, no. 6 (Nov./Dec. 1982), p. 56.

[33]Although we argue for a socialist-feminist perspective that does not privilege gender and that provides the basis for a political world view, we also recognize that in practice many socialist feminists tend to organize with women and around women's issues, although not only in the organizations of the women's movement but also in the trade union movement, the NDP, etc. However, for socialist feminism to develop as a significant informing politic, socialist feminists will need to widen the scope of their political practice.

[34]Barbara Smith makes a similar point in her discussion of the relation between racism and feminism: 'The reason racism is a feminist issue is easily explained by the inherent definition of feminism. Feminism is the political theory and practice to free all women: women of colour, working class women, poor women, physically challenged women, lesbians, old women, as well as white economically privileged women. Anything less than this is not feminism.' In *This Bridge Called My Back*, quoted in Kandace Kerr, 'Experiencing *Women, Race and Class*, Personally', *Kinesis* Sept. 1985.

[35]'The cultural politics of . . . the early seventies [were] extraordinarily, if naively, optimistic that as women we could change our lives and those of others once we saw through "male lies". Many feminists were eagerly attempting to change every aspect of their lives: how we lived with and related to other adults and children, how we worked and developed new skills, how we saw ourselves. . . . Much of the cultural feminism of today, in contrast, is less concerned with change: it calls upon the timeless truths of women's lives, sufficient in themselves, but threatened by the perpetual and invasive danger of men. It suggests that women do not need to change their lives, other than to separate themselves from the lives of men, and that there is lttle hope of men themselves changing.' Lynne Segal, *Is the Future Female?* (London: Virago, 1987), pp. 68–9.

[36]'In 1983, 77 per cent of all female employees worked in just five occupational groups-clerical, service, sales, medicine and health and teaching. This was only a three percentage point drop from what the proportion had been in 1975. By contrast, these occupational groups represented just 34 per cent of employed males in 1983' (*Women in Canada: A Statistical Report*, Statistics Canada, 1985, p. 43).

[37]'In 1983, there were 956,000 children under 6 and 1,320,000 children aged 6–12 with

mothers in the labour force. Yet, in 1983 there were only 139,070 licensed group and family home care spaces in the whole country.' From Information Sheets from the Canadian Day Care Advocacy Association, n.d.

[38]Martin Meissner studied the sexual division of labour inside Canadian households and concluded: 'In couples without a child under 10 and wife without employment, husbands do an estimated 3.2 hours of regular housework a week [of a total of 99.3 hours of housework], increasing it by an insignificant 6 minutes when their wives go out to work. In couples with a young child, things are only slightly better. The husbands' 5 hours of regular housework increase by one hour a week when their wives work for pay [of a total of 125.6].' See Martin Meissner et al., 'No Exit for Wives: sexual division of labour and the cumulation of household demands', *Canadian Review of Sociology and Anthropology* vol. 12, no. 4 (part 1), (Nov. 1975), p.436. See also Meg Luxton, *More than a Labour of Love: Three Generations of Women's Work in the Home* (Toronto: Women's Press, 1980).

[39]In 1983 52.6 per cent of women were in the labour force (compared to 76.7 per cent of men). Women made up 41.7 per cent of the paid work force in that year (*Women in Canada: A Statistical Report*, Statistics Canada, 1985, p. 47).

[40]*Women in the Labour Force, 1986–7 Edition*, Labour Canada, Women's Bureau, 1987, p. 3.

[41]*Women in Canada: A Statistical Report*, Statistics Canada, 1985, p. 64.

[42]'. . . data from the 1971 census for women in Ontario illustrate that Black women do tend to have higher employment (and unemployment) rates when compared with other women. . . . 49 per cent of Black Canadian-born respondents, and 68 per cent of Black immigrant women were employed in 1971, as compared with 43 per cent of all other Canadian-born women and 42 per cent of all other immigrants.' Adrienne Shadd, '300 Years of Black Women in Canadian History: circa 1700–1980', *Tiger Lily* vol. 1, issue 2 (1987), p. 11.

[43]The understanding of the state put forward in the following section has been influenced by helpful discussions with Kari Delhi, Alice de Wolff, and Roxana Ng in the context of the Organizing Committee for the Conference on Women and the Canadian State held at the Ontario Institute for Studies in Education in February 1986.

[44]One piece of evidence is the proportion of income tax paid by corporations and individuals. In 1983 more than 79,000 profitable corporations with total earnings of $13 billion paid no corporate income tax, despite the fact that 64 of them had more than $25 million each in profits. Further, in 1984 corporate income taxes totalled $12 billion, while personal income taxes were 37.7 billion. In 1951 the proportions were almost equal. Figures based on a NDP study and reported in '79,000 big firms paid no tax . . .', *Toronto Star* 25 Sept. 1986.

[45]Ed Finn in 'Unsafe workplaces are a form of violence against workers', (*Toronto Star* 7 Dec. 1984) reports that 'occupational hazards are the third leading cause of death in Canada, surpassed only by heart disease and cancer. And a large number of the cancer deaths can be traced to exposure to toxic chemicals and radiation in the workplace. Every six seconds in this country, a worker is injured on the job. More than 70 million working days are lost every year though job-related injuries and disease.'

[46]Janine Brodie in *Women and Politics in Canada* (Toronto: McGraw-Hill Ryerson, 1985) gives evidence of the gender bias in the composition of elected assemblies in Canada. For example, 'In 1983 . . . only 6% of a total of 1172 provincial legislators were women. . . . At the federal level, a mere sixty-five women have become members of Parliament between 1921 . . . and 1984' (p. 2).

[47]For an extended discussion of the Canadian state, see Leo Panitch, ed., *The Canadian State: Political Economy and Political Power* (Toronto: Univ. of Toronto Press, 1977).

[48]See Alfred Holden, ' "Spouse in the House" change aids 9000 single parents', *Toronto Star* 29 Oct. 1987; also 'Peel fears end of family life under "spouse in house" law', *Toronto Star* 30 Oct. 1987.

[49]Frances Fox Piven, 'Women and the State: Ideology, Power and the Welfare State', *Socialist Review* no. 74 (March/April 1984). For example, she argues that 'the expansion of social-

welfare programs has created a far-flung and complex infrastructure of agencies and organizations that are proving to be resources in the defense of the welfare state. . . . Women [are] preponderant in this infrastructure and its leadership positions.

'The welfare state also brings together millions of poor women who depend on welfare-state programs. These constituencies do not represent simply atomized and therefore helpless people. . . . Rather the structure of the welfare state itself has helped to create new solidarities. . . .

'The infrastructure of the welfare state also creates the basis for cross-class alliances among women. The infrastructure is dominated by better-educated and middle-class women. But these women are firmly linked by organizational self-interest to the poor women who depend on welfare-state programs' (pp. 17–18).

[50]See Nancy Sagmeister, 'In Sickness and in Health: Spousal Benefits for Gays and Lesbians', *Our Times* vol. 6, no. 6 (Sept. 1987), pp. 33–34, for a discussion of a recent Ontario challenge to this restriction.

[51] Alexandra Dagg, research director for the International Ladies Garment Workers Union, calculates that 25,000 of the 38,654 garment workers in Ontario would lose their jobs under the Free Trade deal. Many of the unemployed would be middle-aged immigrant women whose prospects for job retraining are poor. Reported in the *Toronto Star* 22 Oct. 1987.

[52]For an excellent philosophical discussion of the differences between feminist currents in terms of their understanding of the private and the public, see Alison Jaggar, *Feminist Politics and Human Nature* (Totowa, N.J.: Rowman and Allanheld, 1983).

[53]Carolyn Egan, 'Socialist Feminism: Activism and Alliances', in *Feminism and Political Economy*, eds. Heather Jon Maroney and Meg Luxton (Toronto: Methuen, 1987), pp. 115–16.

[54]It is also the case that radical feminists who focus on the transhistorical reality of patriarchy tend to reach a strategic impasse that takes the form of arguing for a separatist solution; that is, a separate woman culture. It is not hard to see that this would not be attractive to the vast majority of women.

[55]This is a somewhat ahistorical use of the term 'feminist'. Many women who argued for and organized around women's issues in the nineteenth century would not have called themselves feminists. The term 'feminism' was problematic for two reasons. In the first place, in the nineteenth century it had an ambiguous relation to femininity, the two sometimes being confused and the confusion being expressed in attempts by feminists to validate the special nature of women. See Micheline Dumont, *The Women's Movement: Then and Now* (Ottawa: CRIAW, 1986).

Second, the feminist movement in the nineteenth century was overly identified with middle-class and bourgeois women. Although we are now uncovering increasing evidence of organization by working-class women, even around what have been seen to be traditionally middle-class issues such as the vote, it is nonetheless the case that in the nineteenth century the public perception associated the feminist movement with middle-class women. This helps to explain the rejection of feminism by many socialist women.

For a fascinating account of working-class women organizing for the vote in England, see Jill Liddington and Jill Norris, *One Hand Tied Behind Us* (London: Virago, 1978).

[56]'. . . it is worth saying something about "proletarian ethics" or "proletarian sexual morality", in order to criticise the well-worn idea that proletarian sexual morality is no more than "superstructure", and that there is no place for any change in that sphere until the economic base of society has changed. As if the ideology of a certain class is formed only when the breakdown in the socio-economic relationships, guaranteeing the dominance of that class, has been completed! All the experience of history teaches us that a social group works out its ideology, and consequently its sexual morality, in the process of its struggle with hostile social forces.' 'Sexual Relations and the Class Struggle' in *Alexandra Kollontai: Selected Writings*, translated with an introduction and commentaries by Alix Holt (London: Allison and Busby, 1977), p. 249.

[57]Philip Foner, 'Introduction' in *Clara Zetkin: Selected Writings* (New York: International Publishers, 1984), p. 42.

[58]See, for example, 'For the Liberation of Women' (1889), Speech at the International Workers' Congress, Paris; and 'Only in Conjunction with Proletarian Woman will Socialism be Victorious' (1896), Speech at the Party Congress of the Social Democratic Party of Germany. Both are reprinted in Philip Foner, ed. *Clara Zetkin: Selected Writings* (New York: International Publishers, 1984).

Foner tells us that Zetkin 'was the leading advocate of a separate organization for women in the Party, believing that this provided a mechanism whereby socialist women as a minority, could maximize their influence and guarantee representation of their interests. At the same time, autonomy made it possible to maintain the radical nature of the socialist women's movement. . . .' ('Introduction', p. 33).

For a perspective on women's issues inside Canadian socialist and communist parties, see Linda Kealey, 'Canadian Socialism and the Woman Question, 1900–1914', *Labour/Le Travail* vol. 13 (1984); Janice Newton, 'Women and Cotton's Weekly: A Study of Women and Socialism in Canada, 1909', *Resources for Feminist Research* vol. 8 (1979); and Joan Sangster, 'The Communist Party and the Woman Question, 1922–29', *Labour/Le Travail* vol. 15 (Spring 1985).

[59]Barbara Taylor, *Eve and the New Jerusalem* (London: Virago, 1983).

[60]Ibid., p. 285.

[61]Ibid., p. 31.

[62]Ibid., p. 32.

[63]Ibid., p. 52.

[64]Ibid., p. 55.

[65]Meredith Tax, *The Rising of the Women: Feminist Solidarity and Class Conflict, 1880–1917* (New York: Monthly Review Press, 1980), p. 13.

[66]On feminism in the Third World see, for example, Kumari Jayawardena, *Feminism and Nationalism in the Third World* (London: Zed Press, 1986).

[67]Angela Weir and Elizabeth Wilson, 'The British Women's Movement', *New Left Review* 148 (Nov./Dec. 1984), p. 75.

[68]Frigga Haug, 'The Women's Movement in West Germany', *New Left Review* 155 (Jan./Feb. 1986), p. 58.

[69]Monica Threlfall, 'The Women's Movement in Spain', *New Left Review* no. 151 (May/June 1985).

[70]See Theresia Sauter-Bailliet, 'The Feminist Movement in France', *Women's Studies International Quarterly* vol. 4, no. 4 (1981), or Claire Duchen, *Feminism in France: From May '68 to Mitterand* (London: Routledge and Kegan Paul, 1986), especially Ch. 2 'Currents: diversity and conflict'.

[71]Melissa Benn, 'In and Against the European Left: Socialist Feminists Get Organized', *Feminist Review* no. 26 (Summer 1987), p. 88. This article gives a flavour of the current debates among European socialist feminists who have begun meeting regularly at the European level.

[72]Karen Hansen from the University of California (Berkeley), in her paper 'Forging a Class Conscious Feminism: the experiment with socialist feminist women's unions', presented at the 1987 Berkshire Conference, argued that the primary public (audience) of these groups was the left; the autonomous women's movement was a secondary audience.

Hansen also indicated that there had been 18 socialist feminist women's unions (the particular U.S. form of socialist feminist groupings not related to trade unions) between 1969 and 1975. For an assessment of these groups as they were going into decline, see Red Apple Collective, 'Socialist-Feminist Women's Unions: Past and Present', *Socialist Review* 38 (March/April 1978).

[73]Lisa DiCaprio, 'Socialist Feminism USA', reprinted from the *Guardian* 7 Nov. 1984, in *Cayenne* 2 (Feb. 1985), p. 6.

[74]In a conversation with Deirdre English, Barbara Epstein, Barbara Haber, and Judy Maclean, 'The Impasse of Socialist Feminism', *Socialist Review* 79 (Jan./Feb. 1985), p. 101. Judy Maclean, in the same article, suggests pessimistically that socialist feminism 'as a term and as a means of excluding other women . . . is dead' (p. 103).

This is one of a recent series of articles on socialist feminism in *Socialist Review* raising the question: 'Has socialist feminism died?' The discussions in *Socialist Review* present a sharp contrast to the vibrant discussion in *Feminist Review* (no. 23 [Summer 1986]), in England, the latter discussion precipitated by a controversial article by Elizabeth Wilson and Angela Weir on the British women's movement. See Angela Weir and Elizabeth Wilson, 'The British Women's Movement', *New Left Review* 148 (Nov./Dec. 1984).

[75]Socialist-feminist practice must also be understood in relation to the organization of the entire women's movement. The strength and shape of socialist feminism is related to the level of development and strategic choices of other currents of feminism. Unfortunately it is beyond the scope of this book to develop this point in detail.

[76]See, for example, Sheila Rowbotham, Lynne Segal, and Hilary Wainwright, *Beyond the Fragments: feminism and the making of socialism* (Boston: Alyson Publications,1981). See also Monica Threlfall, 'The Women's Movement in Spain', *New Left Review* 151 (May/ June 1985). She discusses the situation after the fall of the Franco regime in which the left attempted to hegemonize the newly emerging women's movement: 'Within the women's movement . . . opinions divided over the question of *doble militancia*, of whether women should spend their time being activists in a political party as well as in a women's group' (p. 46).

[77]For example, the New Democratic Party has a principled commitment to reproductive rights for women and for expansion of and fair access to abortion services. Yet the Manitoba NDP during its stay in power in the late 1980s and under the leadership of Attorney General Roland Penner chose to charge the organizers of a free-standing abortion clinic rather than license it to operate as a hospital.

[78]The NDP has a historic alliance with the trade-union movement in Canada. For a discussion of what these links have meant for union women, see Janis Sarra, 'Trade Union Women and the NDP', in Linda Briskin and Lynda Yanz, eds, *Union Sisters* (Toronto: Women's Press, 1983).

[79]Isa Bakker suggested this way of comparing Canadian and American feminism. It would also be interesting to compare gains made through the public-policy process and those made through the new Canadian Charter of Rights. It is becomingly increasingly evident that the focus on individual rights that is the basis of the Charter can and is being used against women and against the rights of trade unions.

An editorial comment by the staff of *Our Times* stated, 'The Charter places a premium on individual rights. . . . Instead of protecting the majority of Canadians from the power of privileged minorities like employers, we now protect minorities and individuals from "the tyranny of the majority".' *Our Times* vol. 6, no. 4 (May 1987) p. 8.

Doris Anderson has given a few examples of this. For example: 'In Newfoundland a man was charged with sexually assaulting a 14–year-old girl. His lawyer argued that the law is unfair because there is no similar law regarding women who might, but almost never do, sexually assault young boys. His client gets off.' She points out that 'such ludicrous decisions in the courts make the Charter of Rights look like one more cruel joke' ('Women need money to test the Charter', *Toronto Star* 23 May 1987).

[80]The NDP women's committee in British Columbia puts out an excellent publication, *Priorities*, in whose pages this debate has frequently recurred. See, for example, Hilda Thomas, 'Future Perspectives: a discussion paper', *Priorities* vol. 7, no. 5 (July/Aug. 1979); Cynthia Flood, 'Feminists and the NDP', *Priorities* vol. 5, no. 1 (Jan. 1977); Ann Thomson, 'Why are we in the NDP', *Priorities* vol. 5, no. 1 (Jan. 1977); Marianne Gilbert and Other Sister, 'Facing Facts', *Priorities* vol. 4, no. 9 (May 1976).

[81] For example, British Columbia has a right-wing Social Credit government that has system-atically attacked the trade-union movement. For a exploration of some of the resistance to

these attacks, see Brian Palmer, *Solidarity: The Rise and Fall of an Opposition in British Columbia* (Vancouver: New Star Books, 1987).

[82]See Briskin and Yanz, eds, *Union Sisters*, an anthology of thirty articles written mostly by women trade-union militants documenting their struggles and successes.

[83]Heather Jon Maroney, 'Feminism at Work', in Heather Jon Maroney and Meg Luxton, eds, *Feminism and Political Economy* (Toronto: Methuen, 1987), pp. 86–7.

[84]The other anthology published in 1972 was compiled by Margret Andersen and entitled *Mother Was Not a Person* (Montreal: Black Rose, 1972).

[85]'Introduction' in *Women Unite* (Toronto: Canadian Women's Press, 1972), p. 10.

[86]Mariana Valverde, review of Roberta Hamilton and Michele Barrett, eds, *The Politics of Diversity* (London: Verso, 1986) in *New Statesman*, March 1987. Both Heather Jon Maroney and Lorna Weir also take this position in the 1987 collection of articles *Feminism and Political Economy*.

For example, Weir says that 'sexual politics, the struggle for abortion access, and the day care movement are terrains of socialist feminist activism which extend far beyond an abstract notion of a minority of socialist feminists' launching "class intervention" in a preexisting women's movement. In Canada today, socialist feminists are not simply "intervening" but actually helping to define and create significant sectors of the women's movement.' In 'Socialist Feminism and the Politics of Sexuality', pp. 77–8.

[87]As noted earlier, Barbara Epstein, in her assessment of U.S. socialist feminism, attributes its decline in part to its increasing location in the university. Some have also argued that in England socialist feminism is far more developed theoretically than in practice. Often these assessments come from Canadian socialist feminists travelling in England and U.S. who are surprised by the highly academic and theoretical character of socialist feminism.

In her review of 'Women and the State: A Conference for Feminist Activists' (*Feminist Review* no. 26 [Summer 1987]), Lorna Weir says: 'Travelling in England and the United States, Canadian socialist feminists have often been very surprised to discover the strongly academic and weakly activist formation of socialist feminism in these countries. The element of surprise arises from an assumption that the large quantities of English and American socialist feminist literature which we in Canada consume emanate (somehow) from vast systems of socialist feminist political mobilizing. Within Canada, socialist feminists have an ongoing history of participation in popular movements, particularly the women's movement, while comparatively few socialist feminists hold academic positions. Given the sparse number of accounts documenting socialist feminism as an organized political practice, there is an inclination to suppose a rough international uniformity in the political location(s) of socialist feminism. . . . National variations in socialist feminism are constituted organizationally as well as textually, despite our international appearance to each other chiefly as texts' (p. 93).

Lynne Segal also documents the problems with the way that socialist-feminist theory developed in Britain, and its relation to feminist practice. See *Is the Future Female?* (London: Virago, 1987), ch. 2.

This over-identification of socialist feminism with the academy in Britain and the U.S., concomitant with a weak socialist-feminist practice, raises the critical question of the relationship between articulating socialist-feminist discourse and developing socialist-feminist practice.

[88]Wayne Roberts, '"Rocking the Cradle for the World": The New Woman and Maternal Feminism, Toronto, 1877–1914', in Linda Kealey, ed., *A Not Unreasonable Claim* (Toronto: Women's Press, 1979), p. 20.

[89]Ibid., p. 27.

[90]Ellen DuBois, 'The Nineteenth Century Woman Suffrage Movement and the Analysis of Women's Oppression', in *Capitalist Patriarchy and the Case for Socialist Feminism*, Zillah Eisenstein, ed. (New York: Monthly Review Press, 1979), p. 139.

[91]Ibid.

4

The Politics of Making Change

MAKING CHANGE

In this chapter we will translate the analysis of power relations outlined in the last chapter into a perspective on social change. We will systemize what we see to be a socialist-feminist view on change and contrast this to popular ideologies and structures of change that focus on individual solutions and individualism, and on changing values and attitudes. Such ideologies reflect a fear of the collective, and indeed of change itself; identify only the government and elected representatives as the legitimate agents of change; and, in our opinion, combine to produce a fundamental resistance to social change.

In contrast, socialist feminism emphasizes the centrality of human agency and celebrates the possibilities of change. Moreover, it focuses on changing material structures rather than attitudes and values, and highlights the importance of popular movements in making change.

Making change is by definition the goal of the women's movement. To do so is to challenge social inertia, to empower ourselves, and to create a new set of possibilities. But as we pointed out in the introduction to this book, despite rather remarkable successes, the kind of change feminist activists want has not been achieved. In trying to understand why, feminists have a tendency to blame themselves and criticize their efforts, or to attribute the problem to the intransigency of male domination. And although it is necessary both to turn a self-critical eye on the strategic choices of the women's movement and to recognize the depth of women's oppression, we also need to unravel popular consciousness about making change and to analyze the structures and routes to change legitimized by Canadian society. For these are what all feminists confront in trying to make change.

In this chapter we will contend that such ideologies and structures fundamentally limit the process of change. In order to bring about the kind of change the women's movement wants, social consciousness about change must be understood, exposed, and reconstructed.

This means a direct challenge to what we call the 'ideology of change'.

The women's movement has been very concerned with specific change, but we have rarely turned our attention to mainstream structures of, or public consciousness about, change itself. This lack of attention to the process of change has undermined our ability to effect change. We hold up our picket signs to the blindfolded and shout slogans to the deaf. The numbers at our demonstrations are not relevant. We are too often made invisible by a social ideology about the change process.

This ideology of change is directly connected to and reinforces the dominant power relations of patriarchal capitalism. The socialist-feminist analysis of these relations provides the basis on which to challenge popular notions about change and has important implications for how we organize, who we organize, and to what ends. We will begin by exploring the impact of the relations of power on making change, and then turn to a detailed discussion of the ideology of change.

THE IMPACT OF THE RELATIONS OF POWER ON MAKING CHANGE

As we pointed out in the previous chapter, individuals in our society have differential amounts of power and privilege based on their sex/gender, class, race, and sexual orientation. It is not surprising that those with more power have a vested interest in keeping it and therefore tend to defend the status quo. In fact, we might say that resistance to change is fundamentally a resistance to the redistribution of resources. However, we wish to remind readers that this desire for power is not intrinisic to human nature, but is constructed out of the organization and distribution of resources, and the social validation of power and privilege, rather than of co-operation and equality.

These relations of power are embedded in all Canadian institutions, such as schools, workplaces, and the state. They shape the way these institutions function and provide the context within which women organize for change. We can give numerous examples of the resistance of these institutions to change, a resistance organized and controlled by those who have power. A fascinating one is the institutional and individual response to affirmative-action programs designed to deal with historic discrimination against blacks, women, the disabled, native Canadians, visible minorities, and so on. These programs attempt to redress this discrimination by action in favour of the disadvantaged groups and can take a variety of forms: from targeting disadvantaged groups for retraining, to establishing quota systems to ensure that new hirings come from a disadvantaged group. The intention is that over a period of time the imbalance in opportunity, in access to high-paying or non-traditional jobs, will be redressed, thereby making the program redundant.

One of the most widespread reactions to these programs has been to label them 'discriminatory' against men or against whites. This reaction, although apparently a defence of individualism, reflects a resistance to the redistribution of power and opportunity, and an assumption on the part of the dominant group of their inherent rights to those privileges. Thus men assume that they have a right to all the well-paying professional jobs, and that affirmative-action programs that limit their access by sharing it with others is a form of discrimination. These assumptions rest on a denial of, or perhaps an ignorance about, the systematic inequality in distribution of resources and power, and on a rather naive faith in a system of meritocracy.

Another example is the resistance of employers to trade unions. Unions, by collectivizing the process of negotiation, represent one of the few ways that working people can more equitably confront the unequal relations of power inherent in the organization of the patriarchal capitalist workplace. But resistance to the introduction of unions is sometimes overwhelming, despite legislation that gives workers the right to unionize. In recent years the attempts by bank workers to unionize have been unsuccessful, in large part because of the organized resistance of the big banks.[1] In an account describing the impact of the introduction of Instabanks on tellers at the Bank of Montreal, the following story is told:

> One of the tellers that had been demoted to part-time [as a result of the introduction of Instabanks] felt that the branch should be unionized. She spoke to her co-workers and then approached management. Within three days, two men from Charlie Brothers arrived at the bank. Charlie Brothers is the investigation firm the bank uses to screen employees before they are hired. Each teller was interviewed by these men. They were questioned about their interest in organizing a union and were strongly urged not to join. Tellers said that they faced dismissal if they supported a union in their branch. One teller stated that 'after the interviews no one would even mention the word union'. Carole, the teller who initially proposed organizing the branch, left the bank shortly afterwards.[2]

Small employers also successfully resist the introduction of unions. For example, in September 1987 the *Toronto Star* reported the following story:

> About 37 workers at an Etobicoke bakery are out of a job following a series of events in which many were fired, rehired and fired again after efforts were made to form a union. . . . Several employees . . . had been threatened with being fired by the owner, Dr Olinda Casullo, if they didn't sign a paper indicating they wanted no part of the union.
>
> 'He fired us and when we came to collect our paycheques he said he'd take us back if we signed a paper saying we didn't want a union,' Elezar Lopez Mendez said. Workers also claimed they were originally fired last month from their $8–an-hour jobs and rehired on the same day for $6 an hour, only to be fired two weeks later and rehired again strictly on piece work pay.
>
> 'I'm a single mother who needs a job,' said a recent immigrant from Poland, 'I worked sometimes 50 hours a week at normal pay. I never received any overtime pay.'[3]

This story clearly reflects the powerlessness of the workers who do free overtime and take dramatic cuts in pay in order to keep their jobs. It also reflects employers' resistance to changing the patriarchal capitalist relations of power. Furthermore, the lack of neutrality on the part of state agencies such as the police can interfere with organized attempts by women workers to change these power relations. In a famous Ontario instance, however, 120 workers, almost all women, won a union victory against Fleck manufacturing in 1978 despite massive police intervention:

> . . . the strike lasted for six months . . . and culminated in a substantial victory for the women and the union. The victory was won despite the constant intervention of the Ontario Provincial Police, who tried to intimidate the women even before the strike began, argued the company position, arrested union leaders on the first day of the strike, physically attacked the picketers and threw women in snow banks, escorted strikebreakers into the plant, and seized media film as a means to charge workers. At the height of the strike as many as 500 policemen and policewomen were involved—all to control about 80 striking women and a few hundred supporters from the UAW [United Auto Workers, now the Canadian Auto Workers]. The police bill to fight the union was approximately $2 million.[4]

Although in this case the women won, the Fleck strike is a graphic example not only of resistance to a redistribution of power and wealth, but of the lack of political neutrality of state agencies, in this case police bias in favour of employers. To the extent that women's liberation depends upon a redistribution of power between races, classes, and sexes, and between heterosexual and lesbian/gay society, the resistance to change that results from the current relations of power will be a serious impediment.

It is in the context of these relations of power that we can explore what we call 'the ideology of change'—attitudes and structures of change—that helps to conceal rather than reveal these underlying power dynamics and thereby contribute to social resistance to change.

THE IDEOLOGY OF CHANGE

The ideology of change is a set of widely accepted ideas about the nature and possibilities of change, and the mechanisms for it. It is deeply rooted in the consciousness of Canadians and functions to reinforce prevailing power relations in reference to class, gender, sexual orientation, and race, and thereby to restrict our ability to effect change. This ideology is part of the dominant ideology and helps to shape our complex relationship to patriarchal capitalism, to the philosophical principles of liberal democracy (justice, freedom, and equality) and to the practices of representative democracy. Its power is not easily identified or exposed and is therefore considerably more insidious.

This concept of the ideology of change is not meant to be equated with liberalism or liberal democracy. Liberalism as a coherent political philosophy or tradition is more complex, and certainly its practice is not entirely consistent with what we have identified as the key threads of the ideology of change. The ideology of change highlights widely prevalent common-sense notions of change that emerge in part from the hegemony of liberalism and affect the process of making change.

There are four important threads to the ideology of change: 1) belief in individualism; 2) a focus on changing attitudes; 3) a fear of change that is both instilled and exploited by the imagery of 'communism'; and 4) belief in representative democracy as the legitimate route to social change. These four notions participate in creating intense ideological agreement (hegemony) about the process of social change, one that precludes the effecting of significant social change by collective public input and action. We will consider these threads in turn in order to see how each operates to build resistance to change, and then contrast each to a socialist-feminist perspective.

1. Individualism

The dominant ideology in our society propagates a fierce brand of individualism that teaches us to focus on our individual ability to change ourselves. Personal change, negotiated by the individual through determination, will, effort, and discipline, is the most heavily endorsed form of change.

This approach to change rests on certain assumptions: first, that we live in a fundamentally classless society. This implies that there are no vested class interests resisting any particular sort of change, nor are there any irreconcilable conflicts between the needs of individuals. In the classless society of individuals, gender and race are seen to be irrelevant. Needless to say, such a perspective masks gender and race exploitation.

The second assumption is that, with a few exceptions, equality of opportunity exists. Equality of opportunity means that each individual has an equal chance to compete and to change her/himself. This classless reality within which equality of opportunity is seen to exist is the context in which the promises of liberal democracy—justice, freedom, and equality—are supposed to be lived out. Nothing should stand in the way of change, because we are a society with a philosophical commitment to liberal democracy and to the practice of equal opportunity. To the extent that inequality is acknowledged, it is attributed to prejudice (the wrong attitude) rather than to structural inequalities of power, privilege, or opportunity.

Ultimately, the message is that if we work hard, we can 'make it', and if we don't make it—that is, if we fail to change ourselves or our circumstances—then it is our own fault, rather than the result of the class structure of society or any structural limitations. This is certainly one of the recurring messages to the poor and unemployed, a message reinforced by the 'success-story' approach to change, especially in the media.

Socialist feminism challenges this fundamental focus on individual change. In fact, we would argue that individuals' ability to change themselves or, indeed, to exercise control over their lives, is limited by the structures and relations of power. Society is not made up of atomized individuals but of classes, races, and genders who share unequally in the power and privilege and who often face irreconcilable conflicts.

The focus on individual responsibility for success works against the majority of women who are less likely to be able to control or transform the conditions of their lives. Jennifer Gardner addresses this point when she discusses what she refers to as the 'insidious' theory that women oppress themselves. She points out that

> first, women are put down for submitting to unequal, unrespectful treatment without fighting back. Second, they are accused of courting their own oppression. That is, they are accused of behaving in such a weak, passive, dependent way with men that men cannot possibly treat them as equals.[5]

Gardner challenges this perspective by considering the structural and ideological realities that prevent women from shaping their own lives, such as the lack of economic independence and the difficulties of functioning as single women. She concludes: 'the fact that women sometimes blame themselves for their situation may prevent them from becoming strong fighters on their own behalf.'[6]

The notion that our lack of success in transforming ourselves is our own fault shifts attention away from the structures and relations of power and thereby serves to reinforce them. When we fail to change ourselves (get rich, be happy, have power, whatever) we learn to internalize a sense of failure and a feeling of powerlessness. This turning inward contributes to our disempowerment. As we turn further away from a concern with or a belief in social change, we bolster the status quo and add to the social resistance to change.

Since the oppression/exploitation of women is rooted in the material structures of a racist, heterosexist, patriarchal capitalism, individual change and solutions are possible only to a limited extent. Obviously these are more possible for those with economic and social power—that is, for those who have some class, race, or gender privileges. A philosophic commitment to equal opportunity, justice, and so on cannot transcend these constraints.

The rhetoric of individualism has little basis in the structural reality of patriarchal capitalism. To the extent that individual change is possible, it is often reduced to meaningless consumer choice: change the colour of your wallpaper, your hair, the shape of your body, the brand of your toothpaste. Such a focus on consumerism hooks us into the work ethic and the notion that we are what we own while simultaneously concealing our lack of control over the important decisions that afect our lives. Harriet Rosenberg, in her examination of the stress caused by lack of scope for real decision-making in domestic work, quotes a mother of young children:

> It drove me crazy just deciding what to wear or what to eat. Because it wasn't only me, I had to decide for the kids and for my husband. Laundry after laundry . . . meal after meal. And you get to decide

between Cheer and Tide, between Campbell's and Lipton . . . Great choices, eh?[7]

Rosenberg concludes:

> Such pseudo-choices have no fundamental impact on the overall structure of the working conditions of domestic labour. They are simply part of the ideology of 'freedom of choice' under capitalism which diverts attention away from larger issues by focusing attention on the trivialities of minor consumer choices.[8]

We might conclude that on many levels the propagation and internalization of individualism works against social change.

2. Changing attitudes

A second thread of the ideology of change is the focus on changing attitudes. When problems requiring change are identified, the solution is generally seen to be a change in attitudes and values, often through the process of education. For example, to the extent that inequality is recognized in our society, it is often attributed to prejudice—against visible minorities, lesbians, or women. Successfully challenging prejudice is seen to be a solution. This perspective on change is part of what is often called idealism, and can be connected to individualism since it often tends to focus on the attitudes and values of individuals.

Idealism presents a contrast to the materialist perspective of socialist feminism. Idealism attributes a greater degree of power and influence to attitudes and ideas than to material structures and social organization.[9] Rather than focusing on prejudice as the root cause of racism or homophobia, materialists would situate those problems in a structural context, examining the institutions and structures that systematically enforce both racism and the unequal distribution of power and privilege that reproduces racism and homophobia. Such an analysis would provide the context within which individual prejudice could be understood. Prejudice is not seen as the determining factor, however.

The distinction between materialism and idealism is important because it influences how we understand change to take place. For example, it raises the following practical questions. Do we need to change attitudes first? Will a change in attitude lead to change in structures? Is a change in attitude 'real' social change? How can we change structures (like the family or the state) without changing attitudes first? What does it mean to change structures?

Let us take the problem of changing the sexual division of housework. Women's responsibility for that housework produces extensive workplace and household inequality, and there is no doubt that men need to do a larger share. A 1986 Gallup Poll shows that many men agree with this in principle; when asked if they should share the housework 82 per cent agreed (up from 62 per cent in 1976). Yet only 52 per cent said that they regularly helped with the housework and only 42 per cent of married women said that their husbands helped regularly.[10] What this demonstrates is a large gap between the social practice of the sexual division of labour in the household and attitudes about that division of labour. What can we then conclude? In the first place, a change in attitude is not enough, since it will not necessarily translate into a change in social practice. At the same time, a change in attitude is an important contributor to that change.

An idealist might argue that more education is needed to persuade men to do a greater share of household tasks, thus implying that the root of the problem lies in a chauvinist attitude. Although this is true to some extent, a materialist might counter that as long as the sexual division between the household and the workplace persists, which in turn rests on a pattern of women's workplace inequality, the sexual division of labour inside the household will be reproduced. The fact that women's wages are significantly lower than men's reproduces women's economic dependence on them, means that women are seen as secondary workers and less legitimate members of the workforce, and reinforces the notion that women should be primarily responsible for the family and household. Women's segregation in service work, which is seen as an extension of housework, helps to naturalize the household sexual division of labour. This materialist analysis demonstrates that the household sexual division of labour does not simply rest on the attitudes of the members of particular households, but is rooted in social structural factors. As a result, neither individual or attitudinal change will be sufficient to challenge fundamentally the current organization of household tasks.

Although materialism starts with the belief that experience is shaped largely by the material conditions in our lives, materialists also recognize the powerful role that ideology plays in shaping these material circumstances, and perhaps most importantly in influencing whether we accommodate or challenge these conditions.

Materialists believe that there is a complex, rather than a linear or simple, relationship between changing attitudes and changing structures. The question is often strategic: what will work in a particular situation to begin a process of change? In the long run, changing attitudes is insufficient to create a major social transformation—that is, material and structural reorganization—although it might be fertile ground to inspire the process of major social change. It is equally important to stress, however, that changing social and structural organization by fiat of a fascist dictator will also not create the kind of change we want.

3. The fear of change

In contrast to individual change, which receives wide support from our society, social change is seen as threatening the social fabric. Underlying this perception is a fear both of the scope of change (what the world would actually be like afterwards) and of the process of change itself (how the changes would actually come about). In particular, the vision of the 'collective', which is central to socialist feminism both in the changes we would like and in the process of change we envision, is seen as especially disturbing.

There is a persistent social subtext that change in and of itself necessarily leads to chaos and the destruction of democracy, which encourages us to believe that what exists now is not only the best we can hope for, but perhaps even 'natural' and ordained. A common response to the demand for social change is 'Canada is the best place in the world to live'. Notwithstanding the relative truth in this statement, change is always seen as threatening what we have, rather than as creating the conditions for further improvement.

The fear of change is generated and reinforced by the mobilization of images of communism. In terms of the process of change, communism is connected with anarchy, chaos, mob rule, and violence; in terms of the scope of change, it is associated with images of totalitarian regimes. All totalitarianism is linked to communism; conveniently, the totalitarian regimes of the right are rarely the centre of public perception. These confusions are related to a conflation of democracy and capitalism, which leads to the widely held assumption that a defence of capitalism is the same as a defence of democracy; an attack on the patriarchal-capitalist relations of power is therefore seen as an attack on democracy.

As a result anyone who advocates radical change in social organization is assumed to be a 'communist'. It is nothing short of terrifying, the degree to which the very words 'communism', 'socialism', or, for that matter, 'feminism' can be invoked to block a discussion of change. The negative power of these words means that persons or organizations advocating social change can be labelled as adhering to one of those 'isms' and then easily dismissed. The response to these words makes it difficult, even threatening, to ask questions about the organization of society and to be heard. There is no doubt that the power of these words to invoke a kind of social deafness needs to be challenged.

This description certainly does not overstate the problem. For example, in September 1987 revelations concerning lawbreaking in the Canadian Security Intelligence Service (CSIS) led to the removal of its director and to the establishment of a Security Intelligence Review Committee. One issue to emerge from the scandal was the rampant confusion in the CSIS about the difference between legitimate dissent and subversion, a confusion that has led to the surveillance of trade unions, peace groups, and others advocating a change in American foreign policy in Latin America, for example.[11]

Not only does such 'red-baiting' add to a resistance to change, but prevailing views of human nature as greedy and self-seeking mean that desire for social change is often understood as desire for personal, individual power: those who advocate social change must want to gather the reins of power to themselves. Social change motivated by the desire to redistribute power and wealth cannot be understood within the context of the current ideology of change. In general, then, change is always feared and easily dismissed, regardless of what change is actually being advocated. The ideological resistance to social change is focused as much on change itself as on its actual content.

There is a certain irony in this fear of change, for, objectively, our society is always changing. We might go so far as to say that one central contradiction of advanced capitalism is precisely this tension between a conservative ideology that fears change and the reality of people's daily lives. Our lives are full of change: job change, marriage breakdown, forced geographic mobility to look for work, new technology, changing sex roles and patterns of child-rearing, to name a few. These changes are most often perceived as being outside of our control, they are rarely initiated by popular movements, and they contribute, not surprisingly, to the fear of change and the desire for social stability. But social stability is built not on inertia, but on empowerment.

In contrast to the ideology that sustains the underlying fear of social change, socialist feminism is premised on a belief in change, indeed a celebration of change. A historical-materialist approach fundamentally supports this belief. In the first place, a study of the historically specific conditions of a society reveals the way that society works and in so doing unlocks not only what needs to be changed but also how to make that change. In addition, studying history demonstrates that dramatic change has indeed occurred, thereby graphically reminding us of the extent of human agency. This provides us with a fundamental optimism about the possibility for change in the future.

Moreover, the naturalization of what presently exists, and hence its validation as 'best', is challenged by a socialist-feminist analysis of the relations of power. Such an analysis reveals the way in which that naturalism translates into a resistance to and fear of change and becomes an indirect defence of those relations of power. John Stuart Mill, who wrote an influential tract in favour of women's liberation in 1869, made a similar point in his challenge to the argument that male domination is natural:

> But was there ever any domination which did not appear natural to those who possessed it? . . . Did not the slave owners of the southern United States maintain the same doctrine, with all the fanaticism with which men cling to the theories that justify their passions and legitimate their personal interests? . . . Conquering races hold it to be Nature's own dictate that the conquered should obey the conquerors, or, as they euphoniously paraphrase it, that the feebler and more unwarlike races should submit to the braver and manlier. . . . So true it is that unnatural generally means only uncustomary, and that everything which is usual appears natural. The subjection of women to men being a universal custom, any departure from it quite naturally appears unnatural.[12]

4. Representative democracy as the route to social change

The fourth element of the ideology of change is the identification of legitimate routes to social change. To the extent that large-scale social change is legitimized at all, popular ideology and social practice identify the government as the initiator, the site, the nexus of social change. Women often turn to the government to redress social inequality, demanding, for example, changes in the regulation of the family through new divorce laws, the provision of shelters for battered wives, the introduction of equal-value legislation, and the control of sexist representation of women in advertising.

Although it is recognized that the government can prevent the excesses of individualism and act for the larger good, it should also be pointed out that the focus on the government's role in social change co-exists uneasily with the belief in individualism and the commitment to the operation of the free market and free enterprise. Social change as a result of government intervention is often associated with a failure of individual will or with an unacceptable intervention in the operation of the marketplace. For example, when the government provides social-service supports, there may be a grudging acceptance of the need, but there is also a deep-rooted feeling that those individuals accepting government aid should be able to change their circumstances through individual initiative.

In a representative or parliamentary democracy, faith in the government as the agent of change is based on its apparent constitution through a democratic electoral process in which individuals are selected to represent the interests of the majority. As a result of this democratic process, the government is delegated the authority to define areas of public good and to enact legislation. The state then processes that legislation and regulates the social practices connected with it. The fact that the Canadian government functions in a liberal-democratic tradition means a philosophical commitment to the rights of the individual, to justice, and to equality of opportunity. This commitment is expressed structurally, and concretely organized, as representative democracy. By definition, then, a liberal democratic government is committed to responsiveness both structurally (in the form of representative democracy) and ideologically (through its commitment to ideals such as democracy and individual rights). Thus liberal democracy creates the conditions for high aspirations and expectations among its citizens. In contrast, totalitarian traditions, in which there is neither the expectation nor the possibility of government responsiveness, encourages few such aspirations.

Intrinsic to the view of the government as the legitimate route to change is the belief in its political neutrality, as an unbiased and objective arbiter of change that makes decisions in the best interests of the majority. This neutrality stems, in principle, from the process of representative democracy: if the government is the democratically elected expression of the majority—that is, if it governs with the consent of the majority—then by definition it acts in the interests of the majority.

As a neutral and higher authority, the government mediates between what is seen as a variety of equally legitimate interest groups (women, seniors, native people, etc.), weighing and balancing their concerns to enhance the common good; this approach is often referred to as 'pluralism'. Consistent with the view of a classless society, the government is not supposed to privilege one interest group over another, nor is it supposed to have any interests of its own. Seemingly no interest group is advantaged or disadvantaged in the competition to ensure that the government responds to its concerns.

In general, then, the acceptable route to social change in our society and the framework for legitimate political behaviour is one involving government leadership, the principles of liberal democracy, and the practice of representative democracy. It is within these parameters that change is initiated and carried out.

In sharp contrast, socialist feminism exposes the lack of government neutrality and the inefficacy of representative democracy, which is neither as representative nor as democratic as it appears. It challenges the government to live up to the promises of liberal democracy at the same time as it recognizes the deep-rooted contradiction these promises pose for a government so bound to patriarchal capitalism. It argues for more participatory and community-based forms of decision-making and, in contrast to the emphasis on government leadership, it invokes a role for collective action through the auspices of popular political movements such as the women's, trade-union, and peace movements.[13]

In the previous chapter we explored the patriarchal capitalist bias of the state/government. While privileging capitalist/male/white/heterosexual interests over others, the conception of pluralism is cleverly manipulated to make this situation legitimate in the public consciousness and to reinforce the belief in government neutrality. A most interesting example of this manipulation is the fact that the 'business community' is not seen to be a special-interest group. The labour movement, senior citizens, the differently-abled, women, ethnic minorities, and the native community, among others, are all seen as special-interest groups, despite the fact that collectively they represent the vast majority of the population. Providing adequate social services, housing, and family benefits is thus seen as responding to the needs of special, perhaps selfish and self-seeking, interest groups. Yet, unlike them, the business community is not labelled a special-interest group. Its vested interests are assumed to be the same as those of the government, in fact, in the national interest; thus, responding to the interests of the business community is seen as the route to economic health. Belief in the government as a neutral arbiter precludes recognition of its patriarchal-capitalist bias and thus limits the possibilities for real change.

In addition, the lived reality of representative democracy falls short of the ideological commitment to representation and democracy. The problem takes many forms. For example, every individual does not have an equal chance of being elected; party politics, class interests, money, sex, race, and sexual orientation all interfere with access to public office.[14] The process of selecting representatives is not truly democratic, as evidenced in the fact that those elected usually reflect a narrow range of interests (white, middle-class, urban, male). This helps to explain why their decisions so often openly privilege class and corporate interests. Furthermore, the parliamentary process does not incorporate any mechanisms to ensure that elected representatives are accountable to their constituents; politicians can make election promises and then break them, once elected. A striking example was the 1975 election, in which then-Prime Minister Trudeau openly campaigned against the wage-control policy of the leader of the Conservative party, Robert Stanfield. After Trudeau was elected by a landslide victory, at least in part because of his opposition to wage controls, he brought in an extended three-year program of just such controls, a program that was bitterly opposed by the working people of Canada. Brian Mulroney and the Conservative party, who campaigned against free trade in 1983 and were elected, have subsequently negotiated an extensive and fairly unpopular free-trade deal with the United States in 1987. Events such as this make a mockery of the election process and expose the lack of effective representation.

Finally, representative democracy distances the individual from the process of social change. The only participation available to each one of us is the right to vote at election time, a right undermined by the lack of accountability. Elected officials, civil servants, and powerful class interests control the content and process of change. The focus on the government as site and initiator of political and social change limits the degree to which the majority of Canadians participate in shaping our world and in creating change.

The lack of political neutrality and the problems of representative democracy might lead to the conclusion that any attempt to reform the government or in fact to make gains for women through its processes is doomed to failure. This is not entirely the case, however, for though the government is the site of patriarchal-capitalist relations of power, it is also heavily influenced by the traditions of liberal democracy and the practice of representative democracy, which, despite the limitations we have outlined above, create a high level of public expectation.

At times, therefore, the government operates not in the interests of the capitalist ruling class, but in opposition to them. The gains that result are not to be underestimated: more funding for day-care, Secretary of State funding for women's projects, reform in sexual-assault legislation, and so on.

The motive for this kind of behaviour is not readily agreed upon either by feminist activists or by those who study the workings of the government and the state. One end of the spectrum of analysis emphasizes the role of the government in maintaining the patriarchal-capitalist social relations of power. The responsiveness of the government—its acting-out of traditions of liberal democracy—is then understood as its way of exercising social control by co-opting and neutralizing protest in the interests of the status quo. We might say that the capitalists lose a battle (increase welfare benefits, for example) in order to win the war (maintain patriarchal capitalism). This view, held by many socialist feminists, assumes that the government is a monolith, self-consciously manipulating in the interests of patriarchal capitalism.[15] Nicole Laurin-Frenette takes this position:

> The force of feminist protest can be turned against women if, in their struggle against domination, they ally themselves to the power-wielding authorities and institutions of control: political parties, sects and churches of all sorts, the State. . . .
>
> The State has appeared as the privileged interlocutor of the modern feminist movement ever since its beginning, and particularly at its present stage. Appealing to the State, the women's movement has formulated its main claims in the language of the State. . . .
>
> Thus, women have obtained, mainly from the State, recognition of certain rights and the improvement of various conditions. In most cases, these victories of women are also victories of the State; they have, to a certain extent, increased its ability to control women and their movement. . . . [The State has] provided an audience for feminism and a channel for its dynamism, while blunting the movement's subversive potential: its power of liberation.[16]

At the other end of the spectrum is an unquestioning belief in the government as an agent of reform and change, responsive to the concerns of the majority, a neutral and fair arbiter guided by the principles of liberal democracy and the practices of representative democracy—a position often associated with liberal feminism.

In contrast to these positions, we think that it is both more accurate and more useful to see the government as a contradictory set of processes that hang in balance (teeter, perhaps) between the demands of patriarchal capitalism and those of liberal democracy, which sometimes support, but most often conflict with, one another. Central to the contradiction is the fact that patriarchal capitalism is by definition committed to the continuation of unequal class, gender, and race relations, while the tradition of liberal democracy is one of concern for liberty, justice, and equality of opportunity.

More often than not, the government's liberal-democratic commitment is overshadowed by the strength of patriarchal capitalism, a situation exacerbated by the inadequacy of the organizational forms in which responsiveness is organized—in particular, the forms of representative democracy. Despite the fact that the balance of power often resides in the authority of patriarchal capitalism, we maintain that the government does indeed hang in balance between the demands of liberal democracy and the demands of patriarchal capitalism.

The relative strength of liberal democracy as it confronts patriarchal capitalism is determined in historically specific struggles. In each situation the balance of forces will be different: such forces might include the state of public opinion, the degree of mobilization of opposition, the proximity to an election, or the state of the economy. It is our belief that the critical factor in swinging the pendulum toward responsiveness is public pressure; in other words, the balance of forces can be altered by what we do and how we organize. This belief validates the necessity of popular collective movements, a point we will return to in detail later in this discussion.

To the extent that the government remains unchallenged, it will not be responsive—the responsiveness of the government does not occur spontaneously, as an act of generosity or of principle. The actualization of its liberal-democratic nature is a result of a complex process of pressure on the government, most often from extra-parliamentary sources, from popular movements, from anger and outrage. A result of exposing the male domination, class bias, racism, and heterosexism of the government (and the state), and of insisting that it live up to the promises of liberal democracy, is that the government is more likely to act in the interests of women and, indeed, of the majority.

The Canadian government thus has a contradictory nature. It is a site of patriarchal-capitalist relations and is therefore resistant to the kind of changes we would identify as necessary to women's liberation. But it is, at the same time, a liberal-democratic government situated within a tradition of representation, democracy, and equality. The responsiveness embedded in this tradition is not uncomplicated, given the nature of patriarchal capitalism and the structural inadequacies of representative democracy. The responsiveness of the government rests in some complex balance to the pressure exerted on it. This has implications for the way that we pose our demands and for the way we structure our organizations.

For example, it is not enough to ask for equal pay for work of equal value. This demand must be connected to liberal-democratic promises of equal opportunity; at the same time, the reasons why the government resists passing such legislation (for example, because it will cost employers money) must be revealed. The government is torn between liberal-democratic promises and the vested and powerful interests of corporations and employers. The government exposes itself in its response to pressure. The way we structure our demands and the strength of our challenge forces it to show its hand.

Situating our demands in the context of the contradictory nature of the government increases the possibility of making concrete gains. For the exposure of its contradictory nature is partially what motivates it to respond: the government is responsive precisely because its underbelly as patriarchal capitalist has been exposed. This responsiveness reflects the government's need for public credibility and legitimacy, which in turn relates to the fact that its power rests, to a significant degree, on the consent of the governed, however heavily that 'consent' may be manipulated through the mechanisms of the ideology of change. Furthermore, exposing the two-sided reality of the government angers and politicizes people, thus preventing demoralization and empowering many to engage in the struggle for social change. (We will return to this strategic approach in our discussion of feminist practice in the next chapter.)

To the extent that the government responds to pressure it is reshaped and reformed. For example, a government that upholds within its Human Rights Code, as does Canada, women's right to be free of sexual harassment in the workplace is significantly different from one that does not. It is forced to defend this position publicly and occasionally to act on it. Such protection changes not only women's expectations in the workplace but also those of men in general and of employers in particular. It also provides an opening for related demands, such as protection against discrimination on the basis of sexual orientation, thus changing the balance of forces and the context within which the women's movement attempts to make change. Exerting pressure sets in motion a process that alters the possibilities for the future.

Notwithstanding the optimism of this view, it is also important to recognize that the women's movement is changed by the form in which the government responds to us. The funding practices of the state, on which so many women's organizations depend; the establishment of advisory commissions and women's councils that demobilize change through bureaucracy; and the language of legislation, which often limits the actual benefits accruing to women, have all molded and to some extent undermined the struggle of women to make change.[17]

This analysis challenges the government's leadership role, exposes the inadequacy of a representative democracy that limits the agency and intervention of the majority, and identifies the contradictions that arise within a government that is a site both of patriarchal capitalism and of liberal democracy. Such an analysis highlights the importance of popular political movements as agents of change that both represent the marginalized and exert pressure on the government to live up to the promises of liberal democracy.

Popular collective movements as an alternative. Not surprisingly, given the prevalence of individualism, the negative view of the collective discussed in the preceding chapter, and the fear of change that we described above, popular political movements—the practical political expression of the 'collective'—have very limited ideological and structural space within which to participate in making change.

As we pointed out earlier, the collective is associated with a negative image, both as a goal of change and as a mechanism for it. Not only does collective action trigger the fear of change, chaos, anarchy, and mob rule, but the 'collective' is often seen as meaning submission of self, negation of the individual, rather than liberation of self from isolation and competition. Public consciousness, reflected and reinforced by the mass media, dismisses the viability of collective action. As a result the image of collective action is intensely negative. For example, 'joining' is seen as a weakness; it means that you can't make it on your own. Those who participate in public collective action are generally dismissed as weak, as crazies, or as communists.

In this ideological context it is no surprise that the grass-roots women's movement is often made invisible through a focus on the plight or success of individual women rather than on the actions of thousands. The most acceptable change is individual, and as a result the women's movement is liquidated into women's issues and into the problems and successes of individual women.

The ideology of change discredits the role of popular movements in making change and in many particular instances credits the government instead, thereby reinforcing the belief that the government will initiate change on its own. A striking example is the newspaper coverage of the Supreme Court decision to overturn the Canadian abortion law as unconstitutional in January 1988. To read the papers, one would come to the conclusion that Morgentaler, his lawyer, and the courts *gave* women reproductive freedom. What is almost entirely invisible is the massive mobilization by the women's movement for almost twenty years on the issue of reproductive choice. Without this public organizing, it is not at all certain that Morgentaler would have continued his actions in favour of choice, nor that the climate of public opinion would have been one in which the Supreme Court could make such a decision.

Instead of government leadership and the structures of representative democracy, socialist feminists argue for collective action, self-organization, and participatory democracy (a subject we will return to in our discussion of feminist process in Chapter 7) through and in popular political movements. The socialist-feminist focus on the individual within the collective rather than in isolation, and on the underlying belief in the possibility of effective and creative social change, is translated into a commitment to collective action and organizing.

Collective action is the extension of a belief in the collective. Collective action as the route to change empowers people in the face of their individual powerlessness. It encourages the active, on-going participation of large numbers and the pooling of resources by marginalized groups normally excluded from formal political power,[18] and validates both our right and our power to change not only ourselves, but the world around us. Ironically, rather than losing the individual in the collective, it provides the context in which individuals can shape and control their lives; moreover, participation in collective action is often the route to the individual change so greatly valued by the dominant ideology.

Collective action can reshape our lives and the world around us; it can also change the way we see ourselves—not as individuals struggling in isolation to survive, but as part of a collective of shared interest and vision. This can be a transformative and empowering experience and demonstrates in practice the limits of individualism. Changing society is a way of changing ourselves:

> We can only transform ourselves by simultaneously struggling to transform the social relations which define us: self-changing and changed [*sic*] social institutions are simply two aspects of the same process.[19]

Heather Jon Maroney, in her discussion of the famous Fleck strike in 1978, which pitted women at an automobile-parts plant against management and the police, emphasizes the impact of collective organizing on the consciousness of the women strikers:

> By its very nature, a strike situation is an intensive consciousness-raising process. With work rhythms disrupted, the opportunity and the necessity to think collectively and strategically break through the fatigue, political passivity, and mystification of normal production. Militant strike action by women is also an objective challenge to their economic exploitation, their individuation into the illusory privacy of the family, and the ideological construction of women as passive dependents protected by men which is at the core of women's place in the contemporary capitalist sexual division of labour. At Fleck, the strikers explicitly articulated this challenge. . . . The lesson that they confirmed was that, given the right political conditions, self-organization in struggle will radicalize, mobilize and broaden feminist consciousness and action.[20]

Arja Lane describes her involvement in Wives Supporting the Strike (WSS), a volunteer organization that supported the 1978 INCO strike in Sudbury:

> Working with WSS was a politicizing experience. . . . As women we 'came out' in many ways. We became more confident about our ability to use our homemaking skills to organize actions that effected change outside the home. We became less shy about speaking out about the way we saw issues. For many, it was our first time at meetings, and our first exposure to the how's, what's and why's of labour versus management. The information and skills that were shared at meetings and events enabled us to cope better with our everyday lives.[21]

Another member of WSS graphically decribes some of the changes that the collective experience of organizing had on her life:

> My husband saw me in a new way after the strike. He saw me yelling at meetings and going by myself to Toronto to that rally and I realized I had more rights in this family. Some of it is small stuff like now he has to look after the kids once in a while if I want to go away for a weekend. But other stuff is bigger like I say what I think about family plans. And now he listens.[22]

Despite the deeply rooted oppression of women within patriarchal capitalism, the belief in the power of collective action to make change means that the socialist-feminist strategic orientation does not rest on the notion of 'woman as victim'.[23] Rather, we seek to identify the ways in which women have struggled, fought back, been active agents in resistance and in the construction of their own experience.

Women are not passive victims at the mercy of men or capitalism. We are the subjects in our own history, a history shaped by contradiction and struggle. We can make change:

> The portrayal of women as helpless victims is ultimately a 'patriarchal' representation. In explaining the perpetuation of male dominance, all feminists are naturally concerned to avoid blaming the victim and one way of doing this is to emphasize the relative power of men over women. To *over*emphasise this power, however, not only distorts reality, but also depreciates the power that women have succeeded in winning and minimizes the chances of further resistance.[24]

Belief in the intersection of class, race, and sex/gender oppression and in collective solutions means that socialist feminists argue for mass public strategies and build heterogeneous alliances and coalitions around a variety of issues with a wide range of progressive organizations, including trade unions and community-based anti-racist, anti-imperialist, gay, and lesbian groups. In fact, in the long run a broad-based, heterogeneous mass political movement is necessary to bring about the kind of social change that is envisaged.

One of the most interesting and energetic coalitions in recent years has been Women Against the Budget (WAB), which 'formed in July [1983] to oppose the budget, proposed legislation, and social service cutbacks brought in by [British Columbia's] Social Credit government'.[25] The WAB brought together women from 'public and private sector unions, from community groups serving women, from human right's organizations, from women's rights committees, from community college women's programs and from professional women's groups'[26] to highlight the ways in which the budget would hurt women:

> On July 27, the WAB, in conjunction with popular groups, Christian groups and a few local unions, organized the first demonstration against the government's policies. It was a huge success—35,000 women took part! The movement against Bennett and Co. was launched.[27]

Although WAB and the Provincial Solidarity Coalition of which it became a part were unable to alter government plans significantly, they were a powerful voice representing women's concerns and laid the basis for future organizing struggles. In fact, *Kinesis*, the newspaper of the Vancouver Status of Women, characterized WAB as 'the broadest outreach since the struggle for the vote'.[28]

Co-existing with a strategy of alliances and coalitions is a firm belief in the necessity of an autonomous women's movement. Such a movement needs organizational autonomy, but given the nature of patriarchal capitalism it cannot be class and race neutral; in other words, socialist-feminist class and race analysis influences the issues that are prioritized and the allies that are sought out. (In later chapters we will discuss in some detail the building of alliances and the organizational issues of the autonomous women's movement.)

In this chapter we have explored the ideology of change and exposed the way it disempowers us and demobilizes political action. This ideology goes beyond telling us that democracy is exercised and demonstrated through the vote. It makes serious judgements about any challenges to what is seen as the only legitimate liberal-democratic route to change: the structures of representative democracy. There is no doubt that the government does not fulfil its ideological commitment to pluralism or to neutrality. Yet the fact that the ideology of change perpetuates this view of the government influences the majority's expectations of it and, most importantly, their perceptions of the possibilities and parameters of change.

Representative democracy protects capital and corporate interests not only in the actual decisions it makes, but more powerfully in the perception it creates about how the system works. Not only does the government play a key role in organizing change, but it is also central to the construction and reproduction of social attitudes to change, not the least of which is the idea that the government itself must negotiate and organize change. The acceptable route to social change is that directly negotiated and controlled by 'elected' representatives through 'impartial' government structures. Inside this ideology there is no place for collective action, and therefore collective action is, if not invisible, then certainly distasteful to most people. Participating in collective action is seen as a direct challenge to the system of representative democracy, since by definition such action implies that the government is not a neutral arbiter of the public will, and that unless challenged, it will act in the vested interests of men, capital, and corporations.

The power of the ideology of change is evidenced in the fact that despite daily experiences to the contrary, the view of the government as politically neutral is upheld. In our experience we are constantly confronted with challenges to that view, from the actions of police on a picket line to government bail-outs of big corporations, or the refusal of governments to respond to petitions or lobbying for social change. Yet at the same time the notion of government neutrality is constantly reinforced. Why do the majority continue to believe in government/state neutrality in the face of overwhelming evidence to the contrary? Our exploration of the ideology of change has attempted to unravel the answer to this question.

CONCLUSION

Feminists organize because we want change, we make change, we have visions of change. And all of us face resistance to change. The struggle is not only about the issues of women's liberation, but also about the agents of change and the routes to achieve change. It is also necessarily a struggle about the way the patriarchal-capitalist liberal-democratic state responds to its citizens, about the way it organizes and disorganizes change.

We need to recover our own certainty in the power and possibility of change and reclaim our right to make it. We need to reshape public consciousness to legitimize change and the role of popular movements in making it. As part of this process, the fear of social change must be challenged. Our right to ask questions should not be blotted out by invocation—and fear—of words like feminism, communism, and socialism.

The propagation of a limited view of individuality, which actually negates the individual and isolates her/him from the community, needs replacing with a vision of the collective that has as its goal to meet the needs of all individuals. The power of collective action, not as chaos but as effective and meaningful democracy, must be rediscovered.

Exposing the inadequacy of representative democracy challenges it to be both more democratic and more representative, and exposing its limits helps to legitimize, in the public consciousness, other structural routes to change, in particular that of mass-based social movements. Legitimizing social movements breaks the link between the form of liberal democracy (representative/parliamentary structures) and the substance of liberal democracy (individual rights and freedoms, justice, and equality). As a result, the possibility of a serious alternative to representative democracy is posed: mass participation in the process of change.

In the long term the precondition for such a transformation of patriarchal capitalism is the development of a mass political movement. Such a movement will develop only in the context of an overt challenge to the structures and ideology of change. The socialist-feminist perspective provides the basis on which to mount such a direct challenge. Socialist feminism is premised on a critique of liberal individualism, a rejection of electoral process as the only strategy for change, a vision of an altered society—and hence promotion of change rather than fear of it—and a commitment to building popular movements. These are the bases from which it is possible to construct a radical critique of representative democracy, patriarchal capitalism, and the ideology of change.

These two chapters have set the stage for a detailed examination of the grass-roots women's movement in Canada. Chapter 3, on socialist feminism, laid out the theoretical perspective that informs this book as a whole. And although the rest is not restricted in its focus to the socialist-feminist current, the analysis of the practice, organizations, and ideologies of the grass-roots women's movement put forward here is influenced by this theoretical perspective; furthermore, one of our particular concerns in the following chapters is to understand the dilemmas facing socialist-feminist activists in organizing for change.

This chapter on change also provides an important framework for reading the rest of the book. It should remind the reader of the larger context within which the struggle by the women's movement to make change is situated. Not only does it provides a major explanation for the difficulties the movement faces in making change, but it is also suggestive of new and perhaps more effective strategies. Although we will now focus on the more interior processes and contradictions of women's-movement organizing, we will also constantly relate them to the larger questions of the theoretical perspective we have put forward and the resistance to change endemic to Canadian society.

NOTES

[1]See, for example, *An Account to Settle: the Story of the United Bank Workers (SORWUC)* by The Bank Book Collective (Vancouver: Press Gang Publishers, 1979). It also charts some of the resistance of the big unions to feminist union prinicples.

[2]Cyndie Ingle and Julie Martin, 'A Personal Account: Automation at the Bank', *Our Times* vol. 5, no. 5 (Aug. 1986), p. 29.

[3]Bob Mitchell, 'Asked to reject union, fired workers say', *Toronto Star* 10 Sept. 1987.

[4]Paul and Erin Phillips, *Women and Work* (Toronto: Lorimer, 1983), p. 156.

[5]Jennifer Gardner, 'False Consciousness', *Northern Woman* vol. 7, no. 2 (1982), p. 13.

[6]Ibid., p. 15.

[7]Harriet Rosenberg, 'The Home is the Workplace: Hazards, Stress and Pollutants in the Household', *Through the Kitchen Window* (Toronto: Garamond, 1986), p. 42.

[8]Ibid.

[9]For an extended comparison of studying women's work from an idealist and a materialist

perspective, see Pat and Hugh Armstrong, *The Double Ghetto*, rev. ed. (Toronto: McClelland and Stewart, 1984).

[10]Monica Boyd, *Canadian Attitudes Toward Women: Thirty Years of Change*, Prepared for the Women's Bureau, Labour Canada, 1984, pp. 37–41. The 1986 figures are quoted in 'Why Women's Work is Never Done', by Kim Zarzour, *Toronto Star* 16 June 1987.

[11]See, for example, 'Peace groups monitored by spy agency, brief says', *Toronto Star*, 30 Sept. 1987.

[12]John Stuart Mill, 'The Subjection of Women', in Alice Rossi, ed., *Essays on Sex Equality* (Chicago: Univ. of Chicago Press, 1970), pp. 137–8. In a similar vein, Nellie McClung quotes the following in her famous text *In Times Like These*, originally published in 1915 (Toronto: Univ. of Toronto Press, 1972), p. 43.

> I hold it true—I will not change,
> For changes are a dreadful bore—
> That nothing must be done on earth
> Unless it has been done before.
> —Anti-suffrage Creed

[13]It is no small task to comment on the patriarchal-capitalist liberal-democratic state, given its complexity and the extensive feminist and marxist literature on the subject. Examining this literature in detail is well beyond the scope of this discussion; our interest is in exposing the contradictions of the ideology of change. What follows is a schematic picture that fundamentally challenges the ideological view of the state/government as the neutral arbiter of the public will.

[14]See Janine Brodie, *Women and Politics in Canada* (Toronto: McGraw-Hill Ryerson, 1985) and Sylvia Bashevkin, *Toeing the Lines: Women and Party Politics in English Canada* (Toronto: Univ. of Toronto Press, 1985) for discussions of discriminatory patterns against women inside of political parties.

[15]Zillah Eisenstein in her influential book *The Radical Future of Liberal Feminism* (New York: Longman, 1981) emphasizes the 'state's involvement in protecting patriarchy as a system of power, much in the same way as it protects capitalism and racism as systems' (p. 223).

[16]Nicole Laurin-Frenette, 'On the Women's Movement, Anarchism and the State', *Our Generation* vol. 15, no. 2 (Summer 1982), pp. 36–7.

[17]In the Canadian women's publications that we examined, this concern emerged again and again, especially in relation to funding practices. See, for example, Sally Hunter, 'Government Strategies', *Priorities* vol. 5, no. 9 (May 1977); Dorothy Smith, 'Does Government Funding Co-opt?', *Kinesis* vol. 6, no. 11 (1977); Michele Blanchard, 'La Femme et les mouvements féministes', *Canadian Woman Studies* vol. 1, no. 2 (1978/79); Helen Maier, 'We Will Survive', *Kinesis*, June 1984; Isabelle Bouvier, 'Women's Groups and their Relations with the State', *Communiqu'elles* vol. 12, no. 1 (1986).

[18]This focus on pooling of resources is found in Louise Tilly, 'Paths of Proletarianization: Organization of Production, Sexual Division of Labor, and Women's Collective Action', in Eleanor Leacock and Helen Safa, eds, *Women's Work* (South Hadley: Bergin and Garvey, 1986).

Although women's participation in collective action has often been ignored by historians, in recent years this participation is being documented. A new and exciting collection of articles on the history of women's participation in labour organizing is Ruth Milkman, ed., *Women, Work and Protest* (Boston: Routledge and Kegan Paul, 1985.) It is also the case that as a result of feminist scholarship, collective action is being redefined to take into account the unique kinds of political and community organizing in which women are involved.

[19]Nancy Hartsock, 'Fundamental Feminism: Process and Perspective', *Quest* vol. II, no. 2 (Fall 1975), p. 72.

[20]Heather Jon Maroney, 'Feminism at Work', in Heather Jon Maroney and Meg Luxton, eds, *Feminism and Political Economy* (Toronto: Methuen, 1987), p. 94.

162 | Feminist Organizing for Change

[21]Arja Lane, 'Wives Supporting the Strike', in Linda Briskin and Lynda Yanz, eds, *Union Sisters* (Toronto: Women's Press, 1983), pp. 330-1.

[22]Quoted in Meg Luxton, 'From Ladies' Auxiliaries to Wives' Committees', ibid., p. 343.

[23]Wendy Luttrell in 'Beyond the Politics of Victimization', *Socialist Review* no. 73 (Jan./Feb. 1984), stresses the importance of not seeing women as victims. In particular she criticizes socialist feminism for characterizing working-class women as 'victims of a "double burden"' and points out that many working-class women do 'not see themselves as burdened because they raised children. The opposite was more often the case, as many women placed great value and pride in their mothering experience.'

Luttrell goes on to call for a reconceptualizaton of the experience of parenting. 'This reconceptualization must be able to capture the complexity of women's attempt to balance a series of conflicting needs, desires, and responsibilities. Most importantly, this reconceptualization must reclaim women's work and identity—not as victims, as is often depicted by feminism, but also not as mother earth, as is being heralded by the new right' (pp. 45-6).

[24]Alison Jaggar, *Feminist Politics and Human Nature* (Totowa, N.J.: Rowman and Allenheld, 1983), p. 115.

[25]Cynthia Flood, 'Women Against the Budget', *Broadside* vol. 5, no. 2 (1983). See also Carolyn Egan, 'Socialist Feminism: Activism and Alliances', in Maroney and Luxton, *Feminism and Political Economy*, for a discussion of the coalition-building of the International Women's Day Committee (IWDC) in Toronto. In particular she details IWDC's activities in support of the Canadian Union of Postal Workers (CUPW) successful strike for expanded maternity leave in 1981, and their involvement in the Ontario Coalition for Abortion Clinics (OCAC).

[26]Sharon Shniad, 'Women in Solidarity: the story of Women Against the Budget', *Priorities* Nov. 1983, p. 2.

[27]Andrée Côté, 'Autopsy of a Revolt', *Status of Women News* March 1985, p. 20.

[28]'Budget creates unexpected alliance', *Kinesis* Sept. 1983.

III

ANALYZING THE WOMEN'S MOVEMENT

5

Feminist Practice: Organizing for Change

From the outset, the re-emerging women's movement of the 1960s adopted a strong activist orientation and, as we saw in Chapter 2, its early history was characterized by the burgeoning growth of organizations, issues, and actions. In fact, although these early feminists may have been comparatively unsophisticated in their analysis of women's oppression, the amount of energy they devoted to the struggle for change is unparalleled. They recognized that change was not going to occur simply because they acted nicely and got the coffee; women's liberation would be put on the political agenda only if women organized themselves and took action to put it there.

Over the following years the depth and range of feminist analysis has expanded enormously, but the need for action has not diminished. Our analyses continue to form an essential, and now more comprehensive, framework; in themselves, however, they are insufficient for achieving an end to women's oppression. Feminists must continue to organize both themselves and others so that their ideas are transformed into realities: the need to ensure that visions are actually implemented is still implicit in the task of change.

This active organizing for change is what is known as feminist practice: what it is that feminists actually do in order to bring about change. In the next three chapters we will turn our attention towards this critical but complex component of change in order to develop a better understanding of its character.

The various aspects of feminist practice seem easy enough to identify—they centre on concrete questions such as what issues to address, which types of structures or organizations to create, and what tactics are most effective. And with over twenty years of varied and intense experience, feminists have learned a great deal about the specifics of effective organizing. But viewing feminist practice from the standpoint of technique alone is deceptive. Hidden behind our growing expertise about the specific mechanisms and pitfalls of organizing is a maze of issues and problems that make definitive answers to the questions of practice anything but straightforward.

Indeed, despite the increased skills and knowledge of activists, it often seems that we are still back at square one when it comes to answering the basic question of what constitutes an effective practice for change.

One reason for the difficulty is simply that there are different answers to the question: the organized women's movement is not a single entity with a common purpose. In fact, although feminist activists may agree on the need for change, and on the need to actively organize for it, these same activists often differ significantly on how to achieve it. These differences are evidenced in the highly diverse and widespread nature of the movement itself; the often rancorous debate within it suggests that these differences are not minor. Any attempt to analyze and evaluate feminist practice must begin by acknowledging that these differences exist, and by clarifying the basis for them: only in this way can the terms of evaluation be made clear.

Such clarification forms the first part of this chapter. In particular we will examine the differences within feminist practice with respect to: a) the theoretical categories within feminism; b) the concept of different categories of experience; and c) different perspectives on change.

At the same time, it is important not to overstate the divisions within feminist practice, or to isolate and explore only one point of view. Although socialist-feminist analysis informs our overall evaluation of feminist practice, we will not restrict our attention to socialist feminism, since it is not the only, or even the dominant, current. In fact, it would be difficult to argue that any particular issue, tactic, or organization is responsible for the massive impact feminism has had in Canada. This change has occurred as a result of the complex interaction of all feminist practices.

Moreover, although they may have different points of view, feminists do not act in isolation from each other. Rather, as part of an overall movement with a common goal of change, they frequently interact, influencing and supporting each other. For example, the initiative of some feminists to challenge the abortion laws by setting up illegal clinics prompted others across the country to take similar action, and drew the support of thousands more. Feminists are both stimulated and enlightened by the initiatives, and the successes, of others across the movement. This is particularly the case for feminists outside major urban centres, where differences are often overridden by the small size of the feminist community and the overwhelming necessity for feminists to work together.

Thus we are interested in exploring not only the different points of view encompassed within feminist practice, but the whole panorama of feminist practice and its relation to the overall dynamics of change. For this reason, in part two of this chapter we will shift our attention away from the more traditional comparisons to argue for a new model of feminist practice—a model based around what we consider to be the two essential components of making change: what we call 'a politic of disengagement' and 'a politic of mainstreaming'. Our central premise is that all feminist practice is composed of a unique blend of these two politics. It is through exploring the nature and limitations of each that we are able to identify the central strategic dilemma that faces all feminist practice for change, and to locate the practices of different feminist currents with respect to that dilemma. At the same time, this model makes its possible to understand how these different practices intersect, sometimes reinforcing each other, sometimes not. In later chapters we will continue to use this framework as a basis for analyzing both the role of feminist ideology in developing practice and the effect of feminist process on how the women's movement has organized itself.

DIFFERENTIATING WITHIN FEMINIST PRACTICE

1. Theory and practice

Perhaps the most common approach to distinguishing within feminist practice has been to assume that differences can be readily classified according to theoretical categories. The particular choices made by each current of feminism are seen as reflecting their different analyses of the nature of women's oppression—particularly their understanding of the nature and structure of power. Thus each current of feminism is identified as having certain issues and methods of struggle distinct from those of other currents: radical feminists are expected to concentrate on sexuality, the family, and reproduction; liberal feminists on equal-rights issues; socialist feminists on working-class and anti-imperialist struggles.

There is certainly some truth to this paradigm, since different analyses of the roots of women's oppression will obviously have a critical effect on which issues are seen as most strategically important and which methods most viable. However, the separation between the practices of different currents is neither as extreme nor as rigid as this approach tends to suggest. For example, both radical and socialist feminists have participated in the fight to end violence against women. One particularly notable example in Toronto was the 'Snuff Out Snuff' campaign, aimed at ending the screening of a movie that presented a woman's murder as sexually titillating. Liberal and socialist feminists have worked together around employment issues such as job and pay discrimination and co-operated in the Hamilton 'Women Back Into Stelco' and the 'Equal Pay for Work of Equal Value' campaigns. And many women from all three persuasions have come together to demonstrate for abortion rights, as in the Morgentaler defence campaigns, or to support women trade unionists on strike.

The same is true for methods of organizing: theoretical labels do not always offer a very reliable basis for determining which tactics are used by, or appropriate for, different currents. In fact, far from belonging to one current or another, particular tactics have often played different roles at different times, depending on the context. For example, there is a tendency to categorize lobbying as a liberal-feminist tactic, and to view public street demonstrations as the logical extension of socialist-feminist principles. Yet, as recent examples in the day-care and abortion campaigns show, this branding is neither accurate nor very helpful.

In fact, the day-care movement in Ontario has demonstrated how lobbying can be used to achieve very non-traditional results. One way it has used this tactic is to assemble as many groups of individuals as possible to meet their members of Parliament on well-publicized Lobby Days. After their meeting, each group reports to the rest of the lobbyists and to the press. This approach transforms lobbying from a method used only by powerful interest groups or influential individuals to privately solicit the support of government members; it is now a tactic that can be used to bring individual, and sometimes isolated, activists together in a common, politically oriented project. At the same time, lobbying becomes a way of exposing the positions of government representatives to public scrutiny, and of generating collective awareness and support for change; it is no longer an approach that upholds the prevailing belief in the power of the individual to effect change through her/his government representative. Lobbying has been used in a similar way by other feminist organizations, such as NAC, also with positive results.[1]

On the other side of the coin, the use of large demonstrations by anti-abortionists across the country shows the inaccuracy of identifying this tactic as belonging to socialist feminism. Their success makes it only too clear that the fact that demonstrations are mass-oriented does not make them intrinsically progressive or revolutionary. But it is not even necessary to go outside the women's movement to raise questions about the merit of demonstrations. Many feminists themselves have criticized this tactic as over-used and over-rated as a technique for change.[2] Again, the important point is not the tactic *per se*, but how it is used and for what purpose.

In short, then, there is no rigid separation of the issues and tactics of feminist practice into different theoretical categories. On the contrary, members of different currents often agree about many basic demands for women, and frequently organize together.

Indeed, even within a particular category or current, theoretical analyses do not provide clear answers to the specific questions of practice: what issues to take up, what demands to make, what methods of organization to use. In fact, when confronted by the demands of a complex political reality, the straightforward clarity that principles provide in the abstract often becomes opaque and contradictory, and feminists within the same political current can have significant disagreements over political positions or tactics.

Within socialist feminism, for example, there are many differences over which political positions are ideologically correct. One current debate concerns the banning of pornography. Some argue that condoning censorship at any level risks giving undue and dangerously repressive power to the state. The possible—some would argue, highly probable—ramifications include suppression of erotic as well as pornographic material, and a boost to the power of the right-wing in its attempts to define sexuality in strictly monogamist, marital, and heterosexist terms.[3]

This argument derives from the position that the state is fundamentally an instrument of power for patriarchal capitalism and, as such, has interests that are inimical to those of feminism. Calling on the state to rectify the problem of pornography not only fails to specifically identify the patriarchal-capitalist nature and role of the state, but actually ensures that the mythology of the 'protector' state is reinforced.[4] Socialist feminists taking this position could point to the recently proposed federal legislation on pornography to back up their argument.

A contrary position on pornography would compare it to racist or homophobic hate literature, and would be in favour of government action to stop its circulation. This position emerges from a recognition that, while government is the guardian of patriarchal-capitalist interests, liberal-democratic principles of equality and justice are also part of the ideology that surrounds its actions. Calling on the government to stop pornography could be compared to demanding that government provide day-care, or fund free-standing abortion clinics—in short, live up to the promises of equality and justice, and work for women. Refusal to respond only exposes government's true nature. And between these two positions there are many socialist feminists who remain uncomfortable and undecided.

But it is not only socialist feminism that experiences the tension of applying theoretical analyses to the specific issues of practice. For example, the liberal-feminist emphasis on equal opportunity can be translated into different practices also. Some liberal feminists focus on representation in the boardroom, government, and professions—they see equality for women strictly in terms of gaining individual access to positions of power. Others, more egalitarian in their outlook, recognize that equal opportunity is dependent on the provision of social services such as universally accessible child-care and introduction of equal-value legislation, since without these supports the lives of the majority of women will remain unchanged.

In the world of practical politics, then, feminists within a particular current may disagree as often as they agree, both on the correct interpretation of theory and on its practical application. Still, feminists of all persuasions agree on more than their theoretical differences would suggest is possible. This does not mean that there are no theoretical foundations to feminist practice, nor that a consistent strategy is unimportant. On the contrary, theoretical analysis does establish a framework for situating the myriad of issues, details, and decisions of daily politics that often threaten to overwhelm feminist activists. Yet theory is abstract and generalized, while reality is unique and conjunctural. At best, theory can give only a very general sense of how to go about achieving change. Certainly it gives no prescription.

2. *Experience and practice*

Another way of understanding the different orientations within feminist practice is to relate them to what might be called 'categories of experience'. Some feminists are lesbian; some are heterosexual. Some feminists are mothers; others are not. Feminists come from all racial and ethnic groups, all age groups, and different economic strata. Some are disabled. Each of these sets of circumstances can be seen as creating unique interests, which are the natural basis for the political practice of feminists in that group. Thus black women would be expected to see racism as a major focus, while the issues around day-care might be the primary concern of those with children.

Different practices logically arise out of different life experiences and situations.

There are many examples to suggest that identifying categories of experience offers a useful framework for understanding the differences within feminism. One particular example is the conflict that emerged in 1978 while activists prepared for a demonstration on abortion rights in Toronto. Abortion campaigns had traditionally been built around such slogans as 'Free Abortion on Demand', reflecting the concern that women did not have direct control over access to abortion and therefore lacked control over their own bodies. During the planning meetings for this particular action, however, feminists representing immigrant and black women tried to reshape the terms of reference over the abortion issue, arguing that it was inadequate for women in their communities. They proposed the alternative slogan 'We will Bear the Children We Choose to Bear', which reflected their concern over the forced sterilization and compulsory abortion (genocide) experienced by non-white women[5] in addition to their support for the right to choose abortion.

Similarly, we could point to the current debate over racism within the women's movement, a debate that seriously emerged only when black women and women of colour themselves raised a challenge based on their experience of discrimination within the movement. Or there is the struggle that began in the earlier years of the second wave as lesbians confronted the heterosexism of the women's movement. The list could go on.

Recognizing and validating the different categories of experience within feminism has obviously added an important dimension to our understanding of the differences within feminist practice and resulted in a more diverse, responsive, and complex practice. It has also been the impetus for increased theoretical sophistication within the women's movement, in particular in challenging the notion of 'woman' as a overriding, unitary category of experience. Certainly the development of the concept of difference as a central foundation of socialist-feminist theory is at least partly the result of the specific challenges made by different groups. More generally, as we will discuss later in Chapter 6, the importance of 'the personal is political' as a theme within feminist ideology is closely related to the idea of categories of experience, as is the emphasis that feminists have placed on consciousness-raising and the validity of experience as means of understanding the world and testing theory.

Yet, despite these contributions, the idea of separate categories of experience does not offer an entirely adequate explanation for the differences within feminist practice. Different categories of experience, like theoretical categories, cannot be shown to lead to clear or rigid divisions in practice: feminists from diverse backgrounds have frequently been allies around particular issues, and have worked together in common organizations. One reason is that different categories of experience are not mutually exclusive, and women may in fact belong to more than one category. For example, a woman may be both white and working-class, a lesbian and a parent, or black and disabled. Moreover, different life experience is not the only factor that defines the political agenda for feminists— there are other forces that draw women together in struggle. Perhaps the most important of these is the fact that women are oppressed not just because they are black, or lesbian, or welfare mothers, but also because they are women. It is also the case that differences in experience can be cut across by a common theoretical analysis, as in the International Women's Day Committee, or by the emergence of an overriding political issue, such as the Meech Lake Accord.

3. Feminist practice: an orientation to change

It seems, then, that neither the categories of experience nor those of theory offer a sufficient basis for clarifying the differences within feminist practice, although both add to our understanding. In fact, the tendency to rely on one or the other of these approaches as a definitive guide clouds the complexities of that practice, leaving important dimensions unaccounted for.

How can the differences in feminist practice be distinguished? Our discussion above suggests that a third kind of framework is necessary, one that can account for both theoretical and experiential differences, yet explain the fact that feminists often seem to cross these boundaries when making decisions about what issue to fight about and what tactic to use. It must also allow for flexibility in responding to a fluid and complex political reality, yet set some benchmarks by which to judge whether or not a particular issue or tactic is appropriate and effective.

We would argue that such a framework emerges from an exploration of the differences in the way feminist currents understand the overall task of making change, rather than from attempts to categorize issues and tactics. The point is that issues and tactics in themselves do not represent the differences among feminists: what is key is how these issues and tactics fit into an overall perspective on change. In fact, feminists can agree on particular issues or tactics, but the reasons why they do so and the purposes they hope to achieve can be quite different. For example, both liberal and radical feminists may support the right to abortion, but they do so from different perspectives. Liberal feminism sees it as a question of individual rights, while radical feminism sees it as one aspect of the relations of power between men and women. Similarly, women from different categories of experience might organize around separate issues such as racism or union organizing, but be linked by a shared overall vision of change.

Two points in particular serve to distinguish the different feminist views about change: first, analysis of power and vision of change; second, understanding of how change takes place. In what follows, these points will be discussed in relation to the three major currents of feminism.

We will look first at socialist feminism. As discussed in Chapter 3, socialist-feminist analysis emerges out of a materialist, rather than an idealist, approach: it argues that women's oppression is not simply a question of attitude, but is deeply embedded in existing social and economic structures. The liberation of women, then, requires the transformation of the relations of power as they are structured by patriarchal capitalism and the building of an alternative set of public and private institutions that will structure society along collective lines. This analysis of women's oppression defines the first parameter of socialist-feminist practice—that is, the need for socialist feminists to confront the institutions of patriarchal capitalism and wrest power from them. Hence the overall orientation of socialist-feminist practice would be to centre on struggles that pose a challenge to existing institutions and relations of power.

The second benchmark for socialist-feminist practice concerns the way change occurs. From the socialist-feminist perspective the kind of structural change that is necessary can come about only with the mass consent and active support of the majority; those who will be affected by change must be involved in the process of actually making it. Not only does this united participation provide the numbers and power necessary to confront the system; it is also essential to the forging of a new public consensus about the nature and values of the society to be built. Socialist-feminist practice therefore is oriented towards women coming together in a *collective* struggle for social change; at the same time, socialist feminists stress the need for that struggle to be controlled by those who are part of the struggle—in other words, to be *participatory*.

This view of change differs quite substantially from that of radical feminism. Despite the fact that socialist and radical feminisms share a common origin in the grass-roots women's movement, hence a common disbelief in the possibility of change within the existing system, there are important differences in both their visions and their strategies for change.

One key difference is over the nature of the struggle for power. As we saw in Chapter 3, socialist feminism is not only a theory of women's oppression, although certainly this aspect of analysis is most well developed. It is also a radical critique of the institutions and practices of the entire society. As such, it incorporates a challenge to the complex relations of power as they are expressed through class, race, and sexual orientation, as well as those based on gender. Founded on the insights offered through a historical-materialist approach, this analysis of power is confirmed by the reality of personal experience.

Radical feminism, on the other hand, focuses on gender relations of power as key to the struggle for change. At the heart of its theory is the view that biological differences between the genders—and particularly women's role in reproduction—provide the basis for a patriarchal power structure in which men are dominant. At the same time, radical feminism links biological differences to certain inherent qualities of men and women: women's mothering role makes them naturally humanitarian, co-operative, and peace-loving, while man's role is that of aggressor, technician, and competitor. The radical-feminist vision of change looks to restructuring gender relations to end not only the personal power that men wield over women—particularly regarding sexuality—but also the predominance of male culture, and with it many of the problems of our violent, militaristic society.

Radical-feminist theory also differs in its view of how to achieve change. Socialist-feminist strategy emphasizes political confrontation in the public domain—for example, against the government or in the workplace. Radical feminism, however, focuses on the need to withdraw from institutions that perpetuate male domination—in particular those in the private domain, such as the family—and to define feminist alternatives. Thus the locus of practice for radical and socialist feminists tends to be quite different; in addition, radical feminism relies on the personal decision of women to live alternative lifestyles outside the 'male stream', in contrast to socialist feminism with its emphasis on mass-based, externally oriented actions.

Liberal feminism offers a third view of change. While both radical and socialist feminists operate in opposition to the prevailing ideology and institutions of society, liberal feminists focus their efforts

on winning rignts and equal opportunity for women within the existing structures.[6] The primary concern of liberal feminism is not the
nature and structure of social power in itself; rather, it is the fact
that women are excluded from access to that power. Liberal feminists
thus have a more limited analysis of the extent of social change
required for the liberation of women.

Similarly, the liberal-feminist methods of change also fall within
the limits of existing structures and ideas. To the degree that liberal
feminism seeks social change at all, its approach is governmental
and electoral. It urges women to use the structures of representative
democracy by voting at election time or by lobbying, rather than
stressing the direct participation of women themselves in the process
and decisions of change. Liberal feminism also tends to seek change
through individual rather than collective action. It encourages individual women to seek election so that they can exercise legislative
power, or to enter the professions to share in the power of wealth
and status. Those who are successful in the competition for individual power are seen as role models, representing the possibility of
equal access for all women, and as trail-blazers in breaking the
barriers of prejudice. Even when liberal feminism does move outside
the traditional structures of government to build parallel feminist
organizations, such as the National Action Committee, their purpose
is still to create change inside those structures. In short, the liberal-
feminist understanding of how to make change conforms to the
prevailing ideology of change as discussed in Chapter 4, and this
fact alone means that the terms of liberal feminism are more readily
understood, and much more palatable, than those of either radical
or socialist feminism.

In this section we have argued that looking at how different feminisms view making change is a more useful way to distinguish within
feminist practice than the more common approaches, in which these
differences are seen as functions of theoretical categories or as ema-
nating from particular categories of experience. For one thing, it
allows us to understand why different feminisms can at times organize around the same issues and use the same methods, yet at other
times seem to be pursuing their own quite separate paths. For example, the summary of the socialist-feminist view of change allows us
to understand why demonstrations are viewed as the logical method
of struggle for socialist feminists. At the same time, it allows us to
understand why, in the interests of gaining support or of stimulating
public awareness, it is not inappropriate for them to choose lobbying
or guerilla street theatre instead. We can also see why socialist

feminists might argue for united action, yet still recognize the need for diverse communities to organize separately in their own interests. Similarly, this approach enables us to understand why radical feminists are so strongly identified with the creation of a feminist culture through the development of alternative services and community structures, yet turn to large street demonstrations in the struggle against sexual assault. The point is not to attach a label to different issues and methods, but to understand their place within the various feminist perspectives on change. It is only in the context of this understanding that feminists can judge the potential role each can play, and thus develop a practice that can be effective in achieving its particular vision of change.

However, this outline of the different feminist views is primarily explanatory. It compares several different approaches and shows how an understanding of these views helps us to interpret the particular choices of different feminist practices; it does not provide a basis for evaluating their effectiveness in making social change. For that, a different model of feminist practice is needed—one that does not merely view change through the eyes of different feminisms, but directly addresses the problem of making change itself. This model is the focus of the next section.

MAKING CHANGE: A MODEL OF FEMINIST PRACTICE

We suggest that a model for feminist practice needs to be structured around two basic politics: disengagement and mainstreaming. Although each politic encompasses a different attitude to the existing social system and approach to change—as the words themselves imply—they are not opposing politics. As we will argue, each plays its own unique role, yet both are necessary components of any strategy for social change: an overemphasis on one or the other seriously undermines the possibility of making change. In the next sections we will explore these points in more detail: the nature and role of both mainstreaming and disengagement; the relation between these two politics; and, finally, the risks of structuring practice too heavily around one or the other.

1. Disengagement and mainstreaming: the two politics of feminist practice

By definition, all feminisms are critical of existing social and political structures, at least to some degree. What we call a politic of disengagement operates out of this critique, and out of a desire to replace social institutions and practices with alternative modes of functioning. Disengagement emerges out of a vision of what society could, and should, look like if women were no longer oppressed. It is this critique of existing society and this vision for the future that provide the desire for and momentum to achieve change.

A politic of disengagement is not restricted to one particular point of view; the term itself defines neither the specific content nor the degree of the critique being made. In fact, any critique of the system can be seen as a form of disengagement and this politic is characteristic of a range of groups with very different perspectives. In the late 1970s feminists in British Columbia, for instance, critical of male domination of traditional union structures, worked to build SORWUC, a feminist union outside the established trade-union movement; in the same period trade-union feminists in Ontario concentrated on Organized Working Women, which was firmly centred on working within—and changing—those same union structures. Yet the practice of both groups was motivated by a critique of existing structures. A politic of disengagement may operate from an anti-racist, anti-male, anti-heterosexist, or class perspective. The key point is that disengagement is the part of feminist practice that speaks our critique of the existing society, whatever the nature of that critique may be.

As a politic, disengagement takes feminists outside the structures and views accepted by the majority of people. This explains, in part, why feminist ideas are not readily accepted and adopted. At the same time, however, it is precisely this detachment that allows feminists to step back from the immediacy of the situation and grasp the underlying forces at work in society. This larger picture sets a context for understanding how the different aspects of practice relate to each other, and for evaluating the choices being made.

By contrast, a politic of mainstreaming represents the part of feminist practice that attempts to engage with women around concrete issues arising directly out of their personal experience rather than out of an overall feminist agenda for social change. It means, for example, that feminists seeking to help organize bank tellers would not start by raising the need to repeal the abortion law. Nor would feminists organizing support for more day-care start by arguing for an end to patriarchal family structure. Feminist practice that is attempting to mainstream focuses on dealing with what is, rather than on what should be. Perhaps most significantly, it acknowledges how important it is that women themselves set the agendas for change.

The importance of mainstreaming arises out of the need both to alleviate the specific conditions of oppression faced by most women and to actually have large numbers of those women involved in the process of making change. By addressing the issues of the most immediate concern, and by offering concrete, practical solutions, feminists are able to make contact with women in a way that would not be possible if they presented a more comprehensive program for social change. Not only do the larger demands often trigger the fear of change discussed in Chapter 4, and thus tend to close off the possibility of gaining support, but it is also true that the relevance of these changes is simply not clear to many.

This does not mean that mainstreaming requires abandoning overall visions of change or social criticism; rather, it is an acknowledgement of the fact that, in real life, it is often the particular instances of oppression facing women that most anger them and motivate them to act, not the more abstract critique offered by theory. Mainstreaming is the part of feminist practice for change that wants to be concrete and immediately relevant to women's lives; it is the part of practice that wants large numbers of women to participate in the struggle for change. At the same time, becoming involved in these practical issues is often the first step in bridging the gap to a larger vision of change.

Because mainstreaming arises out of the specific realities of women's lives, it must respond to varying political and economic conditions. In British Columbia, for example, after the Social Credit party replaced the NDP as the governing party, the concrete political focus of feminists necessarily shifted. Rather than building on previous successes and expanding the scope of feminist demands for change, possible under a sympathetic NDP government, women were forced to defend previously hard-won gains as the government stripped away funding for such services as shelters for battered women and aid for sexually abused women and children.[7] Similarly, over the years feminists have responded quickly to events such as the Morgentaler arrests, the Meech Lake Accord, or strike situations.

But although the specifics of each situation may vary, there are certain constants to a politic of mainstreaming. The first is that, in order to mainstream its ideas, feminist practice must relate to the key institutions through which women's lives are organized. Naturally one of the most important of these institutions is the family, but the workplace and the various components of the state apparatus are also very significant. For feminist practice to ignore these institutions would be folly: it would simply cut us off from much that concerns women.

The second parameter concerns the prevailing ideology of change. As we argued in Chapter 4, to make change we must not only define what must be changed, but also address the prevailing ideas about how change takes place. These ideas govern the approach taken by the majority of people in our society; to fail to take them seriously, or to simply reject them out of hand, is to ignore the power of these ideas to affect the struggle for change itself.

In summary, we would argue that there are two basic aspects to feminist practice for change. On the one hand, it is clear that social change comes out of a critique of the existing system and out of a vision not only of a new social order, but also of how to end the oppression of women. Without this critique and vision there is no recognition that change is needed, and no momentum to make it take place. Yet it is equally clear that change requires that these ideas be accepted and acted on by the majority of people. To achieve this, feminists also need to develop a practice that engages with the actual concerns of people, and thus with existing institutions and ideologies.

Making change, then, is a question not of choosing between these two approaches, but of reconciling them. Feminists must maintain the integrity of their overall vision of change, yet reach and influence the majority of women who are necessarily focused on the specific concerns of their own lives. Feminists must take their critique— which challenges existing institutions and ideologies, at least to some degree—and make it relevant to a majority who basically accept these structures as they are. To achieve change it is necessary for feminist practice to maintain a tension between the two approaches.

In fact, failure to reconcile these tasks throws up barriers to change. Feminists who act only as critics of the system, and create too much distance from social institutions, run the risk of being unable to reach and activate people. This means that there would not be the mass support necessary to effect change. We refer to this isolation as *marginalization*. At the other extreme, feminists who concentrate on mainstreaming risk straying too far inside the existing social framework, thus losing their perspective and, with it, their ability to make significant change. This process we call *institutionalization*. We will discuss these risks in the following two sections.

2. *Mainstreaming and the risk of institutionalization*

At first glance, it hardly seems possible that emphasizing a politic of mainstreaming could cause difficulties. What problem could there be in organizing around the important issues in women's daily lives and articulating practical solutions? This type of practice would draw support, and it has relevance. In fact, the potential risks of concentrating feminist practice on a politic of mainstreaming do not stem from the attempt to reach out to women in itself. Rather, they arise out of the fact that in relating only to the immediate and expressed concerns of women, feminists often leave their larger criticisms of the system underdeveloped, or unsaid. Their concern is that these criticisms will be incomprehensible or perhaps divisive. Thus, in the effort to build support and unity, feminist demands may never address the terms of existing institutions, or of the ideology that governs our attitude to change. No vision of social transformation is offered as an alternative, and feminist practice simply ends up working within the confines of what is already there.

The problem is that the degree of change possible within these confines is quite limited; and what change can take place often makes little difference to the lives of most women. For example, corporations may remove the barriers to opportunity that now prevent women from achieving executive positions, but while this opens up the opportunity for women who are qualified to obtain jobs previously not available to them, the problem remains that the majority of women cannot expect to achieve these levels at all.

Moreover, the gains women do make are not intrinsic to the existing structures: they can be and are easily taken away if they become too threatening. For example, a corporation may adopt a maternity-leave program, or set up a workplace day-care; it does not, however, go so far as to offer free day-care or fully paid maternity and paternity leave. Moreover, should the profitability of that business become compromised by the support of such programs, limited as they are, the program is gutted. A parallel situation occurs when union members are forced to choose between conceding previous contract gains and the threat of unemployment should the business simply shut down. The demands of capitalist profitability necessarily take precedence over such things as equalizing opportunities for women; if it were otherwise, the corporation could not expect to survive long.

The bottom line is that the nature of power relations within patriarchal capitalism sets certain limits to change. And if feminist practice operates exclusively out of a politic of mainstreaming—that is, without offering a substantive critique of the system and in the context of existing institutions—it is unable to challenge these limits. Such an orientation lacks the necessary critical dimension that would enable it to develop and maintain a larger vision of social transformation, and thus frame demands for change that confront and reveal these limits.

The result is what is known as a process of *institutionalization*. The term refers to the way feminist demands for change are reconstructed and couched in terms of the existing institutions and ideologies. Unlike the term 'absorption',[8] which can imply a disappearance of feminist concerns, 'institutionalization' suggests that there can be some acknowledgement of women's oppression, but that any challenge to it is transformed into something consistent with the existing social and political parameters. In this way the challenge can be met and defused.

The institutionalization of feminist challenges for change occurs for a number of closely related reasons. One factor is the necessity to conform to some degree with the frame of reference of a particular institution in order to be involved with it; that is, feminists must accept at least some of the terms laid out by institutions in order to gain access to them, or to the people working within them. It is unreasonable to expect that organizations would tolerate someone who demonstrated total opposition—someone who was heavily critical of unions would hardly be employed as an organizer; similarly, a bank would not hire a person who refused to abide by its rules and procedures for handling accounts.

This process of conforming is often, rather negatively, labelled co-optation, and is frequently raised as reason for rejecting government funding.[9] It is also seen as a concern when feminists take high-profile jobs, or assume leadership roles in organizations such as unions. However, the process of institutionalization that occurs through institutional conformity is more subtle, even insidious, than the term 'co-optation' suggests. It is not simply a matter of 'buying off' the women's movement with money or power, but of actually engendering a redefinition of the terms of feminist challenge. Thus, as Krin Zook puts it:

When we continue to try to change the institutions we slip into a pattern of upholding them in order to keep our access to them open: for example, not wanting to publicly criticize the police for their use of polygraph because we want continued access to the police college which provides resource people from their training programs. . . . How rape crisis centres are developing as traditional institutions is by rationalizing that it is important to show doctors, lawyers, police and social workers how to better do their jobs, and to believe that it is important to lobby for changes in the law. This supporting of institutions institutionalizes rape as an accepted social reality.[10]

Or, as Dorothy Smith explains the reconstruction of the feminist challenge to men's violence against women:

The issue of men's violence against women in the family setting is being transformed into a professional psychiatric or counselling problem. The 'battered wife' concept is substituted for the political analysis of violence by men against women. There are conferences, a literature, the elaboration of a professional practice. . . . The issue of women's passivity and silence, our socially enforced inability to speak out and to express our anger, these become transposed from a political issue into a technique. We can take courses in assertiveness. We can practice screaming.[11]

The same process has occurred with the issue of equal pay for work of equal value. Rather than developing as a political struggle against the sexual division of labour and the consequent devaluing of women's labour, this issue has been transferred to job-evaluation experts who treat it as a technical question of considering relative levels of qualification, responsibility, difficulty of work, and so on. Similarly, racism, ethnicism, ageism, and sexism are transformed into 'equity' issues, rather than revealed as deeply rooted social problems created by the way power is structured in our society. (It is perhaps significant that the only 'ism' ignored is heterosexism.) And in the media social movements for change are broken down and presented as individual success or human-interest stories, rather than as political struggles.

This list of issues could be extended still further. Again, as Dorothy Smith puts it:

Each [women's movement initiative] is reassembled as a technical or otherwise limited problem. It is relocated into its professional or other institutional setting. It is given a new terminology tying it into the controlled institutional communication and action system. How it becomes visible, can be thought and acted upon, gets restricted to that frame. The problem becomes specific, contained, cut off from its general relation to the whole question of women's oppression in contemporary capitalist society.[12]

The hierarchical and bureaucratic nature of institutions in our society only adds to this risk of adaptation; that is, the very nature of these organizational structures creates and reinforces patterns of uniformity, and makes them inflexible and resistant to change. Not only do is there relentless pressure within the system to conform, but the very immobility of the system is in itself profoundly disillusioning. This is clearly a problem faced by feminists attempting to work with/through government structures. Whether they are working for legislative change, trying to present briefs to public hearings, or employed as civil servants,[13] these feminists experience tremendous rigidity and often feel that they are part of an endless process; it seems they take one step forward only to take two back.

But these pressures also exist within potentially adversarial organizations, such as unions or political parties. Feminists within the NDP have periodically had obstacles put in the path of their attempts to get issues such as abortion onto the floor during policy conventions. Those in SORWUC learned about structural rigidity within the union movement the hard way, as the Canadian Labour Congress consistently failed to support its efforts to organize bank workers, largely because of the challenge SORWUC presented to both union leadership and traditional styles of union organizing.

The power of the pressure to conform to the framework of patriarchal capitalism is even reflected in the way alternative feminist structures develop. Although these structures are set up precisely to provide space for feminists outside the traditional institutions, they too are often forced to reproduce the very norms they have set out to reject, just in order to survive. This problem has been well documented in assessing feminist co-operatives, businesses, and services.[14]

But there is still another reason why working with existing social and political institutions leaves activists vulnerable to pressure to conform: this work often isolates them from a larger social movement. The result is that they lose the power they could wield through being part of a larger constituency,[15] and at the same time are separated from a body of support that could help to offset pressures within the system to conform.

The institutionalization of feminist practice has a number of costs. There is the cost of limiting the scope of the feminist vision of change through adaptation to the institutional framework, as discussed above. But there is also the fact that institutionalization can discourage and demobilize those who seek change. In the first place, it undermines the perception that there is a need for change, because it acts to validate both the traditional structures of power, such as government and police, and the existing ideology of change with its emphasis on individual responsibility. Second, women find it difficult to believe in the possibility of change both because of the limited nature of the changes that have actually been achieved within these institutions and because of the difficulty of trying to effect change through legitimate channels. The result is that a woman's socially ingrained sense of powerlessness is simply reinforced, as there is no apparent solution to her dilemma over how to actually bring change about, and no obvious role for her to play.

Yet the risks of institutionalization do not mean that mainstreaming itself should be abandoned. On the contrary, as we have said, if change is to take place, feminists must reach out to large numbers of women with their ideas. And to reach them, we must engage with the existing political and social institutions; relate to the real concerns of women; and deal in the context of liberal democracy and the ideology of change.

It is necessary to ensure, however, that a politic of mainstreaming is coupled with a politic of disengagement. Disengagement affords feminism the disbelief it needs to maintain a critical distance in the face of pressure to compromise; disengagement allows feminists to understand and resist the possible dangers it faces in mainstreaming.

3. Disengagement and the risk of marginalization

Unlike mainstreaming, a politic of disengagement does not risk compromising its vision of change. Nonetheless, it too is inadequate as the sole basis for feminist practice. The problem with emphasizing disengagement is that feminism then risks separating itself from the lives and consciousness of the majority of women, making it difficult to actually reach and mobilize them. This inability to gain substantial support for a vision of change is what we refer to as marginalization.

In part, marginalization is an inherent tendency in any movement presenting a serious critique of society and attempting to organize mass support for change. As we discussed in Chapter 4, both the idea of wanting social, as distinct from individual, change, and of achieving that change through direct mass action rather than through the processes of representative democracy, simply trigger an endemic fear of change.

But marginalization also results from the fact that many women do not see the larger visions of feminist change as relevant or viable; they do not relate either to the scope of political critique or to the type of solution proposed by feminists. And when feminists situate themselves too far outside what the majority understands about the process, nature, and possibilities of social change, they remove themselves from the audience they most want to reach. They spend their time talking to the already converted.

For example, feminist critiques of the family often do not address the contradictory nature of that institution or the reasons for women's allegiance to it.[16] Even though women's experience within the family is often very negative—involving economic dependence, domestic servitude, diminished status, and, frequently, violence—the family also offers women a kind of social validation through their roles as wives and mothers. Indeed, despite its obvious inadequacies, the family as an institution is still viewed as the nexus of many of the central human expressions of love and caring in our society. Women's economic dependency within the family simply cements this emotional allegiance. The reality is that single women—lesbian, unmarried, widowed, or divorced—are among the poorest in the country.[17]

An implacable theoretical opposition to the family needs to be tempered by a recognition of the very real problems involved in simply abandoning it; otherwise the majority of women have difficulty relating to the critique at any level. Most women do not have the desire to simply abandon home and family—nor are they able to—despite what statistics tell us about marriage breakup and abandonment; indeed, many offer a definite resistance to seeking any changes to the structure itself. By failing to address this reality, feminism only distances itself from people and limits the possibilities of gaining support for its ideas.

A similar problem occurs when feminism fails to address the contradictory character of the state. For example, grass-roots feminism has traditionally focused almost exclusively on the role of the state in maintaining patriarchal capitalism and the limitations of trying to achieve any worthwhile change through governmental measures. This disbelief in the possibility of making concrete gains through intervention in, or working with, governmental structures has often been coupled with a deep fear of being co-opted and of losing control, as discussed in the last section. The result is a strategy that emphasizes non-involvement—a stance reflected in strategic decisions that basically ignore the government completely and direct demands for change towards a generalized public consciousness. Nor is there any serious involvement in election campaigns, which are dismissed as charades.

But while the disbelief in change through government action and the fear of co-optation are based in the reality of the power relations of patriarchal capitalism, it is also true that this is not the belief of most women, and feminists distance themselves by refusing to deal directly with their beliefs. Like it or not, public attitudes are shaped by the prevailing ideology of change, and thus many people view social change as the responsibility of government.

Indeed, in maintaining a critical distance from the goverment and the legitimated processes of change, feminism does more than just isolate itself; it actually disempowers and demobilizes women. By presenting the state as a monolith of patriarchal power rather than as a structure vulnerable to pressure, and by making only criticisms of the state rather than viable suggestions for change, feminism robs women of any belief that social change can take place and that what they do could make a difference. Often women end up seeing no point to activism at all, and turn their attention away from collective political action towards private interests, or 'solutions' such as therapy.

And for those who do remain in feminist political groupings, the isolation created through disengagement often results in a turning inward, which is reflected in an internalized practice involving exclusive organizational, social, and personal norms. We will discuss the problems of this inward focus at greater length in Chapter 7; however, it is certainly clear that it makes reaching out to the majority of women even more difficult, and increases the inaccessibility and invisibility of the women's movement.

Yet the risk of marginalization does not mean that disengagement should be abandoned any more than institutionalization means that mainstreaming should be forgotten. As we have shown, the critical function of disengagement is essential to defining and sustaining the scope of the feminist challenge for change. But disengagement must be balanced by mainstreaming in order to offset the tendency for it to result in marginalization.

4. The strategic dilemma of feminist practice

The uncomfortable reality is that feminist practice is rooted in a central contradiction; it must somehow situate itself with respect to the apparently contradictory demands of two different but equally essential politics. In a sense, it could be argued that mainstreaming and disengagement act as counterweights for each other: together they make it possible to develop a feminist practice that is finely balanced between abstract vision and concrete reality, between the insights of both theory and experience, between the overview and the specific. The necessity of maintaining this balance—and thus avoiding being either marginalized or institutionalized—is what we refer to as the strategic dilemma of feminist practice.

Feminist practice must relate to and use, but at the same time confront, the institutions—and thus the practices and ideas—of our society. By standing outside the system as well as in it, feminists are able to keep a perspective on the role of social institutions and practices in sustaining the oppression of women, yet relate to the majority belief in both. For example, many feminists organizing in the trade unions have argued for the necessity of understanding working-class loyalty to family structures; sometimes this argument has gone so far as to insist that feminists working in the union movement must themselves be married, or have children, in order to relate to the needs and concerns of workers. The point has some validity: it is true that feminists cannot expect an immediate and positive response to demands for 'smashing the family' for reasons discussed earlier. Nonetheless, it is not necessary to abandon feminist critiques of the family completely in order to work effectively in the union movement. Nor should we. The feminist critique of the family is fundamental to its vision of change; to hide it or leave it out implies that feminism is somehow secondary to trade unionism. Rather, these critiques need to be related to the immediate reality of working people's lives—and particularly the lives of working women—and from that foundation developed into a fuller critique.

The need to maintain the creative relationship between mainstreaming and disengagement applies to the whole range of feminist practice for change, including struggles around the family and male-female relationships, workplaces, unions, and so on. However, as we have previously suggested, a strategy for making change particularly requires addressing the prevailing ideology of change.

This means that feminist practice for change must include a clear orientation to the state that both exposes the limits placed on change because of the overall structure of power (disengagement) yet relates to the belief in the possibility of change engendered by the prevailing ideology (mainstreaming). First, this combined approach increases the possibility of making concrete gains. For the threat of exposure is partially what motivates the state apparatus to respond: it hopes that concessions will conceal the underlying power structures and act to mollify an angry population. In many cases, though, success in winning gains, limited as they are, also serves to encourage further mobilization in support of other demands, and validates the role of extra-governmental mass action. On the other hand, should the state refuse to make such changes, the women's movement still gains, because such blatant disregard for the wishes and needs of people tends to provokes anger and disbelief in the promises of the system, and greater willingness to seek its overall change.

Let us consider some actual examples of how this strategy has been used successfully. Take the abortion issue. Gallup polls regularly provide evidence that the majority of the population supports a pro-choice position. If the state were truly representative of and responsive to the concerns of the majority, we would expect the pro-choice position to be legitimized and legalized. Yet the government clearly fails to respond. The pro-choice movement could continue to try to impress upon the government that its position is supported by the majority, and that as a result the law should be changed. This approach is unlikely to be successful.

Much more effective has been the use of a strategy based on exposing the inadequacy of the state's own promises of equal opportunity and justice. The pro-choice movement has highlighted the lack of equal access to abortion services, which is actually a lack of 'equal opportunity'; this 'fairness' approach has mobilized a lot of people and put pressure on the government to respond. In fact, the pressure is so strong that even the candidates for the Ontario Conservative leadership, in November 1985, at one point in their campaign stated that they would force Catholic hospitals to set up therapeutic abortion committees. They were responding not because they believed in the right of women to abortion services, but because the liberal-democratic state's failure to provide equal access and equal opportunity had been exposed. In this situation feminist gains are two-fold: first, in whatever expansion or liberalization occurs in abortion services; and second, in the exposure of the limits of the ideology of change.

In 1984 the co-ordinating committee for the Ontario Coalition for Abortion Clinics wrote an article concerning their strategy with respect to government. In it they make several important points about the value to feminism of developing their practice to include the state:

> Many of us in the women's movement have felt that electoral politics are irrelevant to our struggles. The time has come to reassess this view. Historically, our cynicism of institutionalized politics has allowed us the independence of an autonomous women's movement: fighting in the streets, the press, in our homes and workplaces; through some formidable grass-roots organizations. Our allegiance is with them still. However, in all of these battles we continually run up smack against the power of the state. It is the state, with all of its agencies, that determines our inequality: that limits daycare spaces,

that denies lesbians custody rights, that prosecutes doctors for performing abortions, etc. We have always organized around issues to influence the government. We must also organize around elections to make public our issues.

We have no illusions that elections will solve all of our problems and empower women. However, they do provide at least three options: a forum to educate large numbers of people normally inaccessible to us; a platform by which we might mobilize the women's movement; and a lever by which we might attain feminist goals through political pressure.

This [at elections] is the time that politics becomes legitimate in this country. . . .[18]

The day-care movement has also used the contradictory nature of the state against it. At first, day-care activists tried to prove 'need' by collecting information and writing briefs. They believed that if the government understood the need of a majority of working parents, it would have to respond. Of course this did not happen, and the day-care movement came to understand that a more effective strategy would be one that recognized that the government does not respond to need, but to exposure. As a result activists went on the offensive, demanding not only better day-care services but, more important, a public explanation for the government's failure to respond to the well-documented need and support for more day-care. In this context the government began to respond.

The importance of a strategy towards the state that balances the politics of mainstreaming and disengagement is clear. In the first place, although the gains made through this process may not fundamentally transform the social order, they can provide needed services and legislation, and a sense of victory essential to continued commitment. Second, and as part of a larger strategy for social change, this orientation can serve to expose the limitations of representative democracy and the ideology of change, thus creating the political space for a mass-based struggle for social change to emerge. Furthermore, this exposure also serves to anger and politicize people, thus empowering them to actually play a part in the struggle for social change.

In summary, then, an effective feminist practice for change requires maintaining a tension between a politic of disengagement and one of mainstreaming. It means relating to the specific concerns and beliefs of women, and thus to existing institutions and practices, as well as maintaining a critical distance from these same structures as part of an overall perspective on social change. This approach applies to the full range of institutions and ideas that structure and maintain the oppression of women. We have also argued, however, that a critical component of this strategy must involve engagement with institutions of the state, since it is here that the prevailing ideology of change and equal opportunity directly confronts the reality of the social structure of power. The ongoing power of this ideology poses a major obstacle to attempts to organize a collective struggle for overall social change.

A MODEL OF FEMINIST PRACTICE: SITUATING DIFFERENT FEMINISMS

The practices of all feminist currents combine elements of both mainstreaming and disengagement to some degree; that is, they offer a certain critique of the existing structures, and they want to have their ideas for change accepted. What distinguishes one feminist practice from another is the specific combination of these politics: each has a unique balance that situates it in the overall map of feminist practice. In fact, there is a continuum of feminist practice reflecting various possible combinations of these politics. At one end, practice is dominated by a politic of mainstreaming; at the other, by a politic of disengagement.

How each current of feminism situates itself on this continuum depends on its perspective on making change—that is, its vision of change and understanding of how it takes place. In this section we will examine the three major currents of feminism and their location within our model of feminist practice, using the discussion in the first section of this chapter as a point of reference.

Liberal feminism. Liberal feminism offers the clearest example of a feminist practice based primarily on mainstreaming. As we have seen, its critique concerns the barriers to equality of opportunity that women experience within the system; in general, it accepts the terms of the existing social framework. In fact, we would argue that liberal feminism is, by definition, situated at the centre of acceptable political practice: its commitment to and belief in the prevailing ideology of change means that both its goals and its methods are readily understandable and accessible to the public consciousness.

Liberal-feminist practice demonstrates that there are some obvious benefits to operating primarily within a framework of mainstreaming. Certainly this orientation has meant that the liberal-feminist voice is the accepted public voice of feminism. But it is also true that liberal feminism has helped to increase overall public awareness and acceptance of feminist aspirations for change. Because it expresses its ideas about change for women in the familiar terms of the ideology of change, liberal feminism has made these ideas seem relevant and possible to large numbers of people. In fact, the goal of extending equality of opportunity to women is often seen as a matter of simple justice.

Nor should this goal be dismissed lightly: the concrete advantages of increased opportunities for women are many. Such things as equal-opportunity employment programs, the passing of human-rights legislation, and alterations in the structure and content of education have helped to change ideas about what it is possible for women to do.

In general, however, the history and role of liberal feminism confirm our earlier discussion of the pitfalls of mainstreaming as a primary strategy for change. For one thing, although liberal feminism may have helped to gain a greater overall acceptance of feminism, its program for change has been set well within the terms of the existing institutional framework. More day-care spaces, more services for abused women, more opportunity in the workplace— these types of changes are necessary to the liberation of women, but insufficient for achieving it. As discussed earlier, they are palliatives only and do not alter the basic structure of power. It is also the case that the range of people who have actually benefited by these changes has been quite narrow, compared to the level of need. In fact, some changes made in the name of equality of opportunity have actually worsened the situation of women—for example, the removal of protective legislation requiring employers to provide safe transport for women workers coming off late shifts.

In any case, it needs to be pointed out that the gains were not achieved simply through the mainstreaming efforts of liberal feminism—rather, they were the product of an overall climate of struggle generated primarily by critiques of how the system operates. And while liberal feminism has played some role in these critiques— particularly in pointing out the unequal opportunities available for women—it has largely been the grass-roots women's movement that has created the scandals, identified the problems, and exposed the oppression of women. Moreover, it has been the grass-roots movement's highly visible protests and efforts to mobilize large numbers of people in struggle that have put pressure on the government and other institutions to respond. It could even be argued that the main-streaming approach of liberal feminism has simply provided an 'out';

it offers an avenue for the government and other institutions to appear to respond to demands, when in reality what is taking place is the institutionalization of larger visions of change.

In fact, the problem of institutionalization is one that liberal feminism does not really recognize. Its analysis of oppression is focused not on power relations under patriarchal capitalism, but on individual opportunity within institutions. From its point of view, the institutional structure does not limit change, but provides an opportunity for making change. For this reason liberal feminism can offer little resistance to the constant pressure to reformulate the demands of feminism so that they conform to existing structures and ideas.

Radical feminism. Radical-feminist practice, on the other hand, tends to be centred around a politic of disengagement. Both its vision of change—which argues for the need to end the unequal division of power between men and women—and its method of change—focused on building feminist alternatives—do not simply put radical feminism in opposition to the existing society, but actually take the struggle for change itself well beyond existing structures and levels of consciousness. Indeed, we might say that radical feminism forms a strategic pole opposite to that of liberal feminism. With radical feminism, women separate rather than integrate; they build alternatives rather than seek access to power through traditional chennels.

This emphasis on disengagement is largely responsible for radical feminism's inability to extend its support beyond a small number of adherents. For one thing, its strategy of building feminist alternatives to the dominant 'male-stream' culture has proved to be internalizing and marginalizing. The constant effort it takes to keep such alternatives alive and functioning means that attention is focused inward; moreover, many feminists come to view these alternatives as 'havens', retreats safe from male dominance, and have no particular interest in reaching beyond their confines.[19] At the same time, as we noted earlier, outright rejection of key social institutions, such as the family, as instruments of male power is simply not possible for most women, and by proposing it radical feminism only isolates itself further.

This does not mean that radical feminism has had no impact on the struggle for change. In fact, the radical-feminist critique of male-female power relations has tapped into an enormous amount of personal anger experienced by women over family life, childbearing responsibilities, sexuality, and violence. Its insistence on highlighting the private dimension of women's lives has played a key role in making visible these issues, to the advantage of women today. (We will return to this point in Chapter 6, on the ideology of the women's movement.) Nonetheless, it is instructive to note that radical feminism has had its biggest successes in drawing support when it has concentrated on issues that relate to the immediate life experiences of women, such as sexual assault, and when it has externalized its political actions for change; in other words, when it has mainstreamed, rather than concentrated on disengagement. One example is the series of 'Take Back the Night' demonstrations, which not only dealt with an issue that most women could readily identify with, but also involved women in political action that brought them together in a collective display of power.

The unique role of socialist feminism.   Like radical feminism, socialist feminism faces the problem of marginalization. Both its critique of patriarchal capitalism and its commitment to building a mass movement outside the electoral process make it foreign and threatening in the public's eye. As we discussed earlier, the power of the words 'socialism' and 'collective change' to trigger fear of change should not be underestimated, and the problem is exacerbated by socialist feminists' tendency to employ a technical, abstract jargon that is really accessible only to themselves.[20]

These inherent difficulties are compounded by the fact that socialist feminists also tend to confuse the need for mainstreaming with the problem of institutionalization. They recognize that issues, once mainstreamed or popularized, are frequently institutionalized. But rather than seeing institutionalization as a way of responding to and defusing the power of popular movements, they often assume that it is the inevitable, and undesirable, result of mainstreaming itself. The result has frequently been an abdication of any role but that of cynic; that is, a retreat into the theoretical safety of disengagement.

However, despite the fact that the actual practice of socialist feminism has tended to err on the side of disengagement, its theory makes it uniquely suited for the job of reconciling the two components of change. On the one hand, as we have said, socialist feminism is based on a critique of the entire society: it is centred on a vision of fundamental social transformation in which the existing relations of power, institutions, and ideological practices would be replaced by an alternative set of structures. Its practice then is necessarily structured, at least in part, by a politic of disengagement.

But the critique of patriarchal capitalism is only one aspect of socialist-feminist theory: the other key component concerns the nature of the struggle for social change. According to socialist feminism, change requires a public consensus about and commitment to a new social vision, and the active support and participation of a significant layer of the population in a mass political movement. The approach to change is both collective and participatory.

To build such a movement, socialist feminism must reach out and involve people. This will not be done by standing outside the consciousness of the majority, or outside the institutions that structure the lives of that majority. Socialist feminism is not oriented towards calling in the wilderness, hoping someone will hear—on the contrary, it wants an audience, and to achieve its vision it must go where the audience is. This means that socialist feminists must deal with what women themselves are willing to struggle over, and must actively engage with institutions and the existing level of public consciousness; that is, they must mainstream. In particular, socialist feminists are pushed to deal with the institutions of the state because of the prevailing ideology of change.

In short, then, we would argue that in the context of our model for making change, only socialist feminism actually calls for combining the elements of mainstreaming and disengagement. In fact, the success of its vision depends on successfully linking the two.

THE NEXT STEP

In this chapter we have focused on the nature of feminist practice for change. We were concerned to find a model to help identify the differences within feminist practice, and to evaluate the effectiveness of these different practices with respect to the overall task of making change. This model we saw as being structured around two aspect of the process of change: mainstreaming and disengagement.

Our model, however, is not intended to imply that there are any recipes for social change. The specific character of mainstreaming and disengagement, and what is required to achieve a balance between them, depends on each given situation, not on abstract characterizations. As we have seen, issues and tactics can play different roles under different conditions.

This does not mean that we cannot get a better grasp on the specific questions of practice raised by our model: what works, and how, and why? In the next two chapters we will try to shed some light on these issues through a more detailed examination of past directions and choices. We are not trying to provide an encyclopaedic review, but to capture a sense of the significant features of feminist practice over the last twenty years. In particular, we will examine the ideas of the women's movement and how they shaped the direction of practice, as well as the role played by the feminist organizational processes and structures that emerged. The critical evaluation of past choices is often seen as a negative process. We recognize that we are granted a great deal of hindsight, and it is not our intent to disparage the efforts of the past. Our purpose is to use that hindsight to systematize our experience, and to formulate a more concrete idea of what will help us to achieve change in the future.

The fact that the political, social, and economic climate today is substantially different from that of two decades ago plays an essential role in our ability to activate an ongoing and self-conscious political movement. We are not isolated from the social forces around us; the women's movement does not operate in a vacuum. Nonetheless, the current conjuncture does not excuse us from confronting our past practice. It is only by coming to terms with both our victories and our mistakes that we will be able to gain a clearer sense of the directions we might take.

NOTES

[1] For an interesting discussion of how the women's movement can make effective use of lobbying, see Rosemary Brown, 'On Lobbying', *Kinesis* vol. 6, no. 11 (Oct. 1977).

[2] One such critique is offered by Judy Stanleigh, 'Marching on the Spot', *Broadside* vol.1, no. 10. In this commentary Stanleigh argues that marches actually 'diffuse the emotional rage of the participants', and that 'the traditional march is outmoded, useless, and inconsequential'. She does, however, say that there are times when a march can be effective, as in the Anita Bryant protest and the 'Take Back the Night' march, both of which were immediate and relevant to the situation at hand.

[3] See Varda Burstyn, ed., *Women Against Censorship* (Vancouver: Douglas and McIntyre, 1985).

[4] For a discussion of this problem, see Krin Zook, 'Institutionalized Rape', *Broadside* vol. 2, no. 1/2 (1980; reprinted from *Kinesis*).

[5] This concern is, of course, rooted in reality. Black women do face a pressure to have compulsory abortions and sterilizations that white women do not. One discussion of the orientation black women take to these issues may be found in Makeda Silvera, 'Black Women Organize for Health', *Healthsharing* vol. 2, no. 2 (Spring 1984), pp. 19–22.

[6] Micheline Dumont makes a similar point in *The Women's Movement Then and Now* (Ottawa: CRIAW/ICREF, 1986), when she makes a distinction between a feminism that focuses on rights and one that focuses on power.

[7] Helen Maier in 'We Will Survive', *Kinesis* June 1984, p. 7.

[8] Dorothy Smith uses this term in 'Where There Is Oppression, There Is Resistance', *Branching Out* vol. 6, no. 1 (1979): 'A major danger is the process of institutional absorption. I imagine it to be like a starfish eating a clam, sucking the living tissues from the shell. Institutional structures are set up to organize and control and they do it well. When critical positions and action emerge related to an institutional focus, processes are set in motion

which bring things back in line, which absorb the anomaly, and keep things stabilized. . . . Each new way of absorbing women's movement initiatives into the institutional structure isolates them from the movement and depoliticizes them . . . as the work is absorbed by the ruling apparatus it is withdrawn from the general struggle' pp. 13–14.

9 The issue of co-optation through government funding has been extensively debated within the women's movement. A concise outline of some of the specific pressures that arise through this funding can be found in Dorothy Smith, 'Does Government Funding Co-opt?', *Kinesis* vol. 6, no. 11 (Oct. l977). In addition to noting the ways in which feminist organizations can be distracted by the need to conform to government schedules, and write reports, Smith argues that this funding often reshapes the political direction and organizational structures of the group. For example, funding often necessitates an employer/employee relationship rather than a collective one; it may require that certain categories of people be hired regardless of their political skills or orientation; and it may structure competitive relationships between feminist organizations all seeking funding from the same source. Similarly, groups may design their work with government funding priorities and criteria in mind, rather than continue to play an clearly oppositional, advocacy role. At the same time, however, Smith does not reject funding out of hand: 'because . . . if we are concerned to do things for women politically we also have to take into account the implications of deciding NOT to seek funding which often means that we don't do anything because we actually do depend on it' (p. 5).

10Zook, 'Institutionalized Rape', p. 27.

11 Smith, 'Where There is Oppression, There is Resistance', p. 13.

12Ibid.

13See Sue Findlay, 'Facing the State: the Politics of the Women's Movement Reconsidered', in Heather Jon Maroney and Meg Luxton, eds. *Feminism and Political Economy*, (Toronto: Methuen, 1987) for a description of the process by which the Canadian state integrates the representation of women's issues into the policy-making process, and a discussion of the difficulties faced by feminists working as civil servants in attempting to intervene in that process.

A more pithy view of the same issue is offered by Karen Richardson, 'Alice in Political Land', *Kinesis* vol. 5, no. 53 (March l978).

14For a discussion of feminist businesses and alternative modes of running them, see Jennifer Woodul, 'What's this about Feminist Businesses?' and Maida Tilchen, 'Women's Music: Politics for Sale?', both in Alison Jaggar and Paula Rothenberg, eds, *Feminist Frameworks*, 2nd ed. (New York: McGraw-Hill, 1984).

For a discussion of the impact of government funding on the practice and organization of rape crisis centres, see Toronto Rape Crisis Centre, 'Rape' in Connie Guberman and Marge Wolfe, eds, *No Safe Place* (Toronto: Women's Press, 1985), pp. 82–4.

15See Brown, 'On Lobbying', for a discussion on the importance having public (mass) support in order to exercise power over the government.

16For a discussion of the complexity that characterizes women's relationship to the family, see Meg Luxton, *More Than A Labour of Love: Three Generations of Women's Work in the Home* (Toronto: Women's Press, l980).

17 Statistics on the poverty of single women are common knowledge; statistics pointing out that single women are more mentally healthy than their married sisters, although poorer, are less bruited about. See Dorothy Smith and Sara David, eds, *Women Look at Psychiatry: I'm Not Mad, I'm Angry* (Vancouver: Press Gang, 1975).

18See 'Electoral Exercise' by the Ontario Coalition for Abortion Clinics Coordinating Committee, in *Broadside* vol. 5, no. 10 (Aug./Sept. 1984), p. 5.

19Charlotte Bunch makes the point that 'alternative institutions should not be havens of retreat, but challenges that weaken male power over our lives' ('The Reform Tool Kit', in *Building Feminist Theory: Essays from Quest* [New York: Longman, 1981], quoted in Alison Jaggar, *Feminist Politics and Human Nature* [Totowa, N.J.: Rowman and Allanheld, 1983], p. 336). Recent feminist practice suggests that it is difficult to create an alternative that does not function as a retreat and a haven.

It is interesting to note that Jaggar uses this quote to distinguish between radical-feminist and socialist-feminist alternatives: 'Radical feminists intend their alternative institutions should enable women to withdraw as far as possible from the dominant culture by facilitating women's independence from that culture. . . . Socialist feminists, by contrast, . . . build alternative institutions as a way of partially satisfying existing needs and also as a way of experimenting with new forms of working together' (p. 336).

[20]Lynne Segal discusses this problem with respect to British socialist feminism in *Is The Future Female? Troubled Thoughts on Contemporary Feminism* (London: Virago, 1987), p. 48. A similiar problem within American socialist feminism, but related more to its retreat into academia, is discussed in 'The Impasse of Socialist Feminism, A Conversation with Deirdre English, Barbara Epstein, Barbara Haber and Judy MacLean', *Socialist Review* no. 79, vol.15, no. 1 (Jan.-Feb. 1985).

6

The Ideology of the Women's Movement

While many ideas have come out of the women's movement over the past twenty years, two in particular have stood out as important: 'the personal is political' and 'sisterhood is powerful'. Not only have these ideas been the among the most enduring, but they have also had the widest influence. Indeed, their dominance is such that we would say they have formed a powerful ideological core for the grass-roots women's movement; they have played a key role in shaping the analyses of grass-roots feminism and thus its direction and impact.

But to say these ideas have played a powerful role in shaping the character of grass-roots feminism does not mean that their role has always been positive; in fact, it has been conflicting and ambiguous. On the one hand, as we will show, they offered a powerful challenge to patriarchal capitalism during the early years of the second wave, and in so doing were very important in the emergence of a large and active women's movement. On the other hand, these same ideas have serious limitations as an informing ideology.

This chapter will explore the conflicting role of these ideas. In the first section we will look at 'the personal is political' and its organizational expression, the consciousness-raising group; in the second, at 'sisterhood' and the autonomous women's movement. Each will begin with a look at the formative and positive effect of the idea in question on both our theoretical understanding and our activist approach; we will try to demonstrate why 'the personal is political' and 'sisterhood' had such a dynamic effect on the women's movement, and explore the implications of this dynamism for feminist practice. In particular, we will examine how these ideas fostered a practice that was relevant and involving (mainstreaming), yet at the same time represented a fundamental critique of the existing society and its oppression of women (disengagement). Later in each section we will turn to the limitations of 'the personal is political' and 'sisterhood', and the implications of these limitations for socialist feminism.

'THE PERSONAL IS POLITICAL'

1. The formative role

The catch-phrase 'the personal is political' first emerged during the mid-1960s out of the statements of American feminist organizations such as the Redstockings,[1] and it quickly popularized an understanding about women's oppression that has had far-reaching effects. In particular, this understanding has had a formative influence both on feminist theory and on the emergence and character of a self-conscious grass-roots movement for feminist change.

At the most general level 'the personal is political' was an assertion that the shape of women's personal lives is *not* the result of individual choices, or even 'laws of nature'. In fact, the reverse is true: the overall direction of women's lives—including their ideas, behaviours, and choices—is primarily shaped by the particular way in which society in structured. As it was expressed in the 'Redstockings Manifesto':

> Because we have lived so intimately with our oppressors, in isolation from each other, we have been kept from seeing our personal suffering as a political condition. This creates the illusion that a woman's relationship with her man is a matter of interplay between two unique personalities, and can be worked out individually. In reality, every such relationship is a *class* relationship, and the conflicts between individual men and women are *political* conflicts that can only be solved collectively.[2]

After more than twenty years of struggle by the grass-roots women's movement, this idea of a socially-structured oppression sounds less revolutionary than it did in the late 1960s—although it is still far from universally accepted. At the time, however, 'the personal is political' was nothing less than an ideological watershed. Prevailing theories about the role of women, and of political economy in general, were almost exclusively based on the dominant liberalism: that is, on the separation between the public and the private spheres, the rights and role of the individual, and the concept of governing 'natural' laws. As we discussed earlier, in Chapters 3 and 4, this meant that issues related to family structure, domestic labour, sexuality, and psychology were generally considered to be 'private' or individual areas of concern, and therefore outside the framework of theories that examined political and economic structures and issues. To the extent that these areas were analyzed as social institutions at all, they were seen as essentially autonomous institutions and customs whose development was primarily related to the human (natural) condition and to individual choices, rather than to the nature of the social structures.

For example, people were certainly aware that sexual assault existed. Young women were warned about 'strange' men, and of the dangers lurking in back alleys at night, but discussion of such matters was largely covert, between mother and daughter; the subject was not one for generalized public discussion and intervention. To the degree that sexual assault was publicly acknowledged, however, the conventional wisdom was that it occurred because individual women 'invited' it through some action, such as choosing to walk alone at night, or wearing provocative clothing. Related to this view was a belief in biological imperatives—men are sexual predators and act aggressively by nature. Thus women had to accept being the victims of the immutable 'laws of nature' that determined certain behaviours of the sexes. Change was not possible; the only course open to women was to protect themselves by behaving differently.

Similarly, many believed that women did not have career aspirations because they were not born as ambitious or as intelligent as men. Women's 'natural' role was to nurture, not to lead; this was inherent in male/female hormonal differences. Some also thought that men beat their wives because these women would not submit to the 'natural' order in which the male was dominant over the female. And we could cite dozens of other examples, both major and everyday, in which the assumption was that women's secondary/domestic/passive role was normal, and that women who challenged this role had to take the blame for what happened to them.

'The personal is political', however, challenged the way the private and the public realms were separated into theories of human behaviour and theories of political economy. It argued that the cause of women's problems was neither women themselves nor nature; rather, women were the personal victims of particular political and social structures. Thus violence against women needed to be seen in the context of existing social and ideological structures. It was these structures that gave permission for men to rape and brutalize by objectifying and devaluing women, and by enforcing a power relationship in which men were dominant. In the same way, 'the personal is political' recognized that weaker career aspirations, like passivity and nurturing behaviour, were the logical outcome of female socialization, which trained women from birth to see their futures in terms of being wives and mothers.

Thus 'the personal is political' argued that in order to understand the problems of women—in fact, even to acknowledge their exist-ence—a whole range of questions previously shoved aside as 'pri-vate' had to be analyzed, discussed, and made part of our social theories. Issues of human behaviour and personal interactions could not be left buried in people's private lives, but must be recognized as being socially constructed. 'The personal is political' summarized an important link between personal life and overall political struc-tures, and making this connection had a major impact on the way people understood the world. This change in outlook was reflected in the direction taken by social and political theory, especially with respect to women.

'The personal is political' also challenged the dominant under-standing of how change took place. As the above quotation from the Redstockings Manifesto points out, it suggested that change was not the responsibility of each individual woman and the decisions she made in her own life, nor was it subject to ungovernable 'laws of nature'. In fact, 'personal' concerns were shown to be manifestations of the larger social organization, and revealed as belonging to the 'public', or political, realm. If the lives of women were to be changed in any fundamental way, the social structures that constrained wom-en's choices would have to be changed first. Such change required collective action in the political arena, not individual action in each person's private life.

But the connection between personal problems and political solu-tions did more than direct women's attention towards overall social change: it also helped to break down the numbing isolation of per-sonal experience and to activate women politically. Women were no longer immobilized by the belief that they had only themselves to blame for their difficulties, or that they were helplessly trapped by the natural order of things. Their pain and anger could now be given an external focus and their helplessness transformed into a conviction that social change could be achieved through political action. This change in perception was very liberating and empowering.

The Abortion Caravan of 1970 offers one illustration of the rela-tionship that was effected between women's private experiences and political action. Abortion had long been hidden in back alleys and ignored as a social reality. Women who needed abortions were both isolated and vulnerable; they were also left to assume individual responsibility and blame for the situation in which they had 'placed themselves'. The women's movement changed this by first raising the issue as a social, not an individual, concern, and then taking it across Canada as the focus of a publicly-oriented tour. In making this transition from personal to political, however, the Caravan did not lose its relationship to the personal reality of women. As women travelled with it across Canada, they offered personal stories of the need for abortion, and the horrors of obtaining it illegally, to illustrate the need for change.

However, much of the transformation in political awareness that took place around 'the personal is political' occurred not through such explicitly political campaigns, but rather in connection with consciousness-raising. In fact, the CR format might be seen as the organizational expression of 'the personal is political'. This does not mean that there was a well-organized and sustained network of CR groups in the Canadian women's movement. On the contrary, although the CR group emerged as a unique organizing form early in the women's movement, it has rarely existed as a formal structure in an ongoing way. Nevertheless, there have been many attempts to develop such a structure, and the informal use of CR has continued right up to the present. As Patricia Carey writes:

> The original, formally scheduled meetings attended principally by university-educated women under thirty now take place virtually everywhere—in fact, wherever two or more women are gathered together—at dinner parties, in classrooms, and in editorial rooms. Even glove and hat tea parties reverberate with refrains ranging from sober to hilarious as women name and oppose the patriarchal enemies within themselves as well as without, in the attitudes which colour their environment as well as the institutions which shape it.[3]

Basically, the CR group was a vehicle for women to get together regularly in small groups to talk about their personal experiences and feelings. Instead of internalizing their problems and blaming themselves, through the CR process women learned to share information and experiences. The purpose was not to provide personal therapy, but to allow women to vocalize their often hidden problems and to give them legitimacy beyond each woman's personal experience. As Hester Eisenstein puts it:

> In CR, the point of sharing information about personal life and personal experience was to connect these into something that could transcend the personal. A crucial function of CR was to enable women to connect the personal to the political. Once shared in a small group with other women, individual pain and suffering appeared in a different light. It could be seen that these were not personal, idiosyncratic problems, but ones which fell into a pattern that, with variations, characterized other women's lives as well.[4]

The basis for CR was the belief that the knowledge and ability to create change was rooted in each woman's own experience. The goal was not to study theories of social change and women's oppression, nor was it to recruit women to an organization with already defined goals and strategies outside their frame of reference. On the contrary, the CR process emphasized the need for women to value their *own* perceptions and abilities; it offered them the power to evaluate events and theory on the basis of what they knew from personal experience, and to set their own agendas for change. As the Redstockings Manifesto put it:

> We regard our personal experience, and our feelings about that experience as the basis for an analysis of our common situation. We cannot rely on existing ideologies as they are all products of male supremacist culture. We question every generalization and accept none that are not confirmed by our experience.[5]

Some have suggested that the CR groups isolated women from the 'real' politics of theory and campaigns by focusing on personal issues and experiences. In fact, the reverse is true. Far from being an exercise in self-pity, addressing the significance of personal experience was instrumental in both politicizing and activating women. Most women had been socialized to defer to the knowledge of others and consider their needs as secondary, and it was this view of themselves as unimportant that was depoliticizing. The CR process actually changed that view and consequently empowered women to become politically active. Again, to quote Hester Eisenstein:

> Rather than being the objects of study by psychologists and social scientists, women were the experts, the authorities, the sources of knowledge about themselves. This expertise stemmed, to borrow the title of a work of feminist criticism, from 'the authority of experience'. A woman knew something to be true because she lived through it, and had her own feelings and reactions, rather than the feelings she was supposed to have, or even, than she herself expected to have.[6]

Moreover, as women discovered in CR sessions, it was precisely the separation of these personal issues from the political sphere that permitted the oppression of women to remain invisible:

> Many of the crucial elements of the new knowledge about women's situation contributed by the women's movement were accumulated through accounts first garnered in consciousness-raising groups. The number of women who had abortions, when this was illegal and a taboo subject for discussion; the number of women who had been raped, often by people well-known to them and trusted; the number

of women who had experienced incest, or sexual molestation, within their families, by fathers, brothers, uncles, or other male relatives; the number of women who had been beaten or otherwise physically abused by their husbands—all of these intimate and 'shameful' facts about the lives of individual women, by means of the process of consciousness-raising, and the principles of sharing personal experience, could be seen in a different light. These were not isolated phenomena, illustrating the individual failure of an individual woman within her own family to direct her own life correctly. They were symptoms of a society-wide structure of power and powerlessness, in which *the victimization of women by the men holding the power of official authority, whether husband or public official, was hidden from public view by the mechanism of privatization.*[7]

As long as the structure and role of the family and sexuality in society was not discussed, there were no issues or categories by which to identify women's oppression. By encouraging women to speak about what were apparently 'personal' problems, and by discovering the common character of these experiences, the CR process played a key role in exposing the institutionalized, entrenched oppression of women in our society.

However, exposing the link between women's personal problems and the existing social structures did more than change women's attitudes towards political action—it actually changed the character and scope of political life itself. One example can be seen in the way grass-roots feminists of the late 1960s and early 1970s challenged the social roles assigned to them as women. As feminists gained more understanding of how the social structure penetrated even the most 'private' aspects of life—particularly within the family and sexual relationships—they confronted traditional norms directly. Dress codes, the sexual double standard, monogamy and marriage, compulsory heterosexuality, job definitions, language, beauty contests, the sexual division of labour—all were rejected. Friends, partners, political allies—all were challenged to accommodate the 'new' woman. Although the effort was often tiring and painful, the courage and audacity feminists showed in struggling with the shape of their personal lives were often astounding, and helped to pull women together.

Like consciousness-raising itself, however, this questioning of personal life patterns and choices was frequently called 'apolitical', 'extremist', and even 'ridiculous' by those affronted by such a challenge to long-held prejudices. In fact, the confrontation of traditional norms for females was none of these; the social and personal storm generated by this defiance played a very important role in changing the way politics itself was defined. Since politics did not traditionally include issues of the kind that concerned feminists—as then-Prime Minister Trudeau said, 'The state does not belong in the bedrooms of the nation'—it was necessary to widen the boundaries of what were considered to be political issues. The double day of labour, marriage, sexual harassment, sex-role socialization, and sexuality are all examples of issues that the women's movement confronted in its rejection of defined social roles for female, and that have now been moved out of the privacy of the home into the political realm.

Equally important, these challenges helped women to recognize that political struggle does not take place only in what is traditionally understood as the 'political' sphere. Political action did not need to be restricted to government and elections; it was now seen to include public acts of defiance of all kinds, and in a variety of arenas. The early acts of personal rebellion not only confronted people's preconceptions and forced them to examine the limitations of their thinking; they also took politics into the streets, the schools, and the bedrooms. Ultimately, women's understanding of the scope of political activism was altered and enlarged.

In retrospect, then, it is clear that 'the personal is political' and the CR group were important ideological acquisitions for the grassroots movement, and central to the appeal and character of the women's movement as a whole during its formative stages. In particular, these ideas have had three positive and dynamic effects. First, by challenging the concept of the separation between the public and private spheres, and thus bringing the two together, 'the personal is political' has had a transformative effect on political and social theory. Second, it has refocused women's attention, away from personal solutions and towards a strategy of collective political action. At the same time, the political front itself has been redefined and enlarged to include a wide range of so-called 'personal' issues and extra-parliamentary actions. Finally, women's growing awareness of the connection between their personal problems and a socially constructed oppression of women has been instrumental in actually mobilizing them as active participants in their own struggle for liberation.

2. Implications for feminist practice

The early success of the women's movement in creating a large social struggle for change is instructive for feminist activists today, and in this section we will look at those aspects of 'the personal is political' and consciousness-raising that contributed to this success.

One obvious factor was the ability of 'the personal is political' and CR to link the individual experiences of each woman's life to the wider political context, and thus make sense of them. This link was essential because it provided women with a sense of the direction they needed to take and thus made it possible for them to act together to create change; indeed, without this overview tying together the scattered details of women's experiences, there would have been a continued sense of isolation and helplessness.

On the other hand, the success of these ideas is also a reminder that visions of change need to be rooted in the reality of personal experience. A critique that does not resonate with personal experience is often received with apathy; it is the emotional depth of those experiences that actually fuels the struggle for change. And in this respect the CR group proved a particularly successful organizing vehicle in the earlier period. The more structured political organizations and campaigns that developed later have been essential in co-ordinating and extending the efforts of those women who had already been reached by the ideas of women's liberation, but it was the personal appeal of CR that made it possible to reach and ultimately activate those women in the first place. The reason 'the personal is political' and CR had such an enormous effect on the numbers of women who became active was precisely that they focused attention on issues in which women had vested interest and insight.

In short, then, the success of 'the personal is political' and CR illustrates the importance of developing an analysis of power and vision of change in terms that both include and adequately account for women's actual experience; in other words, the importance of reconciling a politic of disengagement with one of mainstreaming.

The other factor in the success of these ideas was their ability to define a viable and acceptable alternative to the existing ideology and structures of change. And here the fact that 'the personal is political' and CR offered women a personal stake in seeking change was again significant. The point is that CR did not create issues, but acted as a mechanism by which women identified the issues that were most important in their experience, and linked those issues to a larger vision of social change. Nor was this an abstract exercise: in creating this connection the CR process had a transforming effect on women's sense of identity and involvement.

Patricia Carey describes the role of this type of subjective transformation as follows:

> [W]omen could dissociate themselves from feminism as long as they
> believed they, personally, had never been oppressed. . . . When the
> penny finally did drop, we saw that being labelled a dyke, bitch or
> castrator was not worse than being Woman, Other, Outside to male
> values, institutions and respect. At this point of recognition—of iden-
> tifying with the oppressed—a great dividing line separating women
> occurs. Those who make that identification become unapologetic,
> self-declared feminists, almost without exception permanently active
> in feminist causes. Those who do not, say, 'I believe in equal pay for
> equal work, but. . . .'[8]

This involvement, of course, contrasted vividly with the existing
political process in which the theories, programs for change, and
issues of concern were removed from the reality of people's everyday lives and often very remote from the problems faced by women.
In fact, as we have seen, the prevailing ideology of change is based
on the separation of public (political) life and private life—an idea
that renders the oppression of women invisible, and serves to demobilize any impetus for change.

Moreover, this ideology offered women a sense of their own
agency in creating change; they could see that they had a personal
role in both creating and defining political change. In fact, both 'the
personal is political' and consciousness-raising were based on the
concept that the impetus for struggle comes directly from women
themselves, rather than from some outside force.

This practice of indigenous or self- organizing for social change
presented another contrast to the prevailing ideology of change;
specifically, to the idea of being governed by an elected government
of representatives. Representative government was essentially non-
participatory: it distanced people from the act of making change and
tended to engender feelings of ineffectiveness and disinterest. By
defining a role for women in making change, 'the personal is political' and CR acted as antidotes to this political apathy—a fact that
was critical to the capacity of the early grass-roots movement to
develop a collective and participatory approach to making change.

At the same time, however, it was clear that the struggle for change
was to take place at the social level, not the private one. 'The personal
is political' and CR created links among women who were angry
about their lives, and directed that anger out towards the political or

social arena, rather than inwards to the individual herself. By offering such a powerful challenge to the prevailing emphasis on making change through individual choices and actions, both 'the personal is political' and CR helped to counteract women's sense of powerlessness and isolation.

3. Limitations of 'the personal is political'

Yet the role of 'the personal is political' as an informing ideology of the women's movement is not so unambiguously positive as the foregoing might suggest. In fact, far from keeping the women's movement on a consistent path, this ideology has itself been reshaped in the context of different feminist currents. And in the course of this reshaping, the emphasis in 'the personal is political' has tended to shift away from the relationship between personal experience and the nature of the social structures, to centre on the importance of the personal side of the equation only. The result has been a loss of much of the power of these ideas to mobilize an effective feminist movement for change.

In this section we will explore how 'the personal is political' and consciousness-raising have been reinterpreted in the context of different feminisms, and how these interpretations have altered the balance between the personal and the political. We will also explore the implications of this reinterpretation, in particular the way in which renewed stress on the role of personal change strengthens both the push towards marginalization and the pull towards institutionalization.

The push towards marginalization. As we discussed earlier, an essential component of 'the personal is political' and consciousness-raising is the emphasis on connecting women's actual experiences with the overall structures that define their lives. Women used their experiences and, more particularly, the commonality of their experiences both as a means to critically evaluate prevailing ideologies and as a basis on which to develop generalized, or social, explanations. Or, as Nancy Hartsock puts it:

> At bottom, feminism is a *mode of analysis*, a method of approaching life and politics, rather than a set of political conclusions about the oppression of women. . . . [I]n this way, feminism provides us with a way to understand our anger and direct our anger and energy toward change.[9]

Critical to this method of inquiry were the assumptions that all experience was valid input, that experience was an important measure of the accuracy of theory, and that the structure of feminist groups must facilitate speaking out about experience. Kate Lindeman talks about the ways in which the structure of consiousness-raising groups was set up to encourage women to share their knowledge:

> First, the experience is more than communal, it is collective. . . . Second, the group is dialogic and it is without a formal, appointed leader. Honest, mutual sharing without regard to status has been freeing and has generated keen insights for such groups. Third, the group emphasizes non-judgemental listening to the naming of personal experience by other members. All experience, as long as it is owned by someone, is worthy subject matter. Fourth, in the consideration of someone's experience, members respond with supportive, collaborative experience, or with questions to aid clarification or critical reflection. They do not seek to tell, to 'narrate answers to another'.[10]

Over time, however, the relationship between personal experience, theory, and feminist analysis has shifted. Rather than being seen as offering two separate, but mutually enhancing, approaches to analysis, theory and experience are frequently counterposed. And many feminists now view experience as the *only* authentic guide to understanding and organizing around oppression.

This emphasis on experience frequently expresses itself in the suggestion that one cannot understand or comment on a particular form of oppression with any authority if one does not have personal experience of it. Thus a man cannot understand women's oppression; heterosexuals cannot relate to the discrimination faced by lesbians; a white cannot comment on racism; and so on. The impetus for this shift towards experience is understandable and, in fact, the point has validity: the abstractions of theory have allowed women's oppression—and that of others—to remain invisible, and the elevation of theoretical knowledge has worked to exclude the oppressed from power. Indeed, it was precisely for these reasons that women developed and codified the practice of consciousness-raising.

However, making experience the dominant criterion for understanding and organizing around oppression is also problematic. First, experience does not always act as a source of added strength and richness; rather, in the context of an increasingly heterogeneous movement, it can act as a divisive and exclusionary force. Thus the many different experiences women now bring to the movement have added important new dimensions to overall feminist analysis, but they have also served to separate feminists into myriad small groups, each organized around a separate category of experience. This has made it difficult to attract new activists: they often do not have a niche to fit into, or cannot relate to groups they perceive as being isolated and having no common perspective apart from a shared experience of oppression. The same emphasis on experience often inhibits feminists from building social and political alliances with others who do not share their experience of oppression (and thus their central strategic focus). For example, trade-union women who see their relationship with men in a different light from other feminists because of the intersecting oppression of class may be unwilling to take part in an action that excludes men from participation.

These divisions within feminism are only exacerbated by the judgemental attitude that has crept in alongside the emphasis placed on experience as the basis for analysis and practice. It shows up in a tendency to evaluate political positions on strongly personal grounds—for example, to dismiss a woman's political point of view on the basis of her class, race, or sexual preference. It is also evidenced in the fights that can erupt over degrees of oppression, or in guilt-ridden discussions of who is more oppressed than who. Lynne Segal quotes Pratibha Parmer, a black feminist in Britain:

> One of the results of only focusing on separate oppressions is retrogressive. Women have got into hierarchies of oppression saying, 'I'm more oppressed than you because I've got more labels and oppressed status'. I think that has been totally wrong and negative.[11]

The question of the proper feminist attitude towards men, and especially their role in the struggle for women's liberation, has been one particularly volatile area of difficulty; another has been the question of lesbianism and heterosexuality. More recently, racism within the women's movement has occasioned much discussion and debate.

Personal challenge has been an important tactic of the women's movement and has been used effectively to confront prejudices in the world at large and within the movement itself. However, when personal challenge becomes rejection, and when actual experience of oppression becomes the passport to political legitimacy, that effectiveness is lost. Not only does this create a situation in which women may actually be afraid of change because it threatens the political status they appear to gain through their experience of oppression, but the personal edge to political criticism also helps to create a fear and avoidance of political debates. This can only be destructive to the women's movement. The problem is that you cannot make 'wrong attitudes' go away by burying them—on the contrary, failure to discuss issues openly and politically ends up alienating women from each other. Moreover, as we have seen, such tendencies only demobilize activists and drive them away, leaving feminist groups even more isolated and ineffective—that is, marginalized.

In addition, this type of debate is misleading. It focuses feminists' attention on the problems within our organizations, turning feminist against feminist, rather than on the social structures that create and sustain the oppression. The power of 'the personal is political' lay in its ability to cut across the isolation of individual experience, and to situate that experience in the context of a socially contructed oppression of women. By isolating experience and saying that it alone constitutes valid political analysis, we undermined this power. Rather than being a springboard for uniting women in a common struggle for change, the value now placed on personal experience often serves to separate women into their different and isolated realities.

A second problem with emphasizing the personal side of 'the personal is political' is the suggestion that change occurs at the level of the individual. Thus personal choices become essential political acts: if each woman were to change her attitudes, her practices, and her choices, then the society as a whole would be changed. Confronting compulsory heterosexuality, monogamy, marriage, and the family—even clothing and makeup, language, male/female behaviour norms: the individual decisions each feminist makes on these issues become key to challenging women's oppression. In this view women's liberation will occur only when women refuse to be complicit in their own oppression and take steps to change their lives as individuals.

As we have already noted, however, a view of change that places the responsibility for change on the individual is in itself isolating and demobilizing. The notion that a woman's failure to make personal change means she is letting down the whole of womankind only increases the pressure she experiences, and certainly makes it difficult to attract and sustain women in struggle. The following selection outlines a common feeling:

> Partly because feminism was addressing more personal issues, and partly because there was kind of transformative zeal to the women's movement, I felt utterly shut out, and told to run my own life in a way that I didn't want to run it, told that I was a traitor when I tried to pursue issues that seemed very important to me. So I had a lot of bitterness about the women's movement.[12]

Even when the personal changes demanded of individual women are situated within a framework of support from other feminists—as can happen in the alternative feminist communities developed in the radical-feminist model—the pressures of 'living the revolution' can be severe. The personal upheaval and sacrifice required remain significant and, in fact, the co-terminous character of political and personal relationships makes it difficult to avoid acrimony and judgemental overtones, both of which are divisive for the feminist community itself and unattractive to those outside. The net result is that, despite the time, energy and personal struggle involved in developing feminist alternatives, these feminist nucleii remain on the fringes of struggle. In the end, as more and more feminists leave, the primary goal of many of the collectives often becomes the continued existence of the group itself.

But the emphasis on personal life change also seriously misrepresents the nature of women's oppression. Johanna Brand and Ester Koulack noted this problem in their summary of a speech made by Angela Miles:

> . . .they [radical feminists] erred in overemphasizing the importance of personal life. Personal action and lifestyle became their political statement. What follows from this is that women are responsible for their own oppression.[13]

Or, as Lynne Segal puts it:

> An emphasis on interpersonal behaviour, on racism or on class privilege within feminism is misleading if it encourages only individualistic, moralistic self-blame and proposes only personal solutions. For we are up against something much larger if we want to confront the underlying structures of class or race, or of gender domination.[14]

However, to argue that the shift towards the personal in 'the personal is political' has been negative for the women's movement does not mean that the ways in which women experience oppression on the personal level should be ignored. In fact, as the first section of this chapter argues, the reverse is true: the relating of personal experience has been a foundation stone in building both analyses of women's oppression and relevant programs for change. As Barbara Haber argues:

> If the core of the early phase of the feminists movement was the critique of personal life, particularly the family and heterosexual relations, this was neither arbitrary not subjectivist. A politics that attempts to understand and act upon the interwoven systems of class

and sexual oppression must have at its center a cogent analysis of the family and sexual relationships between women and men. It must also have programs aimed at changing the structure and function of those relationships, that offer practical alternatives to them.[15]

Nor does it mean that feminists should not attempt to provide organizational and personal alternatives to the prevailing hierarchical and authoritarian structures. As we will discuss in the next chapter, feminist process has played an important role in building struggle for change. It is also true that struggle at the personal level has helped to bring about the range of feminist services, cultural alternatives, and lifestyle options that women now enjoy. Radical feminism in particular has been responsible for the continued high profile of 'personal' issues and the creation of feminist alternatives.

There is a difference, however, between building alternatives outside the existing society and using alternative forms to help meet the existing needs of women within that society. Proponents of the latter acknowledge that change will not be fully possible until the structures themselves are changed, but recognize the importance of beginning to confront the values engendered by the structure of power in present society. As Patricia Carey puts it:

> Few radical political movements are naive enough to believe revolution in political economic structures is sufficient to change the myriad superstructures—religion, culture, education, language, media—which reinforce governing insitutions. Yet anti-war protesters never fought the private sphere conditioning that breeds boys into soldiers. The New Left (male) leadership was notorious for exploiting women's volunteering and for treating women as a lower class. . . . Conversely, feminists viewed consistency between personal and public revolution as a first principle.[16]

The point remains, though, that an over-emphasis on the personal sphere contributes to the very problem that 'the personal is political' initially resolved: the isolation of individual women in personal struggle to make change and to control their own lives. As we have argued, this is demobilizing and demoralizing for activists; it is not an attractive or effective strategy. Moreover, the elevation of personal experience over theory often masks the underlying forces at work and affords little possibility of understanding different sets of power relations, which may not be part of personal experience. This limits the possibilities for creating an overall movement for social change.

The pull of institutionalization. Nevertheless, in the long term perhaps marginalization in itself is not the biggest problem to result from the increased emphasis on personal change. Rather, it is the failure of this revamped ideology to resist the pull towards institutionalization of feminist demands for change.

Earlier in this chapter we discussed the ways in which 'the personal is political' confronted three central concepts of the ideology of change: the strong belief in individual, rather than social, change; the separation of the private and public, with government intervention in the private strictly limited; and the development of representative democracy to deal with public matters. Critical to this challenge was the way 'the personal is political' situated women's personal experiences in a larger political context, and thus oriented women towards a collective struggle for social change. However, as the emphasis in 'the personal is political' has shifted away from changing society and towards women changing themselves, this tension has been lost. 'The personal is political' no longer offers a serious challenge to the prevailing ideology of change and, as a consequence, can offer no alternative vision capable of offsetting the pressure to conform to the ideological and structural framework that currently prevails.

In fact, the shift in the meaning of 'the personal is political' has actually opened up the possibilities for the institutional reconstruction of feminist demands for change. Whereas once the dominant vision of feminism was one of overall social change and collective action, today the public view of the women's movement is increasingly narrowly defined. The powerful image of the modern superwoman—a strong individual, independent, a trail-blazer who makes things happen for herself—is right in keeping with both the emphasis on individualism in our society and the myths of equality of opportunity and the power of effort.

Barbara Ehrenreich's ideas concerning the changes that have been wrought in feminism have been summarized by Brand and Koulack:

> When the economic expansion to the late 1960s allowed women greater access to the labour market, the cultural ideal also changed. The first inkling of the new image came. . .with the publication of Helen Gurley Brown's *Sex and the Single Girl*. It was the first voice representing a new possibility for women.
>
> Not threatened by this change, capitalism was quick to coopt the demands of the women's movement. In the *Ladies Home Journal*, the words, 'Ladies Home' shrank in size until they are now almost undecipherable. Today's reader is 'the woman who never stands still'. She combines career, children, family, fashion, and consumerism—above

all, consumerism. More consumer goods could be sold to individuals living alone, and to working woman with their own incomes. . . .

Again the psycho-medical establishment provided the 'scientific' rationale. Pop psychology encouraged women to put their own needs first, to take assertiveness training, to do her own thing.[17]

As we discussed in the previous chapter, this institutionalized version of feminism is not only insufficient to end the oppression of women, but does not even address the reality of most women's lives. In fact, Karen Dubinsky quotes Ehrenreich as follows:

Outside the middle classes, lifestyle feminism [also known as the superwoman phenomenon] can be actively repellent. If feminism is for women who are slender, 'intelligent' and upwardly mobile and you are over forty, perhaps overweight and locked into a dead end job and/or marriage then you are more likely to see feminism as a putdown than a sisterly call to arms.[18]

But this institutionalization has also had another, more subtle effect. As feminists observe the way personal life issues are manipulated to serve the needs of the political mainstream, they have become more wary of any struggle on this ground at all. Personal lifestyle struggle of the kind exemplified in the pages of the *Toronto Life* or *Chatelaine* is characterized as 'middle class'. At best it is seen as having no relevance to the lives of working-class women and therefore no role in building a mass movement for change; at worst it is seen as separating us from the realities faced by working women and cutting us off from any future access. As Barbara Haber puts it:

[A more overt political justification] might go like this: 'Only our middle class privilege lets us indulge in that critique and those experimental living situations anyway. Our experience is largely irrelevant to the mass of women who work at regular jobs or who depend on a husband to support them and their children. If we persist in criticizing the family and motherhood we make those women feel guilty and resentful, and we make ourselves politically useless.'[19]

In fact, this characterization is somewhat dangerous. In the first place, working-class, immigrant, poor, lesbian, and black women all face the personal realities of the sexual division of labour and the double day of work, the double standard and marriage inequalities, issues of mental health and psychological treatment, sex-role stereotyping, and so on; day-care, sexuality, and control over reproduction are not issues only for upwardly-mobile career women.

Indeed, many of them are more serious for those who have fewer financial and social resources to combat them.

But there is more at issue here than falling victim to stereotypes. As we discussed in the first part of this section, the struggle around so-called personal issues has played and continues to play a key role in the politicization and mobilization of women. It is important that the women's movement retain the 'personal' roots to its struggle, since it is precisely those roots that have allowed it to gain the mass support necessary to challenge the institutions of power. Moreover, failure to confront 'personal' issues threatens to bring the women's struggle back full circle to the point where we have no categories to identify our oppression. If we have learned nothing else, we have learned that the oppression of women is masked—and often buried—by the privatization of so-called 'personal' issues. At the same time, however, it is important that we not allow these issues to be trivialized as nothing more than 'lifestyle' questions.

4. Implications for socialist feminists

In summary, we would argue that 'the personal is political' has played a contradictory role as an informing ideology of the women's movement. At times it has seemed to focus on the social character of women's oppression, and tied the personal/private realm together with the overall political/public one. In this way it has helped to resolve the central dilemma of feminist practice—that is, the need both to appeal to and mobilize large numbers of women (mainstream) and to offer a critique of the system (disengage). At these times the mass movement for social change has been powerful and dynamic.

At other times, however, 'the personal is political' has been interpreted to mean that personal life experiences and struggle are the keys to making change. As a result women's attention was turned inwards towards the differences in experience within the women's movement, or alternatively, towards finding individual solutions outside the movement. The one led to fragmentation and marginalization; the other, to institutionalization.

The ambiguity of 'the personal is political' and consciousness-raising has been confusing for socialist feminists. On the one hand, history suggests that practice should be clearly oriented around a critique of the overall system, and should avoid the dangers inherent in focusing on personal life solutions. Yet it is also clear that relating to the concrete reality of women's lives has been a key to mobilizing women in collective struggle for social change. Thus there is a tension between identifying the personal roots to struggle and 'bending the stick too far'; it is an ongoing struggle to maintain the balance in the relationship between the personal and political.

Ultimately, of course, this ambiguity stems from the fact that, as an ideology to inform analysis and strategy, 'the personal is political' is insufficient to deal with the complexity of the power relations of patriarchal capitalism. 'The personal is political' may suggest that there is a relationship between women's private lives and the structure of power, but it does not identify the precise nature of that structure. Thus it is possible for radical feminists to put 'the personal is political' in the context of male-female power relations, while socialist feminists would situate it within their analysis of different but intersecting relations of power. It is these differences in the analysis of power—that is, the definition of 'political'—that results in different interpretations and strategies, rather than some inherent contradiction.

These limitations do not mean that 'the personal is political' must be rejected as part of feminist ideology. On the contrary, the very valuable role it is capable of playing must be acknowledged. However, it is important for socialist feminists to keep 'the personal is political' firmly within the context of an overall social and political analysis and sense of strategy.

'SISTERHOOD IS POWERFUL'

1. The effect of 'sisterhood'

Like 'the personal is political', the cry 'sisterhood is powerful' arose early in the history of the re-emerging women's movement, as women began to uncover and react to the discrimination they faced because of their sex. And, also like 'the personal is political', it has exercised a formative influence on both the theoretical and the political development of the women's movement.

First and foremost, the idea of 'sisterhood' asserted that womanhood itself formed a basis that united all women; it acknowledged that there is a common character to women's experiences, and hence a fundamental bond. But 'sisterhood' also symbolized a rejection of the isolation and powerlessness women felt because of the dominant and intensely privatized character of their relationships with men. 'Sisterhood is powerful' was a rallying call for women to move outside those relationships and seek change in a political alliance with other women.

Fundamentally, then, the concept of 'sisterhood' established womanhood as the basis of a common oppression and a common struggle. It not only formed an analytical basis for understanding that women constituted a specific *group* facing a common and unique oppression; it also had a strategic component as 'womanhood' was seen as a basis on which women could unite as a force to fight their oppression.

The profound effect that 'sisterhood' has had in social and political analysis is evidenced simply in the quantity of material for, by, and specifically about women. The common nature of women's experience and situation has acted as the starting-point for a great deal of the analysis of women's oppression, and has resulted in an enormous increase in understanding of the nature and manifestations of women's oppression. In fact, the interest in women's role and place in society was instrumental in creating that completely new field known as 'women's studies'.

But the focus on the category of 'woman' has brought about some very significant changes in social and political theory more generally. For example, radical feminism has developed an analysis of patriarchy that is centred on the idea of women as a social class. Socialist feminism initially represented a fusion between an analysis of the sexual division of power and one centred on class. As we pointed out in Chapter 3, this analysis has now developed into one dealing with all the complex relations of power under patriarchal capitalism, and how they intersect with the structure of power around gender/sex. But even proponents of traditional theories based on liberal individualism have frequently been forced to change. They have had to acknowledge the existence of women as a distinct category and adjust their analyses to account for this. Thus history is now written to include women; there are studies that deal with the socialization process as it relates to sex roles; management theory deals with the style and psychology of the female executive; sociological studies identify single women as among the poorest in Canada; and so on.

'Sisterhood' also had an impact on the character of feminist activism in that it centred attention on issues that specifically addressed the needs of women, and organized women as a group to fight for these issues. Thus feminists have organized primarily around concerns such as access to abortion and birth control, issues of sexuality and marriage, sex-role stereotyping, and equal opportunity for women.

Building the autonomous women's movement was the logical organizational and strategic extension of 'sisterhood'. Initially, the notion of organizing as a distinct group grew out of a simple practical need to separate from men so that women could develop their own skills and leadership abilities, rather than get the coffee and type.

However, the desire to separate went further than just creating an opportunity for women to develop skills. Politically, it was clear that if there were to be a serious struggle around 'women's issues', then women would have to organize that struggle on their own. At first the move to organize independently was a somewhat *ad hoc* reaction against the tendency of men in both mainstream and protest groups to ignore women's issues or to tell women what to do. This was women's struggle, and they could—and would—determine its direction.

Judith Quinlan summarizes the argument:

> We built an autonomous women's movement for the following reasons:
> - because experience had taught us that even within the most liberal of male-led freedom movements, the concerns of women were always ignored, sometimes even resisted;
> - because we understood that the oppression of women was and is basic to the maintenance of all power hierarchies in the world, and that the best way to fight this was as women;
> - because 'including' men always meant excluding some women (particularly lesbian women, but many others too). And our first concern is always for our sisters;
> - because we have seen that even allowing a single well-meaning man into our groups means that many others follow, and soon they assert their birthright of telling us what to do;
> - because we understood that men had gone far riding on the apron strings of women but, like all good mothers, we must push them out of the nest to fend for themselves. Men had to 'grow up' politically and the existence of an independent women's movement gives them the opportunity to do just that.[20]

But the process gradually assumed more formal dimensions as women increasingly asserted their right to define their own issues and organize in their own interests. Building the autonomous women's movement became a strategy for the women's movement, a strategy that reflected a growing awareness of collective oppression and the need for social change. Women saw themselves as an independent movement that was important in its own right and refused to take a back seat to other social and political struggles. And the building of an autonomous movement, with its separate political and organizational identity and its focus on women's issues, did have a huge impact on the numbers of women who became active in the cause for women's rights. In the first place, independent organizing by women for women reinforced the sense of collective power suggested by 'sisterhood'; this was a powerful antidote to the feelings of isolation and powerlessness that women normally experienced. Second, the autonomous women's movement formed a base from which women could raise and define issues on their own terms. The separate organization of women for women was the most effective mechanism for uniting women in struggle against their oppression and ensuring that their voice was heard. Issues did not become buried in a welter of other concerns, or become a hodge-podge of bits and pieces. The fact that these issues were defined by women themselves, not some outside 'authority', has also helped to ensure their continued relevance .

But as the women's movement developed an independent political identity and strength, 'autonomous' came to mean more than organizing separately around women's issues. It came to mean rejecting ways of organizing that were hierarchical, bureaucratic, and competitive. These were precisely the mechanisms used to exclude women from power, and the desire grew to set up alternative structures that would reflect the principles of 'sisterhood' and encourage the participation and development of women. To that end, feminist groups experimented with consensus politics, collective leadership, circle structures, 'leaderless' groupings, and so on. As we will discuss in the next chapter, feminist process and organizing principles formed an important part of the growth and success of the women's movement. The emphasis on sisterhood contributed to a sense of personal safety and helped to develop women's leadership abilities. This, along with the sense of being part of a collective struggle for change, encouraged the participation of greater numbers of women.

Finally, it is important to note that 'sisterhood' began to develop on a personal level as well as a political and organizational one. Women formed networks of friendship and support, provided services for women in difficulty, and helped each other sort through the maze of personal issues. The starting point for these relationships was often the CR session. Women had always formed mutual support systems and friendships, but these networks were different from those of the past.[21] They were not oriented towards 'helping each other out' when husband, house, or children got to be too much, but towards helping each other struggle against helplessness and dependency and providing a base of strength on which to build a struggle for liberation. The personal recognition of another woman as a 'sister' and the sense of personal belonging that came from those friendship networks were very important reinforcements to the growing political ties.

As we have talked about it above, 'sisterhood' took three different forms, each of which played an important role in defining the character of the political challenge offered by the early grass-roots movement. First, 'sisterhood' had an *ideological* component in that it identified and popularized the fact that, as a group, women were oppressed. This contrasted with the prevailing ideology of change and its denial of power structures, and provided a social critique around which women could build a struggle for change. 'Sisterhood' also had an *organizational* component: the building of the autonomous women's movement was both the strategic and structural extension of 'sisterhood'. That is, the autonomous women's movement functioned both as an alternative to existing organizational structures and practices, in its emphasis on non-hierarchical and co-operative process, and as the means by which large numbers of women could unite in collective struggle to make change. Finally, 'sisterhood' had a *lifestyle* component, as women developed personal friendships and support networks with other women. In summary, 'sisterhood' could be said to have structured a powerful feminist critique of the society. Yet at the same time it helped the movement to define issues that were relevant and to develop supportive organizational process.

2. *The limitations of 'sisterhood'*

With the benefit of hindsight, it is now clear that while 'sisterhood' and autonomy made important contributions to the political character of the earlier stages of the women's movement, over the longer term this ideology has not proved to be a sufficient basis around which to structure feminist practice for change. In fact, the emphasis placed on 'sisterhood' and on building the autonomous women's movement has at times created serious political and strategic barriers to developing an effective strategy for social change.

The push towards marginalization. One obstacle posed by 'sisterhood' has been its tendency to suggest an analysis that implicitly, if not explicitly, identifies women as a class within a patriarchal structure of power, and thus to suggest a strategy centred on gender/sexual politics. The locus of power in this approach is situated in the hands of men; the struggle to be waged is against men, or at least against the institutions of the patriarchal structure that give men their power, in particular regarding the family and sexuality.

This analysis has implications for building the autonomous women's movement. Rather than simply expressing the desire to maintain control over the direction of the struggle for liberation, 'autonomous' comes to mean 'separate' and imply a strategy of building feminist alternatives outside male-dominated culture. As the following excerpt from an article by the Political Action Committee of the Ottawa Women's Centre suggests, sisterhood is seen as the basis for establishing boundaries between the women and the rest of patriarchal society, and for building the power of women to reject their oppression:

> Sisterhood is the only viable option we have. . . . We must work together to become the women we would all like to be, and in the process make outselves into a united group of feminists whose growing strength allows us to deny the patriarchy its power over us.
>
> Sisterhood is both the end and the means of our struggle. What are we working for? How do we want to live? We must begin to fantasize in more detail, develop our embryonic ideas of what life could be like without patriarchal oppression, so we know what living in sisterhood could be like. . . . Then we must begin to develop small pockets where we can turn our dreams into reality for at least some women, some of the time.
>
> By withdrawing our labour (underpaid and undervalued as it is) from our oppressors, and by refusing to enter the race, we can damage the capitalist patriarchy and leave ourselves free for some satisfying work and some good times.[22]

In fact, this approach was the basis on which many women's services and businesses were developed. They were intended as alternatives for women—alternatives structured outside male-dominated institutions and culture and reflecting women's priorities as defined by women. They were women-organized and women-led; their structures were based on the principles of sisterhood. One prime example is the network of Rape Crisis Centres. But the list of feminist alternatives also includes publishing houses, coffee houses, film-makers, newspapers, credit unions, musical groups, housing co-operatives, and more.

Nor is the separate organizing of women related simply to service or cultural alternatives within the women's movement itself; it can be extended to include creating feminist unions and feminist political parties outside the traditional (male) structures. A 'women-only' orientation is even reflected in the types of support given to other struggles. For example, some feminists who offered serious support to the Fleck women strikers were reluctant to get involved with the support organization created by wives of INCO workers on strike in 1978.

However, the fact that 'sisterhood' tends to see women's oppression as being structured around gender relations means that a great deal of feminism's political activity is not centred around traditional institutions or forums at all. Rather than orienting towards government or the workplace, 'sisterhood' focuses attention on sexuality and the family—areas that are central to the oppression of women as women.

We have already outlined some of the marginalizing tendencies inherent in a strategy of building feminist alternatives. What is now clear is that part of the reason these alternatives lack relevance and appeal has to do with the concept of a fundamental 'sisterhood' of women. One problem is that, although the intent of 'sisterhood' was to emphasize women's common oppression as a fundamental basis for unity in struggle, it is soon apparent that this vision does not reflect the reality. There are, in fact, significant differences in the situation and interests of different groups of women, and 'sisterhood' is unable to account for or accommodate them within its analytic and strategic framework.

Much of the difficulty here stems from that fact that the basis of 'sisterhood' is fundamentally biological; socially specific factors do not enter into its analysis of power. That is, 'sisterhood' assumes that women's common biology gives them a basic shared interest that crosses over different historical periods and social situations. This assumption becomes the basis for building a movement that defines its audience and membership as female, and the terrain of its struggle as primarily matters of concern to women: the 'autonomous women's movement'.

'Sisterhood', then, means that feminists have no way of understanding differences in power other than those related to gender, except on an 'add-on' basis. In other words, while 'sisterhood' allows for the fact that black and immigrant women, lesbians, and working-class women may have a more difficult time in terms of the degree to which they experience oppression, it does not acknowledge that the character of their oppression is different in any substantive way from that of all 'sisters'. As a basic view of the structure of power, therefore, 'sisterhood' is not inclusive, but very exclusive.

This narrow view also means that, as a central rallying cry, 'sisterhood' actually appeals to a very limited audience. Women of colour, married women, lesbians, mothers, older women, disabled women, trade-union women, and immigrant women are among those who find that 'sisterhood' does not address the overall reality of power as they experience it. In fact, their gender is often not the issue of most immediate significance in their lives, and they are not attracted by a movement that stresses gender issues to the point of excluding other aspects of social reality. Thus, despite the fact that it purports to deal with all women, 'sisterhood' has not only limited the ability of feminists to relate to large numbers of women (mainstreaming), but has actively distanced many. In other words, the ideology of 'sisterhood' often serves to marginalize the women's movement.

Moreover, the inability of 'sisterhood' to accommodate different sets of power relations is divisive. Sometimes this divisiveness takes the form of open competition as each group tries to establish the importance of its specific form of oppression—a sort of hierarchy of oppressions. But often the conflict is rooted in an inability to acknowledge the differences in the realities that women face. By glossing over these differences in search of an undifferentiated sisterhood, the movement renders the concerns of these groups invisible within the women's struggle, and creates a situation characterized by dissension and animosity. One example of the tension that can develop can been seen in the struggle by lesbians to have their specific oppression identified and incorporated into the overall struggle for women's liberation. This was a painful process, but it pointed out that the desire for community alone is not sufficient to offset the reality of difference within feminism.

This is only one of many challenges that the women's movement has to face. For example, as discussed in Chapter 2, the last few years have witnessed the emergence of strong criticisms from black women and women of colour. And they are not the only, nor the last, to question gender as the fundamental basis of unity within the women's movement. Indeed, as the movement becomes more successful in its attempt to reach out to a diverse range of women, it can expect much more questioning to follow. To be able to respond to these questions it will have to come to terms with the limitations of 'sisterhood' as an analysis of the structure of power in society.

The pull of institutionalization. 'Sisterhood' is equally insufficient as a basis for resisting the pressure to institutionalize the feminist struggle for change. Here again, the fact that it does not deal with the reality and complexity of power relations under patriarchal capitalism is a critical factor in its inability to challenge the prevailing ideologies and structures.

In the first place, the concept that women have certain interests in common because of their biology can readily be incorporated into the idea of a 'pluralistic', rather than a class, society. Although pluralism acknowledges that different groups of people may not share the same interests, these differences are not related to the way power is structured within the society. Indeed, the ideology of change holds that it is the role of government, as neutral arbiter, to mediate among and reconcile the various competing interests within the society.

Moreover, because 'sisterhood' masks the underlying relations of power in support of a politically contentless adherence to a common biology, it does not directly address the prevailing individualism. In fact, it can readily be used to justify giving support to individual women seeking leadership roles within the society. The key issue is gender: if she is a woman, by definition she's okay. What remains hidden is the fact that there *are* fundamental differences in power among women depending on their class, race, and sexual orientation.

'Sisterhood' has even been conscripted in support of the practice of networking used by the upwardly mobile career women of the 1980s. The idea here is that if women won't support other women in their attempts to achieve success, then who will? Thus we see the creation of exclusive women's clubs for the casual socializing of up-and-coming career women; specific pleas to women to provide financial and ballot-box support for female political candidates; and 'Women in Leadership' organizations to foster the promotion of women in various organizations. These networks provide the bases of power that allow certain individual women to achieve leadership roles in government, business, social interest groups, and so on.

But perhaps the most insidious use of 'sisterhood' in the service of the existing structure of power is its use as a means of choking off criticism and toning down demands for change. This problem is increasingly evident in the context of the rise of right-wing forces who would turn back the clock on the gains made by women. To quote the Working Group on Sexual Violence:

> In comparison with the threat from these forces, the state can be seen as a friendly and benevolent patriarch whose allegiance we must maintain. . . .
> It is in times like these that the call to unity, the invocation of

sisterhood, is most often heard. Criticism from 'within the ranks' is silenced. Centralization of power is defined as 'practical' and 'necessary'. The basis of agreement becomes the lowest common denominator.[23]

3. Sisterhood and socialist feminism

In summary, then, 'sisterhood' and the autonomous women's movement offer an analysis and a strategic orientation that are too narrow and exclusive in their approach. This narrowness means that feminists are unable to relate to the differences among women along the lines of class, sexual orientation, and race. This inability restricts the appeal and relevance of feminist visions of change and tends to isolate the women's movement from its potential allies. At the same time, however, 'sisterhood' is readily incorporated into the classless ideology of change, and is adapted to fit the needs of liberal-feminist strategies for change.

The narrow analysis afforded by 'sisterhood' and the autonomous women's movement is not one to which socialist feminism subscribes. As we have pointed out, socialist-feminist theory recognizes that there are, in fact, enormous differences between women of different social classes, races, and groups. At the same time, it recognizes the inadequacy of a struggle for change based on gender alone, and the need for unity among all oppressed groups.

This does not mean that socialist feminism must abandon 'sisterhood' or the concept of autonomous organizing. On the contrary, as we have been at some pains to point out, these ideas add an important dimension to the struggle for women's liberation. For socialist feminism the challenge is to incorporate this positive dimension, yet not lose sight of the larger vision of social change.

This is a tension with which socialist feminism has been struggling for a long time; it is not easy to resolve. Yet over the years socialist feminism has developed some important clarifications regarding these concepts. In particular, it has been able to distinguish between a view that sees the autonomous organizing of women as a strict organizing principle, and one that sees it in terms of the right of women to organize separately, and to lead and organize their own struggles. Similarly, socialist feminism has utilized the power of 'sisterhood' as an expression of the solidarity and support that can exist among women and that women can offer to others, rather than as a statement about the exclusive nature of power. As Bell Hooks argues, there is a difference between solidarity and sameness. Feminists do not need to eradicate differences in order to have solidarity. Solidarity is built on a community of interests, shared beliefs, and goals around which to unite.[24] Indeed, it could be argued that our strength comes out of an understanding of our diversity, not out of trying to bypass it.

More recently, socialist feminists have turned towards building coalitions as a way of creating unity among different struggles while maintaining women's organizational autonomy and control. This form of organizing will be discussed at greater length in the next chapter. However, it is clear that this form of organization provides a mechanism by which the women's movement can maintain its distinct character without isolating itself in the struggle for social change. As Lorna Weir argues:

> That we support other popular movements does not at all mean their issues and ours are all the same, nor that there is no distinction between these movements and ours. . . . When discussing coalitions, it is important to remember that the issue at hand is one of solidarity and co-operation among mass movements, not the assimilation or subordination of these movements to one another.[25]

CONCLUSION

In this chapter on ideology we have discussed the fact that the women's movement has been dominated throughout its history by two key ideas: 'the personal is political' and 'sisterhood'. These ideas acted as turning-points in the development and politicization of the women's movement and helped to shape a movement that was able to reach and involve thousands of woman in a collective struggle for social change.

In the longer term, however, the ideological matrix that these ideas represent has proved to be an insufficient basis around which to structure practice. Central to this insufficiency is the fact that neither 'the personal is political' nor 'sisterhood' offers an adequate analysis of power relations under patriarchal capitalism. As a political current, socialist feminism has already begun to address some of the limitations discussed in this chapter. It is critical that this process continue.

NOTES

[1]'Redstockings Manifesto', reprinted in Betty and Theodore Roszak, eds, *Masculine/Feminine* (New York: Harper Colophon Books, 1969), pp. 272–4.

[2] Ibid, p. 273.

[3]Patricia Carey, 'Personal is Political', *Canadian Woman Studies* vol.2, no. 2 (1980), p. 6.

[4]Hester Eisenstein, *Contemporary Feminist Thought* (Boston: G.K. Hall & Co., 1983), p. 35. In this chapter on consciousness-raising and 'the personal is political', Eisenstein explores the role of consciousness-raising in the development of feminist theory and political action.

[5]Redstockings Manifesto, p. 274.

[6]Eisenstein, *Feminist Thought*, p. 37.

[7]Eisenstein, *Feminist Thought*, pp. 37–8 (emphasis added).

[8]Carey, Patricia, 'Personal is Political', p. 5.

[9]Nancy Hartsock, 'Fundamental Feminism: Process and Perspective', *Quest* vol. 2, no. 2 (Fall 1975), p. 71 (emphasis added).

[10] Kate Lindeman, quoted in Alison Jaggar, *Feminist Politics and Human Nature* (Totowa, N.J.: Rowman and Allanheld, 1983), p. 365.

[11]Lynne Segal, *Is the Future Female? Troubled Thoughts on Contemporary Feminism* (London, Virago, 1987), p. 60. This quotation is part of a longer discussion of the problems of using experiences as the major criterion for feminist organizing and analysis.

[12]'The Impasse of Socialist Feminism, A Conversation with Deirdre English, Barbara Epstein, Barbara Haber, and Judy MacLean', *Socialist Review* no. 79, vol. 15, no.1 (Jan./Feb. 1985).

[13]Johanna Brand and Ester Koulack, 'Liberation More than Equality', *Canadian Dimension* vol. 13, no. 1 (1978), pp. 18–21.

[14]Segal, *Is the Future Female?*, p. 61.

[15]Barbara Haber, 'Is Personal Life Still a Political Issue?', *Feminist Studies* vol.5, no. 3 (Fall 1979), p. 76.

[16]Carey, 'Personal is Political', p. 4.

[17]Brand and Koulack, 'Liberation', p. 20.

[18]Barbara Ehrenreich, as quoted in Karen Dubinsky, 'Lament for a Patriarchy Lost: Anti-Feminism, Anti-Abortion and R.E.A.L. Women in Canada (Ottawa: CRIAW/ICREF, 1985), p. 40.

[19]Haber, 'Personal Life', p. 74.

[20]Judith Quinlan, 'Autonomy = independence = separatism revisited', *Kinesis* July/Aug. 1981, p. 19.

[21]Although the coming together in consciousness-raising groups was a new phenomenon, it did resonate with historic traditions of women's intimate friendships, especially in the homosocial world of the nineteenth century. For a description of women's friendships in the nineteenth century, and an exploration of the centrality of these friendships to women's lives, see Carroll Smith Rosenberg, 'The Female World of Love and Ritual: Relations between Women in Nineteenth Century America', *Signs* vol. I, no. 1 (1975).

[22]Political Action Collective of the Ottawa Women's Centre, 'Sisterhood—the only option', *Upstream* vol. 3, no. 8 (Aug. 1979), p. 7.

[23]Working Group on Sexual Violence, 'Better Strident than Silent', *Broadside* vol. 6, no. 6 (May 1985), p. 6.

[24]Bell Hooks, 'Sisterhood: Political Solidarity Between Women', *Feminist Review* no. 23 (June 1986), p. 138.

[25]Lorna Weir, 'Tit for Tat: Coalition Politics', *Broadside* vol. 3, no. 4.

7

Feminist Organizations and Feminist Process

The preceding sections of this book have focused on various aspects of the struggle for change: the ideology of change itself, the history and ideology of the women's movement, and the feminist practice of change. This chapter turns to the structures through which we attempt to make change. These structures are important because they limit and/or facilitate feminist practice for change. Initially there were no organizations in existence that addressed women's concerns, needs, or emerging politics. One of the first tasks of the women's liberation movement was to create structures that would be alternatives through which women could organize. As we have seen, those structures took a number of forms: study groups, CR groups, women's caucuses, women's organizations, women's centres, services, and businesses. Given the large number of these groups currently in existence, it is hard to comprehend that only two decades ago there were virtually no feminist organizations. In twenty short years we have created a diverse and widespread movement. That creation has been a process of rejecting the traditional, experimenting with new forms and structures, and creating feminist alternatives.

In addition to challenging traditional ways of thinking about the world, feminist ideas also challenged how that world was organized. Our experience as women in organizations—whether traditional women's organizations, political parties, workplaces, unions, or left organizations—was one of powerlessness. Within feminist organizations women attempted to understand why we were powerless in those other organizations—not just ideologically, but also structurally. Gradually feminists developed a critique of traditional organizations and began to experiment with new organizational forms and processes.

Feminist ideas criticized traditional organizational forms, and gradually a specifically feminist approach to organizational structure and processes emerged. The feminist model was closely linked to the ideology of the women's movement, particularly the notions of 'the personal is political' and 'sisterhood' outlined in the preceding chapter. The feminist challenge was to develop organizational forms that empowered women and provided an effective base from which to carry out the aims and goals of particular feminist groups. Feminists needed organizational structures and procedures that would be accessible, would make use of our strengths, and would facilitate our making effective and real change.

The feminist critique of traditional organizations did not emerge full-blown, but was pieced together over the early years of the women's movement through experimentation with alternatives. Although there is now an identifiable feminist model of organizational process, the process of experimentation and adjustment is ongoing. Fortunately, the grass-roots movement has largely resisted the pull to name one organizational structure as 'correct'. Instead, each organization takes the grass-roots feminist model (see below) and loosely applies it to its own analysis, goals, and strategies to create an organizational structure and process most useful to its members. Sheila Rowbotham has identified this as one of the strengths of the women's movement:

> As women encounter feminism they can make their own kinds of organising depending on their needs. It is this flexibility which it is extremely important to maintain. It means that for example groups of women artists or groups of women setting up a crèche or on the sub-committee of a trades council can decide for themselves what structure is most useful.[1]

The women's movement is not one organization, but the totality of a variety of organizations and individuals struggling to end the oppression of women. The distinction between movement and organization is an important one. An organization has structural form, organizational norms and goals, and a membership. It can be small or large, it can tend to homogeneity or heterogeneity, it can be focussed on personal or political goals or both. However it is constructed, an organization is identified by a structure, membership, politics, norms, and goals.

A movement, on the other hand, has an amorphous or fluid organizational quality; episodically, a more stable form might emerge. What holds a movement together is more ideological in nature than what is necessary to sustain an organization. So the women's movement, which really has no formal organization *per se*, is held together by a commitment to women's liberation. This is true even though what this liberation means to specific components of the women's movement may differ dramatically. Loosely, then, the ideology of women's liberation gives some coherence to the women's movement.

This chapter is about feminist organizational process. In it we are going to take the issue of feminist organization and process out of the context of the women's movement. Although this approach separates organizations from their context, their tasks, and their strategies, it allows us to begin to examine in detail the specific organizational issues that have confronted the women's movement. While we are examining the structures themselves, it is important to remember that they exist only to facilitate the group's politics and strategies. In the women's movement we know how easy it is to be distracted from the goals by the structure.

FEMINIST CRITIQUES AND MODELS

Second-wave feminists quickly developed two different critiques of traditional organizational methods, which reflected the different origins of institutionalized and grass-roots feminisms. Each of these currents began with a critique and gradually developed a feminist model of organization and process. Organizational models included issues of leadership, membership, voting procedures, committee structure, and education of new members. Process models were designed to address the issues of power, democracy, and equality among group members. Though sometimes organization and process can be easily distinguished, often the two are closely interlinked.

Institutionalized feminism emerged from organizations such as the YWCA and the CFUW, which had traditional hierarchical organizational structures and traditional processes. Such forms include an elected executive (president, vice-president, secretary, treasurer), a committee structure, clear membership criteria (usually requiring a membership fee), and the use of *Robert's Rules of Order* to organize each meeting; decision-making is by majority vote. Because these were *women's* organizations, institutionalized feminists' experience of them was fairly positive: women were the leaders as well as the members, and women made the decisions as well as the coffee. This positive experience of traditional organizational norms helps to explain their continued use despite vociferous criticism by grass-roots feminists.

Grass-roots feminism had a very different origin from institutionalized feminism, and grass-roots feminists did not share a common experience of organizational forms. Many women who entered the grass-roots movement did so as individuals without experience in political organizations. Other grass-roots feminists came from other social movements, such as the student, native, civil-rights, anti-war, new-left, and counterculture movements of the sixties. While these movements were not associated with any particular organizational forms, the individuals who came from them into the women's liberation movement brought along a general, if often unarticulated, critique of traditional organizations. Their experiences in those groups ranged from positive—small groups and shared leadership— to negative—tightly structured organizations with élite leaderships.[2] In addition, some grass-roots feminists came from left organizations such as the Communist Party of Canada, the League for Socialist Action, and the Revolutionary Marxist Group. These women probably had the most experience with alternative organizational structures. Democratic centralism was the theoretical organizational model of left organizations, meaning, in theory, that all group members participated in making a decision (democracy) and then, once it was made, *all* members were responsible for carrying it out (centralism).[3] In practice, the democracy ranged from very traditional voting to other, more inclusive forms of decision-making.

In general, the experience of grass-roots feminists *as women* in the organizations of the 1960s' social movements and left organizations was negative. Despite their critiques of the status quo, those organizations tended to be as hierarchical and male-dominated as traditional organizations. Women's experience was largely one of being members, not leaders, and of making coffee, not decisions— the reverse, as we have seen, of the experience of institutionalized feminists in their own women's organizations. For grass-roots feminists the struggle around organizational issues was in part a reaction against their experiences in other organizations.

Whatever the members' organizational experience—traditional, left, or none at all—the early years of the feminist movement were characterized by women critical of traditional organizing. For reasons discussed above, grass-roots feminists' suspicion of traditional organizational norms and leadership came out of our experience in organizations where we were denied any real access to positions of power. We rejected what we saw as the male, patriarchal, hierarchical, and élitist norms of traditional organizations as models. In the early years the question of organizational norms was high on our political agenda, and an enormous amount of time was spent developing alternatives that emerged slowly out of our feminist practice. In the mid-1960s there were *no* feminist organizations for women to join; we had to create each of the thousands of women's organizations that now exist in Canada and elsewhere. We did not like what existed, so we set out to build strong and effective alternatives.

What emerged from the feminist critique of traditional organizational forms and processes were two very different models, each suited to the politics and strategies of its originators. Institutionalized feminism retained many of the structures and processes of traditional organizations, but modified them to meet its own needs. Grass-roots feminism, on the other hand, initially rejected traditional organizational forms altogether and set out to build a new alternative. The result has come to be called 'the feminist model' or 'the feminist process'.

1. The modified traditional feminist model

Institutionalized feminism, working largely within traditional organizations and having a strategy focused on changing 'the system' from within, chose to modify traditional structures and processes to meet the needs of its members. Although these groups continued to use *Robert's Rules of Order*,[4] maintaining a hierarchical structure[5] with an elected executive and decision-making by majority vote, there was an emphasis on teaching members the rules of order and of ensuring that they were more aware of the executive's activities than in traditional organizations, and more involved. Sometimes, in groups such as NAC, the executive was gradually enlarged to include members-at-large representing regional concerns. In this case, the organization changed its structure to reflect its changing goals and strategies.

Feminists active in trade unions have attempted to work within the traditional hierarchical, male-dominated structure they found there. For many, the discovery that unions are as traditionally structured and as sexist as other institutions in our society has been discouraging;[6] these structures and attitudes often limit the possibilities for organizing women. Debbie Field has pointed out that the dilemma facing women's committees in trade unions is whether to try organizing autonomously, outside the trade-union structure, or within the structure in ways often determined by the (male) leadership.[7] Field concludes by linking the structure of women's committees to their effectiveness:

> In hindsight, and from the vantage point of no longer working at Stelco, I believe we made a mistake forming a women's committee

so closely tied to the leadership. It would have been better to spend time, even a year or two, getting to know women in the plant before moving to structure a formal committee. This approach would have involved experimenting with new forms of organizing. . . .

Unions could generally strengthen membership involvement if more informal methods of meeting and transmitting information were developed. Particularly when trying to mobilize women or new union members, it is important to develop creative tactics to make the union more accessible.[8]

While modified traditional forms work very effectively for some organizations, they are ineffective for others. In NAC the modified traditional structure works fairly well (although members do have criticisms)[9] because the member organizations have all agreed to the organization's goals. For trade-union women the modified traditional structures work less well, because these women are struggling with the contradictions of working in an overall organization that is male-dominated and sexist.

2. *Organizing without organizations: the grass-roots feminist model*

Grass-roots feminism, in contrast to institutionalized feminsim, found traditional structures and processes inadequate and began to develop alternative structures and processes that have come to be called 'the feminist alternative'. Underlying it were three principles: a rejection of the notions of hierarchy and leadership, an emphasis on personal experience, and a belief in the importance of process. Grass-roots feminists totally rejected traditional structures and processes as fundamentally flawed and incapable of being modified to meet the needs of women. This rejection of hierarchy and leadership was a reaction to our perceived powerlessness in traditional organizations. One response was to refuse to consciously build any organization and to regard all aspects of organization—leadership, membership, structure, and decision-making—as innately oppressive to women and at odds with what the women's movement stood for. Initially feminists tried to find ways of organizing without organizations. In 1975, some five to six years after the first women's liberation organizations began in the U.S., Nancy Hartsock, an American feminist activist, wrote that 'we have *only begun* to think about the way we should work in organizations with some structure, as opposed to the way we should work in small groups'.[10]

As Hartsock suggests, the initial organizational structure in the grass-roots movement was the seemingly structureless small group.

In Chapter 6 we discussed the importance of 'the personal is political' to the grass-roots movement; this idea was very influential in how we thought about new organizational forms. It was imperative to recognize the importance of personal experience and to incorporate that into any organization. The organizational expression of this recognition was the small consciousness-raising group, which many feminists identified as basic to feminist organizing:

> The *practice* of small group consciousness raising, with its stress on examining and understanding experience and on connecting personal experience to the structures that define our lives, is the clearest expression of the method basic to feminism.[11]

The committee of the 'Women Organize Alberta' conference in 1981 articulated this link between 'examining and understanding experience' and 'connecting previous experience to the structures in our lives':

> We feel that the act of continously voicing our own realities and informing others of our developing understanding is an essential basis for women's organizing. . . . Working from one's own interests is a personal political action in the context of an organizing process in that it potentially expresses the ways in which our realities are marked.[12]

The final principle guiding grass-roots feminist organizing was a belief in what is frequently referred to as the 'collective process'. Feminists from a range of backgrounds expressed the belief that it was the means, or the process, rather than the end that was central to feminism. In the late 1970s the Combahee River Collective, a small group of black American feminists, wrote:

> In the practice of our politics we do not believe that the end always justifies the means. Many reactionary and destructive acts have been done in the name of achieving 'correct' political goals. As feminists we do not want to mess over people in the name of politics. We believe in the collective process.[13]

Almost ten years later, in the mid-1980s, Gloria Steinem argued a similiar place for the process in feminist practice: 'the integrity of the process of change [is] part of the change itself. . . . In other words, the end cannot fully justify the means. To a surprising extent, the end *is* the means.'[14]

Grass-roots organizations had a particular means of operating. Typically, they were small groups of women organized collectively, with no office and no paid staff. The group met on a regular basis at a specific time, communicating with its members, and with interested women who were not members, through mailings, newsletters, and telephone networks. Membership was rarely formally defined; usually whoever came to a meeting was considered a member and could participate in all decision-making. Regular expenses, such as the cost of the meeting space and mailings, were paid for by donations from members and other interested women or organizations. The group as a whole made decisions for the organization, though sometimes a group would have a committee structure and delegate some decision-making to those committees. Groups frequently had both standing and *ad hoc* committees. The chairing of meetings was rotated among all members, agendas were prepared by the group as a whole, and minutes were sometimes kept and sometimes not. At meetings members sat in a circle.

Although the details of 'feminist process' differed somewhat from group to group, its basic aspects—collective organization, no leadership, rotation of administrative tasks, agreement by consensus, and an emphasis on personal experience—were generally the same. These feminist assumptions emerged from, and are closely linked to, the two central aspects of feminist ideology: 'the personal is political' and 'sisterhood'.

The importance of the feminist challenge to traditional structures and processes should not be underestimated. Both types of feminist organizations provided an opportunity to learn skills (for example, political organizing, lobbying, brief-writing, public speaking, administrative skills) that were frequently unavailable to women in traditional organizations. As a result women gained confidence in themselves, created alternative structures and processes, and built a powerful movement. Today, although traditional organizations are very slow to change, feminist organizational issues and questions are beginning to resonate there.

ISSUES OF FEMINIST ORGANIZING

All feminist organizations have faced two key questions. The first has been to determine what internal processes would best further the group's overall goals. While feminists share a general critique of traditional organizational models, there is no one feminist model of internal process. Internal processes need to facilitate meeting the group's goals; as a result, different women's organizations have chosen different processes, though as we will see, we can identify some specifically feminist approaches to structure and organization.

Once the issues of internal process have been examined, feminist organizations face a second question. That is to determine which overall form or structure is most appropriate to the group's particular feminist agenda. There is actually a cluster of issues within this one question, including the range of issues the group addresses, the size of the organization, and the extent to which the membership is homogeneous or heterogeneous. The decisions on each of these issues are made in the context of the group's political analysis and strategy, and they reflect the group's purpose. While the questions are similiar for all feminist organizations, the answers/solutions differ widely. Below, we will discuss the general issues of organizational types, but these will, of necessity, not be within any political analysis or strategy. It is important to keep in mind that finally it is only within a political analysis that any particular group can make decisions that will help it to make change.

1. Internal process

The following section explores three aspects of internal process in grass-roots feminist organizations: leadership; membership, education, and recruitment; and decision-making and democracy. The initial wholesale rejection of these by grass-roots feminists and the subsequent recognition of the need for alternative models of each, gives grass-roots feminism a complex and contradictory relationship to each of these issues.

Leadership. Out of our critique of the traditional theories of leadership emerged a grass-roots feminist model of leadership that initially tended to reject the very idea of leadership. Instead, the ideology of sisterhood led grass-roots feminists to argue that each woman in a group was a leader who shared an equal responsibility with all other members to facilitate the group's functioning. This approach was in marked contrast to representative forms of leadership in which the individual is absolved of all responsibility except that of voting on the leadership. Feminists believed that the rotation of administrative tasks, chairing meetings, public speaking, writing, organizing, and all other group functions would provide women with the opportunity to learn by doing. Also, the constant rotation of tasks was designed to make it impossible for any one woman or small group to take over the leadership. This rejection of leadership was both a strength and a weakness of grass-roots organizing. While we often created an underground and unrecognized leadership within a group, many women were empowered and learned new skills. Institutional feminism, on the other hand, more or less accepted a traditional notion of leadership, with the result that a small network of women provided the leadership, and many outside of it felt excluded and unsure of how to break in.

A definition of leadership is difficult to formulate because women make many different kinds of contributions to the women's movement, all of which could be aspects of leadership. Our experience is that both the women's movement and specific organizations need women with certain attributes in particular: a capacity for co-ordination, a vision, the ability to plan strategy in light of it, and the interpersonal group skills to facilitate the adoption of that vision and strategy. While these attributes are not the only ones necessary for a successful organization, without a number of women possessing them an organization cannot be politically effective.

Our experience as grass-roots activists is that no matter how much we tried to structure our organizations in ways that eliminated leadership, it did not disappear, and its unacknowledged existence was a constant source of tension.[15] Because we did not recognize and validate it, leadership became covert. The lack of clear leadership meant that it was important to know the right person; this kind of personalism then became a substitute for leadership. Informal decision-making was made by an 'in' group through personal contacts and discussions outside the larger group. The larger group often felt manipulated and unimportant. There was frequently nothing concrete to point to, just a feeling that things weren't quite what they seemed on the surface. This in turn lead to the resentment of 'old' (i.e., experienced) women by 'new' members of the organization. New women found it difficult to break into the (unacknowledged) leadership of the group, and as a result often felt marginal.

Both newer and older members were undermined by these notions about leadership. Experienced women often came to feel they were mistrusted because of their skills. Skilled women who could provide practical and theoretical leadership were frequently accused of being élitist or too theoretical, adopting male models, attempting to control the group, being power-hungry, and so on. Such accusations usually ensured that those women left the organization; after they were gone, the 'problem' was seemingly solved. In 1978 the steering committee of Saskatoon Women's Liberation described this phenomenon:

> Our elites were groups of friends who happened to participate in the
> same political activities and who had lots of time or energy. . . . This

is not to set the women who took leadership roles up as villains. On the contrary, they were primarily victims. They were almost invariably competent, dedicated, talented feminists. As their position as leaders was not acknowledged they were rarely given credit but often blamed. They did almost all of the work and were finally 'burned out'. They had no mechanisms by which to recruit replacements. When they eventually had to withdraw in order to recuperate they took most of the information and the knowledge gained in their years of work with them. New 'elites' had to start from the beginning again. Invaluable women and their experiences were lost.[16]

One aspect of the attitude towards new women was the element of class guilt. A dynamic developed in which less skilled women (usually new to the movement) were regarded as necessarily working class, and skilled women (usually experienced) necessarily middle class. Skilled women were unsure of how to explain their skills and apparent, though unacknowledged, leadership in the group. Because skill level had come to be linked with class, and skilled women regarded as middle-class, these women felt guilty about their (actual or supposed) class privilege. One way to alleviate both the privilege and the guilt was to give way to the less skilled and newer women. The strategy of listening more carefully to new women was not necessarily wrong; what was harmful was the patronizing element. Our attitude was patronizing because it was based on guilt, not on a respect for differences. The organizational and leadership norms remained such that they reflected largely middle-class values and goals. But because those norms were unarticulated, any challenge to them was regarded as disloyalty, and, because of our deep fear of the anger that accompanies such discussion, it has been virtually impossible to deal with the complex issues of class linked to grass-roots feminist notions of leadership.

We see a similar sort of 'racial' guilt operating in parts of the women's movement today. Frequently our response to the whiteness of feminist organizations has been to adopt a woman of colour; white women then use her presence to reassure themselves that their organization does not have a problem with racism. Racist attitudes certainly must be confronted, but an anti-racist stance requires more than that. Groups have to examine their structures and processes closely in order to understand how racism (and sexism, classism, and heterosexism) are built into the organization. White women's fear of change and our lack of a clear sense of an anti-racist practice has lead to tokenism and a patronizing attitude towards women of colour. Instead of taking them seriously, we sometimes tend to accept uncritically any actions or statements made by women of colour and refuse to air any of our concerns or fears. Certainly as white feminists we need to deal with both individual and organizational racism, but when we do it from guilt, the result is patronizing.

Grass-roots feminist organizations have come to terms with leadership in a variety of ways. Many organizations have devised some form of acknowledged leadership. Some chose one or two co-ordinators, others chose a co-ordinating committee, and others continue to operate without an explicit leadership. Although most grass-roots organizations have made an uneasy peace with the notion of leadership, they have rarely articulated their particular processes of deciding what type of leadership best suits them.

Membership, education, recruitment. The notion of sisterhood has been the cornerstone of grass-roots feminist notions of membership, education, and recruitment. Because the assumptions of sisterhood were rarely articulated, grass-roots feminist organizations, on the whole, have experienced a number of problems in these areas. The lack of an analysis of difference made it difficult to define membership criteria, establish educational programs, and do effective recruitment to a particular organization.

Membership has been an issue for grass-roots organizations because we have been reluctant to establish membership criteria, especially clear *political* criteria. Because grass-roots feminists were in the process of developing a politic, it was difficult to present new members with a clear statement of the group's analysis. The fear of excluding interested women also made feminist organizations reluctant to require all members to agree with a specific list of political statements. For example, the constitution of Saskatoon Women's Liberation had four requirements for membership, one of which read: 'Members must read all adopted papers of SWL and be prepared to publically support these positions, although they may disagree internally.'[17] This example reflects grass-roots feminism's concern that women with different ideas and opinions be able to coexist within an organization, but also that organizations be able to take articulated political positions on issues.

The view that the women's movement should be open to all women, that it belongs to all women, has been translated in practice into the view that women's organizations should also be open to all women regardless of their politics. The concept of building a movement by including everyone in organizations has meant that there is no clear relation between organization and politics. Anyone who is biologically a woman, not just those who agree with a certain politic, can often join a particular organization. The very idea of membership criteria is considered anathema. What this means is that organizations are not constructed on a political basis; women are recruited to a specific politic only after joining an organizations. This has meant that the integrity of the organization and its politics is constantly challenged and threatened. Although this process can sometimes be creative, it is more often destructive.

Establishing membership criteria pushes an organization to articulate its political positions, strategies, and goals. It also pushes groups to be clear about their structure and their leadership; otherwise, new members have no clear place or role in the organization. New members need to know what is expected of them in terms of time, participation, and political work, and whether or not they will be getting feedback from the group as to how they are doing. The question of membership inevitably leads to questions of recruitment, because without membership criteria that are political, organizations have no basis on which to recruit. They also have no clear basis for an educational program because it is not clear whether women are being educated to build skills and/or to develop a political perspective. Only a clear sense of political perspective and strategy, with resulting organizational norms and membership criteria, can lead to coherent educational and recruitment policies.

One of the keys to recruitment is an educational process; education leads to an understanding of what is needed to change the world. The process of educating women about their rights and revealing the oppressiveness of their situation has been instrumental in building the women's movement. Education within the movement includes many different kinds and levels: consciousness-raising, study groups, skills, women's studies courses, and so on. Initially our approach to education was through CR groups. The purpose was to understand our personal lives and experiences, not to build a mass movement. This was an important and positive approach to education at that time; unfortunately, the women's movement ceased to refine its educational process as it continued to develop and become more complex.

Grass-roots feminists have acted on two assumptions that have made it difficult, if not impossible, to develop an educational process. The first is our assumption that what is important is the experiential and personal; many grass-roots feminists have rejected education as inherently middle-class and androcentric. The second assumption is that 'we are all the same': no leaders, no acknowledgement of different skills, etc. The result has been that the women's movement has discarded education and teaching in much the same way we rejected leadership, instead of putting forward a popular education model that could have used the insights gained from consciousness-raising groups without denying the need for teachers and the differences in our experiences.

Decision-making and democracy. Out of grass-roots feminists' experience of being excluded from the power and decision-making structures within traditional organizations came a commitment to a model that included all members in decision-making. The decision-making model that seemed to best meet these criteria was consensus. Consensus allowed each woman to participate equally in decision-making; for the first time we had a say in the decisions that affected how our group functioned. Many of us learned to analyze and to strategize in those tedious but exciting meetings. The process not only allowed each woman a role in the decision-making, but meant that until each woman had agreed to the decision, the discussion continued; in other words, each decision had to be unanimous. Such decision-making was highly centralized—the entire group had to make every decision; delegation cannot exist with consensus decision-making. R. Seyd, a member of the Red Ladder Theatre collective in England in the mid-1970s, described such a group:

> Essentially, the group was structured so that every decision, however small, needed the unanimous agreement of every individual on it before it could be acted upon. Of course, in theory, this seems the perfect democratic approach. In practice it meant that those with the strongest personalities (the pushy ones) dominated the group. Through the course of an argument, those in a minority would eventually put up their hands and make the decision unanimous even when they did not agree with it, just so that the work could continue. . . . When resentments built up to an intolerable level, explosions occurred, and often we would sit down for days in order to work out the problems. Because we believed there could be nothing wrong with the structure, since it was so democratic, this working-out led us into people's individual personalities and psychologies. The effect of this ultra-egalitarianism, this idealistic democracy, was in fact to individualise everything.[18]

The problem for the grass-roots women's movement was not with consensus *per se*, but rather with the way we analyzed the problems connected to it. Our fear of conflict stifled the potentially positive and creative ideas about how a group could function that might have been generated out of consensus decision-making.[19]

The grass-roots feminist belief that consensus was the 'politically correct' form of feminist decision-making, together with a generalized fear of conflict, had several consequences. First, it meant that alternative models of decision-making, such as voting, committee structures, or delegation of decision-making, were rarely explored, although in practice we frequently used them—often with a sense of guilt. Second, it prevented feminists from developing a critique of consensus and thus validating the use of other forms. It also meant that women who disagreed with a general decision had to either 'give in' to the group or 'hold out' and stop any decision from being made—in other words, we pushed ourselves to homogeneity. For women who were new to the group, shy, or unsure of the group's politics and hence unsure of speaking, consensus decision-making reinforced the informal and unacknowledged leadership within the group. Although it appeared that all members made the decision, frequently the informal leadership was responsible. In such a situation the centralization of decision-making in the group as a whole is as problematic as the notion of consensus itself. The result was that we held ourselves hostage to our fear of conflict without understanding what was happening.

Conflict and disagreement are necessary and healthy signs that a group is functioning well. Conflict generates creativity, especially in the context of decision-making by consensus, and the resolution of conflicts can be energizing and empowering for the group. When groups create norms that discourage conflict, and when disagreement is seen as destructive to the group's unity, those members who have questions or who disagree with the generally accepted position silence themselves, usually by leaving. And the result is that, in trying to be democratic, the group comes to function in an undemocratic fashion.

The resolution of conflict in a healthy way has been difficult for many grass-roots feminist organizations, which have responded to conflict in one of two ways. Either the group would minimize the importance of dealing with conflict and maximize the importance of 'getting on with it', because time was of the essence, our numbers small, and the tasks we were undertaking large, or it would focus entirely on conflict resolution and tend to turn the disagreements into personal ones. In 1978 Saskatoon Women's Liberation decided not to operate by consensus, and explained how their decision-making procedures avoided both these pitfalls: 'We expect and welcome

244 | Feminist Organizing for Change

differences and debate. It can be one of our most constructive practices. We advocate majority decisions that will be acted upon (or at
least not acted against) by every member of the group. Debate on
the issue, though, may continue indefinitely.'[20] This group also recognized the tendency to turn political differences into personality
conflicts and cautioned against it. Like swL, many grass-roots feminist organizations ceased to use a consensus model but retained the
original feminist concern that every member's voice be heard.

The general approach of the grass-roots women's movement to
democracy and decison-making can be seen as a form of participatory democracy. The thrust of participatory democracy is that everyone should participate in the group and that everyone is equally
responsible for and to the group. Sheila Rowbotham has summed
up the problems with participatory democracy:

> If you are not able to be present you can't participate. Whoever turns
> up next time can reverse the previous decisions. If very few people
> turn up they are lumbered with the responsibility. It is a very open
> situation and anyone with a gift for either emotional blackmail or a
> conviction of the need to intervene can do so without being checked
> by any accepted procedure. Participatory democracy only works if
> everyone accepts a certain give and take, a respect for one another's
> experience, a desire and need to remain connected. If these are not
> present it can be a traumatic process.[21]

As Rowbotham's comments suggest, consensus decision-making
works only in small, homogeneous, stable groups. When those conditions exist it is a very democratic and empowering form of decision-making; when they do not, consensus decision-making is
inappropriate. The most suitable form of decision-making for an
organization is closely related to size, homogeneity, heterogeneity,
and type of organization. The processes most appropriate to a particular organization can be decided only by examining those issues
in light of each other and of the group's political analysis, goals,
and strategies.

2. Issues of form

The second set of issues facing feminist organizations includes type
of organization, size, and homogeneity or heterogeneity. Like issues
of feminist process, these choices are finally made in the context of
a politic and strategy. We will now examine the general issues facing
organizations in each of these areas.

Type of organization. The first question facing an organization is the range or scope of the issues it will address. It can choose to be an umbrella organization or coalition, a multi-issue, or a single-issue organization. This political and strategic decision has important organizational or structural components. All three types of organizations can be successful, as we will see below, but the organizational issues facing each are somewhat different.

An umbrella organization, or coalition, is an organization of groups; it may or may not permit individual memberships.[22] Various groups agree on a basis of unity for the coalition, but each member group remains independent. One of the most effective examples in Canada is NAC, founded in 1972 and with a current membership of approximately 530 organizations, representing some three million women. The goal of such an organization must be either very specific or very general in order to hold together a range of groups that likely have more differences than similarities. Including groups with identified politics that cover the whole range of institutional and grass-roots feminisms, NAC has a general goal: to 'unite women and women's groups from across the country in the struggle for equality'. Such an approach allows the wide range of its member groups to work together within the context of that general goal and, at the annual general meeting of member groups, set specific policies by majority vote.

An example of an umbrella organization with a very specific goal is the Ontario Coalition for Abortion Clinics (OCAC), which focuses on the establishment and legalization of free-standing abortion clinics in the province. Like NAC, OCAC is a long-term organization with staff, membership fees, and so on. But many other coalitions are formed to work around a particular issue or to plan a particular event, and are seen as short-term from the start. In cities across Canada, for instance, coalitions are formed every year to plan celebrations for International Women's Day.

Umbrella organizations and coalitions have become an important form of feminist organization as the women's movement has come to comprise many organizations with clearly defined political analyses, strategies, and goals. The positive aspect of this way of organizing is that it focuses on what large numbers of organizations and individuals within the movement can agree on, and is thus able to validate the differences among groups while concentrating on their shared viewpoints. This type of organizing presents a powerful unified face to the world and is often effective in achieving change. The challenge is to present at the same time the complexity and diversity of the women's movement.[23] As the critique of the movement by women of colour, lesbians, and disabled, francophone, native, and immigrant women shows, it has not often—some would say, rarely—been successful at balancing sisterhood and difference. As we suggested earlier, this is the current challenge facing the women's movement.

Multi-issue organizations are single groups that share a common political analysis and/or agree on a series of goals. These groups address a wide range of issues and are frequently members of coalitions. Examples include women's centres and groups that agree on a series of goals or services rather than a shared politic. For example, the Port Coquitlam Area Women's Centre states its objectives as follows:

> To be a women's drop-in, information-referral centre, serving women of all ages; to offer information and support through various programs; to offer volunteer opportunities for skill development, finding goals and breaking out of isolation; to provide a central place for women to meet; and to inform our elected representatives of the needs and concerns of the members.[24]

Another example of a multi-issue organization arising from a common political analysis is the International Women's Day Committee of Toronto, a socialist-feminist organization. The IWDC's goal is twofold: to work for 'immediate concrete gains, as well as a much larger process of building alliances for a longer-term struggle for a transformed society.'[25]

The strength of multi-issue organizations is that they address a range of issues from a shared political analysis and/or set of goals, and thus are able to link together the range of issues that feminism addresses and present them as a package. These organizations play an important role in linking single-issue concerns to feminism as a whole. Also, because these groups struggle to understand issues and action in the context of an overall political analysis, they have often been the initiators of important new practices. For example, in Toronto the IWDC played an important role in bringing many organizations into coalitions in the late 1970s. The group focused especially on making links with trade-union women, which in turn led them to recognize the different needs of immigrant women and, finally to recognize the importance of the issue of racism to the women's movement.

Single-issue organizations focus on *an* issue. Often these groups are made up of individuals with many different political analyses, but with agreement on the one issue and a strategy for change related to it. The single-issue group is now probably the most common type of feminist organization. The strength of these groups is that they bring a wide range of skills, experience, and numbers of members to focus on one issue. Thus the chance of 'winning' is, obviously, greater than that of seeing a package of issues accepted, and single-issue groups therefore have clear successes and failures in a way that umbrella and multi-issue groups do not. And as Charlotte Bunch has said: 'Women need to win. . . . Victories and programs, especially when linked to specific organizations, give us a clearer sense of what we can win and illustrate the plans, imagination, and changes that women will bring as they gain power.'[26]

The struggle to legalize and implement midwifery in Ontario is an excellent example of a single-issue campaign led by several fairly small groups of midwives and consumers. Prior to 1986, the practice of midwifery in Ontario was in the twilight zone, neither legal or illegal. Concerned consumers and practising midwives came together to form the Midwifery Task Force and the Ontario Association of Midwives, both fairly small organizations.[27] These groups decided on a specific focus: the legalization of midwifery as a self-regulating profession. Their struggle took place in the context of a Health Disciplines Legislation Review, without which their victory would have been much more difficult, if not impossible. This small group of activists learned the political skills of lobbying, brief-writing, and building a large base of support. In 1986 the Ontario government made midwifery legal and set up a Task Force on the Implementation of Midwifery in Ontario. Again, the midwifery community mobilized its support and has been very influential with the committee; in October 1987 the task force made recommendations that largely reflect its demands. Such 'wins' are important not only because they improve the conditions of women's lives, but also because they give us a sense of our strength.

Size. Size of organization—the optimum or desired number of members—is another important issue, though one that is often not recognized. The feminist assumption that we are building a mass movement of women has meant that we have assumed we are building large organizations. The reality of most organizations—and groups like NAC are exceptions—is that our membership has been small, rarely more than thirty or thirty-five regular and active members.

Often this was a puzzle to us—we wanted to build large organizations and we were open to all interested women, but we rarely grew beyond a basic core. Why? There are several aspects to the answer. The first is that we usually did not articulate our assumption that we wanted or needed large organizations, and so could not explore the issues involved. Obviously movements need large numbers of people actively involved if they are to be effective. But, as we have seen, movement and organization are not the same. Size seems to be related, at least in part, to type of structure. An umbrella organization or coalition will obviously be large in the sense of representing a lot of people, although the actual number of individuals who participate in its daily work may be quite small. Single-issue groups also have the potential to be large organizations, because the members need only agree on one issue. Multi-issue groups, which require a more comprehensive basis of unity or shared political analysis, have tended to be smaller.

Like type of structure, optimum size depends on the group's political agenda and strategy. It may change over time, and certainly it varies from organization to organization. Some fairly small groups of women, such as the Ontario midwives and their supporters, have been very successful in making change, so effectiveness is not linked necessarily to size.

A number of other factors have contributed to the smallness of many women's organizations. These include our unarticulated desire to remain small in order to foster and protect personal networks; problems of integrating new members; conflict between 'old' and 'new' members; and an inability to resolve conflicts.

Heterogeneity/homogeneity. The issues of heterogeneity (the differences among feminists) and homogeneity (the similarities) have both arisen from our assumptions about the sisterhood of women. Grass-roots feminists are often torn between these two views of women. In the early years of this wave of the women's movement, we saw ourselves first as homogeneous—feminists, *the* women's movement, sisters; yet at the same time we experienced ourselves as heterogeneous—a wide variety of kinds of groups with differing political perspectives, objectives, and organizing methods; as lesbians and heterosexual women, as working-class and middle-class women, as white women and black women and women of colour. We are, of course, both things at once—the same and different. As we noted in Chapter 3, categories of difference are not neutral, but reflect complex relations of power. And for grass-roots feminists the understanding of difference is complex because it includes two different kinds of difference. One expression of difference is through the 'politics of identity'; this includes the categories of race, class, ethnicity, and sexual orientation.[28] The other kind of difference is that of political strategies. Grass-roots feminists have had difficulty recognizing these two differences and often assumed that a political strategy flows directly from identity. Our problem has been not only a lack of understanding of our complex relationships, but also a failure to acknowledge ourselves as both homogeneous and heterogeneous. This failure is the structural expression of the feminist struggle to understand the complex relationship between sisterhood and difference.

Inside most feminist organizations that we have participated in, women have felt uncomfortable with heterogeneity, conflict, and change. The fact that these organizations too often played the role of personal networks meant that there was a drive to homogeneity, sameness, inside the organization. Groups often kept themselves small (and comfortable) by pushing out those who disagreed or who wanted to implement non-personal organizational norms. Desire for this kind of homogeneity was connected to creating a feeling of safety, which in turn was related to the role of the organization as a haven. Because differences are so threatening to a group where personal rather than political interactions dominate, it is difficult to acknowledge them openly. The more difficult this is, the less likely it is that the organization will be able to develop norms to deal with the differences.

The most recent example of this type of issue is the critique of the women's movement by women of colour. Black women, native women, and other women of colour have argued for the centrality of their difference—race—to their feminist politics. The issues raised by women of colour are questions of power relations, and they remind us that organizational structures and processes, even feminist ones, are not neutral. Power relations are built into those structures and processes, and one of our tasks as feminists is to understand and expose them. Women of colour have criticized feminist structures and processes for allowing those power relations to exclude them:

> I've been working in women's organisations for years and I think there has been a serious attempt to try and have structures that are quite contrary to hierarchical, patriarchal structures. That is something we do not have in our history that we can build from. At the same time, there are things that are quite manipulative of immigrant women. On the one hand, you rotate chairs, minute taking, and so on, so that there will be some level of skill sharing between all

members of the collective. There are clearing sessions where people can talk about how one person got to monopolize the chair. So there is some room to raise issues, but there are unspoken leaders . . . I feel that these women do manipulate the young, new, naive women in the group. You have to know how to talk like them, you have to be articulate, you have to know when to raise your voice.

When I came over here, one of the things I didn't know was how meetings were conducted. I had never heard of *Robert's Rules* so I didn't know you had to speak through the chair. You couldn't come in and just say what you wanted to say. I was rendered completely neutralized, completely powerless by the structure of the meeting.[29]

For many of the reasons discussed above, women's organizations continue to have difficulty translating an anti-racist politic into concrete behavioral and structural changes. While this is a difficult process, it is a necessary one.

SOCIALIST FEMINISM AND ISSUES OF ORGANIZATION

As we discussed in Chapter 3, the socialist-feminist politic is based on a radical critique of the entire society, in particular of ideological practices, relations of power, and existing institutions. Our particular dilemma as socialist feminists is to combine diversity with unity, wide scope with focused action, and participation with direction. For socialist feminists, the feminist model of organization and process must be placed within this context as we try to avoid both marginalization and institutionalization.

Successful socialist feminism, as we noted in Chapter 5, depends on balancing a politic of mainstreaming and a politic of disengagement, and thus avoiding both marginalization and institutionalization. It is this unique pattern that helps to explain the difficulties of building socialist-feminist organizations, which must accommodate both the 'inside' and the 'outside' dimensions of the socialist-feminist task.[30] Socialist feminists face three dilemmas in building organizations, and they emerge directly out of our politic and practice.

In the first place, the concomitant pulls of disengagement and mainstreaming create a dilemma about what kinds of organizations are appropriate. Disengagement suggests the building of specifically socialist-feminist organizations. These might take the form of socialist-feminist political organizations, such as the International Women's Day Committee of Toronto or Bread and Roses of Vancouver, or a feminist trade union such as SORWUC.[31] Mainstreaming suggests entering into and participating in mainstream organizations from the standpoint of a socialist-feminist politic. This can take the form of organizing a women's caucus or committee inside a mainstream institution like a trade union. Inside such an organization (for example, the Toronto-based Action Day Care) socialist feminists, often unnamed as such, would fight for better day-care.

Although these choices are not necessarily mutually exclusive, it is difficult to sustain both strategies at once, as the above examples suggest. And when the decision is to disengage and build alternative organizations, the latter are often marginalized; SORWUC provides a clear and somewhat painful example of this process.[32] If the choice is to mainstream, co-optation and institutionalization often occur; the difficulty faced by trade-union women's committees in sustaining their challenge to the goals and practices of unions is one example.[33] Another is the difficulty Action Day Care faces in maintaining a radical position.

For socialist feminism the more difficult part of this dilemma is often that of marginalization. Many socialist feminists, among them Charlotte Bunch, argue that one way of building power is by creating alternative institutions 'such as health clinics that give us more control over our bodies or women's media that control our communications with the public'. However, Bunch recognizes the danger of such alternatives, and adds that, 'alternative institutions should not be havens of retreat, but challenges that weaken male power over our lives'.[34] Alison Jaggar argues that in that sentence Bunch sums up the difference between socialist-feminist ideas of building alternative institutions and the radical-feminist conception of a woman-culture, which would allow women to withdraw from the dominant culture.[35]

Second, the centrality of 'difference' to the socialist-feminist politic and practice creates some contradictions around the building of socialist-feminist organizations. A politic of building sisterhood on the basis of difference is expressed organizationally through alliances and coalitions, rather than through large, homogeneous political organizations.

Inside such coalitions socialist feminists are torn between two political tasks: the need to build a broad-based, heterogeneous mass movement that can challenge dominant ideologies and practices (mainstream) and the need to win women to an alternative socialist-feminist vision (disengage). The first goal lends itself to the building of alliances constructed on a limited basis of unity, which would not offer much opportunity to highlight socialist feminism; the second suggests an explicit focus on building a socialist-feminist organization or current—that is, attempting to win women to a socialist-feminist perspective. The former functions in a politically heterogeneous environment; the latter aims for a degree of homogeneity and is, by definition, threatening to the coalition process.

Finally, the socialist-feminist belief in the necessity of a fundamental social transformation that challenges not only gender relations but also relations of class, race, and sexual orientation implies a commitment to the building of a mass heterogenous political movement. In principle this means forming alliances with organizations outside the women's movement, such as trade unions and progressive community groups that organize around peace, anti-racism, and environmental issues, and, if they exist, parliamentary and extra-parliamentary socialist and communist parties. In all these cases such a commitment also means organizing with men, which raises complex questions about the relation between the building of such alliances and autonomous feminist organizing.

The building of these kinds of alliances also constantly raises the strategic question of whether it is more appropriate to build socialist-feminist organizations or to enter into existing organizations and tranform them. One of the dilemmas that arises here concerns the internal process of organizations. Feminists have developed an extensive critique of the process and practices of most social institutions (including the democratic centralism of far-left organizations), and have attempted to develop, although not always successfully, an alternative feminist process. The fact that feminist process is most easily developed and expressed in alternative organizations presents some difficulties for socialist feminists, who reject alternatives as an adequate political strategy and yet who simultaneously reject the practices of mainstream institutions.

As socialist feminists our particular strength in taking feminism out into the world is in the area of education. Socialist feminism unmasks how the system works; makes known the limitations of conventional political routes, thus empowering people with that information and perspective; and links one feminist issue to another to provide a complete picture of women's oppression. However, recruitment to socialist-feminist organizations is difficult because of anti-communism, the fear of change, and other factors discussed in Chapter 4. That difficulty might suggest that socialist-feminist organizations need to concentrate on the areas of education and outreach.

It is not so easy to juggle these various options, and in Canada, certainly, this has most often meant that building explicitly socialist-feminist organizations has not been a priority for many socialist feminists.[36] Moreover, it is important to point out that there is no consensus among socialist feminists that creating such organizations *per se* is the best strategy. And of course, at different historical and political conjunctures such organizations might be more or less viable. Notwithstanding, it is useful to situate the discussion of whether or not socialist feminists should focus their political energy on building such organizations inside the particular dilemmas that face such a project. In fact, it might be appropriate to suggest that part of the reason such organizations have so often failed, or that the project has been avoided, is precisely the contradictory nature of the task. Building socialist-feminist organizations is complex because we are pulled in different directions.

CONCLUSION

In building organizations, grass-roots feminists frequently got caught up in the organizational process itself, even when the organization in question was no longer effective. Organizational process can and does obscure the larger political goals that organizations set themselves, and also leads us to lose sight of the movement we are building. As we noted earlier, organizations are not a substitute for a movement, they are part of a movement; movement is a larger category, which gives meaning to individual organizations.

Organizational structures and processes do not exist for themselves. They have a purpose: to facilitate the political effectiveness of the organization. It is in the context of a particular group's political analysis and strategy that its structure and process must be evaluated. And though there has been a tendency in the grass-roots movement to regard 'feminist process' as the correct way to structure every organization, the discussion above has demonstrated that different structures and processes are suited to different agendas. No one structure can meet the variety of political agendas found in the women's movement.

For socialist feminists the strengths and weaknesses of feminist organizational models can best be understood in terms of the balance between disengagement on the one hand and mainstreaming on the other. Certainly the feminist model was a rejection of mainstream organizational theories and attempted to provide alternative structures using feminist process; as such it was a politic of disengagement. The danger of such a politic is that it can easily lead to marginalization and invisibility. And in fact, as we have seen, the practice of feminist process has been contradictory: while the theory operated as a politic of disengagement, the practice was often one of marginalization.

NOTES

[1]Sheila Rowbotham, 'The Women's Movement and Organising for Socialism', in Sheila Rowbotham, Lynne Segal, and Hilary Wainwright, *Beyond the Fragments* (London: Islington Community Press, 1979), pp. 40–1.

[2]See Jo Freeman, 'The Tyranny of Structurelessness' in Jane P. Jaquette, ed., *Women in Politics* (New York: John Wiley & Sons, 1974), pp. 202–14 and Myrna Kostash, *Long Way from Home* (Toronto: Lorimer, 1980) for more detailed discussion.

[3]For a fuller discussion of democratic centralism, see Rowbotham et al., *Beyond the Fragments*.

[4]*Robert's Rules of Order* was first published in 1876 by U. S. Army general Henry M. Robert. Part I is subtitled 'A Compendium of Parliamentary Law, Based Upon the Rules and Practise of Congress', and Part II is subtitled 'Organization and Conduct of Business: A Simple Explanation of the Methods of Organizing and Conducting the Business of Societies, Conventions, and other Deliberative Assemblies'. In North America these rules of order have come to be regarded as the standards for running a meeting and are very widely used. They are periodically revised and updated, and many organizations adapt them to their own needs.

[5]Hierarchical organizations have a structure that gives the most power to one or a few people and then gradually spreads different amounts of power to increasingly larger groups. There is a clear sense of power and authority *descending* from a few at the top down to those at the bottom.

[6]Linda Briskin, 'Women and Unions in Canada: A Statistical Overview' in Linda Briskin and Lynda Yanz, eds, *Union Sisters* (Toronto: Women's Press, 1983); Julie White, *Women and Unions* (Ottawa: Canadian Advisory Council on the Status of Women, 1980).

[7]Debbie Field, 'The Dilemma Facing Women's Committees', in Briskin and Yanz, *Union Sisters*, pp. 293–306.

[8]Ibid., p. 300.

[9]For example, see OCAC's proposal for structural change at the 1986 annual general meeting (CWMA/ACMF).

[10]Nancy Hartsock, 'Fundamental Feminism: Process and Perspective', *Quest* vol. 2, no. 2 (Fall 1975), p. 78 (emphasis added).

[11]Josephine Donovan, *Feminist Theory* (New York: Frederick Ungar, 1985), p. 85.

[12]Alice de Wolff, Judy Dragon, Julie Ann Le Gras, Trudy Richardson, Sandy Susut, Derwyn Whitehead, 'Women Organize Alberta: Discussion Paper' (1981), p. 2 (CWMA/ACMF).

[13]Donovan, *Feminist Theory*, p. 87.

[14]Ibid.

[15]Freeman, 'Tyranny of Structurelessness'.

[16]CWMA/ACMF, Saskatoon Women's Liberation papers, Steering Committee, Constitution Proposal, Jan. 1978, p. 3.

[17]CWMA/ACMF, SWL papers, Constitutional Proposal, Jan. 1978, p. 6.

[18]C. Landry, D. Morley, R. Southwood, P. Wright, *What a Way to Run a Railroad: An Analysis of Radical Failure* (London: Comedia Publishing Group, 1985), pp. 11–12.

[19]For examples of forms of conflict resolution see Joan Holmes and Joan Riggs, 'Feminist Organization Part II: Conflict and Change', *Breaking the Silence* vol. 3, no. 1 (Fall 1984), pp.16–22.

[20]CWMA/ACMF, SWL papers, Constitutional Proposal, Jan. 1978, p. 4.

[21]Rowbotham, *Beyond the Fragments*, p. 40.

[22]For a fuller discussion of this topic see Lorna Weir, 'Tit for Tat: Coalition Politics', *Broadside* vol. 3, no. 4 (Feb. 1982), pp. 10–11.

[23]See Weir, 'Tit for Tat', for the challenges of working with non-feminist groups in a coalition.

[24]Bev Le François and Helga Martens Enns, *Story of a Woman's Centre* (Vancouver: Press Gang, 1979), pp. 28-9.

[25]Egan, p. 113.

[26]Quoted in Allison Jaggar, *Feminist Politics and Human Nature* (Totowa, N.J.: Rowman and Allanheld, 1983), pp. 335-6.

[27]Based on discussions with Vicki van Wagner and Rena Porteous, fall 1987.

[28]Linda Briskin, 'Socialist Feminism: From the Standpoint of Practice' (paper given at the 3rd International Interdisciplinary Congress on Women, Dublin, Ireland, July 1987), pp. 3-4.

[29]'Organizing Exclusion: Race, Class, Community and the White Women's Movement', *Fireweed: A Feminist Quarterly* no. 17 (Summer/Fall, 1983), pp. 57, 59.

[30]It is useful to note a distinction between organizing for change and building organizations to facilitate that process.

[31]For a detailed discussion of the attempts of SORWUC (Service, Office and Retail Workers Union of Canada) to organize the bank workers, see The Bank Book Collective, *An Account to Settle* (Vancouver: Press Gang, 1979).

[32]Rosemary Warskett, in 'Legitimate and Illegitimate Unionism: the Case of SORWUC and Bankworker Unionization' (unpublished paper prepared for the Political Economy Sessions of the Canadian Political Science Association, June 1987) documents the process of SOR-WUC's being constructed as an 'illegitimate' union. In the language of this book, we might label this process marginalization.

[33]For a discussion of the difficulties of building trade-union women's committees and the conditions under which such committees get co-opted, see Field, 'Dilemma Facing Women's Committees'.

[34]Quoted in Jaggar, *Feminist Politics*, p. 336.

[35]Ibid., p. 336.

[36]Some exceptions are Saskatoon Women's Liberation, the International Women's Day Committee of Toronto, and Bread and Roses of Vancouver.

8

Conclusion

We were young and vigorous and full of ambition. We would rewrite
our history. We would copy no other country. We would be ourselves
and proud of it.[1]

As this quotation from Nellie McClung reminds us, the era of the
present women's liberation movement is not the first time women
have sought change. Nor is it the first time women have believed in
their ability to make that change happen. In fact, this description of
how Canadian suffragists felt about the possibility of change could
just as well be used to convey the optimism of the re-emergent
feminist struggle of the 1960s and early 1970s. At that time, as in
the previous era, feminists felt that something new and powerful had
been discovered: the ability and strength of women to fight against
their subjugation, and to win.

It seems clear that the feminist perspective on change in the late
sixties and early seventies was unself-conscious and theoretically
unsophisticated. Initially it was not rooted in a systematic historical
or political explanation either of women's oppression or of the process of change. In fact, feminists were not even really aware that
there was a history of women's oppression, or of women's struggle
against it. The vibrancy of the movement came straight out of a very
immediate awareness of women's oppression, and as women cata-
logued their experiences it seemed that the enormity of that oppression cried out for change. Feminists thought that simply exposing
the extent of this oppression would itself create change. There were
no insurmountable barriers to change: it seemed obvious that, once
revealed, the oppression of women would no longer be tolerated.
All things were possible; change would result from recognizing the
need for it.

And in 1969 it was easy to believe that in ten years the world
would be a different place, that women's oppression would be
entirely eradicated. The numbers of women who, apparently over-
night, rallied to the cause; the proliferation of groups, issues,
actions; and the growth of ideas and theories—all contributed to the

sense of excitement, power, and possibility. This feeling was captured by Elaine Dewar:

> It was magic. Suddenly the idea of women's liberation was everywhere and women started banding together in little groups to talk about 'the problem'. . . . We vibrated with the joy of discovery: women had things to say to each other besides 'How's hubby?' and 'Where didya get that dress?' We examined ourselves in consciousness-raising groups, agonizing over the crucial moments at which we had been stopped, shunted onto the narrow track that ran straight to wifehood and motherhood.
>
> The vision, when it came, was a blinding light, a flashing awareness that everything about our social lives was wrong, insane, twisted. Marriage oppressed us. Sex roles constrained us. We were chattels. Men were the enemy. Since everything needed a complete makeover, we would make over everything.
>
> We began to organize. We wrote briefs, gave speeches, appeared on TV, picketed, marched, changed ourselves. From 1969 to 1972 a new breed of braless women hit the streets. We burned. We raged. The revolution was now and no one would ever hold us down again.[2]

It is important to put this optimism into its historical context. The growth of the second wave of the women's movement coincided with widespread social and economic changes and expansion resulting in greater opportunities for women. It also coincided with the emergence of other social movements—the student movement, the anti-war movement, the Quebec nationalist movement and the American civil-rights movement—the combination of which created a belief in, and an enthusiasm for, the possibilities of change unparalleled in recent history. In this sense, the women's movement was part of a larger movement for change.

But that optimism was also very much in keeping with the prevailing ideology of change. It reflected a belief in the promises of individual justice and equality and a conviction that no social-structural class barriers stood in the way of change. Change was a question of making people aware of the existence of women's oppression.

Belief in the possibility of change provided the basis for the strength of the early grass-roots challenge to the system. Those feminists were not afraid of change, and their belief in the possibility of it made them feel powerful; in fact, did make them powerful. Because it felt powerful, the movement was able to act. The combined sense of optimism and outrage had a dramatic mobilizing effect on women in the late 1960s and early 1970s, just as it had during the earlier period when women struggled to be acknowledged as 'persons' in their own right, and for the right to exercise their power as persons through the vote.

This explosion of anger and feminist consciousness gradually gained more focus and direction as efforts were made to analyze and explain the roots of women's experience, and those experiences were put into larger social and historical perspectives. At the same time, recognizing the initial eclecticism of the movement and the fluidity of its organizational forms, feminists attempted to create and sustain long-term structures and memberships, and to define the venues for struggle more clearly.

The process of solidification was as tempestuous and challenging for feminists as the beginning stage had been. It was a time for organizational consolidation, for theoretical and historical analysis, for political debate and differentiation. Political meetings took place every night of the week; feminist organizations proliferated; from a few cherished books, the literature about and by feminists became impossible to keep up with. In the process of all this discussion, the movement grew more sophisticated and self-conscious in its efforts to organize for change.

Coming out of that period, however, it seemed that while the movement had gained in theoretical and political terms, something else had been lost. The more that was understood about women's oppression, the more overwhelming the task of change appeared. Increasingly, the vision of social change became more attentuated and abstract, based more in feminist theories about change than in the anger of experience.

At the same time, despite all the effort, change was not occurring as quickly as expected, and when it was, the result was not always the one desired. It often seemed that the earlier sense of power was an illusion, that social change of the sort envisioned in those heady earlier days was not really possible. In part, this pessimism was related to what seemed to be a move towards a more limited vision of change, towards more 'realistic' goals within the framework of the system. As the Working Group on Sexual Violence put it in 1985:

> At some time during the past ten years, the word 'liberation' disap-
> peared from the Women's Liberation Movement. Our analysis was
> softened so as to reach the ears of those who govern even before we
> said it out loud to each other. Our demands became polite requests,
> and our reality became a negotiable position.[3]

In short, many believed that the optimism that had inspired women to act around radical visions of social change had dissipated, leaving what remained of the women's movement in the hands of institutional feminism. Again, to quote Elaine Dewar:

> The optimism of the early 1970s—'You've got it, we want it, and we're going to get it' was one of our slogans—has dried up and with it have gone most of the radical women who forced the issues on the public. The women's liberation movement has narrowed to a pallid lobby for equal rights; the radical lifestyle questions that caught the public's imagination have been shunted aside. Without the radical debate, the movement is missing something basic.[4]

Yet cries that the grass-roots women's movement was dead—that it had been superceded by superwomen in business suits—were not accurate. There were still many feminists continuing to work for fundamental social change—organizing for day-care, equal pay, and abortion rights, and against compulsory heterosexuality and violence against women; involved in a whole range of issues surrounding women's oppression. The problem was that these efforts were often diverse and seemingly unconnected, and the sense of movement often weak. This feeling of fragmentation was heightened as many grass-roots feminists expanded their political activity beyond the traditional boundaries of the women's movement to include such concerns as racism or anti-nuclear issues, and to become involved in other organizations such as trade unions or solidarity movements.

Indeed, since the mid-seventies it has often seemed that the main issue facing the grass-roots women's movement was how to recapture some of the early momentum and unity—and with it some of the earlier sense of certainty about change. Time and time again, it seemed, feminists built campaigns, raised and defined issues, recruited support, and created organizations. But we did not achieve the breakthrough we wanted, and the task of mobilizing support for social change only seemed to get harder with the passing years. Twenty years later, we, like Dewar, were asking: 'So where has all the shouting gone? Where the hell is the WOMEN'S LIBERATION MOVEMENT now?'[5]

In fact, it was with just such a feeling of demoralization, confusion, and even anger that we set out to write this book. We wanted to sort out why the women's movement had 'failed' to live up to its promise, why it was fragmented, why it was becoming harder to activate support—and, in our disappointment, our first tendency was to look for a place to lay the blame. Had the women's movement been 'bought off', or, at the other extreme, were our goals too extreme and unrealistic? Did the problem lie in poor organizational ractices, inadequate outreach, or weak leadership and a lack of commitment among activists?

Yet, although we started out feeling angry and discouraged, these feelings changed as our sense of the richness of the women's movement gradually re-emerged. As our discussions reminded us, the women's movement has had a varied and complex history, which in Canada alone spans two centuries. The most recent wave began in the favourable conditions of the late 1960s and early 1970s in the midst of considerable social and political tumult and openness to change; but it has continued to organize through economic downturn and the rise of conservative ideology.

At the same time, the movement has taken great strides forward in terms of its own complexity and development. Over twenty years it has changed in a qualitative way—grown, developed, diversified, and matured. It now encompasses a number of different theoretical perspectives and organizes around an ever-increasing number of issues that reflect the wide scope of its concern. It has organized itself using a variety of structures: from consciousness-raising groups to collectives, from caucuses to coalitions. Originally the movement in Canada arose out of the idealism and aspirations of white, middle-class, and educated young women; over the years it has found the range of its activity challenged by the self-organization of women from many different situations, including black, native, and working-class women. At the same time, it has been forced to confront the ageism, racism and heterosexism within its own ranks.

The truth is that the history of the women's movement is not one of failure and decline or of bad leadership and lack of commitment; in fact, as we described in the introduction to this book, overall the movement has had an enormous impact both on the specific character of women's lives and on the more general political situation. The problem was that much of the excitement of this history, and much of the sense of development, remained hidden in the memories of earlier feminists. It was inaccessible to many newer ones; even for those who had lived through the experience, it was too often buried by the tasks of the day. It seemed, then, that our first task in this book was simply to introduce the women's movement—its history, its forms of organization, its practice, its ideas—to those outside it, and to jog the memories of those who had been there. This we tried to do not only in Chapter 2, which is specifically about the history of the movement, but throughout the book as we analyzed some of the key ideas and decisions of the past twenty years.

But if writing this book has helped us to recover our sense of optimism about the women's movement, it is an optimism tinged with wariness. We are much more aware of the complexity of the struggle for change than in earlier days, and much more realistic about the difficulties to be faced in achieving it. Change is not just a matter of getting more people out to demonstrations, or writing more leaflets, or making more demands—the process is not as straightforward as many of us once imagined.

Thus our second purpose in this book has been to try to come to terms with the complexity of making change. And for that we have developed some conceptual tools that help to clarify the nature of the task, and serve as a framework for evaluating the role the women's movement has played.

One central foundation to our analysis was the idea of a prevailing 'ideology of change' that governs how people view the process of change. Although confronting the ways in which women are oppressed and pressing for change is obviously important to feminist practice, it is also necessary for feminists to change existing ideas about how this change will take place. In particular, the prevailing ideology of change and its emphasis on individualism engender a fear of both collective power and social change, and thus act to limit the possibility of wide acceptance for feminist visions.

We also introduced the idea that certain distinct ideas and organizational practices have been characteristic of the women's movement throughout its history, and that these have played a significant, although contradictory, role in shaping feminist practice. On the one hand, we showed how both the movement's central ideas—'the personal is political' and 'sisterhood'—and its alternative organizational processes were critical to its early growth. Yet those ideas and processes also limit the abilities of the women's movement to organize effectively. It is important to acknowledge the existence of these defining elements in the movement, and to understand the role they have played.

But the key tool in our analysis of making change is our model for feminist practice. We have argued that, to be effective in organizing for change, feminist practice needs to combine a politic of mainstreaming with a politic of disengagement. We believe this model allows for a less sectarian and rigid approach to understanding and situating different feminist practices than either of the more traditional categories of theory or experience, and thus provides a wider perspective for evaluating the role different feminist practices have played in making change. Our model also facilitates a better understanding of the apparently contradictory demands inherent in the task of making change itself, and thus acts as an important framework for grappling with the concrete decisions of practice.

However, this book goes beyond simply analyzing the task the women's movement faces in making change: it is also a call for activism. It tries to show that 'believing in equal rights' is not enough: to make change, women need to both identify themselves as feminists and recognize the need to organize. Moreover, it argues that in the context of feminist organizing for change, socialist feminism in particular offers a penetrating analysis for understanding the nature of women's lives, and a coherent basis on which to build an effective strategy for the future. Indeed, we believe this book itself makes a significant contribution to the elaboration of socialist-feminist analysis, particularly in Chapter 3, and opens up some important issues for socialist feminism to address concerning the nature and future direction of its practice.

And it is a challenging future that we face. On the one hand, there is the increasing external pressure exerted by worsening economic conditions and the rise of the new conservatism; on the other, the tensions created by the growing diversity and sophistication of our movement itself. These conditions add new dimensions to the already complex problem of organizing to bring about social change and an end to women's oppression. Can the grass-roots women's movement—and, in particular, socialist feminism—meet these challenges? We are now more optimistic that it can.

NOTES

[1] Nellie McClung, *The Stream Runs Fast*, p. 135, quoted in Veronica Stong-Boag, 'Introduction' to Nellie McClung, *In Times Like These* (Toronto: Univ. of Toronto Press, 1972).

[2] Elaine Dewar, 'Beyond Sisterhood', *Optimst* no. 12 (1977), p. 11, reprinted from *The Vancouver Sun, Weekend Magazine*.

[3] Working Group on Sexual Violence, 'Better Strident than Silent', *Broadside* vol.6, no. 6 (May 1985).

[4] Dewar, 'Beyond Sisterhood', p. 11.

[5] Ibid.

Appendix A: Documents

We have included the following documents because such material is no longer available to most women, and we feel it provides a sense of the women's movement that our words alone cannot give. The documents here represent the three currents of feminism, lesbian feminism, and women of colour. Most are from the early to mid-1970s, because these are the documents least familiar today, and most of them have been edited. The originals are available at the Canadian Women's Movement Archives/Les archives canadiennes du mouvement des femmes (P.O. Box 128, Station P, Toronto, Ontario M5S 2S7).

1.   PURPOSES OF THE VOICE OF WOMEN

The Voice of Women was founded in 1960 and has numerous chapters across Canada. The following is an excerpt from the Voice of Women Constitution, adopted in 1961.

To unite women in concern for the future of the world;

To help promote the mutual respect and cooperation among nations necessary for peaceful negotiations between world powers;

To protest against war or the threat of war as the decisive method of exercising power;

To appeal to all national leaders to cooperate in developing methods of negotiations;

To appeal to all national leaders to cooperate in the alleviation of the causes of war by common action for the economic and social betterment of all people;

To provide a means for women to exercise responsibility for the family of humankind.

2. EDITORIAL FROM *THE NEW FEMINIST*

The New Feminists split from the Toronto Women's Liberation Movement in 1969 because they objected to the TWLM's stress on class and its lack of stress on sexuality, particularly lesbian sexuality. They began to publish their own newsletter; the following editorial is taken from vol. 1, no. 5 (March 1970). The New Feminists called themselves 'radical feminists' and this editorial is a partial statement of their politics.

MYTHS, LIKE GHOSTS, are hard to lay. One myth has it that New Feminists are a-political.

True, we have not tied our movement to a political prophet, dogma or a sacred scripture that describes the millennium.

We all, as individuals, have our faiths and we have our hopes. But as a group we grant impartial credence to the Gospel according to Mark, to Marx or Marcuse, to Mohammed or Malcolm X. The Koran and Das Kapital are both on our reading list. Trudeau and Trotsky are just another pair of men.

But politics are the heart of our concern. Not the narrow 18th century view of politics as coextensive strictly with the state. In current thinking, politics is about all power. Political systems are all systems of power, where one person or group systematically control another.

The family is a political system. Power in the family system is unequally divided according tothe categories of age and sex. An adult male, if there is one about, is 'head' of the household and gives it his name. In the family, nascent personalities receive the first imprint of sexism.

The schools are themselves power systems; but their greater importance comes from the fact that they socialize young humans to fit into unequal power roles based on sex (as well as class). The economy is a vast network of power systems. In all its parts women are in effect excluded from control positions and channeled into positions of powerless, poorly rewarded drudgery. The state is a power system more or less controlling all other systems in the society, and it has always been commandeered by males to reflect their prejudices and protect their prerogatives. Finally, confirming and sanctifying the unequal distribution of power in society, religion has placed the seal of God's approval on the subordination of women.

Every act to change a power system is by definition a political act. It is a political act to change the power balance of the sex roles within the family.

A political act to purge religions of their anti-feminine superstitions. A political act to pressure the schools into desisting from socializing children into a caste system based on sex. It is a political act to exert whatever leverage is necessary on the economy to eliminate sex roles as a basis for locating and rewarding people in its structures. It is a political act to get sufficient control of the state that laws are passed which emancipate women rather than oppress them.

The total society is based on discrimination of sex roles, and the total society must be changed. Any act, in any sector of the society, that changes the unequal power balance between men and women has necessarily political consequences.

We are totally, radically, opposed to a society in which sexuality is destiny. But because we are a radical movement, we must guard against other radical movements which will try to foist their own dogmas off on us. Our strength is in the singleness of our purpose. If we confuse that purpose by associating it with one or another of the plethora of splinter movements vying for influence and members on the fringes of society, we will ourselves become just another splinter and lose all influence over the potentially large constituency of discontented women.

We are radical feminists. Our friends are those who support our goals—whether these friends are found on the left, the right or the center. Our enemies are those—whatever their other political persuasions—who threaten the realization of our radical feminist goals.

3. A PAPER FROM THE LEILA KHALED COLLECTIVE

The Leila Khaled Collective was formed in Toronto in late 1970. They were a group of women who withdrew from the Toronto Women's Liberation Movement because they felt TWLM should focus more on solidarity with Third World struggles and so named themselves after a Palestinian revolutionary. This position paper outlines the politics of the collective. It is not dated, but was written in late 1970 or early 1971.

. . .[W]e see a women's movement in North America attacking symbols (bras and beauty contests) and not the oppressor, concerned with individual liberation while black sisters are beaten and tortured, demanding freedom and equality from a decaying society where no one can be free and equal. The world has changed—has been transformed by the Vietnamese, the Panthers and the FLQ—and we have to figure out our responsibilities all over again before we go any further.

Women's Work and Anti-Imperialist Politics

We began the women's Liberation Movement with the correct understanding that women's oppression was basic to imperialism and that women must struggle politically to achieve their liberation. What resulted, however, was a split between organizing women and anti-imperialist politics.

We decided to meet as a separate group because we understood that women were already moving around those issues which affected them. We also recognized how male chauvinism had prevented us from taking ourselves seriously as political people. However, we falsely identified the problem as 'male' rather than an abstract and incorrect politics.

Women's Liberation, therefore, began on a basis of false unity. Our unity and our loyalty were based on the fact that we were political women. We recognized in a rhetorical way that the structures of imperialism were our enemy (not men). In practice and in our ongoing debates, however, we treated women's oppression as special and related to other people's oppression only in a mechanical way. We thus reinforced the same abstract politics that had originally frustrated us. We related to the problem of male chauvinism as something that could endure the revolutionary process. Women's real interests were not seen as central to smashing imperialism but a women's group was necessary to insure that the revolution included 'women's needs'. When it was suggested that the group take initiative around the people's struggle in Quebec, we discovered that the links between the English Canadian Women's movement and the Quebecois were not obvious to everyone. Our anti-imperialism had been assumed and tasked [sic] on. It was not a part of the daily political struggle and practice of the Women's group. Our conception of women's oppression had become insulated from the questions and the problems of the rest of the movement (the left as a whole).

. . . When we say that we must understand our oppression as women before we can understand other people's oppression, we make a split that most women cannot make. We fail to see that women are among the strongest people in this society, precisely because they fight so hard for their own survival, for the survival of their husbands, their children and their communities under capitalism. While it is true that women have always been socialized to care for others at the expense of themselves, their capacity to support and fight for others is a strength and not a weakness. In many ways, women's liberation up till now seems to have been saying it is a weakness. This contradiction can be resolved in a more revolutionary way. Women are struggling for the liberation of all people. . . .

Part of our unity as T.W.L.M. was based on an assumption that we shared a correct class analysis. We have understood well what is incorrect about feminism. Feminism comes from a middle class consciousness and therefore, could not speak to the lives of most women. Since many of us come from middle class backgrounds, we have known that we must educate ourselves and overcome a socialized chauvinism towards working class sisters. That is, we have talked about class in many good ways, but there has also been much in the talk of 'organizing working class women' which we must reassess critically.

. . . As the Women's Liberation Movement we made a distinction between ourselves and the feminists because we were concerned with organizing working class women. We have pointed out some of the errors in our conception of 'working class', however, there is a further way in which our analysis must be reevaluated. We must make the decision about where we as revolutionary women will work on the basis of *where we can best give* leadership. The question should not be posed as: 'to work or not to work with men'.

We know that across North America women's consciousness is growing. A large autonomous women's movement exists now and will continue to exist. Sectors of this movement are feminist and given their class interests will continue to be feminist. A substantial sector of this movement has revolutionary potential and revolutionary women must understand their responsibility to provide the leadership so that this potential becomes a reality.

Theory and Practice

Our practice in the T.W.L.M. has been of three kinds—the integration of new women into the group, serve the people projects around day-care and abortion and actions like the Abortion Caravan and the Waterloo Beauty Contest. . . .

Our continual concern with integrating new women came partly from a confusion about what building a women's movement was all about. We have tended to confuse building a movement with building a women's group, eg. we have conceived of the women's groups as a mass movement which grew by recruiting and integrating new members one by one. All we have to offer new women is an education process to make them more politically aware. This meant the composition of the group was bound to remain mostly young, unmarried women with more academic experience than most. Although we did serve the needs of these women to some extent, it didn't help them to move forward as revolutionaries in any major way. Women with little time, little education, with families and jobs or women who have to fight hard to survive on welfare aren't interested in coming to weekly meetings to talk about sexuality or to read Engels.

We never felt very happy about this process of internal education and last winter our frustration led us to the conclusion that the only way we could overcome the stagnation within the group was to undertake public actions. . . .

Our third type of practice has been to set up services which we hoped would not only meet a pressing need but be a means of politicizing women. Many of us worked hard at the day-care center and in the abortion referral service—we have accomplished much and learned a lot but we must not be blind to the limitations of this work. Politically we have set ourselves up as a kind of manipulator—we have helped some women with an immediate need and then we have asked them to rise above this need and jeopardize the security of their assistance by broadening the struggle. We get a woman an abortion and then ask her to fight out of gratitude to us for abortions for other women.

In the University of Toronto Collective, our basis for collectivity was common work. When the women in the New Left Caucus split from the men, we understood our priorities as developing a collective sense of our own politics so that we could challenge the apolitical nature of the women's group. Our working together on a series of seminars did not resolve any of the political differences that existed among individual women nor did it deal with those of the larger group. We did not struggle through such basic political questions as imperialism or racism even within our own collective. In effect, we insulated ourselves within the collective, unable to challenge the women's movement even through the back door. We did not raise the question of when it would be politically strategic to work with men. Without our collectivity being based on a common understanding of politics, our collective work would only be a substitute for political struggle.

We realize that our political differences cannot be settled by merely working together on certain projects. We have to ask the question of how to develop the highest possible level of political unity among women. How do we do mass organizing in a revolutionary way?

Our unity can no longer be a clinging together, it has to be an agreement to increase each other's strengths and diminish each other's weaknesses. The women's group has helped a lot to break down our dependencies on men but it has to do more than that. It has to make us more capable of loving and working with men and women as revolutionaries or it does nothing at all.

ALL POWER TO THE PEOPLE!

4. SUMMATION OF THE STRATEGY FOR CHANGE CONVENTION

This document is the summation by the National Action Committee of the 'Strategy for Change' Convention of Women in Canada, Toronto, 7–9 April 1972.

The enormity of the task undertaken by the Steering Committee of [NAC] in calling a conference of Canadian women in early April would have caused anyone who was not aware of the February Impending-Election fever to quail, deferring action until 'proper planning' could take place. It is a credit to the Committee's imagination and to the courageous leadership of Chairperson Laura Sabia that the moment for [NAC] to act in support of its priorities was recognized immediately following the Submission to the federal government. . . .

Hindsight indicates that more adequate facilities should have been provided in the press room; we cannot do without the media—we want to maintain our visibility. Closer attention might have been given to the control of public access to the conference; the publications display was jeopardized and uninvited demonstrators created disturbances.

We regret that representation from the gamut of Canada's women was not ideal, and we recognize that a longer time spent in planning would have permitted more thoughtful selection of delegates by constituent organizations, many of which exist at a national level only as consultative bodies. A future conference and the on-going [NAC] should incorporate a procedure for delegate accreditation. Without this, voting indicates only the responses of those present, with or without credentials, and cannot be taken as a formal result of a controlled polling. . . .

. . . [T]he conference represented an honest beginning by a significant sector of Canadian women who want to work together in matters of common concern.

Delegates persevered through a forest of diversities: 'the generation gap' was found to be a myth; leadership ability abounded; cultural variety was enriching. Many participants commented on increasing personal consciousness and reassurance in finding so much in common with other women. They resolved to follow-through on municipal and provincial levels. In the near future, regional committees will undoubtably assume much greater importance in the overall effort toward implementation of RSCW recommendations. Reports are also being made to appropriate groups in areas both geographically and organizationally distant from the present [NAC]. To this end, local programs of study, investigation and public relations are being organized.

It was obvious that the philosophic underpinnings of the RCSW do not satisfy everyone. More dialogue on issues is needed; more time to talk; more information—for everyone at the conference did not begin discussion of strategy from a basis of knowledge of the REPORT. Herein lies the value of exposing varying degrees of commitment and revealing the extremes of current attitudes. To see that this could happen was of benefit to delegates who, not always willingly, sublimated concern for issues to the discipline of devising ways and means.

The conference brought into focus the need for the [NAC] to define its own limits: membership, structure, objectives, relationship to constituent organizations and to governments, etc. Can such a body work on a presumption of consensus? How will it deal with objective methods while maintaining democratic procedure? We became aware of the lack of structure which is necessary to put our proposed strategies into effect.

As the delegate for the Yellowknife YWCA said: '. . . if the purpose . . . was viewed as intending to *consider* strategy for change, the conference was highly successful. On the other hand, if . . . to *determine* strategy . . . it was somewhat less successful, such intention perhaps being premature.'

A prime value of the conference was a two-fold realization: on the one hand, by 'conservative' elements, that confrontation techniques are some-times effective strategies in situations where change is not part of normal expectations; on the other, by 'radical' elements, that reasoned argument based on substantiated fact goes further in the pursuit of real justice than does partisan emotion.

It is, for instance, essential to know that *behind* some apparent flagrant discriminations there exists historical oversight—even a cultural barrier which should not be interpreted as intentionally hostile. It is essential, too, for women seeking change to understand thoroughly the practical proce-dures and legislative 'machinery' so that they can harness, rather than destroy, the potential energy of established political, economic and social power.

We agreed that a certain amount of tension is healthy. If we want our movement to be dynamic, we must accept the clash of forces which creates the all-important *process* of change. Many of the recommendations approved by the conference reflected this rejection of the comfortable status quo.

We had a sense of participating in a unique event—of witnessing an inevitable collision of viewpoints—of uniting to assume the heritage of the suffragettes. The impact of the conference is difficult to assess, but we know that action has been started which otherwise would not have been considered. If such a distance was measured at the first conference, it is encouraging to speculate how far the next step may carry us.

At the introduction of the theme, the conference paused to reflect: 'And miles to go . . .', but now at the conclusion, no matter what path each member organization may choose to follow in reaching the common goal, the same words, 'And miles to go . . .' may be given as a ringing exhortation.

5. STATEMENT OF A 'RADICAL CAUCUS OF WOMEN'

This statement was included in the final report of the 'Strategy for Change' Convention of Women in Canada, sponsored by the National Action Com-mittee on the Status of Women and held in Toronto, 7–9 April 1972. It was written by a group of feminists who considered themselves 'radical' in relation to the majority of women attending the NAC conference. They were not using the term 'radical' as it was later to be used to mean 'radical feminism'.

The following statement, received from a radical caucus formed outside the planned programme of the Convention, represents the views of a limited group of women who demanded to be heard.

'Over sixty women met last night in an emergency session to discuss issues they found missing from the National Action Committee on the Status of Women in Canada. The following statement was drawn up:

'We feel that the basic issue which had been ruled out of discussions was that it is not only the status of women which is wrong, but that it is in fact only symptomatic of what is wrong. This being the system itself. We believe women want to work for the benefit of all the people of Canada rather than to jockey for positions in corporations, most of them U.S. dominated, that exploit all Canadians and Canadian women in particular. From our experiences at this conference we suggest that should there be future conferences they be:

a) located in simpler surroundings, in a place not owned by a large U.S. corporation such as I.T. & T. which produces anti-personnel weapons for destruction of life and vegetation in Viet Nam.

b) that natural foods be provided

c) that table service be carried out by the participants

d) that entertainment be provided by women concerned about the cause of women and be non-sexist in nature

e) that film crews and other media personnel be all-women, to promote the hiring of women in this field and to encourage understanding coverage

f) that conference committees should be more flexible to reschedule time to provide for special needs which might arise.

'At a future conference on the Status of Women the following should be debated in full:

a) child care in state supported child care centres as a right for every child, as education is a right

b) community control of education at all levels

c) the including of sexuality in the human rights code

d) the elimination of poverty which calls for radical change of the whole structure of this society. For we as women understand that the relationship between women and poverty is a necessary and basic part of the present system.

'We demand that the conference support demonstrations, boycotts, strikes and other such actions as a means of public education and of effecting change; that it recognize that all levels of actions are necessary and in a spirit of sisterhood all women support such actions in the manner they feel to be the most valid.

'We feel further that an illustration of how we cannot solve the question of women's exploitation without understanding how a huge international corporation like Kraft is destroying farming communities in Canada. We suspect the use of Kraft cheese at a luncheon. We therefore demand that five minutes be allocated for a presentation of the reasons behind the Kraft Boycott.'

6.   MONTREAL WOMEN'S LIBERATION

Montreal Women's Liberation was formed in Montreal, Quebec, in 1969. The following document is not dated, but was certainly written after 1 June 1970 the date of Morgentaler's first arrest. It focuses on the structure of the organization.

We have started, we all wanted to be sisters, together, without leaders or élites.

Instead, because one of our problems as women is thinking we can't think, speak, or act, we were all scared and separate.

Those who had previous political experience, or who just were able to talk more easily, seemed like 'heavies' to the others and scared them more.

When they realized that they were coming on too strong, they felt guilty and tried not to come on at all.

We had lots of arguments in the big meetings about whether we should ACT or THINK.

We finally knew we needed both. So we tried to set up some structure.

We had from the start had small groups to raise our consciousness.

So we decided those groups should take turns making presentations for discussions at the big meeting, on some aspect of women's oppression. We hoped they would be analytical, historical, and suggestive of action.

The consciousness-raising groups didn't pull it off, though. And on the side, many of them fell apart.

New women came and were often confused by our confusion, frightened at evidence of hostility and lack of togetherness, and turned off by our lack of effectiveness.

Because we had no separate way of incorporating them into the movement, they sometimes provided distractions as well [in] those big meetings, by asking questions irrelevant to our discussion which couldn't be coped with easily in the large group, or by opposing a policy of ours out of ignorance, e.g. our press policy, for reasons many of us might have felt before being involved and which they themselves would probably change later, etc. In addition, because they were new and often unfamiliar with the jargon, we often either avoided pursuing a political argument to its conclusion for fear of alienating them, or just the opposite, fell into sloganism as a substitute for analysis out of sheer frustration and inexperience.

Meanwhile, someone told us about the Abortion Cavalcade and we jumped on. Some of us worked very, very hard and lots of us went to Ottawa.

But on Sunday, the Montreal action was a bust. Some of us were too tired from Saturday. Some of us were embarrassed or scared. Some of us didn't know what the point was anyway. Some of us just had other things to do.

So afterwards, we tried to have self-criticism. But either because we didn't want to criticize our sisters, or because we just found it too confusing as a whole, we said very little.

Then we decided what we needed all along was a Political Analysis. So we set up study groups.

Meantime Morgentaler was arrested and some of us set up an Abortion Committee.

Welfare wanted our help, so others of us set up a Welfare Committee.

A conference was suggested, so we set up a Conference Committee.

We found an office, and naturally, an Office Committee.

We became fragmented.

And that meant:

Actions had not enough political understanding and *strategy* based on that.

Study groups tended to become abstract. If we wanted to talk about concrete problems, we often felt apologetic.

Many times in consciousness-raising groups, we would end up talking about our past.

Our fear of elitism meant we had no leadership at all, no one to accept responsibility. Without being able to ascribe responsibility, we didn't know how to make collective criticism—and so we all felt individually shitty.

Or else we saw the group as something other than ourselves and blamed it.

Meanwhile, a kind of élite did grow up, who were too frightened at the thought of acknowledging themselves as an élite to get together, though they did manage to sway decisions of the large group.

Throughout all this, commitment was a large problem.

But to be committed to something, unless one is a masochist, means to see it as related in a real way to your own needs.

As long as it remains a purely individual decision to help or not to help on any particular project, or keep one's small group from falling apart, etc., people are bound to be scared, discouraged, and eventually turned off.

And as long as we are fragmented in our groups, people will be turned off.

Only when we work through small units which genuinely do function as collectives where consciousness-raising, political reading and discussion, and actions become integrated, will we begin to learn to:

- trust each other

- overcome our personal feelings of insecurity

- express disagreement without appearing or being hostile; to learn to express anger positively

- see the movement as a movement, which needs analysis, strategy, and lots of time and work

- be able to make political and therefore meaningful decisions about whether or not to support an action, staff the office, etc.

Let's say we had three groovy collectives based on particular areas of concentration. One member from each would serve on a coordinating body, which would do just that, coordinate the various collectives. The members would rotate, each serving 6 weeks. . . . The c.b. would meet once a week, so that each collective's representative would report on where they were at, and take back to her collective a report on where the others were at. . . .The c.b. would decide which collective would make a presentation at the bi-weekly meeting. . . .

Some of the advantages of such a structure:

- Works against élitism without eliminating leadership.

- Combines the now fragmented functions of personal, theoretical, and action. Should become much closer, much more like sisters, and thus much better able to support each other in personal problems, when we are working and thinking together as well.

- Thought should become less abstract and more related to practise.

- Our actions should be more thought out and certainly more frequent and more fully supported, because people will know why they are taking place and how to relate to them.

- Helps us better (by virtue of small groups) cope with the problems of talking too much or too little, taking on too many tasks or too few, by those problems becoming part of the group's problems instead of just the individual's; by our simply feeling more comfortable with each other; and by our having better political perspective in which to see these problems, rather than considering them as personal weaknesses simply.

- Tries to deal in a much less distracting way with new women, because it talks to their specific needs, while really trying to bring them into the movement as a whole.

- We should be able to begin to think in terms of long-range strategy aswell as short-range.

- Easier to identify self with movement instead of seeing it as other.

- More committed because more involved, more of own needs being met.

- It's a better way for all of us to learn the skills of coordinating, calling meetings, speaking, writing, organizing, listening to each other, etc.

- The more we act collectively, the more likely we are to help each other when we become discouraged or make mistakes, and the more we are likely to stick with our work. (For example, if a collective takes karate together, they would talk about it afterwards, about their fears of hitting or being hit, about their attitudes towards competitiveness and helping each other, those of us who took karate this summer did not do that as a group, and many of us dropped out.)

Sounds pretty cool, huh?

But there are lots of problems:

- Some people don't want to break up their present consciousness-raising group or study group, if they really derive support or stimulation from them, and don't want to be in different collectives from their members.

- We'd have to avoid thinking that unless our collective was going to be the All-Time Best Collective, it wasn't worth starting or working on. In other words, we'd have to be ready to realize that no structural change brings immediate utopian results, and we'll have to struggle hard to make this work.

- How do we avoid becoming issue-oriented? It seems obvious that no one aspect of women's oppression should be viewed out of context of that overall oppression, and that one can't talk about welfare, for example, without talking also about abortion, shift work, high schools and education and training in general, discrimination about jobs, and the whole bit. Still, this is something we would have to be careful about. Likewise in our reading, although it would make sense to read things written specifically about the problems we are dealing with, it would be a mistake, surely, not to go on reading general background political things.

Finally, why talk about structure at all?

It seems clear that matters of relating well individually, of reaching out to new women who are oppressed, and of making effective decisions about actions and published analysis, can really all be fucked-up by bad or no structures. All the problems we've talked about—shadowy élites and no leadership, fragmentation, hostility, bad actions, lack of political perspective, lack of commitment, etc., reflect that.

Structure is never an answer by itself—but we shouldn't automatically equate it with bureaucracy and authoritarianism. Like most things, it can either be in the interest of the State (the few who actually make decisions) or in the interests of the People (all those others affected by the decisions). There can be democratic structures through which people grow, and it is often, as in our case, I think, true that lack of structure leads not to real collective decision-making and work-sharing, but to the behind-the-scenes manipulation, however undesired or unintended by the very people who do it, what we feared in the first place.

7. NAC AND IWY

This document is taken from *The Status of Women News*, the publication of the National Action Committee on the Status of Women, vol. 2, no. 3, November 1975. Written by NAC president Lorna Marsden, it represents NAC's summary of International Women's Year (IWY).

I don't think anyone can deny that International Women's Year has had an impact on the women's movement in Canada. The question is, what sort of impact?

In the National Action Committee our emphasis is upon bringing about legislative changes which will be the underpinnings for change in society and in the lives of women. We are not especially happy with progress in IWY. Some housekeeping has taken place with the passage of the Omnibus Bill.

The Human Rights Legislation has been introduced and if passed in an amended form may give some hope to working women. But by and large no woman in Canada is able to wield legal power to redress the wrongs she encounters in the workplace.

In assessing the impact of IWY, however, we must consider other changes which have occurred.

At the level of community interest and action, there has been change. Evidence of this is membership in Status of Women organizations and other of our member groups. Women across the country are flocking to join up and participate. Women who always denied that they had ever been discriminated against, who argued that women just didn't 'go out and fight' for their rights, or who classified us as 'loudmouthed' and 'angry' are now aware that there are issues of real importance for the direction which this society will take in the priorities, of the women's movement. They also recognize the kinds of structural discrimination implicit in government which continues to assume that housework will be done but go unrecognized and unrewarded if a marriage breaks up after twenty years, in a labour force where most women are in the tedious and poorly paid jobs and most men in the more interesting and better paid jobs, in a social climate which characterises all women in one way ('bitching after the fact') instead of looking at an individual's talents and merit.

But it is not only the differentiation and discrimination built into our legal and social system which confronts us. This year, more than ever, women are aware of what it takes to bring about changes at home. Daughters recognize the subtle pressures that parents are putting on them when they assume that girls will have short term careers and therefore don't deserve as extensive a training as boys. Mothers are conscious of the fact that their sons may have to learn to cook and their daughters learn to fix their cars and understand insurance policies. Husbands seem to trail behind the Movement in many families—believing in equality intellectually but becoming bewildered when confronted with change. The ways in which one brings about permanent change in the daily schedule of the home, in the language used by members of the family, in the relationships with friends are being worked out and used, not only among 'Libbers' but everywhere.

Is there a backlash? Probably. But that's not a bad thing if we know what we are after and what we have to do to resist it.

At the Annual Meeting of the National Action Committee in the spring of 1976, we will consider these questions: policy, tactics, and the future.

1975 was only one year in a long and slow process of social change. But in sum, I believe it has helped. It has made legitimate the goals and aspirations of all women in Canada. Now that governments, business and most people are willing to *talk* about equality, let's make them *do* something about it.

Tributes to the creativity and hard work of all the women of Canada who have made IWY a special year are in order. But questions about how we are going to proceed now are even better.

8. POSITION PAPER FOR SASKATOON WOMEN'S LIBERATION

Saskatoon Women's Liberation was formed in Saskatoon, Saskatchewan, in about 1969. The following document, dated 14 October 1977, is a political position paper outlining the politics of this 'feminist-socialist' organization.

Since the autumn of 1976 there have been important developments within the women's milieu in English Canada and Quebec. The quiescence of the past few years has undergone a change, one which is quite apparent in Saskatchewan. The reconstitution of women's groups in Regina and Saskatoon is part of a national reactivation that is taking place in Vancouver, Winnipeg, and Kingston, and to some extent in Ottawa and Toronto. In at least some of these centres, if not all, women are attempting to clarify where they stand politically through study and collective action.

This renewal is the external manifestation of a ferment among women that is taking place on a broader scale, a ferment that is the result of the massive contradictions of capitalism. On the one hand there exist today the economic preconditions for absolute equality for women, technological sophistication, development of the productive forces to the point where the socialization of reproductive tasks is materially possible, and rising expectations that such equality should become a fact. On the other hand exists the reality: women remain superexploited in the workforce and subjugated in the family. These contradictions cannot be resolved under the present system, since the oppression of women is essential to the maintenance of capitalism, just as the exploitation of the whole working class, female and male, is essential. Hence the contradictions can only deepen, and women who challenge traditional mores and roles in effect change the whole system.

Despite its explosive potential, the present revival of struggles for woman's equality remain limited in nature and their existence is tenuous. It is becoming increasingly clear to many of us that in order to maintain the present momentum and to develop it to its fullest strength, we must consciously build a vehicle to carry out our struggles. The vehicle is an autonomous women's movement. In constructing a new women's movement we can build on the acquisitions of the women's movement of the late sixties and early seventies, both its successes and the conditions that lead to its ultimate impasse.

It is a major thesis of this paper that women can achieve their ultimate liberation only through a world socialist revolution and not by any reform of the present system.

Women's oppression is an essential feature of class society. Its origins are economic and social in nature, not biological. In primitive society, before classes were established, social production was organized communally and its products shared equally. In that period of history, although women's reproductive function was the same as it is now, both sexes participated in assuring the sustenance and survival of all, with women playing a leadership role in some instances. The social status of women reflected their real equality in social production and everyday life. However, as human productivity increased—the result of the domestication of livestock and better methods of agriculture—there developed an increasing social surplus which came to be privately appropriated—usually by men.

. . . In sum, the oppression of women that originated with class society and the development of the family, can only be eradicated with the abolition of private ownership of wealth and the means of production, and the transfer to society as a whole, first, of the wealth and control now exercised by a minority, and second, of the social and economic responsibility now borne by the individual family.

While women have struggled over the centuries to overcome their oppression, the first major and successful battles were conducted in the late 19th century. It is the struggles of women in this period that set the preconditions for those of today.

. . . While the fundamental oppression of women does not lie in the formal denial of equality and the law, but goes much deeper, the extension of democratic rights to women helped masses of women to fight more effectively and assisted in exposing the deeper roots of their problems.

The resurgence of the women's movement in the sixties came about in those countries where many democratic rights had been won and where there continued to be a tradition of militant struggle. But the radicalization did not remain isolated to North America. In country after country, primarily in the advanced capitalist world, increasing numbers of women have raised demands for complete equality in all forms of economic and cultural activity—equal education, equal access to jobs, equal pay, and equal work. At the heart of all these struggles has been the fight for abortion. The right to control their own bodies, to determine if they will bear children, when and how many, is seen by millions of women as a fundamental precondition for their liberation.

Women's radicalization has a dynamic of its own because of the pervasive nature of our oppression. While we are not mechanically dependent on other social forces or subordinate to their leadership, we are not isolated from them either. This analysis is important if we are to understand the pressures acting on the women's movement of the sixties, and the different forces that we may be subject to. During the past few years the women's movement has been on the rise in a number of European countries—Britain, France, Italy and Spain particularly. It is no coincidence that in these countries there has been a general rise in militancy of the working class and students as well.

In Canada, however, working class and student struggles have not been nearly as pronounced as in Europe, and the mobilization of native peoples has not reached the proportion the blacks achieved in the U.S. in the sixties. It is this quiescence of the working class which has been largely responsible for the impasse reached by the Canadian women's movement in the past.

It was in many ways responsible for the inability of women to deal with the issue of class society, since there was no visible working class taking up issues which vitally affected all society. The confusion of the women's movement was further exacerbated by the method of 'consensus' operating. Going by 'consensus' meant that there was no clear recognition that political differences would inevitably spring up inside the women's movement and that there had to be a mechanism for dealing with these differences without jeopardizing the movement. Consensus tended to deny the existence of these differences and to impose a superficial unity based on a rather apolitical notion of sisterhood. Arguments about the strategic direction of the movement, once they did emerge, tended to have a rather destructive dynamic. They often took the form of personality conflicts and power struggles which were seen in largely personalist terms. The result, we now see, was damaging, unnecessarily so.

Since 1975, however, there has been a change in the economic and political scene in Canada. The economic crisis has struck; wage control and cutbacks were implemented in the fall of 1975, all of which have the most pronounced effect on women. In this situation we will most certainly see an even greater rise in struggles around women's issues.

This analysis is intended to provide a framework for the pressing questions before us—how to orient to these struggles? How to build an independent women's movement, not only in Saskatoon or Saskatchewan, but nationally? What should be the principles around which we organize?

The first requirement is women who will provide an organizing nucleus and leadership, more women than are presently consistently active. While it is difficult to remain active in the present period without becoming demoralized, given the lack of activity generally and the conservatism of Saskatchewan people, and while many of us are absorbed in our personal lives and problems, still political activity must become a priority for us if the women's movement is to survive and advance.

It is important that Women's Liberation be solid organizationally, with an elected leadership, delegated tasks and an established communications network. We must begin to structure meetings with agendas, speakers' lists, formal debate, motions, etc. In this way we will be able to carry out democratic debate and to deal with differences when they arise so as not to repeat our earlier mistakes.

We must set our sights on building a women's movement of hundreds, and then thousands, of women. A mass women's movement composed of alliances of women's groups would be heterogeneous politically, and it is essential that such a movement avoid political sectarianism. It must be the democratic right to contribute and to form tendencies to develop strategy. Policy must be set after formal, democratic debate and vote, with majority decisions abided by. In such a movement we would attempt to play an educational and leadership role in winning women to a feminist-socialist perspective. An independent movement must also be independent of the bourgeois political parties and the NDP (although this does not mean that we would not support progressive policies of the NDP). Finally, we must remain independent of the state—place no confidence in it alleviating our condition in any significant way, realize that grants of women's groups are essentially a means to control discontent and channel it into acceptable projects.

Finally, while it is necessary to maintain independence, it is equally important to overcome any tendency to go to the other extreme—remaining a small 'pure' and isolated grouping, turned inward.

It is essential that Saskatoon Women's Liberation affirm that it is a feminist-socialist women's group, with the perspective that women's true liberation will occur only under socialism, and that socialism will only be established with the liberation of women. However, to state our maximum goal is not enough. We need specific demands which will lead to the accomplishment of that goal. Existing and forthcoming papers of Saskatoon Women's Liberation will elaborate our demands and programs.

—Political Positions Committee

9. CONSTITUTION PROPOSAL (STEERING COMMITTEE, SASKATOON WOMEN'S LIBERATION)

This document, dated January 1978, is the introduction to a proposed new constitution. The fate of this proposal is not known, but it is interesting as another examination of the issue of structure and its relation to politics.

One of the tasks of the Steering Committee of Saskatoon Women's Liberation in 1977 was to draw up a formal organizational structure for Saskatoon Women's Liberation. Such a proposal may still seem alien to many of us as 'structurelessness' has been an integral part of the women's movement for the last ten years. 'Structurelessness' was part of our strength and one of our symbols. It distinguished us from all of the male-dominated movements of the time (as, of course, did our political emphases!). It was a major break with the patriarchal, capitalist system that we were and are struggling to overthrow. It was a manifestation of our noblest concept: Sisterhood. All women could and would work together for our common victory and we refused to replace the old oppressive authority structures with our own oppressive authority structure.

It has since become apparent that 'sisterhood' is not a universal given and we now treat it as a goal rather than an actuality. We believe that the women's movement has also outgrown the notion of 'structurelessness'. It was facilitative several years ago when the women's movement was primarily a myriad of consciousness-raising groups trying to define our problems and goals. From this stage most groups have moved on to a service orientation and disjunctive political actions. The last few years have been disastrous. Between 1974 and 1976 almost every Canadian women's group (except the major revisionist groups like Status of Women) went into a slump so serious that it appeared that we had perished.

We considered that there were several reasons for this temporary demise:
1. The political climate of the time;
2. The successful crippling by the state of so many women's centres in our acceptance of state funding;
3. The lack of political direction and goals of the movement;
4. And the lack of formal structure and organization of the various women's groups.

It is on this last point that we wish to concentrate.

'Structurelessness' is a myth. The nature of human groups is such that informal structures inevitably develop within them. All groups are structured. We can only decide whether or not our structure will be formal or informal.[1] The women's movement of the late 1960s and early 1970s operated on a very personal basis and called itself 'structureless'. For consciousness-raising groups an informal structure is the correct one. For any larger action or service-oriented groups it is not. We did not change our form when we changed our function and ended up disorganized as well as unorganized. Believing in this myth and thus refusing to build a formal

---

[1]For an excellent elaboration of this matter and its effects see 'Tyranny of Structurelessness' by Joe Freeman in *Radical Feminism*, eds. A. Koedt, Ellen Levine, and Anita Rapone.

framework for our groups had grave detrimental effects on our capacity for action and continued existence.

Probably the most obvious result of our lack of organization was our 'crisis in leadership'. This manifested itself in various ways. As Jo Freeman points out, we were led by informal elites. 'An elite refers to a small group of people who have power over a larger group of which they are part, usually without direct responsibility to that larger group, and often without their knowledge or consent.'[2] The leadership that we had was neither responsible nor recallable because it was not acknowledged. Our elites were groups of friends who happened to participate in the same political activities and who had lots of time or energy. Participation in them was not based on 'one's competence, dedication to feminism, talents or potential contribution to the movement.[3]

This is not to set the women who took leadership roles up as villains. On the contrary, they were primarily victims. They were almost invariably competent, dedicated, talented feminists. As their position as leaders was not acknowledged they were rarely given credit but often blamed. They did almost all of the work and were finally 'burnt out'. They had no mechanisms by which to recruit replacements. When they eventually had to withdraw in order to recuperate they took most of the information and the knowledge gained in their years of work with them. New 'elites' had to start from the beginning again. Invaluable women and their experiences were lost.

Another aspect of the 'leadership crisis' was our lack of accountable spokespersons. No one was given the responsibility and no one was trusted to act as such. Thus women who somehow 'made it' in the ordinary world, such as authors, editors and tennis-players, who professed feminism were taken by the media to be our representatives and presented to the public as our spokespersons. We all resented it but as we had no alternatives to offer we had no way of combatting it.

In summary, democratically elected/approved leaders and spokespersons are both responsible and recallable. Organization will give us more control over our movement. It can also prevent the debilitation of many good women and facilitate the passing on of cumulative knowledge.

The principle of sisterhood under which we originally operated implied that women were equal in all respects. This denied differences of interest and experience. We asked women who were just becoming involved in the movement to take full responsibility in the group, to make decisions for the whole group and to learn skills by trial and error. This has had an inhibiting and demoralizing effect on many new women. Only the already self-confident persisted. At the same time women who had been active in the movement for several years were forced to stay low key so as not

---

[2]Ibid.
[3]Ibid.

to intimidate new women. They were asked (only implicitly) not to develop and use their full potential in all or any one area. This practice was an attempt to insure that no one woman or small group of women had any more influence on the movement than any other women. This was both a disincentive to new women and a waste of the potential of our veterans.

In a formal organization women can choose which positions they are interested in holding and those in which they feel competent. We can recognize women's differences without giving anyone more than their democratic share of power.

In a group that has no formal decision-making process, decisions can be made by anyone at anytime and overturned as easily. Previously in Saskatoon decisions that no one was bound to were made and remade depending on who attended what particular meeting. We went in circles. It is a means of accomplishing a minimal rather than a maximal amount. It insures that we will not have a consistent direction for any length of time. It is self-defeating for any group that hopes to effect drastic, long-term social change.

We believe the decisions made democratically after considerable thought and all necessary debate will contribute immeasurably more to our changes of success, even small scale successes. But we will not operate under a consensus orientation. We expect and welcome differences and debate. It can be one of our most constructive practices. We advocate majority decisions that will be acted upon (or at least not acted against) by every member of the group. Debate on the issue, though, may continue indefinitely.

This brings up another disadvantage of operating on a personal and consensus basis as opposed to a formal, democratic framework. In the past we let political differences create personality conflicts. Personality differences were also allowed to act as serious rifts within the group. We do not underestimate the importance of either. It will probably continue to be the case that women leave our group over both factors. We do not claim that we can prevent this—only that we can turn some of it into a constructive process rather than a destructive one. It is only through a dialogue between several existing theoretical orientations that we can develop the socialist-feminist analysis we are striving for. And we cannot ignore the fact that the larger our group the more public impact we are able to have. Many differences can be worked out within the group rather than acting as a barrier to our growth.

Any structure that we develop now must be changeable over time. Such organization must also be done firstly at a local level to suit the specific situation. We submit this proposal as only being suitable for here and now. We hope that the condition of women and women's movement will change and that our organization will evolve appropriately.

There is nothing inherently evil about structure itself—only its excess or misuse. We must learn from our previous mistakes or we can expect history to repeat itself. The previous period of the women's liberation movement in Saskatoon lasted only six years. All of us realize that the dramatic social, economic and political changes required for the true liberation of women cannot and will not happen in a few years. In the political context of Canada we may have decades of struggle ahead of us. In 1976 we had to begin again from almost nothing. We must try to insure that this common cycle is not repeated. We must provide for continuity and direction. We believe that the existence of a solid, permanent structure and organization for Women's Liberation groups locally, nationally and finally internationally will provide us with an immensely greater chance of achieving our goals.

10. IWDC BASIS OF UNITY

The International Women's Day Committee was formed in Toronto in the late spring of 1978 as an anti-capitalist, anti-patriarchal organization. The following document is the basis of unity the group adopted in the summer of 1979. Later the group came to call itself a socialist-feminist organization.

Our Goal
The International Women's Day Committee stands for the complete social, political, economic, sexual, psychological, and cultural liberation of women. We stand opposed to the oppression of women in all its manifestations.

Our Enemy
We find the oppression of women rooted in the patriarchal capitalist system. Our oppression is determined by the mutual interdependence of the capitalist relations of production and the relations of patriarchal domination, particularly the institution of the family and the sexual division of labour. Male privilege and patriarchal ideas have been incorporated into the structure of capitalism and act to support it and legitimize its practices. Thus, the liberation of women in the long run must involve not only an attack on these ideas, but also profound and radical changes in the very structure of our society.

Furthermore, we cannot see the Canadian government as a neutral bystander in our struggle. Government structures at all levels are component parts of the capitalist system charged with the task of defending and maintaining this system and the values and practices that are central to it. Government must be seen as part of the problem—not part of the solution.

Our Task
It is clear from this that we have little to gain by lobbying the government. Rather, we must put our energies into building mass actions and a mass, united movement of women which can begin to challenge the system in a

more direct and serious way. We will need allies for this battle. Our primary allies are to be found in the various groups which presently form the women's movement. We also want to work with all those who challenge the economic, social and governmental forces which promote our oppression. In particular, the trade union movement can become an important and powerful force for the liberation of women.

11. LESBIAN ORGANIZATION OF TORONTO—A HERSTORY

The Lesbian Organization of Toronto (LOOT) was formed in 1977. The following document, written in mid-1979, recounts the history of that organization and explains some of the political perspectives of the lesbian movement.

The history of LOOT goes back farther than we think. It is as old as Sappho and all the lesbians to come after her. Since the beginning of the patriarchy, of the domination of men over women, our sexuality has been repressed and our identity denied and, at times, we have even been killed as witches. We must remember our roots and make our history now for those who will follow us.

LOOT's very existence is a political act in itself. Two years ago, we defined ourselves as lesbians. Without this definition, without this house, both the gay movement and the women's movement in this city would lack strength.

From the first days of CHAT,[1] lesbians were active and fighting, arguing and debating with gay men over the role of women in a gay group. From the first days of the recent women's movement, lesbians were putting forward their views within women's liberation. In the spring of 1971, the first public statement of lesbians was made at the Indo-Chinese Women's Liberation Conference here in Toronto. The group called the Women's Liberation Movement in Toronto was holding lesbian rap groups since the beginning of 1971.

Let us not forget that 1971 was also the year of great turmoil within the American women's movement over the issue of lesbianism, leading to the formation of separate lesbian groups. Here, in Canada, lesbian autonomy was retarded by a different evolutionary process.

How many of us remember The Other Woman feminist newspaper which was first produced and sold by five lesbians in the spring of 1972? It was that first issue which caused a scandal among the feminist community by daring to print more than one article of interest to lesbians.

The Woman's Place began in the summer of 1972 as a centre for feminist organizing. Many members of LOOT came out as lesbians through involve-

---

[1]Community Homophile Association of Toronto.

ment in the women's centre. But for those who were already lesbian, it was a struggle to maintain a separate identity. For about a year, we held Friday night Lesbian Drop-Ins and, from this, we developed rap groups. It was also at this time that the Toronto Sun was condemning the women's centre for being run by marxist-lesbians!

The first Canadian lesbian conferences took place in Montreal in the winters of 1974 and 1975 co-ordinated by anglophone lesbians. The second one took place during one of the worst snowstorms of that winter but the conference carried on with 200 lesbians. This was the first time that lesbians danced and listened to an all-women's band. To many women here today who have been immersed in a lesbian culture of art and music, it is difficult to describe the emotions felt that night.

Aside from these large events, it is time to reclaim our own local history. How many know that the first lesbian conference ever was held right here in Toronto in the summer of 1973 at the old YWCA at 21 McGill St. Probably very few. After all, it was only a local affair. Organized by lesbians from the Woman's Place, it was one in a series of attempts to bring lesbians in Toronto together.

342 Jarvis St. was a woman's space for over a year before it became LOOT. After the closing of the women's centre, women signed a lease to open a coffeehouse in 1975 but found too many problems over zoning bylaws and several lesbians moved into the house for the next year. During that winter of 1975, some frustrated lesbians opened the Three of Cups, a social space being badly needed.

In all this time, the community was growing and changing. In May of 1976, the Kingston gay group held a conference on Women and the gay liberation movement, at which the need for lesbian autonomy was expressed. The National Gay Rights Conference the following September in Toronto was the scene of a heated dispute over feminism.

Immediately afterward, the newly formed lesbian group in Ottawa (LOON) sponsored a national conference on the Thanksgiving weekend bringing together all the changes in the last two years. Two women from Toronto came to the conference and handed out a leaflet describing the need they felt for a space in Toronto for their lesbian identity. This one leaflet created both curiosity and excitement; it was obviously time for something important to happen.

Several Sundays later, the first meeting took place at the old CHAT Centre. Many ideas floated around; everybody wanted something—women's rock band, women's centre, lesbian centre, information network, etc. After the second meeting, a 'task force' was set up to look for a physical space for the idea that was taking shape in our discussions. From this two years later, we have our house, our idea called LOOT and we now also have a women's rock band.

At the same time, the lease on this house was expiring and the present members of LOOT who had lived there for a year were moving out. Both

The Other Woman newspaper and The Three of Cups were looking for a better and more permanent living space of their own. The problem was both time and money; it had to happen right away; so it did. Nobody had any money and yet we were taking on the burden of a $300 house and all its gas bills.

But the lesbian group now had a name and the task force ran its first lotolesbian to meet rental payment in February for its office. That was an incredibly hard winter; nobody was prepared for the gas bills, never mind the rent. Our meetings were sometimes complete confusion over who pays what and whose duty it was to clean the house. We kept saying: if only we can get through the first year. We'll be all right. There was never enough time to plan for the future of our lesbian centre.

That May LOOT's counselling service and the newsletter put us into business. There was an Open House to introduce ourselves to other groups. All of the social events of LOOT have been immensely successful in building a community for ourselves. The Task Force continued to meet as a coordinating body to look after finances and endless details while the phone line built up the house from drop-ins and pot luck suppers. Early on, the social committee grew out of the activity of running the drop-ins.

By the time of the first New Years dance, we had managed to build a supportive environment for everyone and made our presence known in the city with an ever-growing mailing list. However, the political action committee had continued to remain the background through the fall, until LOOT decided to take part in the coalition against Anita Bryant that January.

Our brunches, concerts, dances, coffeehouses have all contributed to our lesbian identity but none of these can influence our direction by themselves. The discussion last spring on child sexuality from a lesbian viewpoint and the transsexual discussions are all responses to issues coming from outside the house. With the LOOT sponsored conference this May, we will finally have a chance to act on a political identity of our own as Toronto lesbians.

12. TOWARDS A CANADIAN FEMINIST PARTY

The following statement was published by the Feminist Party of Canada in April 1979, about two months after its founding meeting.

. . . Government is affecting all our lives to an ever-increasing degree. And this broadening of powers brings with it the possibility of real threat to our way of life unless it is accompanied by a genuine sense of moral responsibility to all those who are being represented. It is that moral sense that has been missing from politics.

It is the aim of those who are now working towards creating a feminist party that women's full participation in the political arena will bring a new perspective and a new direction to government in general. For the feminist perspective is an all-encompassing view of the world—life becomes a multifaceted whole, no single facet of which can be ignored or treated as separate. Thus politics, in the feminist view, is seen not as a business set apart from life as it is lived, but rather as an integral part of our communal existence, a very necessary forum for the public discussion of the concerns that so intimately affect our lives and the tenor of our society.

The vision women will contribute to politics is that same vision we have always been depended on to bring to our more traditional spheres. In the family we have provided a moral base; in the wider world we have consistently struggled to humanize our environment—humanize it too for the men who share it with us—whether it be the neighbourhood, the workplace, or any of the many other institutions which structure our communal lives.

Traditionally, politics has not been one of the areas defined by society as the sphere of women, nor have women's interests been seriously articulated there. Traditionally, so-called women's interests have been consigned to so-called women's realm, and the designation has tended to be a derogatory one. But although the role that women play in society has historically been imposed on us and defined for us, it has in effect made us the custodians of those concerns that are most fundamental to a functioning society. Moral values, social relationships—women have taken historic responsibility for all that which renders communities more fully human. If politics is the process through which society safeguards the humanity of its members, then women belong in politics; and if politics is not such a process, then clearly women are needed to make it so.

The political process as it is now practised is not based on human or moral consideration, but on values which, at best, are not conducive to the creative resolution of the problems our country faces. Life, to fulfill its highest potential, depends on integration, on creativity, and politics must be redefined to incorporate these qualities.

A change is in order. A political party with a feminist perspective can be both the focus and the vehicle for that change.

13. GAY PRIDE DAY SPEECH

This speech was given on behalf of the Lesbians against the Right (LAR) in mid-1981 by Lorna Weir. Addressed to an audience of lesbians (feminists and non-feminists) and gay men, it examines the relationship of the lesbian movement to the women's movement and the gay movement.

Lesbianism is a political issue. It is something more than a private sexual orientation to be tolerated among so-called 'civilized' people. The liberation of women will not be accomplished until lesbians are free.

I'm going to be talking about lesbians and the women's movement for a while. This does not mean that every dyke is feminist, though I wish we all were. However, what's new in lesbian organizing over the past ten years and the distinctive form of lesbian politics in the 70s was the result of the emergence of lesbian feminism.

The women's movement emerged in the late 60s after about 30 years of inactivity. Lesbians were active in the new women's movement from the first because it spoke to our concerns as women about such issues as decent wages, daycare and violence against women. It wasn't until the early 70s that lesbianism became an important issue for the women's movement as a whole to deal with. What Stonewall was to the gay liberation movement, Kate Millett's 1970 coming out statement was to the lesbian movement. . . .

. . . A lot of feminists wished Millett had never opened her mouth, but she had, and it was clearly important to defend her because the entire women's movement was being trashed. How exactly to do this was the real question. Do you say, yes, there are dykes in the women's movement, but don't feel threatened because most of us are straight? Or, lesbians are part of the movement, and we are fighting for their civil rights? Or, maybe you say that all women have reason to support a woman's right to love another woman.

In the attack on Millett, the movement had to understand how the accusation of lesbianism has been used to divide women from each other. Any independent woman is liable to be called a dyke. Calling a woman a lesbian is an attempt to break her attachment to other women and to summon her back to the role of helpmate to men. Lots of us have had the experience of being hustled by a man, telling him to get lost and then being called a dyke in the hopes we'll defend our honour by having sex with him. What happened to Millett is that this kind of lesbian-baiting was being used against the women's movement as a whole. We were being told to continue to define our lives and our politics in terms of men. By supporting Millett and other lesbians, the women's movement is defending the right of all women to work with and care for other women. Individually and collectively, we need to be able to decide what to do with our lives and to define our politics on our own terms independently of men.

I think part of the reason for the anti-feminist and anti-lesbian stance of the New Right is the fear of women's autonomy. When women say we want our own movement, people panic because they think that the world will be left without comfort after we've had our way. In a world in which women have a virtual monopoly on nurturing and men on social power, women's claims to self-determination and power are felt as an attack on people's emotional security.

Lesbians are women whose primary emotional and sexual committment is to other women. By the way we live, lesbians claim economic and emotional independence from men. We take the power to explore and discover women's sexuality on women's terms. Lesbians act on women's rights to be with other women, to enjoy the company of women and to organize with women. All feminists, heterosexual and lesbian, are engaged in these struggles to create a culture and a society which validates women's experience. So feminists do fight for civil rights for lesbians, and also, more importantly, see the lesbian movement as a magnificent social experiment to discover the meaning of what it is for women to identify with other women in every way, including sexually, an experiment in which all women have a stake.

Not everything was or is rosy for lesbians in the women's movement. We came to see the need for an autonomous lesbian movement partly because of our need to be together and partly because of the problems lesbians face in the women's movement and other radical movements such as the gay liberation movement. Despite real gains over the past ten years, lesbians are still fighting social invisibility. When I'm walking down the street with my lover, and somebody calls us faggots because bigots don't even know how to insult lesbians accurately, it's for sure we've got a way to go fighting lesbian invisibility. Partly as a result of so many dykes coming out in the women's and gay liberation movements, and partly because there is a growing awareness that women can indeed be sexual, more people than ever before now know that lesbians do exist. And that means we're starting to become targets for attacks. Police harassment of lesbians is on the increase, street assaults are more frequent and we were even privileged with special mention in the hate literature dumped on Toronto over the past few months.

The lesbian movement is starting to regroup in order to fight back. It's true that over the past year we've had two setbacks which still have us reeling: the closing of our bar, the Fly by Night and the folding of LOOT although the phone line continued in operation. The closing of the Fly was a brutal lesson in the ghetto business mentality. The new owner's need to make a buck cost lesbians the loss of our most important social centre; we all felt the loss of a sense of collectivity and power when the Fly folded.

Things clearly couldn't remain in this sad state long. Lesbian groups have started to reform. A lesbian speaker's bureau has been set up and a new lesbian-feminist political organization interested in fighting the right wing attacks on us is being created. . . .

. . . I've been talking about lesbians working together and in the women's movement. But why are some of us here today, with gay men? Working politically with gay men is a very controversial subject among lesbians. The politics of lesbian feminism and the politics of gay liberation are different, because the life experiences of lesbians and gay men are not the same. Our social and sexual lives are organized very differently, and this is reflected in our politics.

I think lesbians are here today partly because the Lesbian and Gay Pride Day Organizing Committee showed a real awareness of the differences and had a willingness to work things out. We are here because this day is a way to publicly fight our invisibility as lesbians. Some of us are here because we have worked in the gay movement in order to fight the oppression of lesbians. We're here because lesbians and gay men are both called 'homosexuals', and we both have a common battle against compulsory heterosexuality in a society which thinks of us as deviant and sick. Both lesbians and gay men demand the right to control our own bodies, to give our bodies to people of the same sex, to choose our own sexuality and define it on our own terms. We claim this choice to be legitimate and good.

The past year has made it clear to lesbians and gay men that we face a common enemy in the New Right. We don't necessarily have exactly the same fight, and we must do some hard thinking in the next while about the terms of our alliance in the fight against the right. The autonomous lesbian movement gives lesbians the political and personal base needed to join together to define our priorities and then hopefully to work together in cooperation with the gay movement and other progressive movements. Being clear on who we are as lesbians will permit us to join with our gay brothers in our common struggles with goodwill and solidarity.

14. WOMEN AGAINST VIOLENCE AGAINST WOMEN STATEMENT: INTERNATIONAL WOMEN'S DAY 1983

WAVAW began in Toronto in late 1977. While its politics were not clear at their founding, it soon became clear that it was a radical feminist organization. The following is a statement of WAVAW's political position, dated 5 March 1983.

WAVAW maintains that sex oppression is universal and functions as the model for all other systems of oppression. Violence against women flows from sex oppression. This oppression, the denial of self-determination for women, is violent in itself. We live in a sex-caste system in that our sex determines our status and role in society. Men have power by virtue of being born male. Women may have 'power' and 'privilege' because of their economic, class, or family relationships to men. However, women in significant positions of 'power' have thoroughly internalized the values and practices of the patriarchal death culture. Ultimately the male ruling class throws these token women into the face of the feminist movement as examples of our pseudo equality.

Men have created the nature-destroying and woman-hating culture. The nuclear arms race and possible annihilation of human existence is a product of this destructive masculinist culture. This ultimate form of the conquering of nature correlates directly with male colonization and destruction of female existence. Men have created the structure of society and, as a whole, are the oppressors of women. Class, race, and national divisions are all products of masculinist ideology. Men define, maintain, and profit from the sex-caste system. However, just as the destruction of the planet is not in the interest of women or men, the continued annihilation of women is against the interests of all of humanity.

Internationally, the patriarchal structure protects perpetrators of misogyny and the destruction of women. The ever-famous guise for this is 'culture and tradition', under which the hideous crimes against women are performed, condoned, and justified. No matter which country or culture, WAVAW condemns the following atrocities against women and names them the ongoing Female Holocaust:

Denial of the right to self-determination and self-value
Compulsory heterosexuality/denial of freedom of sexual expression
Rape and sexual assault of women and girls
Woman battering and femicide
Sexual harassment in the home, on the street, at the workplace
Pornography and sexism in the media
Denial of reproductive rights—restricted abortion, forced sterilization, ineffective and dangerous contraceptives
Drugging and incarceration of women
Forced marriage
Worldwide genital mutilation of tens of millions of women and girls
Seclusion and veiling of women
Forced prostitution
Female slavery
The dowry system and the wife murders that follow
World hunger/refugees—most of the hungry and homeless of the world are women and children
Female infanticide
Forced economic dependence
Denial of education and technical knowledge
Gynecological, obstetric and psychiatric abuses
Crippling and sexually objectifying fashions
Female poverty
Erasure of our herstory and cultural contributions
Subordination of women in and through religion

During the late 1970s and early 1980s we have witnessed an increasing backlash against feminism from both the right and the left. Leftist political ideologies have failed to internalize feminist theory and practice. They have subordinated sex oppression to struggles for class, race, and national liberation. Third World women in particular, apart from struggles against the vestiges of colonialism and imperialism, are struggling against their own local patriarchal oppressions. Men, by ignoring the analyses of sex oppression, are guilty of condoning the above-named crimes against women. It is time for us as women to reaffirm fundamental feminist premises: Whether we choose to work with men or not, we must re-examine our involvement in the male political world. We must act upon feminist principles to bring about truly social change through the elimination of sex oppression.

Women's existence is being threatened *now*. Many of the gains we have made are being lost. Sexism still goes unnoticed and accepted. Abortion rights—always meager—are diminishing. Pornography (the extreme representation of male sexual colonization of women) is increasingly being presented as an accepted norm for a sexually liberated society. Pornography must be viewed in its true form: women-hating propaganda.

The patriarchal death-culture is pornographic, woman-hating, and nature-destroying, and must be exposed as such. We call on our sisters to struggle against this destructive force and unite to overthrow it. WAVAW maintains that women's bonds and solidarity transcend all male-created economic, social and political institutions as well as all class, race, and national boundaries. Sisters, join together to uncover women's spiritual, physical, emotional, intellectual, and political power and energy! To overcome patriarchy is to effect the liberation of all.

15. FIGHTING RACISM AND SEXISM TOGETHER

This speech was the keynote address for Toronto's 1987 International Women's Day Celebrations, which had as its theme 'Fighting Racism and Sexism Together'. Carol Allen, a black women, and Judy Persad, a South Asian woman born in Trinidad, gave the speech jointly on behalf of the March 8th Coalition of Toronto.

Last year on International Women's Day we said we were going to build a new women's movement in Toronto—a women's movement which will integrate the fight against racism and the fight against sexism. Racism and sexism have to be integrated into the movement because they are already in our lives. The women's movement must represent all women—the fight against racism is everybody's fight. . . . Since its beginning it has been a predominantly white women's movement. Last year women of colour, black women, and native women challenged this structure. And this year we are beginning to see the results of that challenge. We have to continue.

We do not believe that racism is merely a misunderstanding among people, a question of interpersonal relations, or an unchanging part of human nature. Racism, like sexism is an integral part of the political and economic system under which we live. This system uses racism and sexism to divide us and to exploit our labour for super-profits and it gives some women privilege. They must fight this in their daily lives. You cannot just educate racism away, and even legal reforms are not enough. We must change the economic and political structures which maintain the oppressions which we face.

A women's movement which does not represent and include all women cannot be called a true women's movement. An anti-racist women's movement has to include women of colour, black women, and native women.

It has to address issues which affect our lives. The past shows us that issues which affect the lives of women of colour, black women, and native women are not seen as feminist issues—these are seen as 'other' issues which the feminist community may or may not pay attention to at any one time. Well, these are not to be classified as 'other'. These are issues which affect us as women and the movement has to pay more than just token attention to them. The movement must focus on racism and its effect in women's lives.

An anti-racist women's movement has to include an anti-racist analysis of each and every issue. Racism has been seen as an issue—an issue to be added to a list of items. *Racism is not an issue.* Racism, as sexism, is part of each issue. For women of colour, black women, and native women racism and sexism are part of every day.

What is using an anti-racist perspective?

Well, it is *not* paying lipservice to issues concerning women of colour, black women, and native women;

It is *not* looking for speakers from these communities at the last minute for a conference you're organizing;

It is *not* going through a speech and putting in the words 'women of colour', 'black women', 'native women', and 'immigrant women' where it can fit or where it sounds good;

It is *not* white women being defensive because racism has been the focus of the 1986 and 1987 International Women's Day.

What it *is*—is the acknowledgement that racism and sexism are integral parts of every issues—for example—a conference on gay rights, or on pornography and prostitution, or on sexuality should not need a workshop on racism to address its effects; racism should be integrated into every workshop.

What it *is*—is the integration of anti-racist perspective into analysis and practice. . . .

Some black women, native women, and women of colour who were involved last year are not involved this year, while there are some who have returned. There are also quite a few women of colour, black women, and native women who are participating in the coalition for the first time this year.

Some of us choose to work only within our communities and some of us choose to work within the broader women's community. At times this choice has created conflict between us. It is important to see this conflict as a difference in strategy, not a difference between us. Some of us do work in both communities. It is important that we see the integration of our work in the overall struggle for the liberation of people of colour, black people, working class people, native people, gays and lesbians, and disabled people. We must create and strengthen alliances between us and work together.

The distrust women of colour, black women and native women feel towards the women's movement is justified. We have felt continuously excluded from the women's movement. . . . Although we share a common oppression as women, we must work together to overcome the issues that divide us. This will not be easy because the society we live in continuously tries to highlight the differences between us and make it difficult for us, as women, to come together, acknowledge our differences and find ways to move forward together.

[W]e, women of colour, black women, and native women . . . who have chosen to work in the coalition have made a political decision to develop a strong anti-racist consciousness in the broader women's movement. We expect white women to fight racism on all levels—economic, political, and personal. Structures maintain racism in our society and individual racism helps to perpetuate it. White women must deal with their racism in their lives and politics, while the women's movement organizes against the racism and sexism of the state and other structures in society.

There are many barriers which divide women and in order to work together we have to recognize these differences. If we don't, we end up with a movement that's representative of only a small number of us.

The question is: Should we work together? The answer is yes! . . . [N]umbers influence change: one stick is easy to break, but five sticks side by side are harder to break.

This year's International Women's Day is an example of how we want to build a new women's movement. The analysis of racism and sexism have been integrated into our subthemes of native self-determination, employment equity, choice, and housing. Next year our theme won't be *fighting racism and sexism together*, but whatever the focus is of next year's International Women's Day, racism and sexism will be incorporated.

The cost of not doing so will be too high. It would be taking a step backwards. *We must move forward.*

Appendix B: Abbreviations

AUCE	(B.C.) Association of University and College Employees
B & Ps	Business and Professional Women
BCFW	British Columbia Federation of Women
CARAL	Canadian Abortion Rights Action League, formerly Canadian Association for the Repeal of the Abortion Law
CCLOW	Canadian Congress of Learning Opportunities for Women
CEW	Committee for Equality of Women in Canada
CLC	Canadian Labour Congress
CR	consciousness-raising
CCSP	Centre for Spanish Speaking Peoples (Toronto)
CUPE	Canadian Union of Public Employees
CWMA	Canadian Women's Movement Archives/Les Archives canadiennes du mouvement des femmes
FLQ	Front de libération du Québec
FFQ	Fédération des femmes du Québec
IWD	International Women's Day
IWDC	International Women's Day Committee (Toronto)
IWY	International Women's Year
LIP	Local Initiative Programme
LSA	League for Socialist Action
MACSW	Manitoba Action Committee on the Status of Women
MLA	Member, Legislative Assembly
MP	Member of Parliament
MPP	Member of Provincial Parliament
NAC	National Action Committee on the Status of Women
NDP	New Democratic Party
NOW	National Organization of Women (U.S.)
OCAC	Ontario Coalition for Abortion Clinics
OFL	Ontario Federation of Labour
OFY	Opportunities for Youth
OPSEU	Ontario Public Service Employees Union
OWW	Organized Working Women (Ontario)
RCSW	Royal Commission on the Status of Women in Canada
REAL	Realistic, Equal, Active for Life Women
RMG	Revolutionary Marxist Group
RWL	Revolutionary Workers League
SDU	Students for a Democratic University
SORWUC	Service, Office & Retail Workers Union of Canada
SPC	Socialist Party of Canada
SUPA	Student Union for Peace Action
SWL	Saskatoon Women's Liberation Group

SWW	Saskatchewan Working Women
TAC	Therapeutic Abortion Committee
TWLM	Toronto Women's Liberation Movement
UN	United Nations
VOW	Voice of Women
WAB	Women Against the Budget (B.C.)
WAVAW	Women against Violence against Women
WCEC	Women's Community Employment Centre (Toronto)
WCTU	Women's Christian Temperance Union
WLWG	Women's Liberation Working Group (Toronto)
WSS	Wives Supporting the Strike (Sudbury, Ont.)
WWIW	Women Working With Immigrant Women
YS	Young Socialists
YWCA	Young Women's Christian Association

Appendix C: Selective Chronology, 1867–1988

1867   Dr Emily Stowe becomes first woman doctor to practise in Canada

1876   Toronto Women's Literary Club formed

1883   Toronto Women's Literary Club changes its name to Toronto Women's Suffrage Association
National Women's Christian Temperance Union founded
The first of three suffrage bills introduced by Sir John A. Macdonald is tabled; all three bills are defeated
National Young Women's Christian Association founded

1886   University of Toronto admits first women students

1889   Dominion Women's Enfranchisement Association formed, later called the Canadian Suffrage Association

1890s   Icelandic Women's Suffrage Association founded in Manitoba

1893   National Council of Women founded

1894   National Council of Jewish Women founded
Women's Enfranchisement Association founded, St. John, N.B.

1900   Coloured Women's Club of Montreal founded

1907   Fédération Nationale Saint-Jean-Baptiste, Québec, founded

1912   Political Equality League, Winnipeg, founded

1914   National Union of Woman Suffrage Societies of Canada founded

1916   Women given provincial vote in Manitoba (January), Saskatchewan (April), Alberta, and British Columbia

1917   Women given provincial vote in Ontario

1918   Women given full federal franchise; women given provincial vote in Nova Scotia

1919   Women given provincial vote in New Brunswick
Federated Women's Institutes founded
Canadian Federation of University Women founded

1922   Women given provincial vote in Prince Edward Island

1925   Women over 25 given provincial vote in Newfoundland

1929   Persons Case: Privy Council in London rules that 'women are persons'
Ligue des Droits de la Femme formed in Quebec

1930   Federation of Business and Professional Women's Clubs formed

1940   Women in Quebec given provincial vote

1951   The Canadian Negro Women's Club formed

1960   Voice of Women founded
Birth-control pills go on sale

1962   Voice of Women campaign for legalization of birth-control information

1963   Betty Friedan's *The Feminine Mystique* published

1966   Association féminine d'éducation et d'action sociale (AFEAS)
        founded
        Juliet Mitchell's 'Longest Revolution' published
        Committee for Equality of Women in Canada recommends a
        royal commission on the status of women
        Fédération des femmes du Québec (FFQ) formed

1967   SUPA has a separate women's caucus
        Federal government appoints a royal commission on the status
        of women in Canada (RCSW)
        'Sisters, Brothers, Lovers. . ..Listen' published

1968   *Birth Control Handbook* published by McGill student society
        Women's Caucus of Simon Fraser SDS formed
        Toronto Women's Liberation Movement (TWLM) formed

1969   TWLM splits, New Feminists formed
        Amendment to the Criminal Code passed, removing as an off-
        ence the dissemination of information relating to birth control,
        and making abortion legal if approved by a theraputic abortion
        committee (TAC)
        Anduhyaun Native Women's Centre established
        University of Toronto Homophile Association has first meeting
        First issue of *The Pedestal*
        Waffle women of the NDP form a women's caucus
        National Farmers' Union forms a Women's Division
        (Sept.) Halifax Women's Caucus formed
        Saskatoon Women's Liberation formed
        Montreal Women's Liberation movement formed

1970   Report of the Royal Commission on the Status of Women
        Abortion Caravan travels from Vancouver to Ottawa
        First women's studies course given at University of Toronto
        Indochinese women's Conference in Toronto
        Nov. 21–22, first National Conference of the Canadian Wom-
        en's Liberation Movement held in Saskatoon; 200 women
        attend
        Regina Women's Liberation formed
        First public forum of Fredericton Women's Liberation Move-
        ment held, 150 attend

1971   A Woman's Place, Toronto, opens
        (Feb.) first Canada-wide day of abortion demonstrations held
        Ontario Association for Abortion Law Repeal formed
        Indian Rights for Indian Women formed
        First issue of *The Body Politic*
        Federal cabinet minister responsible for Status of Women
        appointed, Hon. Robert Andras
        Germaine Greer speaks in Montreal
        Centre des femmes started in Montreal

1972   Women's Press formed and *Women Unite!* published
National Action Committee on the Status of Women founded
The Other Woman begins publishing
Interval House Shelter, Toronto, opens
Women for Political Action formed
SORWUC and AUCE organized in British Columbia
Vancouver Rape Relief opens

1973   Canadian Advisory Council on the Status of Women established
in Ottawa
Canadian Association for the Repeal of the Abortion Law, later
Canadian Abortion Rights Action League, formed
Selma James from England's Wages for Housework campaign
tours Canada on a speaking tour
Réseau d'action et d'information pour femmes (RAIF) formed
First National Lesbian Conference held in Toronto (June)
Morgentaler tried and acquitted on charge of illegal abortion;
Quebec Court of Appeals reverses this decision; Supreme
Court of Canada upholds reversal
First issue of *MS* magazine

1974   Toronto Rape Crisis Centre opens
Mother-Led Union (welfare moms and social workers) formed
Second National lesbian conference held in Montreal
British Columbia Federation of Women founded
First woman accepted by RCMP
Native Women's Association of Canada formed
Women Working with Immigrant Women formed in Toronto

1975   International Women's Year
NAC rejects Wages for Housework analysis
Feminist News Service formed by women in Canadian Univer-
sity Press Association
National Association of Women and the Law formed
Toronto Women's Credit Union opens
(June) first national conference of rape crisis centres (22 attend)
First issue of *Atlantis*
'Carrefour' provincial meeting of Quebec women held at Laval
University

1976   Canadian Labour Congress organizes a Women Trade Unionists
Conference
(March) Organized Working Women founded in Toronto
Parti Québécois allows abortion in community health centres in
Quebec
Third national lesbian conference held in Ottawa
Canadian Research Institute for the Advancement of Women
founded
Women's Bureau, Canadian Labour Congress, opened

Les Tête de Pioche, a radical-feminist newspaper, published in Quebec

Quebec equal-pay legislation passed

1977 *Weekend Magazine* (Toronto) says 'the Women's Movement is Dead'

Lesbian Organization of Toronto formed

Badgely Report on abortion released

OPSEU votes to appoint a full-time equal-opportunity co-ordinator

5 Nov. National Day of Protest against violence against women

Canadian Women's Movement Archives/Archives canadiennes du mouvement des femmes founded

1978 Lesbian Mothers' Defense Fund founded

International Women's Day Committee (Toronto) formed

CLC holds second national women trade unionists conference

First Take Back the Night March in Toronto

Le Regroupement des femmes québécoises founded

1979 Action Day Care founded in Toronto

Feminist Party of Canada formed

Native women organize 100–mile march to demand changes to the Indian Act

Saskatchewan Working Women founded

1980 OFL and ONDP conventions take up day-care

Changes in NAC make it more nationally representative—10 regional representatives are chosen

First National Women in Trades Conference held in Winnipeg

1981 Federal Ad Hoc Conference on the Constitution

OFL women's committee decides on strategy of promoting mandatory affirmative action

Canadian Congress for Learning Opportunities for Women (CCLOW) formed

Doris Anderson resigns as President of the federal Advisory Council on the Status of Women in protest of government manipulation of council executive (Jan.20)

1982 Ontario Coalition for Abortion Clinics (OCAC) founded

R.E.A.L. Women formed

Appointment of first woman to Supreme Court of Canada

22 Nov. Red Hot Video store in Vancouver fire-bombed by the Wimmin's Fire Brigade

1983 Visible Minority Women's Coalition formed

1984 NAC TV debate by candidates in the federal election

Federal task force on child-care established

Canadian Human Rights Tribunal imposes first mandatory affirmative action program on CN Rail

Ontario jury acquits Morgentaler on charges of performing an illegal abortion

1985   Section 12(1)(b) of Indian Act repealed, allowing native women
          to marry non-natives without losing their Indian status
        Disabled Women's Network formed
        L'R des centres de femmes du Québec (Quebec coalition of
          women's centres) formed
        Manitoba government passes pay equity legislation.
1986   Federal government passes Bill C-62 dealing with affirmative
          action for women, visible minorities, and the disabled
        Toronto lesbian wins the right to dental and health insurance
          benefits for her female lover and her lover's two children
        MACSW opens branch in Thompson, Man., for northern
          feminists
        Ontario government passes Bill 7 prohibiting discrimination on
          the basis of sexual orientation
1987   Ontario government recognizes midwifery as a legal and self-
          regulating profession
        Federal government puts forward a National Child Care Policy
        Coalition of women's groups organized to protest Meech Lake
          Constitutional Accord
1988   Supreme Court decision on abortion declares TACs
          unconstitutional
        Alberta Union of Nurses goes out on an illegal strike over wages
          and working conditions

Appendix D: NAC Member Groups

NATIONAL

ACTION EDUCATION DES FEMMES
ACTRA ALLIANCE OF CAN. CINEMA,
TELEVISION & RADIO ARTISTS
ANGLICAN CHURCH OF CANADA
ARAB CANADIAN WOMEN'S NETWORK
ASSOCIATION FOR WOMEN'S EQUITY
IN THE CANADIAN FORCES (AWECF)
ASSOCIATION OF UNITED UKRAINIAN
CANADIANS
CANADIAN ASSOCIATION FOR ADULT
EDUCATION
CANADIAN ASSOCIATION FOR THE
ADVANCEMENT OF WOMEN AND
SPORT
CANADIAN ASSOCIATION FOR WOMEN
IN SCIENCE, CAWIS
CANADIAN ASSOCIATION OF ELIZA-
BETH FRY SOCIETIES
CANADIAN ASSOCIATION OF UNIVER-
SITY TEACHERS
CANADIAN ASSOCIATION OF WOMEN
EXECUTIVES & ENTREPRENEURS
CANADIAN AUTO WORKERS -
WOMEN'S DEPARTMENT
CANADIAN CONGRESS FOR LEARNING
OPPORTUNITIES FOR WOMEN,
CCLOW
CANADIAN DAY CARE ADVOCACY
ASSOCIATION
CANADIAN FED. OF BUSINESS &
PROFESSIONAL WOMEN'S CLUBS
CANADIAN FEDERATION OF STUDENTS
CANADIAN HOME ECONOMICS
ASSOCIATION
CANADIAN LABOUR CONGRESS -
WOMEN'S BUREAU
CANADIAN ORGANIZATION FOR THE
RIGHTS OF PROSTITUTES

CANADIAN PSYCHOLOGICAL ASSO.
SECTION ON WOMEN & PSYCHOLOGY
CANADIAN RESEARCH INSTITUTE FOR
THE ADVANCEMENT OF WOMEN
CANADIAN TEACHERS' FEDERATION
CANADIAN TEXTILE & CHEMICAL
UNION
CANADIAN UNION OF PUBLIC
EMPLOYEES, CUPE
CANADIAN WOMAN STUDIES (YORK
UNIVERSITY)
CANADIAN WOMEN'S MOVEMENT
ARCHIVES
CANADIAN WOMEN'S MUSIC AND CUL-
TURAL FESTIVAL
CARAL - CANADIAN ABORTION RIGHTS
ACTION LEAGUE
CHINESE CANADIAN NATIONAL COUN-
CIL, WOMEN'S ISSUES CTTEE.
COMMUNIST PARTY OF CANADA,
WOMEN'S COMMISSION
CONFEDERATION OF CANADIAN
UNIONS
CONGRESS OF BLACK WOMEN OF
CANADA
CONGRESS OF CANADIAN WOMEN
D.E.S. ACTION / CANADA
ECONOMISTS', SOCIOLOGISTS' & STAT-
ISTICIANS' ASSO. (ESSA)
FEDERATION OF JUNIOR LEAGUES OF
CANADA
FEMINIST PARTY OF CANADA
INFACT CANADA (INFANT FEEDING
ACTION COALITION)
INTERNATIONAL INSTITUTE FOR
PUBLIC HEALTH
LIBERAL PARTY OF CANADA,
WOMEN'S LIBERAL COMMISSION

MEDIA WATCH: EVALUATION - MEDIAS
NATIONAL WATCH - IMAGES OF
WOMEN
NATIONAL ASSOCIATION OF WOMEN
AND THE LAW
NATIONAL FEDERATION OF PAKISTANI
CANADIANS
NATIONAL HOUSEHOLD CAREERS
NATIONAL UNION OF PROV. GOVT.
EMPLOYEES WOMEN'S COMMITTEE
NDP PARTICIPATION OF WOMEN
COMMITTEE
NDP RESEARCH
P.C. NATIONAL FEDERATION OF
WOMEN
PIONEER WOMEN NA'AMAT
PLANNED PARENTHOOD FEDERATION
OF CANADA
UNITARIAN UNIVERSALIST WOMEN'S
FEDERATION
UNITED CHURCH OF CANADA,
MINISTRY WITH ADULTS - WOMEN
UNITED CHURCH OF CANADA,
WOMEN'S CONCERNS COMMITTEE
VOICE OF WOMEN / LA VOIX DES
FEMMES
WEB - WOMEN'S INFORMATION
EXCHANGE SOCIETY
WOMEN'S CANADIAN ORT
WOMEN'S COMMITTEE OF NACOI,
CANADIANS OF ORIGINS IN INDIA
WOMEN'S INTERNATIONAL LEAGUE
FOR PEACE AND FREEDOM
WOMEN'S LEGAL EDUCATION AND
ACTION FUND (LEAF)
WORLD FEDERALISTS OF CANADA,
WOMEN & WORLD ORDER COMMITTEE
YMCA OF CANADA

ALBERTA

ABORTION BY CHOICE
ALBERTA FEDERATION OF LABOUR
WOMEN'S COMMITTEE
ALBERTA NEW DEMOCRAT WOMEN'S
SECTION
ALBERTA STATUS OF WOMEN ACTION
COMMITTEE
ALBERTA UNION OF PROVINCIAL
EMPLOYEES
BOW VALLEY WOMEN'S RESOURCE
CENTRE
BUSINESS & PROFESSIONAL WOMEN'S
CLUB OF GRANDE PRAIRIE
C.N.P. WOMEN'S RESOURCE & CRISIS
CENTRE
CALGARY ASSO. OF WOMEN & LAW
CALGARY BIRTH CONTROL
ASSOCIATION
CALGARY SEXUAL ASSAULT CENTRE

CALGARY STATUS OF WOMEN ACTION
COMMITTEE
CALGARY WOMEN'S EMERGENCY
SHELTER
CANADIAN UNION OF POSTAL
WORKERS - EDMONTON
LOCAL CELEBRATION OF WOMEN IN
THE ARTS
EDMONTON WORKING WOMEN
FEDERATION OF MEDICAL WOMEN OF
CALGARY
HECATE'S PLAYERS
LETTER CARRIERS UNION OF CANADA
- LOCAL 15 WOMEN'S CTTEE.
NEWSMAGAZINE FOR ALBERTA
WOMEN
NORTH WEST MEDIA NETWORK GUILD
NORTHERN LIGHTS RESOURCE CENTRE
ASSOCIATION

OPTIONS FOR WOMEN
ORGANIZATIONAL SOCIETY OF
SPOUSES OF MILITARY MEMBERS
PLANNED PARENTHOOD ALBERTA
POSITIVE IMAGES: WOMEN BY WOMEN
RED DEER STATUS OF WOMEN
SECOND WREATH
SEXUAL ASSAULT CENTRE OF
EDMONTON
SOUTH PEACE REGIONAL COUNCIL OF
WOMEN
VOICE OF WOMEN - EDMONTON
WELLSPRING WOMEN'S ASSOCIATION
OF WHITECOURT
WOMEN OF THE NORTH
WOMEN'S PROGRAM & RESOURCE
CENTRE, FACULTY OF EXTENSION
WOMONSPACE
YWCA OF CALGARY

BRITISH COLUMBIA

ARMSTRONG WOMEN'S ASSOCIATION
B.C. FEDERATION OF LABOUR
B.C. GOVERNMENT EMPLOYEES'
UNION
B.C. NDP WOMEN'S RIGHTS
COMMITTEE
B.C. TEACHERS' FEDERATION
B.C. WOMEN'S LIBERAL COMMISSION
B.C. YUKON ASSOCIATION OF
WOMEN'S CENTRES
BATTERED WOMEN'S SUPPORT
SERVICES
CAMPBELL RIVER AREA WOMEN'S
RESOURCE SOCIETY
CANADIAN FEDERATION OF STUDENTS
- PACIFIC REGION
CARAL - FRASER VALLEY CHAPTER
CHETWYND WOMEN'S RESOURCE
SOCIETY

CONCERNED CITIZENS FOR CHOICE ON
ABORTION (CCCA)
CONGRESS OF CANADIAN WOMEN -
B.C. CHAPTER
CONTACT WOMEN'S GROUP
CRANBROOK WOMEN'S RESOURCE
SOCIETY
DISABLED WOMEN'S NETWORK
(DAWN) - B.C.
FEMINIST GRANDMOTHERS OF
CANADA - B.C.
FERNIE WOMEN'S RESOURCE AND
DROP-IN CENTRE
FORT NELSON WOMEN'S CENTRE
FORT ST. JOHN WOMEN'S RESOURCE
CENTRE
GAZEBO CONNECTION
GOLDEN WOMEN'S RESOURCE CENTRE
HOUSEWIVES/HOUSEWORKERS IN
TRAINING & RESEARCH

HOWE SOUND WOMEN'S CENTRE
KAMLOOPS WOMEN'S RESOURCE
CENTRE
KELOWNA WOMEN'S RESOURCE
CENTRE
LANGARA WOMEN'S CENTRE,
LANGARA STUDENTS' SOCIETY
MATERNAL HEALTH SOCIETY
MIDWIFERY ASSOCIATION OF BRITISH
COLUMBIA
NORTH SHORE CRISIS SERVICES
SOCIETY (EMILY MURPHY HOUSE)
NORTH SHORE WOMEN'S CENTRE
OKANAGAN WOMEN'S COALITION
PACIFIC WOMEN'S RESEARCH
INSTITUTE
PENTICTON & AREA WOMEN'S CENTRE
SOCIETY
PORT ALBERNI WOMEN'S RESOURCES

PORT COQUITLAM AREA WOMEN'S
CENTRE
PRINCE GEORGE WOMEN'S RESOURCE
CENTRE
QUESNEL WOMEN'S RESOURCE
CENTRE
RAPE RELIEF & WOMEN'S SHELTER
RICHMOND WOMEN'S RESOURCE
CENTRE
SHUSWAP AREA FAMILY EMERGENCY
SOCIETY (SAFE)
SOCIETY OF TRANSITION HOUSES B.C./
YUKON
SOUTH OKANAGAN WOMEN IN NEED
SOCIETY
SOUTH SURREY/WHITE ROCK
WOMEN'S PLACE
TAMITIK STATUS OF WOMEN

TERRACE WOMEN'S RESOURCE
CENTRE SOCIETY
UNIVERSITY OF BRITISH COLUMBIA
WOMEN'S COMMITTEE
UNIVERSITY WOMEN'S CLUB OF
NORTH VANCOUVER
UNIVERSITY WOMEN'S CLUB OF
VANCOUVER
VANCOUVER ASSOCIATION OF WOMEN
& THE LAW
VANCOUVER SOCIETY ON IMMIGRANT
WOMEN
VANCOUVER STATUS OF WOMEN
VANCOUVER WOMEN IN FOCUS
SOCIETY
VANCOUVER WOMEN IN TRADES
ASSOCIATION

VICTORIA STATUS OF WOMEN ACTION
GROUP
VICTORIA WOMEN IN TRADES
WEST KOOTENAY WOMEN'S
ASSOCIATION
WINS TRANSITION HOUSE (WOMEN IN
NEED SOCIETY)
WOMEN AGAINST VIOLENCE AGAINST
WOMEN RAPE CRISIS CENTRE
WOMEN SKILLS
WOMEN'S ECONOMIC AGENDA
WOMEN'S RESEARCH CENTRE
WOMEN'S RESOURCE CENTRE FOR
CONTINUING EDUCATION
YWCA OF VANCOUVER

MANITOBA

HERIZONS
MANITOBA ACTION COMMITTEE ON
THE STATUS OF WOMEN

MANITOBA ASSOCIATION OF WOMEN &
THE LAW
NORTHERN OPTIONS FOR WOMEN
CO-OP INC.

RESEAU
THOMPSON CRISIS CENTRE INC.
WOMEN'S HEALTH CLINIC
YMCA OF WINNIPEG

NEW BRUNSWICK

CANADIAN CONGRESS FOR LEARNING
OPPORTUNITIES FOR WOMEN, N.B.
F.R.A.P.P.E. - MONCTON
FREDERICTON RAPE CRISIS CENTRE

L'ASSOCIATION DE FEMMES DE RADIO-
CANADA A MONCTON
NEW BRUNSWICK WOMEN'S NET-
WORK/RESEAU

SAINT JOHN WOMEN FOR ACTION GROUP
TOBIQUE WOMEN'S GROUP
UNIVERSITY OF NEW BRUNSWICK
STUDENT WOMEN'S COMMITTEE

NEWFOUNDLAND

BAY ST. GEORGE STATUS OF WOMEN
COUNCIL
CORNER BROOK STATUS OF WOMEN
COUNCIL
GANDER STATUS OF WOMEN COUNCIL
GANDER WOMEN'S CENTRE
GATEWAY STATUS OF WOMEN COUNCIL
KIRBY HOUSE
LABRADOR NATIVE WOMEN'S
ASSOCIATION
LABRADOR WEST STATUS OF WOMEN
COUNCIL

LIBRA HOUSE
MOKAMI STATUS OF WOMEN COUNCIL
MULTICULTURAL WOMEN'S ORG. FOR
NEWFOUNDLAND & LABRADOR
NEWFOUNDLAND ASSOCIATION OF
PUBLIC EMPLOYEES
NEWFOUNDLAND ORGANIZATION OF
WOMEN (NOW/NDP)
NEWFOUNDLAND TEACHERS' ASSO.,
WOMEN'S ISSUES COUNCIL
PLANNED PARENTHOOD NEWFOUND-
LAND/LABRADOR

PROVINCIAL ASSOCIATION ON FAMILY
VIOLENCE
RIGOLET WOMEN'S GROUP
ST. JOHN'S STATUS OF WOMEN
COUNCIL
TRANSITION HOUSE
WOMEN'S CENTRE, CENTRAL NEW-
FOUNDLAND - STATUS OF WOMEN
WOMEN'S COUNCIL
WOMEN'S RESOURCE CENTRE OF
MEMORIAL UNIVERSITY

NOVA SCOTIA

ANTIGONISH WOMEN'S ASSOCIATION
CANADIAN RESEARCH INST. FOR
ADVANCEMENT OF WOMEN N.S.
CAPE BRETON TRANSITION HOUSE
ASSOCIATION
CARAL - HALIFAX
DALHOUSIE ASSOCIATION OF WOMEN
& THE LAW
DALHOUSIE WOMEN HEALTH AND
MEDICINE (WHAM)
EASTERN SHORE LEARNING OPPOR-
TUNITIES FOR WOMEN
HALIFAX TRANSITION HOUSE
ASSOCIATION

INSTITUTE FOR THE STUDY OF WOMEN
LUNENBURG COUNTY WOMEN'S
GROUP
MOTHERS UNITED FOR METRO
SHELTER (M.U.M.S.)
N.S. CONFEDERATION OF UNIV. FAC-
ULTY ASSOC. STATUS OF WOMEN
NDP NOVA SCOTIA WOMEN'S RIGHTS
COMMITTEE
NOVA SCOTIA ASSO. OF SOCIAL WORK-
ERS, WOMEN'S ISSUES GROUP
NOVA SCOTIA ASSOCIATION OF
WOMEN & THE LAW
PANDORA PUBLISHING ASSOCIATION

PICTOU COUNTY WOMEN'S CENTRE
SECOND STORY WOMEN'S CENTRE
SUPPORTIVE ACTION FOR WOMEN
TEARMANN SOCIETY FOR BATTERED
WOMEN
TOWN DAYCARE CENTRE
UNIVERSITY AND COLLEGE STAFF UNION
WOMEN UNLIMITED
WOMEN'S ACTION COALITION OF
NOVA SCOTIA
WOMEN'S EMPLOYMENT OUTREACH
WOMEN'S HEALTH EDUCATION INFOR-
MATION NETWORK (WHEN)
ZONTA CLUB OF HALIFAX

NORTHWEST TERRITORIES

BUSINESS & PROFESSIONAL WOMEN'S
ASSO. OF YELLOWKNIFE

HAY RIVER WOMEN'S CENTRE
SOCIETY AGAINST FAMILY ABUSE

YWCA OF YELLOWKNIFE

ONTARIO

ACTION DAY CARE
AFFIRMATIVE ACTION ADVISORY COM-
MITTEE, GEORGE BROWN COLLEGE
ALGONQUIN COLLEGE, THE WOMEN'S
PROGRAM
ALMONTE COMMUNITY SERVICES
CO-ORDINATORS
ASSOCIATION OF WOMEN & THE LAW
OTTAWA COMMUNITY CAUCUS
ASSOCIATION PARMI-ELLES INC.
AU FEMININ: SPORT & FITNESS
AVOCA FOUNDATION
BAN RIGH FOUNDATION FOR CONTINU-
ING UNIV. EDUCATION
BARBARA SCHLIFER COMMEMORA-
TIVE CLINIC
BEACHES WOMEN'S GROUP
BIRTH CONTROL AND VD INFORMA-
TION CENTRE
BRANT WOMEN'S NETWORK
BUSINESS & PROFESSIONAL WOMEN'S
CLUB OF HAMILTON
BUSINESS & PROFESSIONAL WOMEN'S
CLUB OF LAKESHORE

BUSINESS & PROFESSIONAL WOMEN'S
CLUB OF NORTH TORONTO
BUSINESS & PROFESSIONAL WOMEN'S
CLUB OF ONTARIO
BUSINESS & PROFESSIONAL WOMEN'S
CLUB OF OTTAWA
BUSINESS & PROFESSIONAL WOMEN'S
CLUB OF STRATFORD
BUSINESS & PROFESSIONAL WOMEN'S
CLUB OF TORONTO
BUSINESS & PROFESSIONAL WOMEN'S
CLUB OF TORONTO EAST
BUSINESS & PROFESSIONAL WOMEN'S
CLUB OF TORONTO WEST
BUSINESS & PROFESSIONAL WOMEN'S
CLUB OF SAULT STE. MARIE
CAN. FED. OF UNIVERSITY WOMEN
YORK REGION - WOMEN'S ISSUES
CANADIAN UNION OF EDUCATIONAL
WORKERS - LOCAL 3 – WOMEN'S
CAUCUS
CARAL - LONDON
CARAL OTTAWA CHAPTER
CARLETON WOMEN'S CENTRE

CHATHAM KENT WOMEN'S CENTRE
CHOICE IN CHILD CARE COMMITTEE
CIVIL REMEDIES & RIGHTS COMMIT-
TEE (CRRC)
CLEF EN MAIN
CO-OPERATIVE HOUSING FEDERATION
OF TORONTO INC.
COMMITTEE AGAINST PORNOGRAPHY
COMMITTEE FOR '94
COMMUNITY RESOURCES FOR WOMEN
CONCERNED WOMEN
CORNWALL WOMEN'S NETWORK
COSTI IIAS IMMIGRANT SERVICES
DISABLED WOMEN'S NETWORK -
ONTARIO
DISABLED WOMEN'S NETWORK -
TORONTO CHAPTER
DISABLED WOMEN'S SUPPORT GROUP
DURHAM INTERNATIONAL WOMEN'S
DAY COMMITTEE
EDUCATION WIFE ASSAULT
ELIZABETH FRY SOCIETY OF OTTAWA
ELIZABETH FRY SOCIETY OF TORONTO
EMILY STOWE SHELTER FOR WOMEN

EQUAL PAY COALITION
ERNESTINE'S WOMEN'S SHELTER
F.A.K.E. WOMEN (FEMINISTS FOR ALL KINDS OF EQUALITY)
FAMILY CRISIS SHELTER
FEDERATION OF WOMEN TEACHERS' ASSOCIATION OF ONTARIO
FIREWEED
FRANCO-FEMMES
GUELPH WELLINGTON WOMEN IN CRISIS
HABITAT INTERLUDE
HALTON WOMEN'S PLACE
HAMILTON STATUS OF WOMEN SUB-COMMITTEE
HAMILTON WOMEN TEACHERS' ASSOCIATION
HAVEN HOUSE (MANITOULIN FAMILY RESOURCE CENTRE)
HYSTERIA
IMMIGRANT WOMEN'S CENTRE
IMMIGRANT WOMEN'S INFORMATION CENTRE - WINDSOR
INDUSTRIAL TRAINING CENTRE FOR WOMEN OF SUDBURY INC.
INTERFACULTY COMMITTEE OF WOMEN'S STUDIES
INTERNATIONAL WOMENS' DAY COMMITTEE
INTERVAL HOUSE
INTERVAL HOUSE OF OTTAWA-CARLETON
KABABAYAN COMMUNITY CENTRE WOMEN'S COLLECTIVE
KENORA FAMILY RESOURCE CENTRE
KITCHENER-WATERLOO STATUS OF WOMEN GROUP
L'ESCALE, CENTRE DE RESSOURCES POUR FEMMES
LABOUR COUNCIL OF METROPOLITAN TORONTO, WOMEN'S COMMITTEE
LANARK COUNTY INTERVAL HOUSE
LAURENTIAN WOMEN'S ASSO./ASSO. DES FEMMES DE LA LAURENTIENNE
LEEDS & GRENVILLE INTERVAL HOUSE
LINCOLN WOMEN TEACHERS' ASSOCIATION
LONDON BATTERED WOMEN'S ADVO-CACY CLINIC INCORPORATED
LONDON STATUS OF WOMEN ACTION GROUP
METRO ACTION CTTEE. ON PUBLIC VIOLENCE VS. WOMEN & CHILDREN
MIDWIFERY TASK FORCE (ONTARIO)
MIDWIVES COLLECTIVE OF TORONTO
MOTHERS ARE WOMEN (M.A.W.)
NATIONAL ASSOCIATION OF WOMEN & THE LAW, OSGOODE CAUCUS
NATIONAL ASSOCIATION OF WOMEN & THE LAW, OTTAWA CAUCUS
NATIONAL ASSOCIATION OF WOMEN & THE LAW, QUEEN'S LAW FACULTY
NATIONAL ASSOCIATION OF WOMEN & THE LAW, TORONTO AREA CAUCUS
NATIONAL ASSOCIATION OF WOMEN & THE LAW, WINDSOR CAUCUS
NDP ONTARIO WOMEN'S COMMITTEE
NDP WOMEN'S COMMITTEE - ALGOMA
NEW EXPERIENCE FOR REFUGEE WOMEN
NIPISSING TRANSITION HOUSE
NORFOLK WOMEN TEACHERS' ASSOCIATION
NORTH BAY WOMEN'S CENTRE
NORTH YORK WOMEN TEACHERS' ASSOCIATION
NORTHERN WOMEN'S ACTION GROUP
NORTHUMBERLAND & NEWCASTLE WOMEN TEACHERS' ASSOCIATION
NORTHWESTERN ONTARIO WOMEN'S CENTRE
NORTHWESTERN ONTARIO WOMEN'S DECADE COUNCIL
NURSES FOR SOCIAL RESPONSIBILITY
ONTARIO ASSOCIATION OF INTERVAL AND TRANSITION HOUSES
ONTARIO COALITION FOR ABORTION CLINICS
ONTARIO COALITION OF RAPE CRISIS CENTRES
ONTARIO COMMITTEE ON THE STATUS OF WOMEN

ONTARIO CONFEDERATION OF UNIV. FACULTY ASSOCIATIONS (OCUFA)
ONTARIO FEDERATION OF LABOUR, WOMEN'S COMMITTEE
ONTARIO FEDERATION OF STUDENTS
ONTARIO NURSES' ASSOCIATION, LOCAL 88
ONTARIO PUBLIC SERVICE EMPLOYEES UNION (OPSEU)
ONTARIO STATUS OF WOMEN CTTEE. CAN. FED. OF UNIV. WOMEN/ CFUW
OPPORTUNITY FOR ADVANCEMENT
OPSEU REGION 5 WOMEN'S CAUCUS
ORGANIZATION FOR WOMEN IN LEAD-ERSHIP, BOARD OF EDUCATION
ORGANIZED WORKING WOMEN
OSSTF STATUS OF WOMEN COMMITTEE
OTTAWA RAPE CRISIS CENTRE
OTTAWA WOMEN'S LOBBY (OWL)
OTTAWA WOMEN'S NETWORK
OUTREACH, A WOMAN'S ACTION GROUP (DURHAM)
P.C. ASSOCIATION OF WOMEN OF ONTARIO
P.C. WOMEN'S CAUCUS OF PEEL-HALTON (FEDERAL)
P.C. WOMEN'S CAUCUS OF METRO TORONTO (FEDERAL)
P.C. WOMEN'S CAUCUS OF OTTAWA
PEEL WOMEN TEACHERS' ASSOCIATION
PERTH COUNTY STATUS OF WOMEN ACTION COMMITTEE
PETERBOROUGH WOMEN'S COMMITTEE
PINK RIBBON COMMITTEE
PLANNED PARENTHOOD ONTARIO
POLITICS OF CUSTODY COALITION
POR NO WOMEN
PROFESSIONAL WOMEN'S ASSO., UNIVERSITY OF WATERLOO
PROJECT MAYDAY
QUEEN'S WOMEN'S CENTRE
RAPE CRISIS CENTRE - HAMILTON
REGISTERED NURSES' ASSOCIATION OF ONTARIO
RENFREW COUNTY WOMEN'S INITIA-TIVE NETWORK
RESEAU DES FEMMES DU SUD DE L'ONTARIO
RESOURCES - FEMINIST RESEARCH/ DOC. SUR RECHERCHE FEMINISTE
REXDALE COMMUNITY MICROSKILLS DEVELOPMENT CENTRE
REXDALE WOMEN'S CENTRE
RIVERDALE WOMEN'S ACTION COMMITTEE
RYERSON WOMEN'S CENTRE STUDENT UNION (SURPI)
SCARBOROUGH WOMEN'S CENTRE
SEXUAL ASSAULT CENTRE LONDON
SEXUAL ASSAULT CRISIS CENTRE, KINGSTON
SEXUAL ASSAULT SUPPORT CENTRE
SISTERING: A DROP-IN CENTRE FOR HOMELESS WOMEN
SOUTH RIVERDALE COMMUNITY HEALTH CENTRE
STORMONT, DUNDAS & GLENGARRY WOMEN TEACHERS' ASSOCIATION
SUDBURY SEXUAL ASSAULT CRISIS CENTRE
SUDBURY WOMEN TEACHERS' ASSOCIATION
SUDBURY WOMEN'S ACTION GROUP
SUDBURY WOMEN'S CENTRE/CENTRE DES FEMMES DE SUDBURY
THUNDER BAY PHYSICAL AND SEXUAL ASSAULT CRISIS CENTRE
TIMES CHANGE WOMEN'S EMPLOY-MENT SERVICE
TIMMINS SEXUAL ASSAULT CENTRE
TORONTO BIRTH CENTRE INC.
TORONTO BOARD OF EDUCATION WOMEN'S LIAISON COMMITTEE
TORONTO DISARMAMENT NETWORK
TORONTO HADASSAH-WIZO
TORONTO RAPE CRISIS CENTRE
TORONTO WOMEN IN FILM & VIDEO
TORONTO WOMEN TEACHERS' ASSOCIATION
TORONTO WOMEN'S BOOKSTORE

TORONTO WOMEN'S CHIROPRACTIC COUNCIL
TORONTO WOMEN'S HEALTH NETWORK
TORONTO WOMEN'S HOUSING CO-OPERATIVE (THE BEGUINAGE)
UNITED JEWISH PEOPLES ORDER, TORONTO WOMEN'S COMMITTEE
UNITED STEELWORKERS OF AMERICA DISTRICT 6
UNIVERSITY OF TORONTO STAFF ASSOCIATION
UNIVERSITY OF TORONTO, SAC WOMEN'S COMMISSION
UNIVERSITY OF WESTERN ONTARIO WOMEN'S ISSUES COMMISSION
UNIVERSITY WOMEN'S CLUB OF BURLINGTON
UNIVERSITY WOMEN'S CLUB OF NORTH TORONTO
UNIVERSITY WOMEN'S CLUB OF NORTH YORK
UNIVERSITY WOMEN'S CLUB OF OAKVILLE
UNIVERSITY WOMEN'S CLUB OF ST. CATHARINES, WOMEN TODAY
UNIVERSITY WOMEN'S CLUB/OTTAWA STATUS OF WOMEN COMMITTEE
WENTWORTH WOMEN TEACHERS' ASSOCIATION
WEST BAY HOMEMAKERS' CLUB (ANISHNABEQUEK)
WEST END / WOMEN ENTERING MACHINING
WESTERN'S CAUCUS ON WOMEN'S ISSUES
WILFRED LAURIER UNIVERSITY FACULTY OF SOCIAL WORK
WINDSOR WOMEN'S INCENTIVE CENTRE
WOMANPOWER INCORPORATED
WOMEN ACTIVE IN SPORT ADMINIS-TRATION (WASA)
WOMEN EDUCATORS IN SUPPORT OF PUBLIC EDUCATION
WOMEN FOR POLITICAL ACTION
WOMEN FOR WOMEN, SAULT STE. MARIE DISTRICT
WOMEN HEALTHSHARING
WOMEN IN CRISIS, NORTHUMBERLAND COUNTY
WOMEN IN PLANNING
WOMEN INITIATING RESPONSIBLE CHANGE
WOMEN LIKE ME
WOMEN OF HALTON ACTION MOVEMENT
WOMEN PLAN TORONTO
WOMEN TODAY
WOMEN WORKING WITH IMMIGRANT WOMEN
WOMEN ZONE
WOMEN'S ACTION COUNCIL OF PEEL
WOMEN'S CAREER COUNSELLING SERVICE
WOMEN'S CENTRE AT UNIVERSITY OF TORONTO
WOMEN'S COMMUNITY HOUSE SEMJA INC.
WOMEN'S COUNSELLING, REFERRAL AND EDUCATION CENTRE (WCREC)
WOMEN'S GROUP, FIRST UNITARIAN CONGREGATION OF TORONTO
WOMEN'S HABITAT
WOMEN'S HEALTH INTERACTION (WHI)
WOMEN'S PLACE KENORA
WOMEN'S PLACE/PLACE AUX FEMMES
WOMEN'S PRESS
WOMEN'S SELF-HELP GROUP
WORKING SKILLS CENTRE
YELLOW BRICK HOUSE PROJECT H.O.S.T.E.L.
YORK REGION WOMEN TEACHERS' ASSOCIATION
YORK UNIVERSITY - GRADUATE POLIT-ICAL SCIENCE WOMEN'S CAUCUS
YORK WOMEN'S CENTRE (YORK UNIVERSITY)
YWCA OF KITCHENER-WATERLOO
YWCA OF METROPOLITAN TORONTO
YWCA OF PETERBOROUGH
YWCA OF ST. CATHARINES

YWCA OF ST. THOMAS
YWCA OF SUDBURY

ZONTA CLUB OF BURLINGTON
ZONTA CLUB OF GUELPH AREA

ZONTA CLUB OF HAMILTON II, STATUS
OF WOMEN COMMITTEE
ZONTA CLUB OF MISSISSAUGA

PRINCE EDWARD ISLAND

CARAL - PRINCE EDWARD ISLAND
NATIONAL ASSOCIATION OF WOMEN
AND THE LAW, PEI CAUCUS

PRINCE EDWARD ISLAND COALITION
AGAINST PORNOGRAPHY
PRINCE EDWARD ISLAND RAPE & SEX-

UAL ASSAULT CRISIS CENTRE
PRINCE EDWARD ISLAND WOMEN'S
NETWORK INC.

QUEBEC

ACTION FEMMES HANDICAPPEES
MONTREAL (D.A.W.N. MONTREAL)
ACTION TRAVAIL DES FEMMES DU
QUEBEC INC.
ASSOCIATION DES FEMMES
COLLABORATRICES
ASSOCIATION OF FAMILY LIFE EDUCA-
TORS OF QUEBEC
AU BAS DE L'ECHELLE - RANK AND
FILE INC.
BUSINESS & PROFESSIONAL WOMEN'S
CLUB OF MONTREAL
CANADIAN CONGRESS FOR LEARNING
OPPORTUNITIES FOR WOMEN-
QUEBEC
CARREFOUR DES FEMMES DU GRAND
LACHUTE
CENTRE D'EDUCATION ET D'ACTION
DES FEMMES DE MONTREAL
COMITE DE CONDITION FEMININE -
FED. QUE. DES INFIRMIER(E)S
COMITE DES FEMMES AFRO-
ASIATIQUES DU QUEBEC
COMITE ET RESEAU DE LA CONDITION
DES FEMMES CEQ
COMITE NATIONAL DE LA CONDITION
FEMININE DE LA CSN
CONCORDIA WOMEN'S COLLECTIVE,
CUSA

CONGRESS OF BLACK WOMEN -
MONTREAL COMMITTEE
CONSEIL D'INTERVENTION POUR
L'ACCES DES FEMMES AU TRAVAIL
EQUAL RIGHTS FOR NATIVE WOMEN
FED. NATIONALE DES ENSEIGNANTS
ET ENSEIGNANTES/QUE. FEMMES
CSN
FED. SYN. PROF. D'INFIRMIERES ET
D'INFIRMIERS DU QUE. - FSPIIQ
FEDERATION DES FEMMES DU QUEBEC
FEMMES AUTOCHTONES DU QUEBEC/
QUEBEC NATIVE WOMEN'S ASSO.
GATINEAU VALLEY HOUSE/MAISON DE
LA VALLEE DE LA GATINEAU
GROUPE D'AIDE ET D'INFORMATION
HARCELEMENT SEXUEL AU TRAVAIL
INDIA CANADA ASSOCIATION OF
MONTREAL
L'R DES CENTRES DE FEMMES DU
QUEBEC
LA FEDERATION DES ASSOC. DE FAM-
ILLES MONOPARENTALES DU QUE.
LA MAISON LE PRELUDE INC.
LA VIE EN ROSE
LENNOXVILLE & DISTRICT WOMEN'S
CENTRE
LIGUE DES FEMMES DU QUEBEC
LIGUE OUVRIERE REVOLUTIONNAIRE

MAISON HALTE SECOURS INC.
MONTREAL WOMEN'S NETWORK
MOUVEMENT CONTRE LE VIOL, COL-
LECTIF, FEMMES DE MONTREAL
NACOI - MONTREAL (NAT'L ASSO.
CANADIANS OF ORIGINS IN INDIA)
NACOI SOUTH SHORE (NAT'L ASSO.
CANADIANS OF ORIGINS IN INDIA)
NOTRE DAME DE GRACE WOMEN'S
ACTION
PLANNED PARENTHOOD VILLE MARIE,
INC.
PROJECT MOM
QUEBEC TASK FORCE FOR IMMIGRANT
WOMEN
REGROUPEMENT DES GARDERIES DU
QUEBEC
SIMONE DE BEAUVOIR INSTITUTE OF
CONCORDIA UNIVERSITY
SOUTH ASIA COMMUNITY CENTRE
VOICE OF WOMEN QUEBEC
WEST ISLAND WOMEN'S CENTRE
WOMEN'S PARTICIPATION GROUP
WOMEN'S STUDIES STUDENT ASSO.
SIMONE DE BEAUVOIR INSTITUTE
WOMEN'S TIME OUT
YWCA OF MONTREAL
ZONTA CLUB OF MONTREAL

SASKATCHEWAN

ALTERNATIVES FOR SINGLE PARENT
WOMEN (ASPW)
IMMIGRANT WOMEN OF SASKATCHE-
WAN (IWS)
NORTH WEST STATUS OF WOMEN
REEL WOMEN'S CABLE COLLECTIVE

REGINA HEALTHSHARING INC.
SASKATCHEWAN ACTION COMMITTEE
ON THE STATUS OF WOMEN
SASKATCHEWAN TEACHERS'
FEDERATION
SASKATCHEWAN WOMEN'S AGRICUL-
TURAL NETWORK (SWAN)

SASKATCHEWAN WOMEN'S
RESOURCES
SOROPTIMIST CLUB OF REGINA
WORKING FOR WOMEN
YWCA OF PRINCE ALBERT
YWCA OF REGINA
YWCA of SASKATOON

YUKON

NDP WOMEN'S COMMITTEE, YUKON

VICTORIA FAULKNER WOMEN'S
CENTRE

YUKON STATUS OF WOMEN COUNCIL

Bibliography

This bibliography is divided into three sections: the contemporary women's movement in Canada, which includes, at the end, a separate list of the historical references on the first wave cited in the text; the women's movement in western Europe and the United States; and, finally, other sources cited in the text.

As we discovered in writing this book, little scholarly or even systematic research has been done on the contemporary Canadian women's movement. As a result of our commitment to relying on Canadian sources and the Canadian experience, we sought out archival and journalistic sources, in addition to the few articles and book that are widely circulated or easily available. These we have compiled into a bibliography on the contemporary Canadian women's movement, which we hope will provide a starting point for future research in the area.

In contrast to the paucity of academic writing on the women's movement, there exists a remarkable and lengthy list of Canadian feminist periodicals, journals, bulletins and newspapers, some of which have survived for many years, some of which lasted only for a few issues. Unable to search systematically all the existing material, we selected a representative list, which we examined in detail. The list of these journals/newspapers with publishing history, place and years of publication follows:

Alberta Status of Women News, Edmonton: Alberta Status of Women Action Committee; vol. 1, no. 1, 1980—.

Atlantis, Halifax: Mount St. Vincent University; vol. 1, no. 1, 1975—.

Branching Out, Edmonton: New Women's Magazine Society; vol. 1, no. 1, 1974—vol.7, no. 2, 1980.

Breaking the Silence, Ottawa: Carleton University; vol. 1, no. 1, 1982—.

Broadside, Toronto; vol.1, no. 1, 1979—.

Canadian Woman Studies/les cahiers de la femme, Downsview: York University; vol. 1, no. 1, 1978—.

Cayenne, Toronto; vol. 1, no. 1, Nov./Dec. 1984—.

Common Ground, Charlottetown: Women's Network Inc.; vol. 1, no. 1, 1982—.

Communiqu'elles, Montreal: Women's Information and Referral Centre; May, 1981—; formerly *Bulletin*, Dec. 1978—April 1981; formerly *Women's Information and Referral Centre Newsletter*, 1975—Nov. 1978.

Feminist Action/féministe, Toronto: National Action Committee; vol. 1, no. 1, 1985—; formerly *Status of Women News*, vol. 1 no. 1, 1973—vol. 10 no. 4 1985.

Herizons, Manitoba; vol. 1, no. 1, 1983—vol. 5, no. 2, 1987; formerly *Herizons Newsletter*, vol. 2, no. 1, 1981—vol. 2, no. 7, 1983; formerly *Manitoba Women's Newspaper*, vol. 1, no. 1, 1981—vol. 2, no. 1, 1981.

Kinesis, Vancouver: Vancouver Status of Women; Jan. 1974—; formerly *Vancouver Status of Women Newsletter*, July 1973—Jan. 1974; formerly *Status of Women Action and Coordinating Council Newsletter*, Spring 1971—July 1973.

Northern Woman, Thunder Bay; vol. 1, no. 1, 1973—.

Optimst, White Horse: Yukon Status of Women Council; no. 1, 1975—.

Prairie Woman, Saskatoon: Saskatoon Women's Liberation; vol. 1, no. 1, 1977—Jan. 1981; formerly *Saskatoon Women's Liberation Newsletter*, Jan. 1975—July 1977. *Priorities*, Vancouver: Standing Committee of Women's Rights of the British Columbia New Democratic Party; vol. 1, no. 1, 1973—.

Rebel Girls Rag, Toronto: International Women's Day Committee; vol. 1, no. 1, 1987—; formerly *International Women's Day Committee Newsletter*, 1979—1986.

Upstream, Ottawa: Feminist Publications of Ottawa; vol. 1, no. 1, 1976—July 1980.

Selecting the references to include in the bibliography was not always easy. We wished to focus on the women's movement itself rather than the issues it has addressed, but this is a difficult distinction to maintain. Often the most coherent discussions of strategy and organization are situated within debates about specific issues such as day-care, abortion, or lesbian rights. And there is no doubt that certain issues tend to generate particular kinds of debate about strategy and organization; for example, concerns about violence against women may more often give rise to strategic discussions about the exclusion of men or the development of alternatives than discussions of union organizing. In addition, though many of the pieces are short and newsy, we have included a number of them as a means of documenting the history of the contemporary women's movement. Finally, we would point out that the listing on the first wave of the women's movement in Canada at the end of the first section of the bibliography includes references only to works actually cited in the text.

The second part of the bibliography brings together a selected list of resources on the women's movement in western (and to a limited extent, southern) Europe and the United States. As with the bibliography on Canada, we have tried to select references that deal with organizing and strategy in the women's movement. The quantity of material available is much more extensive, and the list is therefore somewhat selective in terms of our political perspective; we actively sought discussions of socialist-feminist organizing. The third part of the bibliography includes all other sources cited in the text.

1. The Contemporary Canadian Women's Movement

Adamson, Nancy, and Kathy Arnup. 'A Committee for All Seasons'. *Broadside* vol. 3, no. 5 (March 1983), p. 4.

Adamson, Nancy, and Anne Molgat. 'NAC' 86: Who's In and Who's Out?' *Cayenne* vol. 2, no. 4 (Fall 1986), pp. 20–2.

Adamson, Nancy, and Susan Prentice. 'Toward a Broader Strategy for Choice'. *Cayenne* no. 3 (May-June 1985), pp. 3–8.

Adamson, Nancy, et al. 'What are our Options?' In *Still Ain't Satisfied*, pp. 300–12. Edited by Maureen FitzGerald, Connie Guberman, and Margie Wolfe. Toronto: Women's Press, 1982.

Bacave, Christiane. 'The Women's Movement in Quebec'. *Status of Women News* vol. 8, no. 3 (1983).

Bank Book Collective. *An Account to Settle: the Story of the United Bank Workers (SORWUC)*. Vancouver: Press Gang, 1979.

Bannerji, Himani. 'Popular Images of South Asian Women'. *Tiger Lily* Nov./Dec. 1986.

Barrett, Michele, and Robert Hamilton. 'Introduction'. In *The Politics of Diversity*. Edited by Robert Hamilton and Michele Barrett. Montreal: Book Centre, 1986.

Battered Women's Support Services. 'Defining Feminism'. *Optimst* vol. 11, no. 3 (1985).

Bell, Sharon. 'More than a Rhetorical War'. *Broadside* vol. 4, no. 8 (1983).

Bill C-127 Working Group. 'Lobby Logistics: Bill C-127'. *Broadside* vol. 4, no. 3 (1982).

Black, Ayanna. 'Working with Collectives: An Interview with Toronto Women's Press'. *Tiger Lily* vol. 1, no. 2 (1987).

————— . 'Working with Collectives: An Interview with Larissa Cairncross and Nila Gupta from Toronto Women's Press'. *Tiger Lily* vol. 1, no. 3 (1987).

Blanchard, Michele Miville. 'La femme et les mouvements féministes'. *Canadian Woman Studies/les cahiers de la femme* vol. 1, no. 2 (1978–79), pp. 94–5.

Bouvier, Isabelle. 'Women's Groups and Their Relations With the State'. *Communiqu'elles* vol. 12, no. 1 (1986).

Brand, Johanna and Ester Koulack. 'Liberation: More than Equality'. *Canadian Dimension* vol. 13, no. 1 (1978).

Briskin, Linda. 'Socialist Feminism: From the Standpoint of Practice'. Paper given at the 3rd International Interdisciplinary Congress on Women, Dublin, Ireland, July 1987.

————— .'Toward Socialist Feminism?' *Our Generation* vol. 10, no. 3 (Fall 1974).

Briskin, Linda, and Lynda Yanz, eds. *Union Sisters: Women in the Labour Movement*. Toronto: Women's Press, 1983.

Broduer, Violette, et al. *Le mouvement des femmes au Québec*. Montreal: Centre de formation populaire, 1982.

Brown, Heather. 'New Times—New Tactics'. *Broadside* vol. 1, no. 1 (1979).

————— . 'The Press vs. the Feminist Party'. *Broadside* vol. 1, no. 1 (1979).

Brown, Rosemary. 'Feminism and Socialism'. *Priorities* vol. 3, no. 6 (1975).

———— . 'Rosemary Brown on Lobbying'. *Kinesis* vol. 6, no. 11 (1977).

Bruners, Daina. 'The Influence of the Women's Liberation Movement on the Lives of Canadian Farm Women'. *Resources for Feminist Research/ Documentation sur la recherche féministe* vol. 14, no. 3 (Nov. 1985).

'Budget Creates Unexpected Alliances'. *Kinesis* Sept. 1983.

'Building the Feminist Network'. *Saturday Night* vol. 93, no. 7 (1978).

Burgess, Jean. 'Power is not Electoral'. *Branching Out* vol. 4, no. 5 (1977).

Burstyn, Varda (producer). *Feminism in the Political Arena.* ('Ideas' transcript) Toronto: CBC, 1983.

———— . 'The Age of Women's Liberation'. *Canadian Dimension* (Oct./Nov. 1984), pp. 21–6.

———— , ed. *Women Against Censorship.* Vancouver: Douglas and McIntyre, 1985.

Burt, Sandra. 'Women's Issues and the Women's Movement in Canada since 1970.' In *The Politics of Gender, Ethnicity and Language in Canada* vol. 34: Studies Commissioned as part of the Research Program of the Royal Commission on the Economic Union and Development Prospects for Canada, co-ordinated by Alan Cairns and Cynthia Williams. Toronto: Univ. of Toronto Press, 1986.

Carey, Patricia. 'Feminist Party of Canada'. *Canadian Woman Studies/les cahiers de la femme* vol. 1, no. 4 (1979), pp.119–20.

———— . 'Personal is Political'. *Canadian Woman Studies/les cahiers de la femme* vol. 2, no. 2 (1980).

Cartlidge, Thora, and Sharon Batt. 'Our Readers on the Women's Movement'. *Branching Out* vol. 6, no. 1 (1979), pp. 18–21.

Cheda, Sherrill. 'Indian Women: An Historical Example and a Contemporary View'. In *Women in Canada* (rev. ed.) pp. 195–208. Edited by Marylee Stephenson. Don Mills: General Publishing Co., 1977.

Cheda, Sherrill, Johanna Stuckey, and Marilyn Kantaroff. 'New Feminists Now'. *Canadian Woman Studies/les cahiers de la femme* vol. 2, no. 2 (1980).

Cherniak, Donna, and Allan Feingold. 'Birth Control Handbook'. In *Women Unite!.* Toronto: Women's Press, 1972, pp. 109–13.

Cleveland, John. 'The Mainstreaming of Feminist Issues: the Toronto Women's Movement, 1966–1984'. Ms., York University, 1984.

Clio Collective. *Quebec Women: A History.* Toronto: Women's Press, 1987.

Cohen, Yolande. 'Thoughts on Women and Power'. In *Feminism in Canada: From Pressure to Politics.* Edited by Angela Miles and Geraldine Finn. Montreal: Black Rose Books, 1982.

Cole, Susan G., et. al. 'What Price Status?' *Broadside* vol. 2, no. 4 (1981).

Colley, Sue, and Weisia Kolasinska. 'Action Daycare'. *Broadside* vol. 5, no. 4 (1984).

Conn, Heather. 'Native Women Take Action—And the DIA Office'. *Kinesis* Sept./Oct. 1981.

Côté, Andrée. 'Autopsy of a Revolt'. *Status of Women News* vol. 10, no. 3 (1985).

Cousinea, Lea. 'Les Québécoises'. *Canadian Dimension* vol.13, no. 1 (1978), pp. 31–4.

Creet, Julia. 'A Test of Unity: Lesbian Visibility in the British Columbia Federation of Women, 1974 & 1975'. Unpublished essay, 1986. CWMA/ ACMF.

Cull, Elizabeth et al. 'Socialism, Feminism and the Urban Environment'. *Priorities* vol. 4, no. 5 (1976).

de Wolff, Alice, Judy Dragon, Julie Ann Le Gras, Trudy Richardson, Sandy Susut, Derwyn Whitehead. 'Women Organize Alberta: Discussion Paper', 1981. CWMA/ACMF.

de Grass, Jan. 'Coops: Tools for Social Change?' *Kinesis* Sept./Oct. 1981.

De Rosa, Susan, and Janou Gagnon. 'The Second Conference of the L'R des Centres de Femmes du Quebec'. *Communiqu'elles* vol. 12, no. 5 (1986).

Den Hertog, Johanna. 'Where are We Going?' *Kinesis* vol. 6, no. 1 (1976).

Dewar, Elaine. 'Beyond Sisterhood'. *Optimst* no. 12 (1977).

Diamond, Sara. 'From Our Past'. *Kinesis* July/Aug. 1983.

————— . 'Working Class Women: Caught in the Gender/Class Squeeze'. *Kinesis* Sept. 1985.

Dick, Jane. 'Why Not? Because. . .'. *Branching Out* vol. 2, no. 6 (1975).

Dillon, Shelly. 'Individual vs. Collective Action'. *Priorities* vol. 2, no. 7 (1974).

Dixon, Marlene. 'Women's Liberation: Opening Chapter Two'. *Canadian Dimension* vol. 10, no. 8 (June 1975), pp. 56–68.

Dubinsky, Karen. *Lament for a 'Patriarchy Lost'? Anti-feminism, Anti-abortion and REAL Women in Canada.* Ottawa: CRIAW/ICREF, 1985.

Duckworth, Janet. 'Native Women Struggle: Four Circles of Strength'. *Kinesis* Dec./Jan. 1984/85.

Dumont, Micheline. *The Women's Movement: Then and Now.* Ottawa: CRIAW/ICREF, 1986.

Edwards, Val. 'The Invisible Community' *Broadside* vol. 1, no. 10 (1980).

Egan, Carolyn. 'Socialist Feminism—A Challenge to Marxism'. *Fireweed* no. 19 (Summer/Fall 1984), pp. 45–53.

————— . 'Sexual Politics'. *Rebel Girls Rag* vol. 1, no. 3 (1987).

————— . 'Toronto's International Women's Day Committee: Socialist Feminist Politics' In *Feminism and Political Economy.* Edited by Heather Jon Maroney and Meg Luxton. Toronto: Methuen, 1987.

Egan, Carolyn, and Lynda Yanz. 'Building Links: Labour and the Women's Movement'. In *Union Sisters.* Edited by Linda Briskin and Lynda Yanz. Toronto: Women's Press, 1983.

Ellis, Jennifer. 'What Does the NAC Do for Us?' *Optimst* vol. 13, no. 2 (1987).

Ellis, Megan. 'The Anti Porn Movement in B.C.'. *Canadian Woman Studies/les cahiers de la femme* vol. 4, no. 4 (1983), pp. 50-2.

Estable, Alma. 'Money, Women and Power: Where is the Women's Credit Union Going?'. *Breaking the Silence* vol. 3, no. 3 (1985).

_____ . 'Immigrant Women: From the Outside Looking In'. *Breaking the Silence* vol. 4, no. 3/4 (Spring/Summer 1986).

Farkas, Edie. 'Canada's Women's Year'. *The Last Post* vol. 4, no. 8 (Aug. 1975).

Feminist Party of Canada. 'Towards a Canadian Feminist Party'. *Atlantis* vol. 5, no. 1 (1979).

_____ . 'Feminist Party of Canada: First Principles'. *Broadside* vol. 1, no. 7 (1980).

Feminist Practice in Quebec. Special issue of *Resources for Feminist Research/Documentation sur la recherche féministe* vol. 15, no. 4 (Dec. 1986).

'Feminist Process and Union Democracy'. n.p., n.d.

Findlay, Sue. 'Facing the State: the Politics of the Women's Movement Reconsidered'. In *Feminism and Political Economy*. Edited by Heather Jon Maroney and Meg Luxton. Toronto: Methuen, 1987.

Fitzgerald, Maureen. 'Toronto International Women's Day Committee'. *Canadian Woman Studies/les cahiers de la femme* vol. 2, no. 2 (1980).

_____ . 'Vancouver Rape Relief: Frustrations With the Fortress Mentality'. *Broadside* vol. 4, no. 2 (1982).

Fitzgerald, Maureen, and Daphne Morrison. 'Lesbian Conference: Agony and Audacity'. *Broadside* vol. 2, no. 9 (1981).

Fitzpatrick, Katherine. 'Northern Women Branch Out to Form Action Group'. *Herizons* vol. 4, no. 8 (1986).

Fletcher, Joan. 'Liberal Feminism'. *Priorities* vol. 2, no. 7 (1974).

Flood, Cynthia. 'Feminists and the NDP'. *Priorities* vol.5, no. 1 (1977).

_____ . 'Solidarity Coalition: Women Against the Budget'. *Broadside* vol. 5, no. 2 (1983).

_____ . 'Solidarity Update'. *Broadside* vol. 5, no. 3 (1984).

Forrest, Mona. 'Feminists Knock NAC'. *Communiqu'elles* vol. 10, no. 5 (1984).

Foster, John. 'Sussex Day Care'. In *Women Unite!* Toronto: Women's Press, 1972.

Fourt, Anne. 'Strategies for Daycare'. *Cayenne* Spring/Summer 1987, pp. 2-7.

Frank, Ellen. 'On The Crisis Line'. *Broadside* vol. 4, no. 9 (1983).

Fulton, Margaret. 'Taking Charge'. *Northern Woman* vol. 8, no. 1 (1983).

Gagnon, Lysiane. 'En Douceur et Mine de Rien: Le Women's Lib. Version Québécoise'. *Maintenant* vol. 140 (Nov. 1974).

Galey, Sherry. 'Nairobi Notebook: A Personal Voyage of Discovery'. *Breaking the Silence* vol. 4, no. 1 (1986).

Gardner, Jennifer. 'False Consciousness'. *Northern Woman* vol. 7, no. 2 (1982).

Gilbert, Marianne, and Other Sisters. 'Facing Facts'. *Priorities* vol. 4, no. 9 (1976).

Godin, Pierre, and Micheline Lachance. 'La Guerre n'est pas fini'. *L'Actualité* vol. 3 (1978).

Gordon, Shelly. 'Articulation of the Women's Movement'. *Prairie Woman* vol. 2, no. 2 (1978).

Gottlieb, Amy. 'Double Oppression: Mothers, Sisters, Lovers, Listen'. In *Still Ain't Satisfied: Canadian Feminism Today*. Edited by Maureen FitzGerald, Connie Guberman, and Margie Wolfe. Toronto: Women's Press, 1982.

Greenberg, Shirley. 'Lorenne Clark: Creating a Feminist Politic'. *Upstream* vol. 2, no. 5 (1978).

Harding, Ruth L. 'White Women's Movement Keeps Black Women Out'. *Kinesis* Sept. 1985.

Herland, Karen. 'Abortion Coalition in Quebec Pushes for Legislation'. *Herizons* vol. 4, no. 4 (1986).

Hernandez, Carmencita R. 'The Foundation of NOIVMWC'. *Canadian Woman Studies/les cahiers de la femme* vol. 8, no. 2 (1987).

Hilderbrandt, Heather. 'Sorry, Sisters, Women's Lib Only Trades One Tyranny for Another'. *Maclean's* no.84 (1971).

Hillmer, Sandra. 'Prelude to IWD'. *Branching Out* vol. 1, no. 5 (1974).

Holmes, Joan, and Joan Riggs. 'Inside Feminist Organizations: Part One'. *Breaking the Silence* vol. 2, no. 2 (Spring/Summer 1984), p. 7–15.

——————. 'Feminist Organizations, Part Two: Conflict and Change'. *Breaking the Silence* Fall 1984, pp. 16–22.

Hotte, Gabriel, and Michele Jean. 'L'Education et la formation a la Fédération des femmes du Québec'. *Canadian Woman Studies/les cahiers de la femme* vol. 1, no. 1 (1978), p. 20.

'How to Organize Your Own Community'. *Kinesis* vol. 7, no. 12 (1979).

Hughes, Patricia. 'Fighting the Good Fight: Separatism or Integration?'. In *Feminism in Canada: From Pressure to Politics*. Edited by Angela Miles and Geraldine Finn. Montreal: Black Rose Books, 1982.

Hunter, Sally. 'Government Strategies'. *Priorities* vol. 5, no. 9 (1977).

Hynes, Maureen. 'We Need a National Network of Power Brokers'. *Branching Out* vol. 4, no. 5 (1977).

——————. 'Feminist Party of Canada: Entering the Electoral Mainstream'. *Branching Out* vol. 7, no. 1 (1980).

Immigrant Women. Special Issue of *Resources for Feminist Research/ Documentation sur la recherche féministe* vol. 16, no.1 (March 1987).

Isis. 'Feminism and Anarchism'. *Kinesis* Sept. 1984.

IWDC Newsletter Committee. 'International Women's Day Committee Newsletter'. *Broadside* vol. 5, no. 4 (1984).

Jackman, Nancy. 'Conference Reconstituted'. *Broadside* vol. 2, no. 9 (1981).

_____ . 'Staying Together: An Approach to Differences Within Feminism'. *Status of Women News* vol. 8, no. 1 (1983).

Jean, Michele. 'Two Decades of Feminism in Quebec: 1960–1979'. *Fireweed* vol. 5/6 (Winter/Spring 1979/80).

_____ . 'Où va le mouvement des femmes?'. *Canadian Woman Studies/les cahiers de la femme* vol. 2, no. 2 (1980).

Jean, Michele, et al. 'Nationalism and Feminism in Quebec: The "Yvettes" Phenomenon'. In *The Politics of Diversity*. Edited by Roberta Hamilton and Michele Barrett. Montreal, Book Centre, 1986.

Kaetz, Deborah. 'IWY Conferences in Mexico City'. *Atlantis* vol. 1, no. 2 (1975).

Kerr, Kandace. 'Experiencing *Women, Race and Class*, Personally'. *Kinesis* Sept. 1985.

Killan, Melody. 'Children are only Littler People or the Louis Riel University Family Co-op'. In *Women Unite!*. Toronto: Women's Press, 1972.

Kome, Penney. *The Taking of 28: Women Challenge the Constitution*. Toronto: Women's Press, 1983.

Kostash, Myrna. 'The Spirit is Still Willing but the Flesh is Bone Tired'. *Maclean's* vol. 88, no. 9 (Sept. 1975).

_____ . *Long Way From Home: The Story of the Sixties Generation in Canada*. Toronto: Lorimer, 1980.

_____ . 'The Rising of the Women'. *Broadside* vol. 2, no. 5 (1981).

Krakauer, Renate. 'Strategies for Survival'. *Status of Women News* vol. 4, no. 3 (1978).

Lachapelle, Caroline. 'Beyond Barriers: Native Women and the Women's Movement'. In *Still Ain't Satisfied: Canadian Feminism Today*. Edited by Maureen FitzGerald, Connie Guberman, and Margie Wolfe. Toronto: Women's Press, 1982.

Laidlaw, Janet. 'Forum 85: The "Unofficial" Conference'. *Canadian Woman Studies/les cahiers de la femme* vol. 7, no. 1/2 (1986), pp. 7–10.

Lambert, Zoe. 'Feminists are Isolating Poor Women'. *Kinesis* Oct. 1985.

Lamoureux, Diane. 'Nationalism and Feminism in Quebec: An Impossible Attraction' . In *Feminism and Political Economy*. Edited by Heather Jon Maroney and Meg Luxton. Toronto: Methuen, 1987.

Lancaster, Jean. 'British Columbia Federation of Women'. *Canadian Woman Studies/les cahiers de la femme* vol. 2, no. 2 (1980).

Lane, Arja. 'Wives Supporting the Strike'. In *Union Sisters*. Edited by Linda Briskin and Lynda Yanz. Toronto: Women's Press, 1983.

Laundau, Reva. 'Choosing Sides Wisely'. *Broadside* vol. 5, no. 1 (1983).

Laurin-Frenette, Nicole. 'On the Women's Movement, Anarchism and the State'. *Our Generation* vol. 15, no. 2 (Summer 1982).

Le François, Bev, and Helga Martens Enns. *Story of A Women's Centre*. Vancouver: Press Gang, 1979.

Le Gras, Julie Anne. *Pursuing the Limits: Reflections on Alberta Women's Strategies for Action*. Edmonton: Unique Publishing Association, 1984.

Lester, Tanya. 'In Support of Support Groups'. *Herizons* vol. 2, no. 2 (1984).

Lorenzo, Marie. 'Two Wings of the Same Bird: An Interview with Chai Chu Thompson'. *International Women's Day Committee Newsletter* Sept. 1984.

Lowenburger, Lois. 'IWD: Lip Service to Feminism'. *Broadside* vol. 4, no. 6 (1983).

Luxton, Meg. 'From Ladies' Auxiliaries to Wives' Committees'. In *Union Sisters*. Edited by Linda Briskin and Lynda Yanz. Toronto: Women's Press, 1983.

Lynne, Judy, and Kate Nonesuch. 'Talking Directions for the Women's Movement: Re-radicalizing Ourselves'. *Upstream* vol. 4, no. 5 (1980).

McDermott, Pat. 'Pay Equity in Ontario: Coalition Politics'. *Cayenne* Fall 1987.

McDonald, Lynn. 'The Evolution of the Women's Movement in Canada'. *Branching Out* vol. 6, no. 1 (1979), pp. 39–43.

_____ . 'The Evolution of the Women's Movement, Part II'. *Branching Out* vol. 6, no. 2 (1979), pp. 31–9.

_____ . 'Women and the Left'. *Canadian Forum* May 1979, pp. 13–14.

McIntyre, Sheila. 'FPC Growing Pains'. *Broadside* vol. 1, no. 9 (1980).

McKenzie, Maxine. 'You Mean, I Still Ain't: Racism in the Women's Movement'. *Breaking the Silence* vol. 5, no. 3 (March 1987).

Macpherson, Kay. 'The Seeds of the 70's'. *Canadian Dimension* vol. 10, no. 8 (June 1975), pp. 39–41.

_____ . 'Politics Within the Women's Movement'. *Status of Women News* vol. 5, no. 4 (1979).

_____ . 'Persistent Voices: Twenty Five Years with Voice of Women'. *Atlantis* vol. 12, no. 2 (Spring 1987).

Macpherson, Kay, and Meg Sears. 'The Voice of Women: A History'. In *Women in the Canadian Mosaic*. Edited by Gwen Matheson. Toronto: Peter Martin Associates, 1976.

Maier, Helen. 'We Will Survive'. *Kinesis* June 1984.

Makin, Kirk. 'And the Verdict Is. . .'. *The Globe and Mail* 23 Jan. 1988, pp. D1, D8.

Marie, Gillian. 'NAC Conference: Whose Interests Were Served?'. *Kinesis* April/May 1979.

Maroney, Heather Jon. 'Feminism at Work'. *New Left Review* no. 141 (1983), pp. 51–71.

Maroney, Heather Jon, and Meg Luxton, eds. *Feminism and Political Economy: Women's Work, Women's Struggles*. Toronto: Metheun, 1987.

Martin, Mary, et al. 'Group Process'. *Optimst* vol. 11, no. 3 (1985).

Masters, Philinda. 'Toronto Women's Credit Union: Merging Ahead?'. *Broadside* vol. 2, no. 8 (1981).

_____ . 'The Man Question'. *Broadside* vol. 5, no. 6 1984.

Meissenheimer, Joyce. 'An Alligator Speaks Out'. *Priorities* vol. 1, no. 7 (1973).

Miles, Angela. 'Feminist Radicalism in the 1980's'. In *Feminism Now: Theory and Practice*. Edited by Marilouise and Arthur Kroker, Pamela McCallum, and Mair Verthuy. Montreal: Culture Texts Series, 1985.

Miller, Joni. 'Living'. *Kinesis* June 1984.

Mills, Chris. 'Strategy for Choice: An Interview with Judy Rebick'. *Cayenne* no. 2 (Feb. 1985), pp. 22-8.

Morris, Cerise. 'Determination and Thoroughness: The Movement for a Royal Commission on the Status of Women in Canada'. *Atlantis* vol. 5, no. 2 (Spring 1980).

——————— . 'Pressuring the Canadian State for Women's Rights: The Role of the National Action Committee'. *Alternate Routes*. Ottawa: Carleton University, 1983.

'Movement Across the Province'. *Kinesis* vol. 7, no. 7 (1978).

Msimang, Nonqaba. 'National Action Committee: Power in Diversity'. *Herizons* vol. 4, no. 2 (1986).

Nelson, Lou. 'Recognizing Our Labour or The Dinner Party That Never Was'. *Kinesis* Feb. 1982.

Nerimoff, Greta Hofmann. 'The Hard Task of Getting Women Together: Women's Conferences'. *Communiqu'elles* vol. 10, no. 6 (1984).

——————— . 'NAC: Striving to Sweet Reason'. *Broadside* vol. 8, no. 8 (1987).

Nemiroff, Greta Hofmann, and Susan McCrae van der Voet. 'Feminist Research: Does it Affect Government Policy?'. *Communiqu'elles* vol. 2, no. 5 (1985).

Ng, Winnie. 'Immigrant Women: The Silent Partners of the Women's Movement'. In *Still Ain't Satisfied: Canadian Feminism Today*. Edited by Maureen FitzGerald, Connie Guberman, and Margie Wolfe. Toronto: Women's Press, 1982.

Norman, H. E., and A. Micco. 'A History of the Women's Movement in Prince George, 1972-1985'. Typescript. CWMA/ACMF.

O'Brien, Mary. 'At School on the Street'. *Canadian Woman Studies/les cahiers de la femme* vol. 1, no. 1 (Fall 1978).

O'Connell, Dorothy. 'Income Makes All the Difference'. *Breaking the Silence* vol. 4, no. 3/4 (1986).

O'Donnell, Susan. 'Our Taxes are for Us'. *Kinesis* June 1984.

O'Shea, Marie. 'Clerical and Secretarial Workers: Why Some Women Remain Outside the Women's Movement'. *Breaking the Silence* Spring/Summer 1986.

Ontario Coalition for Abortion Clinics Coordinating Committee. 'Electoral Exercise'. *Broadside* vol. 5, no. 10 (1984).

'Organizing Exclusion: Race, Class, Community and the White Women's Movement'. *Fireweed* 17 (Summer/Fall 1983).

Parker, Sandra. 'Deferred Debate'. *Broadside* vol. 8, no. 8 (1987).

Perston, Shirin. 'Domestic Stress'. *Broadside* vol. 8, no. 9 (1987).

Phillip, Marlene Nourbese. 'Solitary Dialogue'. *Broadside* vol. 7, no. 5 (1986).

Pierre-Aggamaway, Marlene. 'Native Women and the State'. In *Perspective on Women in the 1980s*, pp. 66–73. Edited by Joan Turner and Lois Emery. Winnipeg: Univ. of Manitoba Press, 1983.

Political Action Collective of the Ottawa Women's Centre. 'Leadership—Yes or No'. *Upstream* vol. 3, no. 5 (1979).

_____ . 'What Are Collectives?'. *Upstream* vol. 3, no. 6 (1979).

_____ . 'Sisterhood—The Only Option'. *Upstream* vol. 3, no. 8 (1979).

Preston, Patricia. 'Confrontations'. *Branching Out* vol. 6, no. 1 (1979), pp. 32–4.

Prieur, Deborah. 'Community Economic Development: Promising a New Future'. *Kinesis* July/Aug. 1987.

Quinlan, Judith. 'Autonomy Independence Separatism Revisited'. *Kinesis* July/Aug. 1981.

'Racism and International Women's Day in Toronto'. *Cayenne* vol. 2, no. 2/3 (June/July 1986), pp. 25–44.

Randall, Nora. 'How Long Will We Be Adhoc?'. *Kinesis* June 1984.

Randell, Melanie. 'Defining Feminism . . . An Interview'. *Resources for Feminist Research/Documentation sur la recherche féministe* vol. 14, no. 3 (Nov. 1985), pp. 2–6.

Reid, Alison. 'Woman's Programs Funding: There Must Be a Better Way'. *Optimst* vol. 7, no. 3 (1981).

_____ . 'Feminists Talk About Own Race and Class Bias'. *Optimst* vol. 12, no. 2 (1986).

Richardson, Karen. 'Alice in Political Land'. *Kinesis* vol. 5, no. 53 (1976).

_____ . 'The Feminist Revolution? Nowhere in Sight'. *Kinesis* vol. 6, no. 1 (1976).

Ricks, Francie, George Matheson, and Sandra Pyke. 'Women's Liberation: A Case Study of Organizations for Social Change'. *Canadian Psychologist* vol. 13, no. 1 (1972).

Ridington, Jillian. 'NAC: Should We Hang in There?'. *Kinesis* April/May 1979.

Riggs, Joan. 'National Action Committee on the Status of Women: Responsive or Redundant?'. *Breaking the Silence* vol. 5, no. 3 (March 1987).

Ryan, Kay. 'Fusion—Feminism and Socialism'. *Kinesis* vol. 5, no. 50 (1975).

Sarra, Janis. 'Trade Union Women and the NDP'. In *Union Sisters*. Edited by Linda Briskin and Lynda Yanz. Toronto: Women's Press, 1983.

Scher, Ruth. 'Speaking Up: A Labour Women's Roundtable'. *Breaking the Silence* vol. 4, no. 3/4 (Spring/Summer 1986), pp. 18–20.

Shniad, Sharon. 'Women in Solidarity'. *Priorities* vol. 11, no. 4 (1983).

Silvera, Makeda. 'Black Women Organize for Health'. *Healthsharing* vol. 1, no. 2 (Spring 1984).

Silvera, Makeda, and Cy-Thea Sand. 'Two Feminists in Dialogue'. *Kinesis* March 1985.

Smee, Susan. 'Women's Movement Blues'. *Prairie Woman* vol. 2, no. 6 (1978).

Smith, Dorothy. 'Does Government Funding Co-opt?'. *Kinesis* vol. 6, no. 11 (1977).

————— . 'Where There is Oppression, There is Resistance'. *Branching Out* vol. 6, no. 1 (1979), pp. 10–15.

Smith, Dorothy, and Sara David, eds. *Women Look at Psychiatry: I'm Not Mad, I'm Angry*. Vancouver: Press Gang, 1975.

Stanleigh, Judy. 'Marching on the Spot'. *Broadside* vol. 1, no. 10 (1980).

Stasiulis, Daiva. 'Rainbow Feminism: Perspectives on Minority Women in Canada'. *Resources for Feminist Research/Documentation sur la recherche féministe* vol. 16, no.1 (March 1987).

Stein, David Lewis, and Erna Paris. 'Has Feminism Fizzled Out?'. *Chatelaine* vol. 51 (July 1978).

Stephen, Jennifer. 'Women's Centres Unite'. *Broadside* vol. 7, no. 5 (1986).

Stevenson, Judi. 'Fighting Racism in the Women's Movement: An Interview with Carol Allen'. *Cayenne* vol. 3, no. 1 (Winter 1987), pp. 14–16.

Stickney, Janet, et. al. 'Conferring With Reality'. *Broadside* vol. 7, no. 5 (1986).

Sugiman, Momoye. 'Asian Women in Canada: Coming Together With Obsoletes'. *Northern Woman* vol. 5, no. 1 (1979).

Sundberg, Laura. 'Rural Canadian and Third World Women Come Together'. *Herizons* vol. 2, no. 5 (1984).

Swartz, Jacqueline. 'Lysistrata at the Summit'. *Broadside* vol. 8, no. 4 (1987).

Teather, Lynne. 'The Feminist Mosaic'. In *Women in the Canadian Mosaic*. Edited by Gwen Matheson. Toronto: Peter Martin Associates, 1976.

Thomas, Hilda L. 'Future Perspectives: A Discussion Paper'. *Priorities* vol. 7, no. 5 (1979).

Thomson, Ann. 'Why are We in the NDP?'. *Priorities* vol. 5, no. 1, (1977).

Toronto Rape Crisis Centre. 'Rape'. In *No Safe Place*. Edited by Connie Guberman and Margie Wolfe. Toronto: Women's Press, 1985.

Turner, Joan, and Lois Emery. *Perspectives on Women in the 1980s*. Winnipeg: Univ. of Manitoba Press, 1983.

Upstream Collective. 'Upstream Says Good-bye'. *Upstream* vol. 4, no. 5 (1980).

Vallee, Evelyne. 'The First National Women's Network Conference'. *Communiqu'elles* vol. 8, no. 7 (1982), pp. 15–16.

Vancouver Women's Studies Group. *Women and Socialism: Accounting for Our Experience*. Nov. 1979.

Verrall, Marg. 'Has the Women's Movement become a Club for Correct-Liners?'. *Kinesis* Aug. 1980.

Walter, Lisa. 'Celebration and Work in Conflict'. *Alberta Status of Women Action Committee Newsletter* vol. 5, no. 7 (1984).

Waslycia-Leis, Judy. 'Overhaul the Women's Movement'. *Priorities* vol. 6, no. 1 (1978).

Waugh, Phyllis. 'Statement on Alter Eros Festival'. *Broadside* vol. 5, no. 6 (1984).

Weir, Lorna. 'Tit for Tat: Coalition Politics'. *Broadside* vol. 3, no. 4 (1982), p. 10–11.

_____ . 'Socialist Feminism and the Politics of Sexuality'. In *Feminism and Political Economy*. Edited by Heather Jon Maroney and Meg Luxton. Toronto: Methuen, 1987.

_____ . 'Women and the State: A Conference for Feminist Activists'. *Feminist Review* no. 26 (Summer 1987).

Weir, Lorna, and Brenda Steiger. 'Coming Together in a Hot Gym'. *Broadside* vol. 2, no. 10 (1981).

Weir, Lorna, and Eve Zaremba. 'Boys and Girls Together: Feminism and Gay Liberation'. *Broadside* vol. 4, no. 1 (1982).

'What Women Want Now'. *Maclean's*, November 16, 1986.

Wildeman, Marlene. 'Timely Funding'. *Broadside* vol. 6, no. 10 (1985).

Willick, Liz. 'Working to Organize Rural Women in Canada'. *Canadian Woman Studies/les cahiers de la femme* vol. 7, no. 1/2 (1986), pp. 168–9.

Willick, Liz and Sue Berlove. *Building the Women's Movement: From One Women's Centre to Another*. Kitchener, Ontario: Kitchener-Waterloo Women's Place, 1975.

Wilson, Debbie. 'The Selling of Solidarity: A Story About Women and the B.C. Budget'. *Herizons* vol. 1, no. 12 (1984).

'Women of Conviction: Ten Dynamic Women Share Their Views'. *Herizons* March 1987.

Women's Liberation Working Group. 'Principles in Action'. *Broadside* vol. 5, no. 7 (1984).

Woo, Maylynn. 'Autonomy of the Women's Movement'. *Prairie Woman* vol. 2, no. 2 (1978).

Woo, Maylynn, and Prabha Khosla. 'The Politics of Visibility—Addressing Third World Concerns'. *Kinesis* Sept./Oct. 1981.

Wood, Jean. 'Who Represents Canadian Women?'. *Status of Women News/ La revue statut de la femme* vol. 7, no. 1 (Fall 1981), p. 4.

Working Group on Sexual Violence. 'Better Strident than Silent'. *Broadside* vol. 6, no. 6 (1985).

_____ . 'Reclaiming a Feminist Voice'. *Kinesis* May 1985.

Wright, Cynthia. 'Fighting Racism is a Feminist Issue'. *International Women's Day Committee Newsletter* Summer 1985.

Yanz, Lynda. 'Socialist Feminists Speaking About the Women's Movement'. *International Women's Day Committee Newsletter* May 1984.

_____ . 'Talking to Socialist Feminists'. *International Women's Day Committee Newsletter* Sept. 1984.

Yanz, Lynda, and David Smith. 'A Response to the Lesbian Caucus'. *Kinesis* vol. 7, no. 3 (1978).
Zaremba, Eve. 'Caught in the Squeeze: Women's Credit Union'. *Broadside* vol. 2, no. 4 (1981).
————— . 'The Art of Panel Handling'. *Broadside* vol. 4, no. 4 (1983).
————— . 'Manoeuvring the Minorities'. *Broadside* vol. 5, no. 3 (1984).
————— . 'IWD 84': Reaction to Action'. *Broadside* vol. 5, no. 4 (1984).
Zook, Krin. 'Institutionalized Rape'. *Broadside* vol. 2, no. 1&2 (1980).

1.a. The First Wave: Historical Sources Cited

Bacchi, Carol Lee. *Liberation Deferred? The Ideas of English Canadian Suffragists, 1877–1918*. Toronto: Univ. of Toronto Press, 1983.
Cleverdon, Catherine. *Woman Suffrage in Canada*. Toronto: Univ. of Toronto Press, 1950.
Cook, R., and Wendy Mitchinson, eds. *The Proper Sphere*. Toronto: Oxford Univ. Press, 1976.
Gorham, Deborah. 'Flora MacDonald Dennison: Canadian Feminist'. In *A Not Unreasonable Claim*. Edited by Linda Kealey. Toronto: Women's Press, 1979.
Kealey, Linda, ed. *A Not Unreasonable Claim*. Toronto: Women's Press, 1979.
————— . 'Canadian Socialism and the Woman Question, 1900–1914'. *Labour/Le Travail* vol. 13 (1984).
McClung, Nellie. *In Times Like These*. Toronto: Univ. of Toronto Press, 1972.
Molgat, Anne. '*The Voice* and the Women of Winnipeg, 1894–1923'. M.A. Thesis: Univ. of Ottawa, 1988.
Newton, Janice. 'Women and Cotton's Weekly: A Study of Women and Socialism in Canada, 1909'. *Resources for Feminist Research/Documentation sur la recherche féministe* vol. 8 (1979).
Roberts, Wayne. 'Rocking the Cradle for the World: The New Woman and Maternal Feminism, Toronto, 1877–1914'. In *A Not Unreasonable Claim*. Edited by Linda Kealey. Toronto: Women's Press, 1979.
Sangster, Joan. 'The Communist Party and the Woman Question, 1922–29'. *Labour/Le Travail* vol. 15 (Spring 1985).
————— . 'The Making of a Socialist Feminist: The Early Career of Beatrice Brigden, 1888–1941'. *Atlantis* vol. 13, no. 1 (Fall 1987), pp. 13–28.
Shadd, Adrienne. '300 Years of Black Women in Canadian History: circa 1700–1980'. *Tiger Lily* vol. 1, no. 2 (1987).
Strong-Boag, Veronica. 'Ever a Crusader: Nellie McClung: First Wave Feminist'. In *Rethinking Canada: The Promise of Women's History*. Edited by Veronica Strong-Boag and Anita Fellman, pp. 178–89. Toronto: Copp Clark, 1986.

Wade, Susan. 'Helena Gutteridge, Votes for Women and Trade Unions'. In *In Her Own Right: Essays on Women's History in British Columbia*. Edited by Barbara Latham and Cathy Kess. Victoria, B.C.: Camosun College, 1980.

2. The Women's Movement in Western Europe and the United States

Allen, Pamela. 'Free Space'. In *Notes from The Third Year: Women's Liberation*, pp. 93–8. New York, 1971, n.p.

Altbach, Edith, et al., eds. *German Feminism: Readings in Politics and Literature*. Albany: State Univ. of New York, 1984.

Bachrach, Amy, and Carisa Cunningham. 'What Do You Mean the Party's Over? We Just Got Here'. *Socialist Review* no. 81 (May/June 1985), p. 53–63.

Balser, Diane. *Sisterhood and Solidarity: Feminism and Labor in Modern Times*. Boston: South End, 1987.

Barrett, Michele. 'Weir and Wilson on Feminist Politics'. *New Left Review* no. 150 (March/April 1985), pp. 143–7.

Barrett, Michele, and Mary McIntosh. 'Ethnocentrism and Socialist Feminist Theory'. *Feminist Review* no. 20 (Summer 1985), pp. 23-47.

Barrett, Michele, et al. 'Feminism and Class Politics: A Round Table Discussion'. *Feminist Review* no. 23 (Summer 1986), pp. 13-30.

Bassnett, Susan. *Feminist Experiences: The Women's Movement in Four Cultures*. London: Allen and Unwin, 1986.

Benn, Melissa. 'In and Against the European Left: Socialist Feminists Get Organized'. *Feminist Review* no. 26 (Summer 1987).

Bhavnani, Kum-Kum, and Margaret Coulson. 'Transforming Socialist Feminism: the Challenge of Racism'. *Feminist Review* no. 23 (Summer 1986), pp. 81–92.

Bradshaw, Jan, ed. *The Women's Liberation Movement: Europe and North America*. Oxford: Pergamon Press, 1982.

Brixton Black Women's Group. 'Black Women Organizing'. *Feminist Review* no. 17 (Autumn 1984).

Bourne, Jenny. *Towards an Anti-Racist Feminism*. London: Institute of Race Relations, 1984.

Bunch, Charlotte. 'Beyond Either/Or: Feminist Options'. *Quest* vol. 3, no. 1 (Summer 1976), pp. 2–17.

Bunch, Charlotte, and Beverly Fisher. 'What Future for Leadership?'. *Quest* vol. 2, no. 4 (Spring 1976), pp. 2–13.

Burris, Barbara. 'The Fourth World Manifesto'. In *Notes from The Third Year: Women's Liberation*, pp. 102–19. New York, 1971, n.p.

Carby, Hazel. 'White Women Listen! Black Feminism and the Boundaries of Sisterhood'. In *The Empire Strikes Back*, Centre for Contemporary Cultural Studies. London: Hutchinson, 1982.

Cassell, Joan. *A Group Called Women: Sisterhood and Symbolism in the Feminist Movement*. New York: David MacKay Co., 1977.

Charlotte Perkins Gilman Chapter of the New America Movement. 'Socialist Feminism: the Inseparability of Gender and Class Oppression'. In *Feminist Frameworks*. Edited by Alison Jaggar and Paula Rothenberg, pp. 152–4. New York: McGraw-Hill, 1984.

Clark, Adele, and Alice Wolfson. 'Socialist-Feminism and Reproductive Rights: Movement Work and its Contradictions, No. 9'. *Socialist Review* no. 78 (Nov./Dec. 1984), pp. 110–20.

Cockburn, Cynthia, ed. 'Trade Unions and the Radicalizing of Socialist Feminism'. *Feminist Review* no. 16 (Summer 1984).

Collett, Christine. 'Taking the Lid Off: Socialist Feminism in Oxfordshire'. *Feminist Review* no. 26 (Summer 1987).

Combahee River Collective. 'A Black Feminist Statement'. In *Capitalist Patriarchy and the Case for Socialist Feminism*. Edited by Zillah Eisenstein. New York: Monthly Review Press, 1979.

Cott, Nancy. *The Grounding of Modern Feminism*. New Haven, Conn.: Yale Univ. Press, 1987.

Crater, Flora. 'Leadership, Growth and Spirit'. *Quest* vol. 2, no. 4 (Spring 1976), pp. 60–6.

Dahlerup, Dahle, ed. *The New Women's Movement: Feminism and Political Power in Europe and the USA*. London: Sage, 1986.

Davis, Angela. *Women Race and Class*. New York: Vintage, 1981.

Deckard, Barbara. *The Women's Movement, Third Edition*. New York: Harper and Row, 1983.

DiCaprio, Lisa. 'Socialist Feminism USA'. *Cayenne* no. 2 (Feb. 1985).

District 65. 'Union Women on Feminism'. *Heresies* vol. 3, no. 1 (issue 9 [1980]).

Dixon, Marlene. 'Where are We Going?'. In *From Feminism to Liberation*, pp. 56–63. Edited by Edith Altbach. Cambridge: Shenkman, 1971.

DuBois,Ellen. 'The Nineteenth Century Woman Suffrage Movement and the Analysis of Women's Oppression'. In *Capitalist Patriarchy and the Case for Socialist Feminism*. Edited by Zillah Eisenstein. New York: Monthly Review Press, 1979.

Duchen, Claire. *Feminism in France; From '68 to Mitterand*. London: Routledge Kegan Paul, 1986.

Easton, Barbara. 'Socialism and Feminism I: Toward a Unified Movement'. *Socialist Revolution* no. 19 (vol. 4, no. 1 [Jan./March 1974]), pp. 59–67.

Ehrenreich, Barbara. 'A Funny Thing Happened on the Way to Socialist Feminism'. *Heresies* vol. 3, no. 1 (issue 9 [1980]).

Eisenstein, Hester. *Contemporary Feminist Thought*. Chapter 4, 'Consciousness Raising: the Personal is Political'. Boston: G.K. Hall and Co., 1983.

Elshtain, Jean. 'Reclaiming the Socialist Feminist Citizen, No. 5'. *Socialist Review* no. 74 (March/April 1984), pp. 21–7.

English, Dierdre. 'The War Against Choice'. *Mother Jones* Feb./March 1981.

English, Deirdre, Barbara Epstein, Barbara Haber, and Judy Maclean. 'The Impasse of Socialist Feminism, No. 10'. *Socialist Review* no. 79 (Jan./Feb. 1985), pp. 92–110.

Epstein, Barbara. 'Thoughts on Socialist Feminism in 1980'. *New Political Science* vol. 1, no.4 (1980).

Evans, Sara. *Personal Politics: The Roots of Women's Liberation in the Civil Rights Movement and the New Left*. New York: Vintage, 1979.

Ferree, Myra, and Beth Hess. *Controversy and Coalition: The New Feminist Movement*. Boston: Twayne, 1985.

Finch, Sue, et al. 'Socialist-Feminists and Greenham'. *Feminist Review* no. 23 (Summer 1986), pp.93–100.

Firestone, Shulamith, and Anne Koedt, eds. *Notes From the Second Year: Women's Liberation. Major Writings of the Radical Feminists*. New York, 1970, n.p.

Flexner, Eleanor. *Century of Struggle*. Boston: Harvard Univ. Press, 1959.

Foner, Philip, ed. *Clara Zetkin: Selected Writings*. New York, International Publishers, 1984.

Freeman, Jo. 'The Tyranny of Structurelessness'. In *Women and Politics*. Edited by Jane Jaquette, pp. 202–14. New York: John Wiley and Sons, 1974.

Gauthier, Lorraine. 'Feminist Politics and Anti-feminist Theory in France'. *Resources for Feminist Research/Documentation sur la recherche féministe* vol. 14, no. 3 (Nov. 1985), pp. 12–15.

Gordon, Linda. 'Review Essay: Nazi Feminists'. *Feminist Review* no. 27 (Autumn 1987).

Haber, Barbara. 'Is Personal Life still a Political Issue?'. *Feminist Studies* vol. 5, no. 3 (Fall 1979), pp. 417–30.

Hartmann, Heidi. 'The Unhappy Marriage of Marxism and Feminism: Towards a More Progressive Union'. In *Women and Revolution*. Edited by Lydia Sargent. Boston: South End, 1981.

Hartsock, Nancy. 'Fundamental Feminism: Process and Perspective'. *Quest* vol. 2, no. 2 (Fall 1975), pp. 67–80.

Haug, Frigga. 'The Women's Movement in West Germany'. *New Left Review* no. 155 (Jan./Feb. 1986), pp. 50–74.

Hellman, Judith. *Journeys Among Women*. New York: Oxford Univ. Press, 1987.

Hooks, Bell. 'Sisterhood: Political Solidarity between Women'. *Feminist Review* no. 23 (Summer 1986), pp. 125–38.

Kelly, Gail. 'Women's Liberation and the New Left'. In *From Feminism to Liberation*, pp. 39–46. Edited by Edith Altbach. Cambridge: Shenkman, 1971.

Kollontai, Alexandra. *Alexandra Kollantai: Selected Writings*. London: Allison and Busby, 1977.

Lees, Sue, and Mary McIntosh. 'European Forum of Socialist Feminists'. *Feminist Review* no. 23 (Summer 1986), pp. 139–45.

Liddington, Jill, and Jill Norris. *One Hand Tied Behind Us*. London: Virago, 1978.

Luttrell, Wendy. 'Beyond the Politics of Victimization, No. 2'. *Socialist Review* no. 73 (Jan./Feb. 1984), pp. 42–7.

Martin, Gloria. *Socialist-Feminism: The First Decade, 1966–1976*. Seattle, Wash.: Freedom Socialist Publications, 1976, 1986.

Masterson, Lorraine. 'Feminist Leaders Can't Walk on Water'. *Quest* vol. 2, no. 4 (Spring 1976), pp. 29–40.

McAfee, Kathy, and Myrna Wood. 'Bread and Roses'. In *From Feminism to Liberation*, pp. 21–38. Edited by Edith Altbach. Cambridge: Shenkman, 1971.

McWilliams, Nancy. 'Contemporary Feminism, Consciousness Raising, and Changing Views of the Political'. In *Women in Politics*, pp. 157–70. Edited by Jane Jaquette. New York: John Wiley & Sons, 1974.

Meulenbelt, Anja, Joyce Outshoorn, Selma Svenhuijsen, and Petra de Vries. *A Creative Tension: Explorations in Socialist Feminism*. London: Pluto Press, 1984.

Mitchell, Juliet. 'The Longest Revolution'. *New Left Review* no. 40. (Nov.—Dec. 1966).

Mitchell, Juliet, and Ann Oakley. *What is Feminism: A Reexamination*. New York: Pantheon, 1986.

Morgan, Robin, ed. *Sisterhood is Powerful*. New York: Vintage, 1970.

————— . 'The National Conference on Socialist Feminism'. *Socialist Revolution* no. 26 (Oct./Dec. 1975), pp. 85–116.

Page, Margaret. 'Socialist Feminism—a Political Alternative?'. *M/F* no. 2 (1978), pp. 32–42.

Payne, Carol. 'Consciousness Raising: A Dead End?'. In *Notes from The Third Year: Women's Liberation*, pp. 99–100. New York, n.p., 1971.

Perrigo, Sarah. 'Socialist-Feminism and the Labour Party: Some Experiences from Leeds'. *Feminist Review* no. 23 (Summer 1986), pp. 101–8.

Petchevsky, Rosalind. 'Dissolving the Hyphen: A Report on Marxist Feminist Groups 1–5'. In *Capitalist Patriarchy and the Case for Socialist Feminism*, pp. 373–89. Edited by Zillah Eisenstein. New York: Monthly Review, 1979.

Phillips, Anne. *Divided Loyalties: Dilemmas of Sex and Class*. London: Virago, 1987.

Piven, Frances Fox. 'Women and the State: Ideology, Power and the Welfare State, No. 4'. *Socialist Review* no. 74 (March/April 1984), pp. 11–19.

Red Apple Collective. 'Socialist Feminist Women's Unions: Past and Present'. *Socialist Revolution* no. 38 (1978), pp. 37–57.

Rossi, Alice. *The Feminist Papers*. New York: Bantam Books, 1974.

Roszak, Betty, and Theodore Roszak, eds. *Masculine/Feminine*. New York: Harper, 1969. (See especially documents from early women's movement, pp. 251–93.)

Rowbotham, Sheila, Lynne Segal, and Hilary Wainwright. *Beyond the Fragments*. London: Islington Community Press, 1979.

Segal, Lynne. *Is the Future Female?: Troubled Thoughts on Contemporary Feminism*. London: Virago, 1987.

'Socialism and Feminism II: The "Principles of Unity" of the Berkeley-Oakland Women's Union'. *Socialist Revolution* no. 19 (vol. 4, no.1 [Jan./March 1974]), pp. 69–82.

Stamiris, Eleni. 'The Women's Movement in Greece'. *New Left Review* no. 158 (July/Aug. 1986).

Tanner, Leslie, ed. *Voices from Women's Liberation*. New York: Signet, 1971. (See especially Documents, pp. 109–56.)

Tax, Meredith. *The Rising of the Women: Feminist Solidarity and Class Conflict, 1880–1917*. New York: Monthly Review Press, 1980.

———————. 'Learning How to Bake, No. 1.' *Socialist Review* no. 73 (Jan./Feb. 1984), pp. 36–41.

Taylor, Barbara. *Eve and the New Jerusalem*. London: Virago, 1983.

Threlfall, Monica. 'The Women's Movement in Spain'. *New Left Review* no. 151 (May/June 1985), pp. 44–73.

Tilchen, Maida. 'Women's Music: Politics for Sale'. In *Feminist Frameworks*. Edited by Alison Jaggar and Paula Rothenberg. New York: McGraw-Hill, 1984.

Tuchman, Gayle. 'The Topic of the Women's Movement'. In *Making News*. London: Free Press, 1978.

Van Allen, Judith. 'Capitalism Without Patriarchy, No. 8'. *Socialist Review* no. 77 (Sept./Oct. 1984), pp. 81–91.

Wandor, Michelene, ed. *The Body Politic: Writings from the Women's Liberation Movement in Britain 1969–1972*. London: Stage One, 1972.

Weir, Angela, and Elizabeth Wilson. 'The British Women's Movement'. *New Left Review* no. 148 (Nov./Dec. 1984), pp. 74–103.

Williams, Brooke. 'The Chador of Women's Liberation: Cultural Feminism and the Movement Press'. *Heresies* vol. 3, no.1 (issue 9 [1980]).

Willis, Ellen. 'Radical Feminism and Feminist Radicalism'. In *The Sixties Without Apology*. Edited by Sohnya Sayres. Minneapolis: Univ. of Minnessota Press, 1984.

Woodul, Jennifer. 'What's This about Feminist Businesses?'. In *Feminist Frameworks*. Edited by Alison Jaggar and Paula Rothenberg. New York: McGraw-Hill, 1984.

Zaretsky, Eli. 'Socialism and Feminism III: Socialist Politics and the Family'. *Socialist Revolution* no. 19 (vol. 4, no. 1 [Jan./March 1974]), pp. 83–98.

3. Other Sources Cited

Abbott, Sidney and Barbara Love. *Sappho was a Right-On Woman*. Toronto: Stern & Day, 1972.

Armstrong, Pat, and Hugh Armstrong. *The Double Ghetto*. Rev. ed. Toronto: McClelland and Stewart, 1984.

Bakker, Isa. 'Free Trade: What's At Risk?'. *Feminist Action/féministe* vol. 2, no. 7 (1987).

Bashevkin, Sylvia. *Toeing the Lines: Women and Party Politics in English Canada*. Toronto: Univ. of Toronto Press, 1985.

Beechey, Veronica. 'On Patriarchy'. *Feminist Review* no. 3 (1979).

Blakely, Mary Kay. 'Who are the real man-haters?'. *Vogue* April 1983. Quoted in Carol Tavris and Carole Wade, *The Longest War*. San Diego: Harcourt Brace Jovanovich, 1984.

Bourne, Paula. *Women in Canadian Society*. Toronto: Ontario Institute for Studies in Education, 1976. Rev. ed. 1978.

Boyd, Monica. *Canadian Attitudes toward Women: Thirty Years of Change*. Women's Bureau, Labour Canada, 1984.

Braithwaite, Rella, ed. *The Black Woman in Canada*, n.p., n.d.

Brief on the 1987 Constitutional Accord. Toronto: National Action Committee on the Status of Women, 1987.

Brodie, Janine. *Women and Politics in Canada*. Toronto: McGrawHill Ryerson, 1985.

Bunch, Charlote. 'Lesbian Feminist Theory'. In *Women and the Politics of Culture*. Edited by Michele Zak and Patricia Moots. New York: Longman, 1983.

Burris, Val. 'The Dialectic of Women's Oppression: Notes on the Relation between Capitalism and Patriarchy'. *Berkeley Journal of Sociology* vol. 27 (1982).

Cohen, Marjorie. *The Macdonald Report and its Implications for Women*. Toronto: National Action Committee on the Status of Women, Nov. 1985.

Crompton, Rosemary, and Michael Mann, eds. *Gender and Stratification*. Cambridge: Polity Press, 1986.

de Beauvoir, Simone. *The Second Sex*. New York: Alfred A. Knopf, 1952.

Donovan, Josephine. *Feminist Theory*. New York: Frederick Ungar, 1985.

Eisenstein, Zillah. *The Radical Future of Liberal Feminism*. New York: Longman, 1981.

Friedan, Betty. *The Feminine Mystique*. New York: Dell Publishing Co., 1963.

Guettell, Charnie. *Marxism and Feminism*. Toronto: Women's Press, 1974.

Hamilton, Roberta. *The Liberation of Women: A Study of Patriarchy and Capitalism*. London: Allen & Unwin, 1978.

Housman, Judy. 'Mothering, the Unconscious and Feminism'. *Radical America* vol. 16, no. 6 (1982).

Ingle, Cyndie, and Julie Martin. 'A Personal Account: Automation at the Bank'. *Our Times* vol. 5, no. 5 (Aug. 1986).

Jackson, Ed, and Stan Persky, eds. *Flaunting It: A Decade of Gay Journalism from the Body Politic*. Vancouver: New Star Books, 1982.

Jaggar, Alison. *Feminist Politics and Human Nature*. Totowa, N.J.: Rowman and Allanheld, 1983.

Jayawardena, Kumari. *Feminism and Nationalism in the Third World*. London: Zed Books, 1986.

Kaufman, Michael, ed. *Beyond Patriarchy: Essays by Men on Pleasure, Power and Change*. Toronto: Oxford Univ. Press, 1987.

Kraemarae, Cheris, and Paula Treichler. *A Feminist Dictionary*. London: Pandora Press, 1985.

Landry, C., et al. *What A Way to Run a Railroad: An Analysis of Radical Failure*. London: Comedia Publishing Group, 1985.

Lenskyj, Helen. 'From Prejudice to Policy'. *Broadside* vol. 8, no. 6 (April 1987).

Luxton, Meg. *More than a Labour of Love: Three Generations of Women's Work in the Home*. Toronto: Women's Press, 1980.

MacLeod, Linda. *Battered But Not Beaten . . . Preventing Wife Abuse in Canada*. Ottawa: Canadian Advisory Council on the Status of Women, 1987.

Meissner, Martin, et al. 'No Exit for Wives: Sexual Division of Labour and the Cumulation of Household Demands'. *Canadian Review of Sociology and Anthropology* vol. 12, no. 4 (part 1 [Nov. 1975]), p. 436.

Mies, Maria. *Patriarchy and Accumulation on a World Scale: Women in the International Division of Labour*. London: ZED Books, 1986.

Milkman, Ruth, ed. *Women, Work and Protest*. Boston: Routledge and Kegan Paul, 1985.

Mill, John Stuart. 'The Subjection of Women'. In *Essays on Sex Equality*. Edited by Alice Rossi. Chicago: Univ. of Chicago Press, 1970.

Mitchell, Juliet. 'Women and Equality'. In *The Rights and Wrongs of Women*. Edited by Juliet Mitchell and Ann Oakley. Harmondsworth: Penguin, 1976.

Morgan, Marabel. *The Total Woman*. Markham: Simon and Schuster, 1973.

Morgentaler, Henry. *Abortion and Contraception*. Toronto: General Publishing Co., 1982.

O'Brien, Mary. *The Politics of Reproduction*. Boston: Routledge and Kegan Paul, 1981.

Palmer, Brian. *Solidarity: The Rise and Fall of an Opposition in British Columbia*. Vancouver: New Star Books, 1987.

Panitch, Leo, ed. *The Canadian State: Political Economy and Political Power*. Toronto: Univ. of Toronto Press, 1977.

Pelrine, Eleanor Wright. *Abortion in Canada*. Toronto: New Press, 1971.
_____ . *Morgentaler: The Doctor Who Couldn't Turn Away*. Toronto: Gage Publishing, 1975.

Phillips, Paul and Erin. *Women and Work*. Toronto: Lorimer, 1983.

Pleck, Joseph. 'Men's Power with Women, Other Men and Society: A Men's Movement Analysis'. In *Men in Difficult Times*. Edited by Robert Lewis. Englewood Cliffs: Prentice Hall, 1981.

Rich, Adrienne. 'Compulsory Heterosexuality and Lesbian Existence'. *Signs: A Journal of Women in Society* vol. 5, no. 4 (Summer 1980).

Rosenberg, Carroll Smith. 'The Female World of Love and Ritual: Relations between Women in Nineteenth Century America'. *Signs* vol. 1, no. 1 (1975).

Rosenberg, Harriet. 'The Home is the Workplace: Hazards, Stress, and Pollutants in the Household'. In *Through the Kitchen Window*. Toronto: Garamond Press, 1986.

Rowbotham, Sheila. *Women, Resistance and Revolution*. London: Allen Lane, 1972.

_____ . 'The Trouble with Patriarchy'. In *People's History and Socialist Theory*. Edited by Raphael Samuel. London: Routledge and Kegan Paul, 1981.

Rubin, Gayle. 'The Traffic in Women: Notes on the "Political Economy" of Sex'. In *Toward an Anthropology of Women*. Edited by Rayna Reiter. New York: Monthly Review Press, 1975.

Sagmeister, Nancy. 'In Sickness and in Health: Spousal Benefits for Gays and Lesbians'. *Our Times* vol. 6, no. 6 (Sept. 1987).

Silvera, Makeda. *Silenced*. Toronto: Williams-Wallace Publishers, 1983.

Smith, Dorothy. *Feminism and Marxism: A Place to Begin*. Vancouver: New Star Books, 1977.

Stanko, Elizabeth. *Intimate Intrusions: Women's Experience of Male Violence*. London: Routledge and Kegan Paul, 1985.

Tavris, Carol and Carole Wade. *The Longest War: Sex Differences in Perspective*. 2nd ed. San Diego: Harcourt Brace and Jovanovitch, 1984.

Tilly, Louise. 'Paths of Proletarianization: Organization of Production, Sexual Division of Labor, and Women's Collective Action'. In *Women's Work*. Edited by Eleanor Leacock and Helen Safa. South Hadley: Bergin and Garvey, 1986.

Valverde, Mariana. *Sex, Power and Pleasure*. Toronto: Women's Press, 1985.

Warskett, Rosemary. 'Legitimate and Illegitimate Unionism: The Case of SORWUC and Bankworker Unionization'. Unpublished paper given at the Political Economy Sessions of the Canadian Political Science Association, June 1987.

White, Julie. *Women and Unions*. Ottawa: Canadian Advisory Council on the Status of Women, 1980.

Wollstonecraft, Mary. *Vindication of the Rights of Woman*. 1985. Reprint. Harmondsworth: Penguin, 1792.

Women in Canada: A Statistical Report. Statistics Canada, March 1985.

Women in the Labour Force, 1986–7 Edition. Ottawa: Labour Canada, 1987.

Index

Aberdeen, Lady, 31

Abortion: 3, 45–6, 48, 57–8, 86, 171, 188; and the new right, 86; Caravan, 86, 201–2; law, 3, 53, 88

Action Day Care, 251

Ad Hoc Committee of Canadian Women on the Constitution, 71

Affirmative action programs: 3; resistance to, 137–8

Agency, 21–2, 207

Allen, Carol, and Judy Persad, 106, 293–5

Alliances: 252; *see also* Coalitions

Alternative services, 56

Anderson, Doris, 41

Association for the Repeal of the Abortion Law, 52

Attitudes, changing, 4, 140, 143–5

Bannerji, Himani, 24n.2

Battered But Not Beaten, 4

B.C. Coalition for Abortion Clinics, 88

B.C. Federation of Women, 58, 60

B.C. Women's Suffrage League, 34

Bernstein, Judy, et al., 50

Biology, 10–11, 32, 99

Birth-Control Handbook, The, 45–6

Birth-control pill, 40

Blakely, Mary Kay, 16

Brand, Johanna, and Ester Koulack, 212

Bread and Roses (Vancouver), 77

Broadside, 73

Bunch, Charlotte, 105–6, 247, 251

Business and Professional Women's Clubs, 42

Canadian Advisory Council on the Status of Women, 62

Canadian Congress of Learning Opportunities for Women (CCLOW), 62

Canadian Federation of University Women, 29, 42, 51

Canadian Labour Congress (CLC), 183

Canadian Secret Intelligence Service (CSIS), 146

Canadian Suffrage Association, 33

Canadian Women's Educational Press, 48, 50, 53, 66, 125

Canadian Women's Movement Archives, 82, 87

Capitalism: and democracy, 145; patriarchal, 99, 112, 140, 142, 145, 151–2, 185, 193

Carby, Hazel, 19, 107

Carey, Patricia, 44, 202, 207, 213

Casgrain, Thérèse, 39

Centre for Spanish-Speaking Peoples (CSSP) (Toronto), 60

Change: and 'the personal is political', 201, 206–7, 214; fear of, 140, 145–7, 178, 184, 193; ideology of, 13–14, 137, 140–59, 179, 183, 184, 190–1; individual, 141, 211–12, 215; making, 7, 13, 99, 136–60, 172–6, 256–62

Charter of Rights, 134n.79

Chatelaine, 41, 51

Child-care: 4, 6, 15; *see also* Day-care

Chisholm, Barbara, 47

Choice: and class, 104; and race, 106; and sexual preference, 106; ideology of, 143

Civil-rights movement, 39

Class: and choice, 104; differences, 103–5; in organizations, 239

Coalitions; 79–81, 157, 245–6, 248; *see also* Alliances

Cohen, Yolande, 32

Collective: action, 13, 155–6, 161n.18; process, 235

Collective, the: 100–1; individuals in, 155; negative image, 154

Colored Women's Club (Montreal), 36

Combahee River Collective, 108, 235

Committee for Equality of Women in Canada (CEW), 51, 52

Communism, fear of, 145–6

Consciousness-raising (CR), 44–5, 204–6, 209, 228n.21, 241

Consensus, 242–4

Constitution, Canadian, 3, 9, 71

Consumerism, 142–3

Corbière-Lavell, Jeannette, 57

Cott, Nancy, 30

Creet, Julia, 60

Cultural feminism: 11, 67; *see also* Radical feminism;

Currents (of feminism): 9–12, 25n.23, 29; co-operation between, 167–8; practice, differences in, 164–95

Davis, Angela, 107

Day-care: 46–7, 168, 189; *see also* Child-care

Decision-making (in organizations), 243

Democracy: liberal, 12, 140, 141, 145, 147–54; participatory, 244; representative, 147–54, 158; within feminist organizations, 242–5; *see also* Collective action

Dempsey, Lotta, 39

Denison, Flora MacDonald, 33

Dependence, economic, 7, 14, 105, 144

Dewar, Elaine, 257, 259

de Wolff, Alice, 73

'Difference': 10–11, 128n.7, 240, 248–9, 251; and sisterhood, 246; class, 103–5; in socialist-feminist theory, 102–10; race, 106–8; sex/gender, 103, 105

Discrimination, 10, 37

Disengagement: 167, 177–8, 250–2; and mainstreaming, 186–90, 190–4, 206; and marginalization, 184–6

Division of labour, sexual, 37, 110–11, 131n.38, 142–3, 144